Climate Risk and Emerging Markets

Climate Risk and Emerging Markets: Valuation, Volatility, and Portfolio Strategies

EDITED BY

AFZALUR RAHMAN
Woxsen University, India

SHAKEB AKHTAR
University of Technology and Applied Sciences, Oman

MAHFOOZ ALAM
University of the People, USA

AND

MOHSIN KHAN
Vellore Institute of Technology, India

emerald PUBLISHING

United Kingdom – North America – Japan – India – Malaysia – China

Emerald Publishing Limited
Emerald Publishing, Floor 5, Northspring, 21-23 Wellington Street, Leeds LS1 4DL.

First edition 2026

British Library Cataloguing in Publication Data
A catalogue record for this book is available from the British Library

ISBN: 978-1-83708-089-2 (Print)
ISBN: 978-1-83708-088-5 (Online)
ISBN: 978-1-83708-090-8 (Epub)

Printed and bound by CPI Group (UK) Ltd, Croydon, CR0 4YY

Contents

List of Abbreviations

Abbreviation	Full Form
ADB	Asian Development Bank
ADF	Augmented Dicky Fuller Test
AI	Artificial Intelligence
ALM	Application Lifecycle Management
AP-2	Activating Protein 2
ARC	African Risk Capacity
ARDL	Autoregressive Distributed Lag
ASEAN	Association of Southeast Asian Nations
ATM	Automated Teller Machine
BCCSAP	Bangladesh Climate Change Strategy and Action Plan
BIC	Bayesian Information Criterion
BRICS	Brazil, Russia, India, China, and South Africa
BSE	Bombay Stock Exchange
CAAR	Cumulative Average Abnormal Returns
CAB	Climate Awareness Bond
CAPM	Capital Asset Pricing Model
CAR	Cumulative Abnormal Returns
CAT Bond	Catastrophic Bond
CBSL	Central Bank of Sri Lanka
CC	Climate Change
CCLIP	Conditional Loan for Investment Projects
CCTF	Climate Change Trust Fund
CETEs	Carbon Emission Trade Exchanges
CFU	Climate Finance Unit
CH_4	Methane
CICERO	Center for International Climate and Environmental Research

CIF	Collective Investment Fund
CO	Crude Oil
CO_2	Carbon Dioxide
COP	Conference of Parties (related to UN Climate Change negotiations)
COVID-19	Coronavirus Disease 2019
CPI	Climate Policy Initiative
CPU	Climate Policy Uncertainty
CRA	Credit Risk Assessment
CRED	Centre for Research on the Epidemiology of Disasters
CREF	Central Renewable Energy Fund
CRFPs	Climate-Related Financial Policies
CRI	Climate Risk Index
CRID	Climate Resilient Island Development
CSA	Climate-smart Agriculture
CSR	Corporate Social Responsibility
CWT	Continuous Wavelet Transform
CWT	Cross Wavelet Transformation
D8	Developing-8 (Bangladesh, Egypt, Indonesia, Iran, Malaysia, Nigeria, Pakistan, and Turkey)
DOLS	Dynamic ordinary least squares
DPIA	Data Protection Impact Assessments
DPO	Data Protection Officer
ECT	Error Correction Term
EEA	European Economic Area
EEA	European Environment Agency
EGARCH	Exponential Generalized Autoregressive Conditional Heteroskedasticity
EIB	European Investment Bank
EKC	Environmental Kuznets Curve
EM DAT	International Emergency Events Database
EMs	Emerging Markets
EPU	Economic Policy Uncertainty
ERM	Environmental Risk Management
ES	ES
ESA	Event Study Analysis

ESG	Environmental, Social and Governance
ETF	Exchange Traded Fund
EU	European Union
EU27	European Union 27 Member States
FAO	Food and The Agricultural Organization
FCPF	Forest Carbon Partnership Facility
FDI	Foreign Direct Investment
FEMA	Federal Emergency Management Agency
FI	Financial Inclusion
FinTech	Financial Technology
FinBERT	Financial Bidirectional Encoder Representations from Transformers
FMCG	Fast Moving Consumer Goods
FMOLS	Fully modified OLS
FSB	Financial Stability Board
FSOC	Financial Stability Oversight Council
GARCH	Generalized Autoregressive Conditional Heteroskedasticity
GB	Green Bond
GBG	Green Banking Guidelines
GBP	Green Bond Principles
GCF	Green Climate Fund
GDP	Gross Domestic Product
GDPR	General Data Protection Regulation
GEF	Global Environment Facility
GF	Green Finance
GFEVD	Generalised Forecast Error Variance Decomposition
GHG	Greenhouse Gas
GHGI	Greenhouse Gas Inventory
GMM	Generalized method of moments
GNI	Gross National Income
GNP	Gross National Product
GPR	Geopolitical Risk
GRI	Global Reporting Initiative
GTFS	Green Technology Financing Scheme
HICs	High-Income Countries

HO	Heating Oil
ICAR	Indian Council of Agricultural Research
ICBC	China's Industrial and Commercial Bank
ICMA	International Capital Market Association
IDB	Inter-American Development Bank
IEA	International Energy Agency
IFC	International Finance Corporation
IFRS	International Financial Reporting Standards
ILO	International Labour Organization
IMF	International Monetary Fund
IMR	Infant Mortality Rate
IPCC	Intergovernmental Panel on Climate Change
IPCC AR6	Intergovernmental Panel on Climate Change Sixth Assessment Report
IRENA	International Renewable Energy Agency
IT	Information Technology
ITC	India Tobacco Company
JB	Jarque-BeraTest of Normality
KP	Kyoto Protocol
KSAPCC	Karnataka State Action Plan on Climate Change
LGPS	Local Government Pension Scheme
LMICs	Low- and Middle-income Countries
MDBs	Multilateral Development Banks
MINT	Mexico, Indonesia, Nigeria, and Turkey
ML	Machine learning
MLF	Medium-term Lending Facility
MMA	Maldives Monetary Authority
MNRE	Ministry of New and Renewable Energy (India)
MPA	Macro-prudential Assessment
MRTW	Mankiw, Romer, and Weil Growth Model
MSAPPC	Maharashtra State Action Plan on Climate Change
MSCCM	Maharashtra State Climate Change Mission
MSCI	Morgan Stanley Capital International
MSPO	Malaysian Sustainable Palm Oil
N_2O	Nitrous Oxide

NAPCC	National Action Plan on Climate Change
NARDL	Non-linear Auto Regressive Distributed Lag
NASA	National Aeronautics and Space Administration
NbS	Nature-based solutions
NCCP	National Climate Change Policy
NDCs	Nationally Determined Contributions
NEG	Negative
NFRD	Non-financial Reporting Directive
NG	Natural Gas
NGOs	Non-governmental Organizations
NLP	Natural Language Processing
NOAA	National Oceanic and Atmospheric Administration
NRB	Nepal Rastra Bank
NRE	Non-renewal Energy
OECD	Organization for Economic Cooperative Development
OLS	Ordinary least squares
OPU	Oil Price Uncertainty
OXERA	Oxford Economic Research Associates
PBoC	The People's Bank of China
PCA	Principal component analysis
POS	Positive
PPP	Public Private Partnership
PRI	Principles for Responsible Investment
PSL	Priority Sector Loan
p-value	Probability Value
QARDL	Quantile Auto Regressive Distributed Lag
R&D	Research and Development
R^2	R-squared (Coefficient of Determination)
RBI	Reserve Bank of India
RBV	Resource-Based View
RCK Model	Ramsey–Cass–Koopmans Model
RE	Renewable Energy
REDD	Reducing Emissions from Deforestation and Forest Degradation
REIF	Renewable Energy Investment Framework

RMA	Royal Monetary Authority of Bhutan
RPA	Robotic Process Automation
S&P	Standard & Poor
SE	Standard Error
SAARC	South Asian Association for Regional Cooperation
SAB	Sustainability Awareness Bond
SBI	State Bank of India
SBP	State Bank of Pakistan
SDG	Sustainable Development Goals
SDM	Spatial Durbin Model
SEBI	Securities and Exchange Board of India
SEC	Securities and Exchange Commission
SEK	Swedish Krona
SLCCS	Sri Lanka Carbon Crediting Scheme
SLF	Standing Lending Facility
SLL	Sustainability Linked Loans
SMEs	Small and Medium Enterprises
SPOC	Sustainable Palm Oil Cluster
SRI	Socially Responsible Investment
STIRPAT	Stochastic Impacts by Regression on Population, Affluence, and Technology
SUR	Seemingly Unrelated Regression
TARCH	Threshold Autoregressive Conditional Heteroskedasticity
TBL	Triple Bottom Line
TCFD	Task Force on Climate-related Financial Disclosures
TERI	The Energy and Resources Institute
TNSAPCC	Tamil Nadu State Action Plan on Climate Change
t-ratio	*t*-Statistic
TVP-VAR	Time-Varying Parameter Vector Autoregression
UK	United Kingdom
UN	United Nations
UN SDG	United Nations Sustainable Development Goals
UNCTAD	United Nations Conference on Trade and Development
UNDP	United Nations Development Program
UNEP	United Nations Environment Programme

UNES	United Nations Earth Summit
UNFCCC	United Nations Framework Convention on Climate Change
USA	United States
USD	United States Dollar
VAR	Value at Risk
VRIO	Valuable, Rare, Inimitable, and Organized
WB	World Bank
WDI	World Development Indicators
WEF	World Economic Forum
WMO	World Meteorological Organization
World Bank	World Bank Group
ZA	Zivot and Andrews
ε	Error Term

About the Editors

Afzalur Rahman is a distinguished academic and finance expert with over 13 years of experience in academia and business. He specializes in accounts, finance, data analytics, and Fintech, and has guided numerous PhD and MPhil students. He has published 29 research papers, authored 2 books, and contributed to 9 book chapters. His expertise extends to algorithmic trading, financial data analytics using Python, and implementing ERP systems like SAP. He has held prestigious positions such as Professor and Head of Department at B.S. Abdur Rahman Crescent University and currently serves as a Professor at Woxsen University. He has received several awards, including the Best HOD Award and Best Innovative Idea in Teaching Award. He has also established international collaborations and modernized departments with IT solutions. An active participant in global conferences, he shares his knowledge through workshops and lectures internationally (ORCID: 0000-0002-1561-561X).

Shakeb Akhtar is currently a Lecturer at the University of Technology and Applied Science, Ibra, Oman. He holds an MFC and PhD in Banking and Finance from Aligarh Muslim University, India. He specializes in accounting and finance-related courses and has over 10 years of teaching experience in accounting and finance at both tertiary and senior high school levels. Previously, he was Programme Director (MBA-FS), Chair Professor, Research Coordinator, and Examination cell head at the School of Business, Woxsen University, Hyderabad, India. Before that he was Division Chair (Area Chair) and Assistant Professor at Galgotias University, Greater Noida, India. His research interest is in the banking industry, behavioural economics, and secondary data analysis techniques namely; static panel estimation, dynamic panel estimation, ARDL panel modulation and time series estimation, efficiency analysis, sustainability, and SDGs with seven years of research experience. He has made research contributions with 31 publications in ABDC, ABS, Scopus, and Web of Science journals (ORCID: 0000-0003-2069-6669).

Mahfooz Alam is an accomplished Assistant Professor of Finance with over five years of academic experience. His research interests include sustainable finance, FinTech, financial markets, asset pricing, and Islamic banking. He holds a PhD in Finance from Aligarh Muslim University, where his thesis focused on the performance of mutual funds in India. He has held faculty positions at several universities, including ICFAI University and GLA University, and is currently a Faculty Instructor at the University of the People, USA (ORCID: 0000-0002-9311-5688).

Mohsin Khan is an Assistant Professor (Senior Grade) in the Department of Commerce at the School of Social Sciences and Languages, Vellore Institute of Technology (VIT), Vellore, Tamil Nadu, India. He holds a PhD in Corporate Finance from the Department of Commerce, Aligarh Muslim University, Aligarh, Uttar Pradesh, India. His research interests encompass finance and accounting, behavioural finance, sustainable financial goals, sustainable development, social sciences and humanities, and corporate employee cognition. He has authored numerous research papers published in esteemed international journals indexed in Web of Science, Scopus, ESCI, and ABDC (ORCID: 0000-0001-7986-9478).

About the Contributors

Mohd Afjal is a Senior Assistant Professor at VIT Business School, Vellore Institute of Technology, India. His impressive educational journey includes a PhD in Economics, an MBA, and a PGDM. He possesses extensive knowledge in subjects such as financial management, managerial economics, security analysis, and portfolio management, among others. His research focuses on financial economics, energy economics, sustainable finance, financial econometrics, blockchain, and FinTech. He has published several papers in highly regarded peer-reviewed international journals in the fields of economics and finance (ORCID: 0000-0002-1234-6055).

Aliza is a Senior Research Fellow (SRF), working in the Faculty of Commerce at Banaras Hindu University. Her main area of interest is in angel investment, start-up funding, innovations in the start-up ecosystem, and alternative financial investments. She has participated in several national and international conferences and workshops. She has received a grant from the Government of India to pursue her doctoral research. Her doctoral research is based on the study of angel investment in the context of Indian start-ups. She is active in research and has authored several book chapters and research articles (ORCID: 0000-0003-1087-7239).

Tanveer Bagh is a PhD candidate at the Central University of Finance and Economics and also serves as Lecturer of Finance at ILMA University. He received the CSC Government PhD Scholarship and CUFE's Doctoral Research Award for excellence in research. His dissertation, 'ESG Investment, Climate Change Risk, and Corporate Value under a Real-Option Framework', explores sustainable finance, corporate resilience, and strategic decision-making. His research has been published in SSCI, Web of Science, Scopus, ABDC, and ABS-indexed journals, including *IRFA*, *RIBAF*, *IJFE*, *IREF*, *Borsa Istanbul Review*, *The Journal of Portfolio Management*, *Managerial and Decision Economics*, *China Finance Review International*, and others. He has contributed to *The Palgrave Handbook of Green Finance* and *Emerald: Climate Risk and Emerging Markets*. A reviewer for top journals, his expertise spans environmental, social, and governance finance, climate risk, corporate sustainability, and green finance (ORCID: 0000-0001-9488-7885).

Medhansh Bairaria is a business enthusiast with a keen interest in finance, analytics, and global markets. He is specializing in computational business analytics at

Mahindra University. He leverages data-driven insights to decode complex financial landscapes. His research interests span climate finance, investment strategies, and the intersection of geopolitics with economic trends (ORCID: 0009-0007-3400-4295).

K. Balaji is an Assistant Professor in Business and Management at Christ University, Bangalore. He holds a PhD from KLU Business School, KL University, Vijayawada, and has 12 years of teaching experience. His expertise lies in accounting and financial management, consumer behaviour, and entrepreneurship studies. Previously, he was associated with Presidency University, Bangalore, and Mohan Babu University, Tirupati. He has organized ten webinars, three faculty development programmes (FDPs), and an international conference on reimagining marketing in the new normal. A recognized reviewer for reputed international publishers, his research interests include artificial intelligence and machine learning in finance, secondary data-based research in econometrics, financial markets, business strategy, and statistical analysis using tools like Stata. He has authored 40 research publications in ABDC, Scopus, and Web of Science-indexed journals, along with books. He has presented over 12 papers at national and international conferences and attended more than 50 workshops, FDPs, and seminars (ORCID: 0000-0002-3065-3294).

Leticia Bosu is a Lecturer at the University of Cape Coast, Ghana, specializing in business education. She holds a PhD in Curriculum and Teaching and has extensive experience in accounting and management education. Her research focuses on business education, teacher training, curriculum evaluation, and educational equity. She has published on pedagogical strategies and career choices in business studies. As Faculty Examination and Registration Officer (2020–2023), she contributed to academic administration. She has presented at international conferences, including the British Education Research Association Conference. Her teaching philosophy emphasizes effective curriculum implementation and student-centred learning. She believes in equipping educators with essential skills to enhance business education. Her work significantly impacts curriculum development and teacher education in Ghana (ORCID: 0000-0002-8119-2010).

Neenu Chalissery is a doctoral student currently pursuing a PhD at Farook College (Autonomous), Kozhikode, affiliated with the University of Calicut. Her research primarily focuses on volatility modelling, investor sentiment, and sustainable finance in emerging economies. Her academic contributions include publications in prestigious journals indexed in Scopus, Web of Science, and ABDC. In addition to publishing, she has presented papers at esteemed conferences organized by the National Institute of Securities Markets and the Malaysian Finance Association. Her academic excellence is reflected in winning the Best Paper Award at conferences held at Taylor's University, Malaysia, and IIM Bodh Gaya (ORCID: 0000-0002-2583-9641).

Boishali Das is currently a Research Scholar at the National Institute of Technology Jalandhar, specializing in sustainable finance. She holds a Master of

Commerce degree in Accounting and Taxation from Tezpur Central University, where she was honoured as a gold medallist for her outstanding academic performance. In addition to her academic excellence, she has cleared the UGC NET and SLET, further demonstrating her proficiency in her field. Her research interests are primarily focused on sustainable finance, where she aims to contribute to the development of financial practices that support environmental and social sustainability. With a strong academic background and a passion for finance, she strives to merge theoretical knowledge with practical applications in her research work (ORCID: 0009-0009-6373-9682).

Arokiaraj David is an accomplished academic and researcher with a PhD in Management from Pondicherry Central University, India. He serves as an Associate Professor at SBS Swiss Business School – ATMS, RAK, UAE. With an MBA in Marketing and Human Resources and an MCom in Finance and Controls, he brings a multidisciplinary approach to his research. A recipient of the UGC's Junior and Senior Research Fellowships, he has over 100+ publications, including 31 Scopus-indexed, 10 ABDC, and 10 Web of Science articles cited by 1,000+ researchers. His contributions extend to 8 patents, 4 authored books, and 16 book chapters, with works featured in Springer. Proficient in SPSS, AMOS, E-Views, STATA, and Smart-PLS, he specializes in digital transformation, data-driven management, and global commerce (ORCID: 0000-0002-9591-2410).

Dhaya M. is presently enrolled in the PhD programme at Vellore Institute of Technology, Vellore. Under the direction of Dr Sundaram N., a Professor at the Department of Commerce with a focus on finance. With a solid academic background and a drive to learn more, she specializes in examining how financial technology affects emerging economies' ability to grow sustainably. She has published one review paper and one analytical work in Scopus-indexed journals with a positive impact factor of 0.8 in a brief one-and-a-half-year period. At an international conference in the same field, she gave a paper presentation. She has participated in five workshops that provide hands-on instruction in econometrics. At the moment, she works on spatial econometrics and panel data analysis. In addition to her studies, she is actively participating in workshops and academic collaborations to expand her horizons and create multidisciplinary networks (ORCID: 0009-0009-0824-0010).

Rui Manuel Teixeira Santos Dias has a postdoctoral degree in Economics/Finance at the State University of Feira de Santana (BR), Department of Exact Sciences; Doctor of Finance degree at the University of Évora – Institute of Research and Advanced Training (PT); and a Diploma of Advanced Studies in Doctoral Studies (DEA), at the University of Extremadura (ES), in the scientific area of Financial Economics. He served as chief financial officer in various companies for 26 years. He is currently an Associate Professor at the ISG Business & Economics School and ESCE at the Polytechnic Institute of Setúbal. In terms of research, he is an Integrated Member of Centre for Research in Management, Business & Economics School (ORCID: 0000-0002-6138-3098).

Divya Meena S. is an Assistant Professor in grade 2 at VIT-AP University's School of Computer Science and Engineering. Deep learning, cloud security, thermal imaging, hyperspectral imaging, and neuro-fuzzy modelling are some of her areas of interest. Recognized with the Azim Premji University Research Fellowship, she has also received accolades for her contributions to participatory planning and women's empowerment. She holds teaching experience of 5.5 years with publications in Scopus and Web of Science with an impact factor of 11.7 and also contributed to four book chapters. Among her notable publications are 'Land Use and Land Cover Classification with Hyperspectral Data: A Comprehensive Review of Methods, Challenges and Future Directions', cited 97 times, and 'An Efficient Framework for Animal Breeds Classification Using Semi-Supervised Learning and Multi-Part Convolutional Neural Network (MP-CNN)', that has been cited 44 times. She has been cited more than 586 times in Google Scholar for her contributions to computer vision and machine learning (ORCID: 0000-0002-5256-5076).

Saib Fakhar has been serving as an Assistant Professor in the Department of Finance at the New Delhi Institute of Management (NDIM) since August 2024. He completed his graduation in Electronics and Communication from Punjab Technical University and earned an MBA in Finance from Aligarh Muslim University (AMU). He further pursued his passion for finance by obtaining a PhD in Finance from AMU. He qualified NET exam twice and also worked as a Senior Research Fellow. Prior to his tenure at NDIM, he worked as an Assistant Professor at Chandigarh Group of Colleges. His research interests include corporate social responsibility, financial distress, corporate governance, and banking. Notably, he co-authored a paper titled "Financial Distress in the Banking Industry: A Bibliometric Synthesis and Exploration" published in Cogent Economics & Finance in September 2023 (ORCID: 0000-0002-7425-9977).

Amrie Firmansyah is an Associate Professor and currently serves as the Head of the Accounting Department and Master of Accounting Programme at Universitas Pembangunan Nasional Veteran Jakarta, Indonesia. He holds multiple master's degrees in accounting, law, economics, administration, and management and earned his PhD in Accounting from Universitas Trisakti. Previously, he served in several strategic positions at the Indonesian Ministry of Finance, including at the Directorate General of Fiscal Balance. His expertise includes sustainability accounting, public sector accounting, taxation, and financial reporting. He is actively involved as a journal reviewer and board member for national and international journals. He has published widely in Scopus-indexed journals and authored multiple financial and sustainability accounting academic books. He also frequently serves as a speaker and trainer in professional and academic forums in Indonesia and abroad (ORCID: 0000-0002-1234-5678).

Harshi Garg is a dedicated PhD Scholar, recognized for her expertise as a market and user researcher and consultant, with a particular focus on digital and social media analysis. Her contributions to the field are marked by a series of notable achievements. Not only has she presented her research findings at international conferences, but she has also authored research papers in prestigious journals and contributed chapters to esteemed Scopus-indexed books (ORCID: 0009-0005-2790-5111).

Prabha Garg is an esteemed Associate Professor with 18 years of teaching experience and is a distinguished academician and researcher. With numerous publications in UGC-approved, peer-reviewed, and Scopus-indexed journals, she actively contributes to scholarly discourse through research paper presentations at national and international conferences. She has authored book chapters, published patents, and organized university-level programmes, including prestigious conferences. A dedicated advocate for gender inclusivity, she serves on the Women's Cell, Gender Sensitization Committee, and Board of Studies, shaping progressive academic policies. She founded the Expression Literary Club, fostering creativity through poetry, debate, drama, and more. Her initiative, *MMaverick*, a university magazine, provides a dynamic platform for intellectual exchange. Through her leadership, research, and mentorship, she inspires students and faculty, enriching the academic community and driving innovation in education (ORCID: 0009-0009-7015-5052).

Shikha Goyal is an Assistant Professor at Amity Law School, Amity University, Noida. She specializes in taxation, banking, sustainability, and insurance. With a strong research background, she has published around 25 research papers in ABDC-listed, Web of Science, and SCOPUS-indexed journals, including prestigious publishers like Taylor & Francis, Springer, Sage, and Wiley. She has also authored one book and contributed five chapters to edited volumes. As a speaker and organizer, she has actively participated in faculty development programmes, workshops, and conferences. She earned her PhD in Finance from Amity University, Noida, and continues contributing significantly to academia through her research and teaching (ORCID: 0000-0002-7634-4403).

Sumit Gupta is an Assistant Professor at Amity University Noida, with over 14 years of teaching and research experience. He holds a PhD from MNIT Jaipur, where he also earned his MTech. His research primarily focuses on sustainable manufacturing practices, sustainable supply chain management, and Industry 4.0. She has published extensively in international journals and conferences, with 49 publications in international journals. He has also contributed to the academic community through book chapters and editorial roles. His work involves exploring the integration of digital technologies for sustainability in manufacturing (ORCID: 0000-0003-3004-8219).

Viana Hassan is a renowned academic and researcher in Tourism and Cultural Management across Lebanon, Malta, and Cyprus. Founder and CEO of the European Tourism and Events Training Academy, she holds a PhD from Saint Joseph University, Beirut, focusing on Medical Tourism in Lebanon. With 19 years in tourism, she has experience in airline sales (MEA) and co-managing

Lebanese travel agencies. She has over 20 years of teaching at institutions like the Lebanese University, the University of Malta, and GBS Malta. Her expertise spans tourism management, event planning, airline business, and medical tourism. She has presented at global conferences, including Expo Dubai 2020 and the Medical Tourism World Summit, contributing to academia and industry in Athens, Paris, Vienna, Dubai, and beyond (ORCID: 0000-0002-7372-5059).

Uvesh Husain is a distinguished academician with over two decades of experience in teaching, research, and academic administration. He currently serves as the Acting Dean at Mazoon College, Sultanate of Oman, where he oversees strategic planning, risk management, and institutional growth. Specializing in Accounting and Finance, he has supervised 30+ postgraduate and 50+ undergraduate research projects. His scholarly contributions include 25 research papers and book chapters published in Scopus and Web of Science-indexed journals. Additionally, he is a reviewer for over 20 international journals, including those under JSS, Inderscience (IJTMKT), and MoHERI's TRC (ORCID: 0000-0002-8502-8488).

Mohammad Irfan is presently working as an Associate Professor at the School of Business and Management, Christ University, Lavasa, Pune, India. He has done his PhD from the Central University of Haryana. He has MBA (Finance), MCom (Account and Law), and MA (Economics) degrees. He has qualified UGC-JRF/SRF/NET in Management and Commerce. He is certified in NSEs (NCFM) and BSEs. He has experience of more than 16 years in the areas of SAPM, artificial intelligence, machine learning, blockchain, cryptocurrency, financial engineering, Fintech, green finance, and alternative finance. He has to his credit more than 72+ Scopus Indexed articles, including *The Journal of Economic Cooperation and Development* (Q2), *International Journal of Business Excellence* (*IJBEX*), *International Journal of Economics and Management* (*IJEM*), *Montenegrin Journal of Economics* (Q2), *Cogent Business & Management* (Taylor & Francis) (Q2), *Indian Journal of Finance* (*IJF*), and *Journal of Islamic Monetary Economics and Finance* (*JIMF*) (ORCID: 0000-0002-4956-1170).

Manoj Suranga Jothimuni is the Head of the Department of Accounting and Finance at Independent College Dublin, The Republic of Ireland. He is a Chartered Public Finance Accountant, a Fellow Chartered Management Accountant, and a Fellow International Accountant. With over 10 years of experience across both the academic and commercial sectors, he has expertise in audit and assurance, financial reporting, and performance management. His professional background spans multiple countries, including Sri Lanka, the Maldives, the UK, India, Singapore, and Ireland (ORCID: 0000-0002-7825-7258).

Mohammad Kashif is a distinguished academician and researcher in the area of management, finance, financial economics, and international business at Graphic Era Deemed to be University, Dehradun, India. He has several publications indexed in Web of Science, Scopus, and ABDC journals. He authored a textbook titled *Financial Management* for undergraduate students. He is the editor of upcoming edited books under Emerald Publishers and Bentham Science Publishers. He is guiding PhD scholars in his area of expertise. Besides, he is a member of several professional bodies at national as well as international level. He has been awarded many academic and research awards by reputed organizations. He has delivered several keynote lectures in faculty development programmes (FDPs) and conferences organized by reputed institutions. He has organized many FDPs and conferences at the national level (ORCID: 0000-0002-4940-8264).

Parvez Alam Khan is a distinguished academic and sustainability expert, currently serving as a Lecturer at the Department of Management and Humanities, UniversitiTeknologi PETRONAS (UTP), Malaysia, since June 2023. With a profound research focus on sustainability, governance, and the United Nations' Sustainable Development Goals, he has made significant contributions to both academia and industry. He holds a PhD in Sustainability from UTP (2022), an MBA (2014), and a Bachelor of Commerce (2012) from Aligarh Muslim University. His academic and professional journey spans over six years of teaching experience and 3.5 years in the environmental, social, and governance (ESG) sector. He is also an active committee member of ESG Academic Malaysia, the Quality Research Association of Malaysia, and the International Sustainability & Carbon Association (Germany) (ORCID: 0000-0001-8200-2461).

Manas Khemka, currently serving as the Secretary of Research at the School of Business and Management, Christ University, Lavasa, Pune. In this role, Khemka actively contributes to fostering a strong research culture by organizing academic initiatives, supporting faculty and peer research, and encouraging analytical thinking. Khemka's interests lie in finance, international business, and entrepreneurship, and is deeply driven by the pursuit of knowledge and practical insights in these areas. Khemka has been a part of various institutional events and committees, where Khemka developed strong leadership, communication, and organizational skills. Khemka is passionate about exploring new ideas, understanding global business dynamics, and creating platforms that inspire innovation and learning. Khemka believes in leading with purpose and constantly seeks opportunities that allow Khemka to grow and make a meaningful impact (ORCID: 0009-0001-6748-4076).

Sinem Derindere Köseoğlu is an Associate Professor of Finance at Istanbul University, specializing in company valuation, capital budgeting, brand valuation, start-up valuation, financial modelling, financial markets, and mergers & acquisitions. Holding SPK Level 3 and Derivatives Licenses, she collaborates with leading institutions, offering consultancy in project feasibility, financial analysis, and alternative financing solutions. As an editor and author of internationally published books on company valuation, start-up valuation, and financial data analytics, she integrates academic expertise with practical insights. Additionally, she delivers training for organizations such as the Public Oversight Authorit, Capital Markets Board, and Turkish Capital Markets Association, contributing to the development of Turkey's financial ecosystem (ORCID: 0000-0001-9478-0666).

Gaurav Kumar has done postdoctoral research in the area of financial data analytics at University College Dublin, Ireland. He has obtained a PhD degree from the Indian Institute of Technology (IIT), Kharagpur, and an MBA degree from the Indian Institute of Foreign Trade, Delhi. He has studied the liquidity of mid-cap stocks as an area of research for his doctoral thesis. He holds an Engineering degree in Computer Science from the National Institute of Technology, Allahabad. He has received many awards and grants including UGC Junior Research Fellowship. His broad research interests include stock markets, corporate finance, and financial analytics. His research work has been presented at various international conferences at the American Economic Association (USA), ICMA Centre (London), Corvinus University (Hungary), La Trobe University (Melbourne, Australia), IIM Ahmedabad, IIT Madras, IIT Kharagpur, and IIT Kanpur (ORCID: 0000-0001-9067-4161).

Sakshi Kumari is currently serving as the Coordinator of CAPS at the School of Business and Management, Christ University, Lavasa, Pune. In her role, she focuses on bridging academic learning with practical industry insights by organizing workshops, training sessions, and development programmes aimed at enhancing professional and personal growth. She is deeply passionate about creating impactful learning experiences and fostering a culture of continuous development. Her work involves close collaboration with faculty, industry experts, and peers to ensure that every initiative is relevant, engaging, and valuable. She has also contributed to several institutional events and committees, which has helped her hone her leadership, communication, and organizational skills. She is driven by a strong sense of purpose and a commitment to excellence in everything she does. She thrives in dynamic environments and is always open to innovative ideas and meaningful collaborations (ORCID: 0009-0006-9449-7311).

Nawazkhan Meeya is a Senior Lecturer at the University of Technology and Applied Sciences in Oman with over 23 years of teaching experience in India, Eritrea, and Oman. He holds dual Master's degrees in Accounting and Marketing, and a Management diploma, and is a gold medallist in MCom. His research, funded by The Research Council of Oman, focuses on the impact of social media on job search, examining platform preferences and effectiveness. He is dedicated to enriching education with innovative methodologies and is affiliated with the Indian Accounting Association and the Institute of Internal Auditors. An accomplished author with three publications, he recently submitted a book chapter draft titled 'Unlocking Talent Acquisition Potential: AI-driven Recruitment Strategies'. His work underscores his commitment to cutting-edge research and active contribution to the academic and professional communities, inspiring fellow scholars through his dedication and expertise (ORCID: 0000-0002-0258-5765).

Rufsha Melath is a Research Scholar at the Department of Commerce, Farook College (Autonomous), University of Calicut, Kozhikode. Her research interests include the stock market, foreign exchange market, commodity market, energy policy, uncertainty, carbon risk, and sustainable development (ORCID: 0000-0002-4506-9621).

Nandita Mishra is an Associate Professor at the Division of Business Administration in the Department of Management and Engineering, Linköping University, Sweden. She is also an Ambassador to IIRC (International Integrated Reporting Council), London and a Country Director of HETL (USA). She is also part of the Sustainability Reporting Board of ICAI (Institute of Chartered Accountants of India) and works closely with the Big 4 in sustainability, communication, and reporting. She holds a PhD in Corporate Governance in the Banking Sector and has over 20 years of experience in corporate and academic settings. She has attended various international seminars and conferences and has publications in well-renowned journals. She has also completed three funded research projects. She is engaged in consultancy work with many companies in which she helps them communicate their sustainability initiative and non-financial reporting (ORCID: 0000-0001-9725-9761).

Sharif Mohd is a distinguished Academic and Researcher in Commerce and Management, specializing in accounting, finance, and sustainability. He holds a PhD in Commerce and has extensive teaching experience at leading institutions, including NDIM Delhi and the University of Delhi. With a strong research portfolio, he has published 15 peer-reviewed papers in UGC-CARE and Scopus-indexed journals and authored a book *International Financial Management*. He has actively contributed to academia through national and international conferences, faculty development programmes, and curriculum development. Beyond research and teaching, he has undertaken key administrative roles, mentored students in major research projects, and served as an examiner for university programmes. His contributions have been recognized with prestigious awards, including the Best Research Scholar Award and Young Researcher Award. As a lifetime member and reviewer for esteemed academic organizations and journals, he remains committed to advancing knowledge and fostering academic excellence (ORCID: 0000-0002-2530-4815).

Pratik More is a distinguished professional with a strong academic background and extensive industrial experience. He holds two Master's degrees, one in Biotechnology and the other in Business Administration. He finished his PhD in Business Administration (Marketing) from the University of Pune. With the industry experience of more than 10 years, he has been associated with a Fortune 500 company and multinational companies in various roles of international marketing, market research, analytics, and healthcare consulting. At Woxsen University, he brings a fresh approach to education with a track record of engaging students in interactive and innovative learning experiences. Leveraging his decade-long industrial experience, he strives to introduce new skills in curriculum, student assessment, and fostering a positive learning environment. He emphasizes experiential learning for students and focuses on hands-on training and experience through live projects. His research interests include business analytics, co-creation, consumer behaviour, and modern technologies in business (ORCID: 0009-0000-6063-410X).

Donkor Nawaah, a citizen of Ghana, West Africa, is an accomplished academician, Assistant Professor, and Programme Director for the BBA Programme at Woxsen University's School of Business in Hyderabad, India. With over 17 years of extensive teaching experience, he has established himself as a distinguished educator and researcher in the fields of accounting, finance, and higher education. An active and prolific researcher, he has published papers in high-impact, peer-reviewed journals indexed in ABDC and Scopus, contributing significantly to contemporary discourse in accounting and finance. His research interests span a diverse range of critical areas, including accounting and finance, climate finance, corporate finance, accounting education, corporate governance and ethics, sustainability reporting, and managerial/cost accounting. He is also deeply engaged in curriculum design and evaluation, ensuring that academic programmes remain relevant and impactful in an evolving business landscape (ORCID: 0009-0008-8508-2207).

Ezutah Udoncy Olugu is an accomplished academic and researcher specializing in industrial engineering and operations management. He holds a PhD in Mechanical Engineering from UniversitiTeknologi Malaysia. His research interests include green manufacturing, supply chain management, and manufacturing process optimization. He has extensive experience in academia, including his current role at the University of the Witwatersrand and previous positions at UCSI University and the University of Malaya. He is a chartered engineer in the UK and Ireland and has contributed significantly to the field through numerous publications and involvement in professional organizations (ORCID: 0000-0003-2557-0168).

Shiva Sai Kiran Pothula is currently an Assistant Professor of Sustainability at the School of Business, Woxsen University, Hyderabad, India. He has a PhD from the prestigious Indian Institute of Science, Bengaluru, in Sustainability. He also has a Master's degree from Indian Institute of Technology Roorkee. He is the recipient of the prestigious 'Sakura Science Programme' grant from JST, Japan and has also participated in the 'Groningen Summer School' through a fully granted research fund from Groningen University. His areas of specialization include sustainability analytics, urban sustainability, business research methods, and analytics (ORCID: 0000-0002-0576-2480).

Sreekha Pullaykkodi is currently serving as an Assistant Professor at the Manipal School of Commerce and Economics in Manipal, which is situated in the Karnataka state of India. In this role, she is responsible for delivering and teaching subjects related to financial markets, international financial management, and international business management for both undergraduate and postgraduate students. Apart from teaching, she is actively involved in research also. She obtained her Doctor of Philosophy (PhD) from the School of Humanities, Social Sciences, and Management at the National Institute of Technology Karnataka, Surathkal, in the year 2024. Before enrolling for the PhD, she completed her BBA from Kannur University in 2013. Following this, she pursued and earned a Master of Business Administration with dual specialization in finance and marketing from Mangalore University in 2015. Her research interests include market microstructure, commodity markets, and energy resources (ORCID: 0000-0003-4911-0043).

Fazla Rabby is a dynamic and innovative business manager with a robust educational background, extensive teaching experience, and a proven track record in academia and industry. He earned his PhD from the University of Southern Queensland while his Master in Information Systems is from Central Queensland University, along with various other credentials that further enhanced his business and information technology skills. He is currently the Director at the Stanford Institute of Management and Technology, where he manages the academic department and oversees regulatory matters in coordination with the government and other key stakeholders. His commitment to research is a cornerstone of his academic journey, manifesting in a series of impactful publications spanning diverse and rapidly evolving fields (ORCID: 0000-0002-2683-7218).

Dhanuskodi Rengasamy is a renowned Professor who has taught and conducted research for more than 36 years. With a PhD in Management, he is the Director of the GRGSMS in Coimbatore. Among his many academic leadership roles are those of Professor at Bharathidasan and Madurai Kamaraj Universities, Director at DDE, and Alagappa University. He has successfully mentored 18 PhD students and authored more than 100 research articles for reputable publications. His areas of expertise include leadership in higher education, marketing, and management. He has played important roles in curriculum development, accreditation procedures, and quality assurance as a highly sought-after academic administrator. In addition to serving as an external examiner worldwide, he has chaired international conferences and given keynote talks. He continues to make a substantial contribution to management education and research and is well-known for his dedication to academic excellence and innovation (ORCID: 0000-0001-5037-3751).

Mahmood Shaik received his PhD degree from the Indian Institute of Technology Jodhpur. He is currently working as an Assistant Professor at Chaitanya Bharathi Institute of Technology, Hyderabad. Prior to that, he worked as a Postdoctoral Researcher at Mahindra University. His research includes signal processing and artificial intelligence applications for power quality assessment, energy markets, financial markets, and forecasting (ORCID: 0000-0003-2895-428X).

Muneer Shaik is currently working as an Associate Professor in Economics and Finance at Mahindra University, School of Management. He has over 15 years of work experience in academia and industry. He has taught courses in finance for undergraduate, MBA, and PhD level students. He acted as a resource person for various management development programmes conducted for multinational corporations like RBS, Larsen & Toubro, Murugappa Group, and AstraZeneca.

His teaching interests are in corporate finance, financial time series analysis, computational finance, econometrics, financial data analytics, derivatives, and risk management. He has published his research in reputable national and international peer-reviewed journals and presented at multiple conferences. Some of his research papers have won the best paper awards. He is a lifetime member of the India Finance Association (ORCID: 0000-0002-3508-1096).

Syed Noorul Shajar serves as an Assistant Professor, Programme Coordinator for the BCom programme, and Department Placement Coordinator at Vellore Institute of Technology, Vellore. Holding an MCom and a PhD in Accounting and Finance from Aligarh Muslim University, India, he has further demonstrated his academic proficiency by qualifying for the UGC-NET in Commerce. He also possesses dual postgraduate specializations, having completed a PGDBA and a PGFM (Executive) degree from SCDL, Pune, and MIT, Pune, respectively. With over eight years of postdoctoral teaching and research experience, his primary areas of expertise lie in accounting and finance. His current research interests are focused on critical areas such as sustainable development goals, corporate finance, corporate governance, and green finance. He actively contributes to his field through presentations at numerous national and international conferences and has a strong publication record in esteemed Scopus, ABDC, and Web of Science-indexed journals (ORCID: 0000-0002-0042-0190).

Vinay Pal Singh is a distinguished academician and researcher currently serving at Quantum University, Roorkee, Uttarakhand, India. With a strong background in management and interdisciplinary research, he has contributed significantly to academia through teaching, research, and administrative roles. His expertise spans areas such as marketing, finance, entrepreneurship, and emerging technologies, with a keen interest in the evolving digital and business landscapes. He has authored and co-authored numerous research papers, book chapters, and edited volumes, addressing contemporary challenges in management and technology integration. His commitment to fostering academic excellence and industry collaboration is evident in his active participation in conferences, workshops, and curriculum development. As a mentor and thought leader, he continues to shape the next generation of professionals, contributing to Quantum University's vision of innovative and experiential learning (ORCID: 0009-0007-1328-614X).

Ram Singh is a distinguished academician with over 17 years of expertise spanning teaching, corporate engagement, and research. He is a Professor and Director of IQAC at Symbiosis University of Applied Sciences, Indore, India, and holds a PhD in Finance and International Business from HNBG Central University, Srinagar, India. He has an extensive research portfolio, comprising 30+ SCOPUS-indexed papers, 37 book chapters, 20 books, and 7 patents. A sought-after resource person and conference chair, he mentors five doctoral scholars and serves on the editorial boards of prestigious journals such as IGI Global and Inderscience. An award-winning educator, he is also the President of the International Academic Research Association. His contributions to academic excellence, research innovation, and institutional development have solidified his reputation as a thought leader in finance and international business (ORCID: 0000-0002-6565-3091).

Sujit Singh is an experienced academician with over 23 years of teaching, research, and academic administration experience. He holds a PhD in Manufacturing Management from the University of Malaya, a Master's in Industrial Engineering from IIT Delhi, and a Bachelor's in Production Engineering and Management from NIT Jamshedpur. His career includes teaching at institutions in India and abroad, such as Woxsen University and Ethiopian Technical University, and he has held leadership roles including Programme Coordinator and Head of the Mechanical Engineering Department. His research interests include operations management, sustainable manufacturing, and quality engineering (ORCID: 0000-0002-3643-5183).

Nikita Singhal is an Associate Professor at IIMT University. Her areas of specialization are taxation, insurance, and banking. She has published around 30 research papers in ABDC listed, Web of Science and SCOPUS index journals, including Journals of Taylor and Francis, Springer, Sage, Wiley and national and international repute conferences. She also has authored two books and five chapters in an edited book. She has spoken and organized various faculty development programmes, workshops, and conferences. She is also a Managing Editor of the *IJAST Journal* of IIMT University. She completed her PhD from the Department of Commerce, Aligarh Muslim University and was awarded JRF (Commerce) in 2013 and JRF (Management) in 2012. She is also an awardee of a major research project titled 'Insurance Claim Settlement During Covid-19: A New Challenge for Indian Insurance Sector" sponsored by the Indian Council of Social Science Research (ORCID: 0000-0002-0700-8086).

Sundaram N. is a Professor (Higher Academic Grade) with more than 33 years of teaching experience and 20 years of research experience in the Department of Commerce at VIT University, Vellore. He is a productive scholar with 42 publications in Scopus, three of which have impact factors and one with an astounding 11.7. He is now overseeing five PhD scholars and has successfully mentored nine others. Numerous research honours and worldwide recognition have been bestowed upon him, including a monetary prize from Kongwon National University in South Korea. In addition to writing two books, he has finished three financed studies on consumer rights and financial inclusion. He is a key figure in establishing academic standards as an adjudicator for many universities and a peer reviewer for high-impact journals. His efforts, which include teaching, research, and academic administration, demonstrate his dedication to using education to promote social and economic development (ORCID: 0000-0002-0801-0428).

Vidya Suresh is currently a Faculty member at the College of Banking and Financial Studies, Oman. She has over 27 years of experience in teaching and research in economics and management. She had previously held key positions, including

Dean of PGDM in a B-School, business analyst with a KPO firm, editor of academic journals, and other administrative services such as placement & alumni relation management and summer internship coordination. She is a passionate case writer and has published cases with the Ivey League and IIM-A case centre. She is an active researcher and has published in ABDC and Scopus-indexed journals. She has obtained a doctorate degree in Industrial Economics with a focus on econometric analysis of the performance of global manufacturing industries. She is also an alumna of the UC Berkeley Center for Executive Education & UC Berkeley Haas School of Business (ORCID: 0000-0001-7356-8228).

Roshaiza Taha is an Associate Professor at the Faculty of Business, Economics, and Social Development, Universiti Malaysia Terengganu. She holds a PhD in Accounting from Monash University, Australia, and an MBA in Accounting from Universiti Utara Malaysia. Her research interests include taxation, financial markets, Islamic accounting, and zakat. Her doctoral work focused on the relationship between tax systems, financial market dynamics, and economic growth in developing Asian economies. She has also explored zakat as a component of Islamic economic development, highlighting its relevance to public finance and social equity. She has published in high-impact journals such as the *Journal of Asian Economics*, *Renewable & Sustainable Energy Reviews*, and *JurnalPengurusan*. She is a member of the Chartered Tax Institute of Malaysia and the Malaysian Association of Tax Accountants. She actively collaborates with institutions such as Monash University and Waikato University (ORCID: 0000-0002-8391-7206).

Furquan Uddin is an Assistant Professor at Aliah University, Kolkata, India. Besides, he has experience of more than 10 years teaching and research at different public varsities in India. He earned his PhD degree from Banaras Hindu University and postdoctoral research from Aligarh Muslim University. His research interests encompass strategic marketing, rural marketing, consumer behaviour, and life insurance. He has many research papers to his credit in national and international journals of repute (ORCID: 0000-0001-6502-8854).

Muhammad Usman is a Senior Lecturer in International Business at the University of Lancashire, UK. He is a member of the Ethics Review Panel and Research Programme Appraisal at UCLan. He teaches various modules at undergraduate and postgraduate levels and supervises students' research projects. He is active in research and published various articles in high-ranking journals such as *Environmental Science and Policy*, *International Journal of Finance and Economics*, and more. His research is in earnings management, corporate governance, environmental disclosure, and corporate finance (ORCID: 0000-0003-1626-8477).

Faisal Usmani is an Assistant Professor at the Department of Commerce at the School of Social Sciences and Languages, Vellore Institute of Technology, Vellore, Tamil Nadu, India. He holds a PhD in Business Administration with a specialization in financial management, along with an MBA in Finance. With over three years of teaching experience and two years of research expertise, his research interests include financial markets, volatility, foreign investment, and valuation. He has authored and published several research papers and book chapters in reputed journals (ORCID: 0000-0002-3653-334).

Sreekanth Peringanam Veluthedan is currently serving as a Visiting Lecturer at the School of Banking and Finance, Management Development Institute of Singapore in Tashkent, Uzbekistan. In this role, he is responsible for delivering and teaching modules related to banking, finance, and accounting to both undergraduate and postgraduate students. He obtained his Doctor of Philosophy from the School of Humanities, Social Sciences, and Management at the National Institute of Technology Karnataka, Surathkal, in the year 2023. Prior to this, he completed his undergraduate studies at Kannur University, Kerala, India, in 2007, with a specialization in finance. Subsequently, he pursued and earned a Master of Business Administration in Finance from Mahatma Gandhi University, Kerala, India, in 2009. He brings extensive academic expertise and a strong background in finance, contributing significantly to the field through his teaching and research endeavours (ORCID: 0000-0002-4573-5911).

Preface

Climate change is no longer a distant threat; it is an urgent reality with profound implications for global financial markets. Nowhere is this more evident than in emerging markets, where economic growth, financial stability, and sustainability intersect in complex ways. The increasing frequency of extreme weather events, shifting regulatory landscapes, and evolving investor preferences all contribute to an environment of heightened uncertainty. As financial professionals, policymakers, and investors grapple with these challenges, understanding the interplay between climate risk and emerging markets is essential.

Our book, *Climate Risk and Emerging Markets: Valuation, Volatility, and Portfolio Strategies*, aims to provide a comprehensive examination of the financial implications of climate change for emerging economies. It brings together leading scholars, industry experts, and policymakers to shed light on key issues, offering innovative insights into risk assessment, portfolio management, and policy frameworks that can drive sustainability. By exploring these topics in depth, this book serves as a crucial resource for academics, practitioners, and students who seek to navigate this evolving financial landscape.

The Need for This Book

Emerging markets play a crucial role in global economic growth, yet they remain particularly vulnerable to climate-related risks. The volatility and uncertainty arising from climate change impact asset valuation, investment strategies, and financial stability in these regions. Investors, businesses, and governments must develop resilient financial models that integrate climate risks into decision-making frameworks. While developed economies have made significant strides in adapting to climate risk through robust financial instruments and regulatory frameworks, emerging markets often lack the same level of preparedness and institutional strength.

This book is structured to address these concerns systematically, beginning with an overview of the landscape, followed by exploring market responses, investment strategies, and policy solutions. The final section presents case studies that provide real-world applications of these principles, offering valuable lessons for stakeholders.

Structure and Key Themes

The book is divided into four parts, each addressing a critical aspect of the relationship between climate risks and emerging markets.

Part I: Understanding the Landscape

The first section lays the foundation for our discussion by examining the role of emerging markets in the global economy and their susceptibility to climate risks. It includes an exploration of the opportunities and risks these economies face, highlighting how climate change exacerbates financial instability. Additionally, it investigates the valuation of emerging markets in BRICS nations in the face of climate disruptions. By transitioning from perceiving climate change as a threat to accepting it as a financial reality, this section sets the stage for deeper analyses in the following chapters.

Part II: Maneuvering Through the Tempest

With the foundation in place, the second section explores how financial markets react to climate uncertainty. It provides a comparative analysis of stock price vulnerability across different economies, demonstrating how climate change can trigger market volatility. The integration of climate risk into portfolio diversification strategies is examined in detail, offering insights into building resilient investment approaches. This section also delves into the interlinkages between financial inclusion, environmental sustainability, and the transition to a low-carbon economy. Further, it assesses the impact of greenhouse gas emissions on economic stability, an issue of paramount importance for policymakers and investors alike.

Part III: Mapping the Path

While risks and volatility dominate much of the climate finance conversation, this section shifts the focus towards solutions. It explores green finance, sustainability accounting for SMEs, and innovations in green banking driven by artificial intelligence. The ripple effects of climate policy uncertainty on financial markets are also examined, highlighting the need for strategic responses from governments and investors. Additionally, financial resilience in emerging markets is discussed, offering frameworks for climate risk mitigation and adaptation. This section underscores the importance of proactive policymaking, financial innovation, and corporate responsibility in ensuring sustainable development.

Part IV: Case Studies

Theory and strategy must ultimately be tested in real-world contexts. The final section of the book presents case studies that illustrate how firms and financial institutions in emerging markets are responding to climate risk. One such case study focuses on ITC Limited, a pioneering firm in India that has actively engaged with climate challenges. These real-world examples provide tangible insights into best practices, innovative solutions, and remaining obstacles in climate risk management.

Contribution to the Field

This book contributes to the growing body of literature on climate finance by addressing the unique vulnerabilities and opportunities present in emerging markets. While extensive research has been conducted on climate risks in developed economies, the distinctive challenges faced by emerging markets have not received the same level of attention. Our interdisciplinary approach bridges this gap, integrating financial theory, empirical analysis, and policy insights to offer a well-rounded perspective.

We hope that this book serves as a catalyst for further research, discussion, and action. Climate risk is a defining issue of our time, and its implications for financial markets cannot be ignored. By equipping investors, policymakers, and scholars with the necessary tools and frameworks, we aim to foster a more resilient and sustainable financial future.

Acknowledgements

This book is the result of the collective efforts of scholars, industry practitioners, and policymakers who have contributed their expertise and insights. We extend our heartfelt gratitude to all contributors for their rigorous research and dedication to this crucial topic. Special thanks go to the editorial team, whose commitment to excellence has been instrumental in shaping this volume.

We also wish to acknowledge the institutions and organizations that have supported this endeavour. Their encouragement and resources have been invaluable in bringing this project to fruition. Finally, we express our gratitude to our readers (academics, professionals, and students) who share our commitment to understanding and mitigating climate risk in financial markets. Your engagement and feedback will continue to inspire future research and policy advancements in this field.

As climate change continues to reshape the global financial landscape, the stakes for emerging markets could not be higher. This book provides a roadmap for understanding, assessing, and managing climate-related financial risks in these economies. By bridging academic research with practical insights, we hope to contribute to a more sustainable and resilient financial system.

We invite you to explore the ideas presented in the following chapters and join us in the effort to build a financial future that is both profitable and sustainable in the face of climate change.

Introduction Chapter of Climate Risk and Emerging Markets Book

Afzalur Rahman[a], *Shakeb Akhtar*[b], *Mahfooz Alam*[c] *and Mohsin Khan*[d]

[a]*Woxsen University, India*
[b]*University of Technology and Applied Sciences, Oman*
[c]*University of the People, USA*
[d]*Vellore Institute of Technology, India*

Chapter 1 provides an in-depth analysis of emerging market dynamics. A detailed study of emerging markets centers on their growth drivers along with investment opportunities and risk assessment and their economic connections to global markets. The chapter utilizes thematic analysis of publications from Scopus-indexed journals. The research investigates the key elements that facilitate economic expansion within emerging markets. The study evaluates investment opportunities and risks while investigating how emerging economies interact with developed economies. The key growth drivers in emerging markets, according to the chapter, are structural changes together with globalization and innovation. The chapter outlines investment opportunities and risks in these markets while stressing the need to comprehend both economic factors and political conditions. The chapter highlights how financial integration and policy spillovers from emerging markets influence global dynamics. This chapter helps readers gain a deeper understanding of emerging markets as drivers of future global growth and prosperity. It also delivers an exhaustive study of market dynamics as well as potential opportunities and risks within emerging economies, which makes it an essential tool for stakeholders who plan to invest in these markets.

Chapter 2 analyzes the impact of climate-related hazards on emerging markets and resource valuation. Emerging markets possess the capacity for expansion fiscally; they are increasingly vulnerable to tangible climate risks such as severe storm incidents and governmental forces associated with worldwide environmental targets. This chapter investigates how hazards related to climate change influence investment approaches and estimation of assets in developing nations through qualitative case study analysis from economic and ecological reports. The present research explains how these risks confront traditional economic models using the

Climate Risk and Emerging Markets: Valuation, Volatility, and Portfolio Strategies, 1–8

Published under exclusive licence by Emerald Publishing Limited
doi:10.1108/978-1-83708-088-520261003

examination of case studies, such as the economic effects of Cyclone Amphan and the drought's impact on the nation's hydro energy growth. The significant role of environmental, social, and governance (ESG) requirements in decreasing climate risk and establishing strong, balanced portfolios of assets for the long-term future is further examined in the chapter. The result of this chapter illustrates how proactive approaches are required to control these dangers and take benefit of the changing prospects of developing nations.

Chapter 3 examines how climate change, which was once a far-off danger, is now a reality and how its effects are felt by the most vulnerable, such as developing nations that must deal with issues of governance, social inequality, and economic instability. The chapter incorporates case studies, empirical data, and policy evaluations, drawing upon multidisciplinary research conducted between 2020 and 2024. Latin America, Africa, and South Asia provide important instances that demonstrate the effects of climate change and the need for immediate adaptation. Given the reliance on climate-sensitive industries and their limited ability to adapt, developing economies are disproportionately impacted by climate change. Technology breakthroughs, nature-based approaches, and more climate funding are examples of scalable, context-specific solutions that are essential. To reduce risks and increase resilience, regional collaboration and inclusive governance are also crucial. This chapter highlights the need for more study on developing-economy-specific adaptation frameworks, focusing on the relationship between socio-economic inequality and climate change. Finally, by emphasizing the unique challenges and prospects encountered by developing countries in tackling the climate problem, this chapter provides policymakers and stakeholders with useful insights.

With an emphasis on the BRICS economic unity, Chapter 4 examines how climate change affects developing markets' market values. With environmental shocks having a direct impact on economic development, climate change presents a danger to economic growth and diversity. To take into consideration unobserved variability unique to each nation, this chapter uses panel data analysis with the fixed effects method. After adjusting for confounding variables, it looks at how temperature changes and CO_2 emissions affect gross domestic product (GDP). Furthermore, the Spatial Durbin Model (SDM), which incorporates economic linkage variables like inflation and foreign direct investment, is used to capture spillover and direct impacts among economically linked nations. Ordinary least squares (OLS) regression and fixed effects results show that factors related to climate change have a major influence on market expansion. The SDM emphasizes both direct and spillover effects, highlighting the significant consequences of carbon emissions and the moderate effects of temperature fluctuations on GDP. These results highlight the significance of risk coverage plans and mitigation initiatives. Finally, by using sophisticated econometric tools to examine the interaction between environmental and economic factors in emerging markets, this chapter adds to the body of knowledge on climate change and economic growth. The chapter also provides fresh perspectives on the function of economic ties in attempts to mitigate and adapt to climate change.

Chapter 5 examines the impact of climate change events on stock price volatility by reviewing and comparing various methodological approaches used in academic research. The chapter conducts a comprehensive review of existing literature, identifying key methodologies used to assess the impact of climate-related disasters on stock prices. The chapter identifies four objectives: (1) defining and identifying climate change events, (2) detecting abnormal returns, (3) adjusting for seasonal noise in stock market data, and (4) estimating the effect of specific events. The comparative analysis includes methods employed in academic research to address each of the objectives. The review highlights the strengths and limitations of each method, showing that while ESA is widely used for identifying abnormal returns, it must be adjusted for seasonal effects. Regression-based approaches, although scarce, provide insights into causal relationships but require careful specification. The chapter emphasizes the need for a multi-method approach to comprehensively assess climate change risks in financial markets. By understanding the applicability and limitations of different methods, the findings provide valuable insights for young researchers, financial analysts, policymakers, and investors seeking to develop robust strategies for assessing and mitigating climate-induced stock market volatility. This chapter fills a gap in the literature by systematically comparing methodological approaches to studying climate change impacts on stock prices. It offers a structured framework for researchers and practitioners to navigate the complexities of financial market responses to climate-related exogenous shocks.

Chapter 6 explores strategies for building resilient investment portfolios by integrating climate and environmental risks into portfolio diversification strategies. It aims to provide a comprehensive framework for balancing financial returns with sustainable, long-term environmental goals in the context of the modern investment landscape. The research investigates contemporary approaches to diversification, focusing on the integration of climate and environmental factors into portfolio management. The chapter reviews innovative financial instruments, such as green bonds (GB) and ESG strategies, and examines case studies of successful integration within both developed and emerging markets. The chapter finds that incorporating climate and environmental risks into portfolio strategies not only enhances resilience but also presents new opportunities for sustainable growth. Successful approaches include active engagement with ESG criteria, the use of environmental risk assessments, and the adoption of climate-aware investment products. However, challenges remain in quantifying environmental risks and aligning financial markets with global sustainability goals. For investors and portfolio managers, the chapter provides actionable insights into integrating climate and environmental considerations into their strategies. It recommends adopting robust risk management tools, enhancing transparency in ESG reporting, and fostering collaboration with policymakers to create a more climate-resilient financial ecosystem.

Chapter 7 investigates the association between financial inclusion (FI) and environmental sustainability (ES). Additionally, it explores the reciprocal impact of ES on FI. The chapter focused on the BRICS group for the time period of 2008–2020. The International Monetary Fund and World Bank are the major sources of data collection for indicators of FI and ES. Separate indexes were created using principal component analysis FI and ES. To identify the association among the variables, i.e., FI and ES and vice versa, the pooled OLS technique was used. The chapter reveals a negative correlation between the variables, i.e., FI and ES. The percentage of the population availing clean fuels and technologies for cooking and forest areas shows a significant but negative association with FI. Carbon intensity also revealed a negative association with FI. The chapter also checked for a reverse causality test where ES was the dependent variable, and the results showed that inclusive finance negatively affects ES. The chapter examines the BRICS countries to assess the effect of inclusive finance and ES and the reciprocal link between the two variables.

Chapter 8 examines the complex relationship between uncertainty and sustainable stock investment. Focusing on the Indian stock market, this chapter examines the return co-movement and risk spillover among economic uncertainty, oil price shock, climate policy changes, and green stock indices. This chapter employs wavelet coherence and time-varying parameter vector autoregression methodologies to examine the return co-movement and risk transmission dynamics among major uncertainty indices, namely, economic policy uncertainty (EPU), oil price uncertainty (OPU), climate policy uncertainty (CPU), and green investments, as represented by the BSE CARBONEX and BSE GREENEX indices, from January 2013 to July 2024. To offer a comparative evaluation, we furthermore include traditional market indices such as the BSE Sensex, BSE 100, and BSE Oil and Gas indices. Wavelet coherence analysis demonstrates moderate co-movement among EPU, CPU, and the returns of green stocks. However, OPU strongly influences the green stock returns across the time period. The time-varying parameter vector autoregression analysis reveals moderate risk interconnectedness, with CPU, OPU, and EPU serving as net risk transmitters. Notably, CPU emerges as the primary contributor, highlighting the vulnerability of green investments to energy market variations.

Chapter 9 examines the impacts of growing investment in GB on non-renewable energy resources. The chapter also explores the asymmetric linkages between GB, crude oil, natural gas, and heating oil spanning over a decade from 2013 to 2023. The long- and short-term asymmetric connectedness between the variables is examined using a non-linear auto regressive distributed lag (NARDL) model. The chapter finds that GB have a significant nexus with oil prices. This chapter also found that oil prices are significantly positively associated with GB, confirming that GB prices increase as oil prices increase. This chapter becomes novel in terms of methodology and data. This chapter uses NARDL to examine the non-linear nexus between variables.

Chapter 10 examines the relationship between greenhouse gas (GHG) emissions and economic stability in D8 countries – Bangladesh, Egypt, Indonesia, Iran, Malaysia, Nigeria, Pakistan, and Turkey. It aims to assess whether emissions, particularly methane (CH_4), nitrous oxide (N_2O), and carbon dioxide (CO_2), serve as economic indicators and how transitioning to renewable energy influences economic growth and ES. The chapter employs statistical analysis using regression models to evaluate the impact of GHG emissions on key economic indicators such as GDP, gross national income, inflation, and energy consumption. Data from the World Development Indicators spanning 2001–2023 is utilized. The Environmental Kuznets Curve and stochastic impacts by regression on population, affluence, and technology models are applied to examine the interplay between emissions and economic growth. Additionally, sectoral analysis is conducted to highlight the role of renewable energy and policy measures in mitigating emissions. The results indicate a complex relationship between emissions and economic stability. Methane and nitrous oxide emissions exhibit a significant correlation with economic performance, whereas CO_2 emissions show mixed effects. Countries investing in renewable energy, such as Indonesia and Malaysia, demonstrate improved economic resilience while reducing emissions. The chapter highlights the need for energy efficiency measures, investment in clean energy, and regional cooperation to balance economic growth with ES. This chapter provides a comprehensive analysis of the economic impact of GHG emissions in D8 nations, offering policy recommendations to achieve sustainable development while maintaining economic stability.

Chapter 11 investigates the development of green finance in South Asia, a region with rapid economic growth and serious environmental issues. This chapter analyzes the influence of policy, financial instruments, and regulations on green finance among major economies of South Asia. A secondary data approach is employed, examining academic research, regulatory publications, and policy papers. Green finance tools such as climate risk disclosures, sustainability-linked incentives, and GB are assessed critically to determine systemic gaps. As regulatory measures and financial innovations sustain green finance, policy fragmentation, lack of consistency in regulations, and limited investor awareness remain challenges. Nonetheless, forthcoming trends around policy harmonization, growth in sustainable financial products, and enhanced climate-related disclosures suggest promising prospects. The chapter presents practical suggestions for policymakers, financial institutions, and regulators to improve green finance mechanisms. Regional cooperation, financial innovation, and regulatory enhancements can stimulate the uptake of sustainable finance in South Asia. This chapter enriches the limited literature on green finance in South Asia, highlighting how global climate policies and financial innovations can enhance regional economic resilience.

Chapter 12 discusses the challenges and opportunities for implementing sustainability accounting in small and medium enterprises (SMEs). The implementation of sustainability accounting standards that are applied globally is not an easy thing for SMEs. On the other hand, implementing sustainability accounting can benefit SMEs in terms of business transparency, investment access, reputation enhancement, and resource management efficiency. This chapter uses a scoping review approach from several works of literature related to implementing sustainability accounting in SMEs. Implementing sustainability accounting for SMEs is not an easy thing to do. The limited resources that SMEs currently have and the lack of optimal government support are challenges for SMEs in integrating sustainability into their businesses. On the other hand, implementing sustainability accounting can provide various benefits, such as increasing SME access to green investment and funding, strengthening business reputation, building strategic partnerships, and increasing resource management efficiency in the long term. In addition, implementing sustainability accounting also helps SMEs to align consumer preferences and sustainability issues globally. This chapter highlights the role of sustainability accounting as a strategic tool for SMEs to improve business resilience and competitiveness amid the increasing global awareness of sustainability. In addition, this chapter emphasizes the importance of the government's role in supporting SMEs in facing sustainability reporting challenges, which has rarely been discussed in previous literature.

Chapter 13 explores the relationship between artificial intelligence (AI) and green banking, techniques of AI used in green banking, current trends, and new strategies used to support sustainable financial services in emerging markets. This chapter begins with a discussion of the concept of green banking and the basic principles that it is based on, which are designed to support the development of environmentally friendly financial products and services. The chapter also details some practices that show how sustainability is incorporated into banking operations in emerging markets. This chapter concludes that financial institutions in emerging markets can leverage the strengths of sophisticated technologies for several purposes, such as AI-enabled risk assessment and ESG reporting, to make sound decisions and adhere to the set sustainability standards. Machine learning-based analysis assists in the identification of eco-friendly investments, thus helping investors to make the right decisions. Real-time monitoring systems prevent violations of environmental laws and regulations and monitor energy consumption. In addition, AI has changed how customers are engaged by promoting sustainable behaviors and efficiency in business by reducing paper usage and energy consumption. This chapter highlighted AI's potential in evaluating environmental risks, building sustainable investment portfolios, implementing paperless and energy-efficient operations, and fostering informed decision-making in green banking in emerging markets.

Chapter 14 examines the impact of CPU in terms of emerging stock markets, emerging bond markets, as well as burgeoning green investment markets on the entire world financial market. It also shows how CPU is a very significant source of volatility, investment risk management, as well as portfolio diversification regarding investments. This chapter seeks to analyze the complexities of how Climate Policy Uncertainty (CPU) acts through the analysis of market volatility, return statistics, and the pattern of green asset behavior during periods of stress in the market. The current chapter, therefore, gives comparative evidence in terms of the short- and long-term impacts of CPU on emerging and green markets. The findings reflect that CPU leads, at high uncertainty time, to increased short-run volatilities and less return in emerging cases. By and large, however, the long run sees markets adjusting to newer regulatory landscapes and possible greater returns. Green assets, more specifically, demonstrate greater return spillovers across distress periods and with an increased overall connection with sustainable investments. The chapter recommends strategic investments in GB and dynamic portfolio reshuffling to buy out some of the effects of CPU. Their focus is also on risk management while achieving these targets through sustainability. This is of more relevance in emerging markets like Vietnam, where big investments have been made into sustainable practices within the country.

Chapter 15 explains the management of the climate change risks that challenge the current financial stability with new tools in climate finance such as GB, carbon pricing, and climate insurance to build financial resilience. Various tools and sustainable investment strategies function to strengthen financial systems against climate-related risks according to this chapter. The chapter combines multiple disciplines to investigate climate finance mechanisms through both empirical research and policy analysis in order to assess their performance. This chapter investigates the revolutionary advantage of blockchain and AI, digital technology to make the climate finance process automatic, enhancing transparency as well as scalability and operational efficiency. The chapter shows how ESG factors play a significant role in robust sustainability goals with financial systems. Emerging climate finance strategies show their capacity to mitigate climate threats while enhancing financial system resilience. The chapter also illustrates how both public and private institutions need to formulate sustainable policies through adaptive methods in order to achieve sustainability. Through its evaluation, the chapter shows that digital technologies boost conventional financial instruments to create stronger accountable system frameworks. The discussion ends by stressing the need for adaptable financial systems because they will ensure economic stability on our climate-challenged planet. The chapter delivers practical recommendations about uniting modern financial advancements with digital resources under policy frameworks to develop stronger climate sustainability.

Chapter 16 analyzes the challenges that are surfaced across the world due to the accelerating pace of climate change with emerging markets facing rapid-growing, urbanizing, and significantly unequal climate-related hazards entailing droughts, extreme heat, and floods. The growth of emerging economies, when accompanied by the development of their population and industries, stands to make significant contributions to international efforts that are geared toward tackling climate change. However, such efforts have to cope with difficulties in several emerging markets like inadequate infrastructure, limited funding, and governance issues. This chapter used a qualitative research approach, i.e., case studies to focus on the risk-mitigation strategies of three southern Indian states (i.e., Maharashtra, Tamil Nadu, and Karnataka) for achieving development goals amid the pressing need for climate action plans. Further, comparative analysis is also conducted for these three state-level climate initiatives – Maharashtra State Action Plan on Climate Change, Tamil Nadu State Action Plan on Climate Change (TNSAPCC), and Karnataka State Action Plan on Climate Change (KSAPCC). This chapter also showcases that practical implications are wide-reaching and are useful for governments and communities in addressing climate change. The chapter informs the creation of effective climate policies by identifying the most efficient strategies that are used by the government for climate resilience. The chapter emphasizes that decentralized approaches and local solutions must be promoted to tackle short-term vulnerabilities with an eye for longer-term sustainability.

Chapter 17 analyzes how climate risks affect financial assets, market stability, and investment. This chapter estimates that climate change may put around 2% of global financial assets at risk by 2100, with the worst-case scenarios estimating up to 10%. The chapter underscores the importance of efficient risk management and adaptive investment strategies toward these challenges. This chapter marries empirical study with financial modeling to evaluate climate-related risks across emerging markets. The chapter examines economic losses in the past, sovereign credit ratings, and asset pricing to measure climate-related financial exposure. Global financial institution data, market analysis, and climate risk evaluation are used to create a practical framework for investors, asset managers, and policymakers. The findings indicate that climate change has already caused a total global economic loss of an estimated $2.8 trillion over the period 2000–2019, or roughly $16 million an hour. Emerging economies like Bangladesh, Brazil, India, and Indonesia are most exposed because of environmental degradation, resource constraints, and adverse weather conditions. These threats severely impact investment inflows, creditworthiness, and economic prospects for growth in these economies. This chapter closes the gap between empirical research and practical application, providing a holistic framework for incorporating climate risk into financial decision-making. Through the provision of actionable recommendations, it enables investors and policymakers to make risk-adjusted, sustainable financial choices. The chapter highlights the imperative for climate-sensitive investment strategies and paves the way for future studies on how to reduce financial vulnerabilities in emerging markets.

Chapter 18 addresses the impacts of climate change highlighting ITC Limited's sustainable business strategy. As illustrated by the case of ITC in the study, companies can learn how to manage the conflict between profit and the environment and people. In this chapter, ITC's sustainability initiatives in water stewardship, renewable energy, climate-smart agriculture, and paperboard recycling are comprehensively explored. The results of the study are based on the data collected from ITC's financial and socio-cultural projects which aimed at enhancing agricultural production, empowering women, and creating rural employment. This chapter also highlights some of the key milestones that ITC has achieved including water positivity, more than 50% renewable energy, and climate-smart agriculture, all due to their sustainable approach. The company also reduced its environmental effects while increasing its socio-economic value, particularly in rural areas of India. This case points out the necessity of the stakeholder's approach and the long-term perspective for a sustainable business. This chapter also provides a rich and practical understanding of how organizations can incorporate sustainability strategies to tackle climate change and thrive. The practices of ITC are exemplary, and this report provides a clear understanding of how sustainability can be incorporated into business strategies. The chapter adds to the growing discussion on corporate sustainability.

Part I

Understanding the Landscape

Chapter 1

Emerging Markets: Growth Drivers with Opportunities and Risks for Global Prosperity

Afzalur Rahman[a], *Uvesh Husain*[b] *and Manoj Suranga Jothimuni*[c]

[a]*Woxsen University, Hyderabad, India*
[b]*Mazoon College, Muscat, Oman*
[c]*Independent College, Dublin, Ireland*

Abstract

Emerging markets (EMs) are increasingly recognized as pivotal engines of global economic growth, offering substantial opportunities for investors, multinational corporations, and local communities alike. The expanding influence of these markets is driven by rapid industrialization, rising consumer demand, and enhanced technological capabilities. This chapter aims to explore how EMs contribute to global prosperity by fuelling innovation, promoting trade, and offering diverse investment opportunities, while also examining the significant risks associated with their development. Amidst the opportunities, the inherent vulnerabilities of these economies such as political instability, limited infrastructure, regulatory volatility, and climate-induced disruptions pose challenges that must be carefully managed. This chapter provides an in-depth analysis of the dynamic factors at play, highlighting the interconnected benefits these markets offer to global stakeholders, as well as the risks that come with dependence on these regions. By understanding the balance between growth opportunities and inherent risks, stakeholders can make more informed decisions, leveraging the potential of EMs for inclusive and sustainable economic advancement while preparing for the complexities they introduce into the global financial landscape.

Keywords: Emerging markets; economic growth drivers; global economy; investment opportunities; global risk

Climate Risk and Emerging Markets: Valuation, Volatility, and Portfolio Strategies, 11–24

doi:10.1108/978-1-83708-088-520261006

1. Introduction

Over the past decades, emerging economies have emerged as a cornerstone of the global economic landscape. With rapid industrialization and digitalization, these economies serve as the main engines for sustainable growth and development. EM economies constitute around 80% of the world's population and almost 70% of the total gross domestic product growth. One of the important trends that we have seen is the rise of EMs has led to the rapid expansion of consumer bases as well as a paramount increase in their global trade networks. It offers significant opportunities for businesses, investors, and policymakers. However, with an exponential surge and vast potential, these fast-paced EMs pose significant inherent risks, including economic volatility, political instability, and vulnerability to external shocks.

The reason for the sudden surge of the EMs is manifold. The growth can be attributed to several key factors, including technological advancements, demographic shifts, and global interconnectedness. Lately, there is empirical evidence suggesting that emerging economies, such as China, Brazil, India, and South Africa, will emerge as the main potential holders for global economic development (Srivastava, 2012). As the world economy is liberated and globalized, it encourages EMs to diversify their economies, reducing reliance on a single commodity or sector. As innovation is at the centre stage, emerging economies leveraged new products, processes, and technologies to bridge the digital divide, empower small- and medium-sized businesses, and enhance productivity. A few of the major economies are focusing on cross-border trade and regions to diversify their reliance and increase their global reach. For example, the Belt and Road Initiative is a massive infrastructural development project led by China to promote economic development and inter-regional connectivity in over 115 countries, exemplifies how emerging economies leverage international partnerships to accelerate economic development and strengthen their global presence (Zhang, 2021). A few of the studies have also emphasized that globalization has facilitated the flow of foreign capital into emerging economies such as China and India, enhancing their competitiveness and economic resilience (Gorodnichenko et al., 2010).

Despite their growing importance and increased market integration, emerging economies still face heightened risks from globalization due to their dependence on foreign investment, technology transfer, and integrated supply chains. For example, disruptions in the global supply chain, rising geopolitical tensions, tariff wars, etc., have brought risks and potential benefits and costs. Due to the dual nature of EMs that offer both immense potential and heightened sensitivity to global disruptions, investigating the role of emerging economies in the modern era assumes significance. This chapter has implications for businesses, policymakers, and investors to explore the complexities of emerging economies to foster sustainable growth, mitigate risks, and contribute to global economic stability. This chapter explores the critical role of EMs in shaping the future of global prosperity, examining their drivers of growth, challenges, and strategic importance in an interconnected world.

2. Objectives of the Chapter

The main purpose of this chapter is to know about the growth engines of EMs, meanwhile, determining what they can offer as well as what risks they hold. The study tries to address a major research gap on how EMs are able to continue growing and survive within the global opportunities and threats. Specifically, the chapter will:

- *Review growth drivers*: Review the main factors responsible for EM growth, such as structural change, globalization, and innovation (Serletis & Azad, 2018; Wu & Pan, 2021). In this section, we will see how these economies can take advantage of their distinctiveness to deal with the constraints on the global economy.
- *Identify opportunities and risks*: Identify the opportunities to invest and develop in EMs, and the risk of economic volatility, political instability, and external shocks (Bhuiyan, 2023; Domínguez et al., 2016). This double assessment will inform stakeholders when they are considering participation in these markets.
- *Study interdependencies globally*: Explore how EMs and developed economies are interdependent, for example, financial integration across the world and the spillover effects of economic policies (Adler & Mora, 2012; Wang & Chen, 2016). Such interdependencies need to be grasped if we are to understand the wider impact of new market trends on prosperity across the world.
- *Policy suggestions*: Based on the analysis, the chapter will propose policy suggestions for improving the resilience and growth of EMs. These will be for improving governance, innovation, and economic stability (Chea, 2021; Mansur, 2017).

3. Research Methodology

The present chapter is aimed at analysing the existing literature to achieve the given objective. The data source to collect the peer-reviewed literature across the various disciplines that facilitate achieving the objective of the chapter is the Scopus Database. The selection strategy is the search for the most relevant paper through the keyword search. The detail of the keywords that are used to complete the different sections of the book chapter is shown in Table 1.1.

However, the final list of references is 51 on completing this chapter. This systematic literature review is rigorous and provides a clear understanding of dynamics of the EMs, with the associated risks and opportunities. It will also help the researchers and the policymakers in making their effort to write directions.

4. Historical Context and Evolution of EMs

EMs have taken different forms in recent decades thanks to economic reforms and geopolitics. In the past, EMs tend to have evolved from closed, centrally planned economies to open market economies. The process of change was driven both internally through reforms and externally by external influences, and so the interacting forces that made up their economies were rather tangled.

Table 1.1 Detail of the Keywords.

Section	Keyword	Paper Referred
Introduction that also includes the research gap	'emerging markets' and 'global economy' and 'economic impact'	42
Historical context and evolution of emerging markets Economic opportunities in emerging markets	'emerging markets' and 'economic history' and 'market evolution' 'emerging markets' and 'economic reforms' and 'geopolitical factors'	58
Financial markets and innovations	'emerging markets' and 'globalization' and 'technology adoption' 'fintech' and 'emerging markets' and 'financial instruments' 'emerging markets' and 'economic growth' and 'sectoral analysis'	55
Risks and vulnerabilities in emerging markets	'political risk' and 'economic risk' and 'emerging markets' 'emerging markets' and 'risks" and 'vulnerabilities'	58
Strategies for sustainable growth and stability in emerging markets	'emerging markets' and 'sustainable growth' and 'economic policies' 'governance' and 'regulatory frameworks' and 'emerging markets'	48
Future directions and research gaps with policy recommendations	Future research and emerging markets and trends Research gaps and emerging markets and economic studies	60

Many EMs started to implement pro-market reforms to liberalize their economies in the late 20th century. These reforms included deregulation, state-owned enterprises, privatization and legal protection of property rights and foreign investment (Wu & Pan, 2021). Developing countries such as India and China, for example, underwent dramatic economic transformations in the 1990s, phasing out socialist models in favour of market-based ones. This not only accelerated economic development but also enmeshed those economies in the world market, which made them a magnet for high levels of foreign direct investment (FDI) (Epor et al., 2024). These markets are becoming super important in the global economy; they might even drive half of the world's growth by 2025 (Ivanović-Đukić et al., 2021).

EMs have been driven by geopolitics too. The end of the Cold War and the consequent globalization of trade and investment opened up opportunities for developing economies to connect with advanced markets (Ugurlu-Yildirim & Ordu-Akkaya, 2022). Yet geopolitical risk, political uncertainty and wars, for example, have remained major hindrances to their growth paths. Political risks can seriously harm the growth of these economies on long term – it's a high-risk, high-reward kind of deal (Ugurlu-Yildirim & Ordu-Akkaya, 2022).

In addition, EMs' history cannot be dissociated from their colonial history, which frequently left legacies of economic dependence and underdevelopment. The switch to market economies has meant that economic reforms have needed to be done, but also their histories, and the socio-economic structures they had created along the way (Popkova, 2023). That's the history that's needed to learn how EMs operate now and what their future holds.

5. Economic Opportunities in EMs

New EMs offer economic opportunities with high growth, sectoral expansion, and rising integration into the world economy. In their developing stages, these economies are already major global market players and have unique opportunities for investment and growth. This section explores how new markets can make money, using industry research and looking at how globalization and technology are changing things.

5.1. Sectoral Analysis of Economic Growth

New markets have diverse economic sectors that make up their economies. Farming, manufacturing, and services are all really important to the economy. For example, agriculture is the backbone of most developing economies, providing jobs, food security, and a foundation for growth in related industries (Wu & Pan, 2021). The manufacturing industry has been also strong, especially in countries such as China and India, where policies have pushed industrialization and export-led growth (Ivanović-Đukić et al., 2021). Industrialization has not only expanded domestic production but also connected these nations to global supply chains, making them more competitive.

The services, especially information technology and financial services, have been one of the major growth sectors for most of the EMs. The web, digital platforms, and e-commerce have upended traditional businesses, creating opportunities for innovation and entrepreneurs. According to Wu and Pan (2021), the quick growth in these industries means emerging economies are becoming more focused on knowledge-based work. This shift is key to a strong and stable economy.

5.2. Globalization and Technology Adoption

The EM economic system has been transformed by globalization. Integration into the world economy has allowed for global markets, capital, and technology, which are key to growth (Chari & Polizzi, 2011). Rising economies have assimilated to globalization more easily and the flood of FDI has buoyed their economies. The World Bank estimates, for instance, that EMs will drive half of the world's economic growth by 2025, which shows how central they are to the world economy (Raza et al., 2021).

The adoption of technology is another major determinant of economic growth in EMs. These economies used fast-changing tech to jump ahead in older development stages, especially in communications and finance. Financial inclusion was transformed through mobile banking and FinTech services, whereby millions of people started to receive banking services for the first time (Gangadharan & Suresh, 2019). This technology innovation is not just increasing productivity but also enabling innovation and entrepreneurship, which is important for economic diversification and resilience.

Moreover, the COVID-19 pandemic has pushed the adoption of digital technologies in all fields, and it also puts emphasis on opportunities in EMs. Remote work, e-commerce, and digital services created new market segments and platforms for the growth of enterprises (Kim & Yang, 2009). As new emerging economies evolve to take advantage of these developments, they will also be more open to investment and talent and will be placed further up in the global economy.

5.3. *Financial Markets and Innovations*

Financial markets and innovation, in a newer way, have become an increasingly prominent aspect of the world economy. The innovations in finance, due to the advancement of technology and the evolving needs of the consumer, changed traditional financial services and opened new doors of expansion and inclusion. This section covers the innovation role of financial markets and the emerging economy impact of FinTech.

5.3.1. Function of Financial Markets in Inspiring Innovation

Financial markets act as innovation hubs by lending capital and infrastructure for start-ups. Access to funding for innovative projects in EMs hinges on the development of robust financial systems. According to Sağ et al. (2019), globalization and digital technologies led multinational companies to look at new markets as places where they can do research and development and enhance innovation in the region. It is not just this trend, new tech and business ideas also boost the economy.

Apart from that, new financial products are popping up everywhere in EMs, helping local businesses and people. In the case of microfinance and peer-to-peer lending platforms, for example, it offered other means of funding to small and medium enterprises (SMEs) who don't normally get an option from banks (Sharma & Jha, 2016). Not only do these innovations increase access to capital, but they also boost entrepreneurship and economic diversification in developing markets.

5.3.2. What Is the Effect of FinTech in Small - and Medium-Sized Markets?

FinTech has become a game changer in the world of financial services, especially in the new economies. This technology has helped bring new financial products to market that are more efficient and accessible. FinTech applications transformed the way users access financial products and made them accessible to individuals and businesses (Nguyen, 2022). It is especially relevant in developing countries where banks might not have a sound banking system.

Mobile banking and digital payments have been one of the key ways that financial inclusion in developing countries has become mainstream. For instance, FinTech solutions have allowed millions of unbanked people to avail of financial services, hence reducing poverty and driving economic growth (Appiah-Otoo & Song, 2021). Then there is the emergence of blockchain and cryptocurrencies that have also opened up new investments and transactions and diversified the economy (Naseema et al., 2024; Nikiforov et al., 2020).

What's more, FinTech is commonly adopted in the EM as a way to solve a certain problem like transaction fees or access to credit is limited. FinTech is more likely to be adopted in countries where financial services are costly or there is not a lot of competition between providers (Frost, 2020). The dynamic makes the space for growth as FinTech firms strive to be more accessible and affordable compared to financial services.

6. EM Risks and Opportunities, A Few of Them

EMs are generally said to have high growth potential, but there are also risk factors and weaknesses which can undermine the stability of their economy and investor attractiveness. Such risks, especially political and economic risks, should be clear to stakeholders interested in making decisions about investment in these markets.

6.1. Political Risks in EMs

Political risk is one of the most important considerations in EMs for investment. It is a set of uncertainties in government policies, political stability, and regulatory climate. Moreover, as Bilson et al. (2000) explain, political risk can have significant consequences on the performance of the stock market; the higher the degree of political instability, the more volatile and less profitable the investment is for investors. This relationship might be stronger in EMs where politics can be more unstable and easily flipped.

Moreover, the political risk does not just affect short-term market response; it can also affect long-term economic development. Lower political risk is a way of attracting more FDI for developing emerging economies, as Girard and Sinha (2008) propose. High political risk, on the other hand, deters investment and slows economic growth, leading to underdevelopment and instability.

The political schism in the EMs is an additional headache. Depending on political fragmentation and volatility, the companies operating in these markets are at different risk levels (Sun et al., 2015). For companies with political ties, the risk might be easier to manage, and for those without it, it will be arduous.

6.2. Economic Risks in EMs

EM economic risks are multi-faceted and can come from various elements such as macroeconomic volatility, inflation, and external shocks. Because the global financial markets are inseparable, emerging economies are extremely sensitive to economic shocks. The COVID-19 pandemic and geopolitical conflicts like the Russia–Ukraine conflict, for example, have underscored the vulnerability of EMs to global economic shocks (Kaylan et al., 2024; Khan et al., 2022).

Prior studies indicate that economic risk, such as the movement of commodities and changes in international financial dynamics, can affect the performance of stock markets in developing countries (Mensi et al., 2015). Added to these risks are structural weaknesses in local economies (like dependence on a small basket of exports, or a weak financial system).

In addition, with EMs increasingly entangled in the world economy, they are now also subject to greater systemic risk. Borri (2018) on local currency systemic risk also underlines EMs' susceptibility to contagion during times of financial crises. These links mean that problems in one part of the world can rapidly extend to other parts of the world, worsening economic precarity.

7. How to Build Growth and Stability for Sustainable Markets?

EMs are in a situation where growth and stability must be sustainable. In order to compete on a global level, these economies will have to pursue integrated economic policies and governance arrangements that enable sustainability while also dealing with vulnerabilities. Here is where we talk about how best to build sustainable growth and stability in EMs, including economic policies and regulatory regimes.

7.1. Economic Policies for Sustainable Growth

EMs need economic policies that put the long term ahead of the short. As per Shahmi (2023), monetary policy interventions can make a real difference in capital flows and overall growth in developing countries. We will need to see policymakers working to create the conditions for investment, and that means macroeconomic stability such as low inflation and stable exchange rates. That stability doesn't just draw in FDI but also helps local companies in their growth paths.

In addition, sustainability should be a policy priority in economic policies. Bongers and Díaz-Roldán (2018), for example, stress that economic policy should be harmonized with social and environmental conservation targets. Such a policy requires the move to green economic policies, encouraging renewable energy, sustainable farming, and clean technologies. Through sustainability, EMs can save the planet and be more resilient in the long term.

Moreover, green bonds have been developed as a sustainable project funding option for the new markets. Similarly, the green bond market in Latin America and the Caribbean shows that sustainable finance could be used to stimulate growth (Argandoña et al., 2022). With green bonds, developing countries could get funding for environmentally sound projects, which would marry economic development and ecological preservation.

7.2. Governance and Regulatory Frameworks

The best governance and robust regulation are most important for sustainable growth in EMs. Strong governance can make economic policies more efficient and accountable (Papargyropoulou et al., 2012). This means transparent regulation to promote free competition, safeguard investors, and responsibly manage resources.

Even regulation will have to be responsive to EMs. 'We must have a regulatory governance that can adjust to the changes brought about by globalised economic dynamics' (Kjaer & Vetterlein, 2018). That flexibility comes in handy when it comes to the changing technology and dynamics of the market. Regulators should make regulations lenient and non-obligatory so that innovation and elasticity are encouraged, and the public interest is protected.

Further, macroprudential measures also aid financial stability in developing markets (Andrieş & Melnic, 2019). Regulators can also be more efficient in managing financial risks and hedging against shocks with macroprudential tools like capital requirements and stress testing.

8. The Next Steps and Research Needs with Policy Directions

As EMs become more dynamic, knowing the next steps and where the economic studies have yet to cover is important for sustainable growth and stability. Here you'll find EM trends, research gaps, and policy tips to make this happen.

8.1. Future Research Trends in Developing Countries

New markets are now the centres of global economic activity as a result of digitalization, globalization, and demographics. The future of research should be into the effects of these trends on economic growth in sectors like FinTech, sustainability, and market integration. For example, FinTech in EMs opens up the potential for financial inclusion and innovation, which requires studies on how FinTech can affect traditional banks and economic development (Bortoluzzi et al., 2018; Hollebeek et al., 2022). What's more, a better appreciation of how EMs can apply technology to improve productivity, and competitiveness will be essential to their success in the long term.

A second frontier for future studies is the link between governance and economic performance in developing markets. Finding out how diverse systems of governance and regulation shape economic results can be informative for policymakers (Gammanpila, 2024; Pham et al., 2022). This research might be about how effective different forms of governance are at fostering transparency, accountability, and economic sustainability.

8.2. Identifying Research Gaps

Although there's a lot of research out there on EMs, it's not entirely covered. One issue is that no one has done systematic research on the long-run impact of economic policies on sustainable growth in these markets. A lot of work addresses short-term economic indicators, but long-term studies need to evaluate the effects of policy choices (Donthu et al., 2021; Line & Runyan, 2012).

There is also a lack of studies focusing on the different issues in different EMs. Most of the research simply generalizes to different settings and does not consider the socio-economic and political conditions under which each market is operating (Ramos, 2023; Sivaraman et al., 2023). It's important to look at future research in a more nuanced manner and to think regionally, in light of variations in globalization and technological change.

8.3. Policy Recommendations

In order to close the research deficits and foster long-term growth in EMs, there are a few policy recommendations that could be applied:

- *Encourage collaborative research activities*: Governments, universities, and the private sector are required to partner and support research that addresses the unique problems and opportunities in the new markets. This can lead to the sharing of information and making sure research is practical and useful (Alam & Akhtar, 2024).
- *Better collect and use data*: To be able to inform policy, better data on economic performance, governance, and social metrics needs to be available and of good quality. Governments should have a data collection platform and be transparent to better assess and make sense of new market dynamics (Jamar et al., 2024; Ladeira et al., 2024; Preece & Kerrigan, 2015; Xu & Meyer, 2012).
- *Redouble the attention on inclusive economic policies*: Policymakers should focus on inclusive economic policies that drive equitable growth and reduce disparities in EMs. These include investing in SMEs, expanding education and training, and innovating by focusing investment in technology and infrastructure (Alam et al., 2024; Bortoluzzi et al., 2018; Hollebeek et al., 2022).
- *Expand regulatory mechanisms*: We need effective regulatory mechanisms to ensure fair competition, investor protection, and sustainability in order to create an environment that will be stable. The public should be consulted to make the rules that will scale up with the rapidly evolving global environment (Appel et al., 2019; Quach & Ngo, 2022).

- *Encourage green innovations*: Governments should encourage enterprises to go green with tax incentives, grants, and green technology assistance. It is not only environmentally friendly but also positioned EMs as pioneers in the global shift towards sustainability (Khan et al., 2021; Owusu, 2023; Rodner & Preece, 2015).

9. Conclusion

The era of EMs is ripe with opportunities and threats that call for focused studies and policy measures. If policymakers could close the research gap and prioritize sustainable growth, emerging economies would become more resilient and competitive in an increasingly globalized world.

References

Adler, G., & Mora, C. (2012). Riding global financial waves: the economic impact of global financial shocks on emerging market economies. *IMF Working Paper*, *12*(188), 1. https://doi.org/10.5089/9781475505368.001

Alam, M., & Akhtar, S. (2024). Introduction to green finance and technology integration. In S. H. Jafar, R. V. Rodriguez , H. Kannan, S. Akhtar, & P. Plugmann (Eds.), *Harnessing blockchain-digital twin fusion for sustainable investments* (pp. 1–19). IGI Global.

Alam, M., Akhtar, S., & Bettencourt, A. (2024). Introduction to fintech in industry 5.0: Companion or antagonist. In S. H. Jafar, H. Kannan, S. Akhtar, P. A. Khan, & H. El-Chaarani (Eds.), *The adoption of fintech: Using technology for better security, speed, and customer experience in finance* (pp. 1–16). Productivity Press.

Andrieş, A., & Melnic, F. (2019). Macroprudential policies and economic growth. *Review of Economic and Business Studies*, *12*(1), 95–112. https://doi.org/10.1515/rebs-2019-0084

Appel, G., Grewal, L., Hadi, R., & Stephen, A. (2019). The future of social media in marketing. *Journal of the Academy of Marketing Science*, *48*(1), 79–95. https://doi.org/10.1007/s11747-019-00695-1

Appiah-Otoo, I., & Song, N. (2021). The impact of fintech on poverty reduction: Evidence from China. *Sustainability*, *13*(9), 5225. https://doi.org/10.3390/su13095225

Argandoña, L., Rambaud, S., & Pascual, J. (2022). The impact of sustainable bond issuances on the economic growth of the Latin American and Caribbean countries. *Sustainability*, *14*(8), 4693. https://doi.org/10.3390/su14084693

Bhuiyan, M. (2023). *Short and long-term forecasting of emerging market data using ARIMA-based and boosting machine learning algorithms*. https://doi.org/10.11159/icsta23.158

Bilson, C., Brailsford, T., & Hooper, V. (2000). The explanatory power of political risk in emerging markets. *SSRN Electronic Journal*. https://doi.org/10.2139/ssrn.808967

Bongers, A., & Díaz-Roldán, C. (2018). *Stabilization policies and technological shocks: Towards a sustainable economic growth path*. https://doi.org/10.20944/preprints201810.0744.v1

Borri, N. (2018). Local currency systemic risk. *Emerging Markets Review*, *34*, 111–123. https://doi.org/10.1016/j.ememar.2017.11.003

Bortoluzzi, G., Kadić-Maglajlić, S., Arslanagić-Kalajdžić, M., & Balboni, B. (2018). Innovativeness as a driver of the international expansion of developing markets' firms. *International Marketing Review*, *35*(2), 215–235. https://doi.org/10.1108/imr-11-2015-0258

Chari, M., & Polizzi, D. (2011). Sustaining superior performance in an emerging economy: An empirical test in the Indian context. *Strategic Management Journal*, *33*(2), 217–229. https://doi.org/10.1002/smj.949

Chea, A. (2021). Doing business in emerging market economies: Challenges and success strategies for western multinational corporations. *International Business Research*, *14*(9), 82. https://doi.org/10.5539/ibr.v14n9p82

Domínguez, B., Garrido, E., & Orcos, R. (2016). Multimarket contact and performance: Evidence from emerging economies. *BRQ Business Research Quarterly*, *19*(4), 278–288. https://doi.org/10.1016/j.brq.2016.02.003

Donthu, N., Kumar, S., Ranaweera, C., Pattnaik, D., & Gustafsson, A. (2021). Mapping of journal of services marketing themes: A retrospective overview using bibliometric analysis. *Journal of Services Marketing*, *36*(3), 340–363. https://doi.org/10.1108/jsm-04-2020-0122

Epor, S. O., Yua, H., & Iorember, P. T. (2024). Foreign direct investment and economic growth in developing countries: the role of international trade and foreign debt. *Modern Finance*, *2*(1), 1–17. https://doi.org/10.61351/mf.v2i1.87

Frost, J. (2020). The economic forces driving fintech adoption across countries. *SSRN Electronic Journal*. https://doi.org/10.2139/ssrn.3515326

Gammanpila, W. (2024). Review on economic analysis of grid-tied battery storage systems and optimization strategies. *CONTRE*, *1*(1). https://doi.org/10.31357/contre.v1i1.7399

Gangadharan, G., & Suresh, N. (2019). Interrogation of a bubble in the Indian market. *Journal of Management*, *10*(3). https://doi.org/10.34218/jom.6.3.2019.008

Girard, E., & Sinha, A. (2008). Risk and return in the next frontier. *Journal of Emerging Market Finance*, *7*(1), 43–80. https://doi.org/10.1177/097265270700700103

Gorodnichenko, Y., Švejnar, J., & Terrell, K. (2010). Globalization and innovation in emerging markets. *American Economic Journal Macroeconomics*, *2*(2), 194–226. https://doi.org/10.1257/mac.2.2.194

Hollebeek, L., Martínez, N., Clark, M., Simanaviciute, A., & Letukyte, N. (2022). Customer engagement in emerging markets: Framework and propositions. *Organizations and Markets in Emerging Economies*, *13*(2), 284–299. https://doi.org/10.15388/omee.2022.13.80

Ivanović-Đukić, M., Rađenović, T., & Talić, M. (2021). Innovative entrepreneurship and economic growth in emerging markets. *Ekonomika*, *67*(4), 65–74. https://doi.org/10.5937/ekonomika2104065i

Jafar, S. H., Rodriguez, R. V., Kannan, H., Akhtar, S., & Plugmann, P. (Eds.). (2024). *Harnessing blockchain-digital twin fusion for sustainable investments*. IGI Global.

Khan, P. A., Johl, S. K., & Akhtar, S. (2021). Firm sustainable development goals and firm financial performance through the lens of green innovation practices and reporting: A proactive approach. *Journal of Risk and Financial Management*, *14*(12), 605.

Khan, P. A., Johl, S. K., & Akhtar, S. (2022). Vinculum of sustainable development goal practices and firms' financial performance: A moderation role of green innovation. *Journal of Risk and Financial Management*, *15*(3), 96.

Kim, S., & Yang, D. (2009). Do capital inflows matter to asset prices? The case of Korea*. *Asian Economic Journal*, *23*(3), 323–348. https://doi.org/10.1111/j.1467-8381.2009.02014.x

Kjaer, P., & Vetterlein, A. (2018). Regulatory governance: Rules, resistance and responsibility. *Contemporary Politics*, *24*(5), 497–506. https://doi.org/10.1080/13569775.2018.1452527

Ladeira, W. J., Santini, F. D. O., Rasul, T., Cheah, I., Elhajjar, S., Yasin, N., & Akhtar, S. (2024). Big data analytics and the use of artificial intelligence in the services industry: A meta-analysis. *The Service Industries Journal*, *44*(15–16), 1117–1144.

Line, N., & Runyan, R. (2012). Hospitality marketing research: Recent trends and future directions. *International Journal of Hospitality Management*, *31*(2), 477–488. https://doi.org/10.1016/j.ijhm.2011.07.006

Mansur, A. (2017). The impact of a loss of confidence in emerging market economies to the world economy: A simulation with the g-cubed model. *Kajian Ekonomi Dan Keuangan*, *1*(2), 143–164. https://doi.org/10.31685/kek.v1i2.148

Mensi, W., Hammoudeh, S., Yoon, S., & Nguyen, D. (2015). Asymmetric linkages between BRICS stock returns and country risk ratings: Evidence from dynamic panel threshold models. *Review of International Economics*, *24*(1), 1–19. https://doi.org/10.1111/roie.12201

Naseema, N., Akhtar, S., & Al Hinai, A. A. (2024). Disrupting financial services: A case study on Capital One's Fintech Odyssey. In S. H. Jafar, R. V. Rodriguez , H. Kannan, S. Akhtar, & P. Plugmann (Eds.), *Harnessing blockchain-digital twin fusion for sustainable investments* (pp. 363–383). IGI Global.

Nguyen, T. (2022). Does financial knowledge matter in using fintech services? Evidence from an emerging economy. *Sustainability*, *14*(9), 5083. https://doi.org/10.3390/su14095083

Nikiforov, P., Babukh, I., & Kinashchuk, S. (2020). Fintech as a driver for today's financial market transformations: the Ukrainian context. *Black Sea Economic Studies*, *51*. https://doi.org/10.32843/bses.51-30

Owusu, F. (2023). Analysis of market volatility and economic factors in emerging markets. *IJMRM*, *1*(1). https://doi.org/10.47604/ijmrm.2093

Papargyropoulou, E., Padfield, R., Harrison, O., & Preece, C. (2012). The rise of sustainability services for the built environment in Malaysia. *Sustainable Cities and Society*, *5*, 44–51. https://doi.org/10.1016/j.scs.2012.05.008

Pham, X., Nguyen, P., & Truong, G. (2022). A co-word and co-citation analysis of digital marketing research. *International Journal of Service Science Management Engineering and Technology*, *13*(1), 1–20. https://doi.org/10.4018/ijssmet.304817

Popkova, E. (2023). Historical review of the Russian market economy formation and development based on the works of doctor of economics, prof. l.s. shakhovskaya. *Rudn Journal of Economics*, *31*(3), 385–399. https://doi.org/10.22363/2313-2329-2023-31-3-385-399

Preece, C., & Kerrigan, F. (2015). Multi-stakeholder brand narratives: an analysis of the construction of artistic brands. *Journal of Marketing Management*, *31*(11–12), 1207–1230. https://doi.org/10.1080/0267257x.2014.997272

Quach, S., & Ngo, L. (2022). Emerging research trends in marketing: A review of Australasian marketing journal. *Australasian Marketing Journal (Amj)*, *30*(3), 214–227. https://doi.org/10.1177/14413582221110450

Ramos, R. (2023). Mapping research in marketing: Trends, influential papers and agenda for future research. *Spanish Journal of Marketing – Esic*, *28*(2), 187–206. https://doi.org/10.1108/sjme-10-2022-0221

Raza, M. A. A., Chen, Y., Abbas, H. S. M., & Ullah, A. (2021). Impact of institutional governance and state determinants on foreign direct investment in asian economies. *Growth and Change*, *52*(4), 2596–2613. https://doi.org/10.1111/grow.12541

Rodner, V., & Preece, C. (2015). Painting the nation. *Journal of Macromarketing*, *36*(2), 128-148. https://doi.org/10.1177/0276146715574775

Sağ, S., Sezen, B., & Alpkan, L. (2019). Determinants of open innovation and their interrelations. *International Journal of Innovation and Technology Management*, *16*(04). https://doi.org/10.1142/s0219877019400017

Serletis, A., & Azad, N. (2018). Emerging market volatility spillovers. *The American Economist*, *65*(1), 78–87. https://doi.org/10.1177/0569434518816445

Shahmi, M. (2023). Analysis of monetary policy intervention and macroeconomic variable shocks against capital inflow in 4 emerging countries ASEAN. *Proceeding of the International Seminar on Business Economics Social Science and Technology (Isbest)*, *3*(1). https://doi.org/10.33830/isbest.v3i1.1222

Sharma, A., & Jha, S. (2016). Innovation from emerging market firms: What happens when market ambitions meet technology challenges?. *Journal of Business and Industrial Marketing*, *31*(4), 507–518. https://doi.org/10.1108/jbim-12-2014-0265

Sivaraman, T., Zahrin, M., Roni, M., & Kanapathipillai, K. (2023). A study on the factors that impact the future trends of marketing: Evidence from the hospitality industry in Klang Valley, Malaysia. *European Journal of Management and Marketing Studies*, *8*(1). https://doi.org/10.46827/ejmms.v8i1.1406

Srivastava, S. (2012). The emerging economies and changing prospects of the multicurrency global order: avenues and challenges in times ahead. *Procedia-Social and Behavioral Sciences*, *37*, 46–56.

Sun, P., Mellahi, K., Wright, M., & Xu, H. (2015). Political tie heterogeneity and the impact of adverse shocks on firm value. *Journal of Management Studies*, *52*(8), 1036–1063. https://doi.org/10.1111/joms.12165

Ugurlu-Yildirim, E., & Ordu-Akkaya, B. (2022). Does the impact of geopolitical risk reduce with the financial structure of an economy? A perspective from market vs. bank-based emerging economies. *Eurasian Economic Review*, *12*(4), 681–703. https://doi.org/10.1007/s40822-022-00219-3

Wang, M., & Chen, T. (2016). Does the spillover of China's economic growth exist? Evidence from emerging markets. *Journal of International Trade & Economic Development*, *25*(7), 992–1009. https://doi.org/10.1080/09638199.2016.1168477

Wu, S., & Pan, Q. (2021). Economic growth in emerging market countries. *Global Journal of Emerging Market Economies*, *13*(2), 192–215. https://doi.org/10.1177/09749101211004405

Xu, D., & Meyer, K. (2012). Linking theory and context: 'Strategy research in emerging economies' after Wright et al. (2005). *Journal of Management Studies*, *50*(7), 1322–1346. https://doi.org/10.1111/j.1467-6486.2012.01051.x

Zhang, K. (2021). Economic structural transformation in emerging market countries. *Global Journal of Emerging Market Economies*, *13*(2), 216–238. https://doi.org/10.1177/09749101211004614

Chapter 2

Climate-related Risks in Emerging Markets: Understanding the Landscape, Challenges and Strategic Solutions

Mohammad Kashif[a], *Harshi Garg*[b], *Syed Noorul Shajar*[c] *and Arokiaraj David*[d]

[a]*Department of Management Studies, Graphic Era Deemed to be University, Dehradun, India*
[b]*School of Commerce and Management, IIMT University, Meerut, India*
[c]*Department of commerce, SSL, Vellore Institute of Technology, Vellore, India*
[d]*ATMS, Swiss Business School, UAE*

Abstract

The impact of climate-related hazards on emerging markets and resource valuation is the primary objective of this chapter's analysis. Whereas emerging markets possess the capacity for expansion fiscally, they are increasingly vulnerable to tangible climate risks such as severe storm incidents and governmental forces associated with worldwide environmental targets. The present research explains how these risks confront traditional economic models using the examination of case studies, such as the economic effects of Cyclone Amphan, and the drought's impact on the nation's hydro energy growth. The significant role of Environmental, Social, and Governance (ESG) requirements in decreasing climate risk and establishing strong, balanced portfolios of assets for the long-term future is further examined in the chapter. The results illustrate how proactive approaches are required to control these dangers and take benefit of the changing prospects of developing nations.

Keywords: Climate change; environment and sustainability; emerging markets; ESG; risks

Climate Risk and Emerging Markets: Valuation, Volatility, and Portfolio Strategies, 25–39

Published under exclusive licence by Emerald Publishing Limited
doi:10.1108/978-1-83708-088-520261009

1. Introduction

The diversity of catastrophes in the environmental system is no longer stable. Consequently, this is probable that the implications of climate change will become more severe throughout the years to come. Large discrepancies are observed in local temperatures as well. These two variables confound the awareness of the global environment, both now and in the future. For environmental risk analysis, researchers use various warming change models. The level of climate risk is established by the combination of three risk elements. They are exposure, vulnerability, and threats. There are multiple approaches to mitigate risk related to climate change. Climate risk protection is a prime instance. This type of coverage is designed to mitigate the financial and other hazards associated with global warming, especially those resulting from severe weather (Gutiérrez-Ponce & Wibowo, 2024). The evaluation of risk involves a collection of measurable ambiguity. These usually appear in the shape of a collection or variety of prospective outcomes, which might include certainty (Hoffman & Maldonado, 2024).

Climate risk has the potential impacts of climate change that could result in problems for environments or societies. Systematic examination of the impacts, likelihoods, and responses to these effects provides the foundation for evaluating climate risk. Opportunities for flexibility might also be determined by sociocultural limitations. The perception of risk differs because of different danger-related priorities and choices. Risk analysis serves as an essential component for numerous risk evaluation and mitigation approaches. Although there are several evident variations, pertaining to climate risk (Depperu et al., 2024). The word 'risk' is utilized in several professional managerial areas. Management, finance, economies, and security are just a few.

The meaning of 'climate change risk' describes the extent to which environments or individuals are anticipated to be affected by climate change. The 'tendency' or inclination to be negatively impacted by global warming is its government classification. Both individuals and the environment can be impacted by it. An element of climate risk is sensitivity. It differs not only between communities, areas, and economies but also within groups. Throughout the years, it could increase or decrease. Individuals in developing nations usually feel more susceptible than those in wealthy nations. War, hunger, and poor management have been correlated with greater instances of exposure. The implications of worldwide warming are more inclined to influence some professions than others. The financial security of fishermen, small-scale ranchers, and cattlemen may be especially at risk. Inefficient land and ocean activity, poverty, exclusion, and past and present patterns of inequalities and poor leadership are other variables that increase vulnerabilities (Tanveer et al., 2024).

The development of climate risk management and understanding over decades is illustrated in Fig. 2.1. In the beginning, the pre-1970s era was defined by ecological understanding and limited limitations. Global action on climate change has been rendered by the development of the green movement and the growing consciousness of degradation in the 1980s. As business responsibilities for ecological impact increased in the 2000s, global agreements such as the

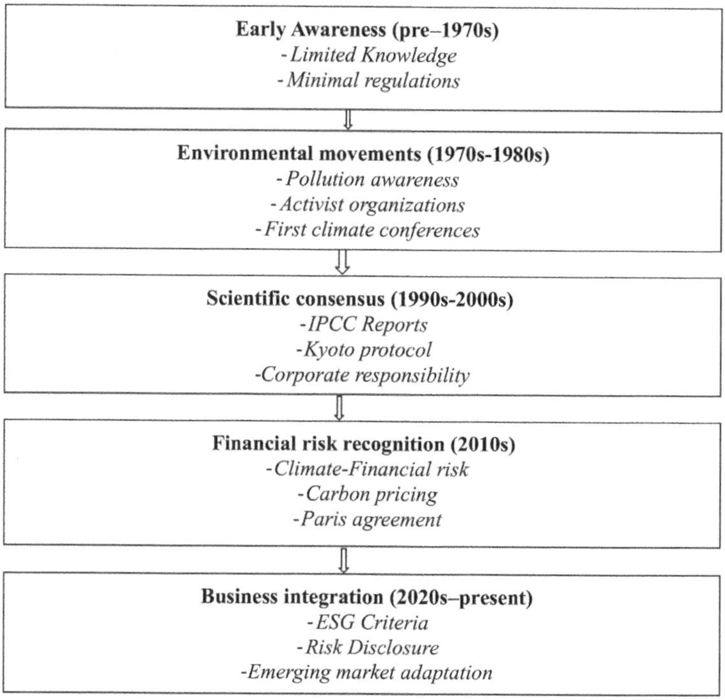

Fig. 2.1. Evolution of Climate Risk. *Source*: Authors' compilation.

Kyoto Protocol were driven by the scientific agreement on climate temperatures. In recent years, ESG standards and risk identification in developing nations are two primary means that environmental danger is deeply embedded in industries and investment operations.

1.1. Overview of Emerging Markets

The commercial sector of a developing nation that is increasing its participation in global markets is referred to as the emerging market economy. Industries that reflect certain but not all of the characteristics of established markets are known as developing market economies. A reliable regulatory environment, steady gross domestic product (GDP) growth, high per capita income, accessible stocks and credit markets, and availability for foreign stakeholders are numerous instances of developing market features (Sungkawati, 2024).

A new market economy evolves, the more closely linked it typically becomes with the wider economy. It could result in higher foreign direct investment, higher trade value, and more stability, in the regional financial and debt markets. It has the power to build relevant economic and regulatory entities. A low-income household, insufficiently developed, usually pre-industrial times is making way for a trendy, manufacturing-based company with a higher life expectancy standard in a newly created market economy (Steiger et al., 2024).

The concept of emerging market can signify that an evolution has started, with financial markets expanding in scope and competence, within modest and apathetic industries, stated the International Finance Corporation (IFC), a division of the World Bank, which developed the word. Any marketplace in an emerging economy can be identified through this name, indicating that all can expand. The overview mentioned was initially set in 1986 when an organization of IFC experts took up the issue of equity market expansion. In 1986, IFC released its first global market fund, with a $50 million corpus and large shareholders who invested in the company's specific emphasis on growing securities markets (Vulturius et al., 2024).

The original description of the IFC was following the economic position of a country. Each market that includes government with middle-class or low-income levels was classified as a developing market. The category was determined by the country's gross national product (GNP) per capita. A nation can be classified as a new market if its per capita GNP did not exceed $9,386 in 1996 (Omole & Olatunde, 2024). The IFC has recently agreed that the financial factors were adequate for identifying developing nations and developed a new, broader description termed the 'developing Stock market standard'. This standard will incorporate already established statistical indicators applicable to the marketplaces, irrespective of the nation's socioeconomic classification. The specification is not yet approved by the IFC.

The purpose is to monitor emerging economies whose GNP has beyond the World's Bank benchmark but whose financial systems remain in their beginnings, and to be able to include industries in wealthy countries, which possess fewer developed financial systems. If a sector fulfils one of the criteria listed above, it would be termed an emerging market. A good deal of rising market studies adopts the IFC definition and the International Monetary Fund (IMF's) new emerging markets because it offers the most extensive and long-term information origin on emerging economies (Jain et al., 2024).

Table 2.1 indicates how emerging economies eventually started to recognize sustainability concerns by the late 1990s, after choosing explosive expansion and overlooking climate issues in the 1980s. Severe storms brought dangers to the forefront in the 2000s, which increased concerns about climate change and encouraged early inclusion of climate issues into financial choices. An essential awareness of how the environment affects these markets contributed to a significant emphasis on adaptation ideas and equitable financing by the 2020s.

2. Literature Review

2.1. Studies Related to the Background of Climate-related Risks

Historical time frame has seen numerous variations in the planet's surface warmth. The typical global heat currently is 15°C. The ambient temperature has changed in earlier times, based on geological records. Researchers fear that climate change caused by humans has displaced the planet's normal variations in temperature (Agbehadji et al., 2024). The word 'greenhouse effect' is often employed. It explains

Table 2.1. History of Climate Risk Considerations in Emerging Markets.

Period	Key Changes	Investor Focus
1970s–1980s	The growth of the industry is fast, and emissions and pollution are high.	Development was given preference over environmental challenges.
1990s	Increasing knowledge about environmental issues and climate change (UNFCCC, 1992).	Minimal risk knowledge and enthusiasm for ESG.
2000s	Severe disasters and the Kyoto Protocol in the 2000s increased awareness of threats.	Awareness of renewable energy is getting started.
2010s	Climate developments in the 2010s, Paris Agreement (2015).	A particular emphasis is on developing climate adaptation.
2020s	Extreme weather impacts in the 2020s (IPCC 2021 report).	Significant emphasis on modification and ecological finance.

Source: Authors' compilation.

how the heat radiated from the earth's surface gets absorbed by the upper atmosphere. The UV rays from the sun's energy enter the ground's ambiance, and they heat the earth's face (Cevik & Miryugin, 2023). The outermost layer of the earth receives solar energy initially, after which it reflects in every single direction.

Numerous elements of the atmosphere of the earth capture the infrared heat that is released. The atmosphere on earth includes greenhouse gases that contribute to keeping our planet alive (Garg et al., 2024). Nevertheless, more substances and a surplus of warming gases in the atmosphere of the plant as an effect of our actions were anticipated calamity. The volume of energy stored in the environment has risen over the years, resulting in burning (Contat et al., 2024). The vast majority of man-made CO_2 greenhouse gases occur through the process of combustion of oil and gas. The elimination of plants worsens this even more.

The regular modification of earth's climate as a consequence of atmospheric shift is what we currently consider to be global warming. The connections are present inside the earth's system between the environment and the many natural, substance, and living substances. The environment can be viewed as more similar to a continuous stream that is always changing (Huang et al., 2018). Many variables, such as sunlight, elevation range guidance, currents in the oceans, plants living on the outermost layer of the earth, and the chemistry of the air affect the features of the environment. A typical description of the climate is the typical weather in a specific area, which is a consequence of several factors like humidity, warmth, and velocity (Garg et al., 2024).

The typical surface temperature of the planet has risen by around 0.75C as confirmed by the IPCC report. The Earth's surface temperature of the earth is not, yet, increasing evenly throughout the entire planet. While the vast majority of the earth is dealing with an environmental issue, certain parts of the Antarctic have experienced extremely cold temperatures (Kashif et al., 2024). The hottest in the past century have all occurred after 1998. The oceans have been reported warmed throughout the following part of the 20th century. It is difficult to question the facts of climate change. To establish that it is true, there are many pieces of evidence. This has been determined carbon dioxide can trap heat (Alam & Akhtar, 2024; Krampe & Mobjörk, 2018).

2.2. *Importance of Climate Risk in Financial Analysis and Investment Strategies*

As financiers consider that environmental-related disruption can have major adverse impacts on economic growth, the relevance of environmental risk in financial assessment and portfolio selection is increasing (Shinbrot et al., 2019). These dangers demand modifications to traditional assessment methods because they entail tangible risks from severe weather incidents and transformational problems associated with the transition to a carbon-neutral economy. Risk evaluation methods are enhanced and more comprehensive and different portfolios are established when social and governance aspects are integrated into financial choices (Adetoyese et al., 2024). Shareholders can more effectively manage the complex dynamics of emerging economies and seek consistent long-term profits by prioritizing climate-resilient investments (Jafar et al., 2024; Volz, 2022).

These days, shareholders include ESG concerns in their ratings since they recognize how essential a business's capacity to endure changing weather is to its financial sustainability. The development of deeper risk evaluation systems that identify both temporal and structural worries comes from this mixture, which ultimately guides the formulation of financing approaches (Pinkse & Kolk, 2012). Climate-resilient expenditures, such as sustainable farming and initiatives involving renewable energy, must be assigned the greatest attention by owners to minimize their dependence on unstable sectors.

The crucial role of environmental risk in financial evaluation and decision-making is crucial which also reveals how it impacts various phases of the purchase process. The study of finances is significantly affected by the increasing knowledge of ecological hazards, which require modifications to traditional valuation procedures to take potential future problems into perspective (Naseema et al., 2024; Yüksel et al., 2024). An economic system that combines specific characteristics of an established industry but falls short of its norms is commonly referred to as an emerging sector, developing society, or emergent industry. This contains regions that have traditionally grown and those that may appear shortly (Adaobi et al., 2024). Emerging economies with lesser, more dangerous, or accessible investment markets are usually referred to as 'Advanced markets' instead of 'arising'. The financial systems of China and India are considered the most significant as of 2006 (Alam et al., 2024; Shajar, Beg, et al., 2024).

The Economic Journal argues that despite several people feeling the phrase to be outdated, no substitute word has become popular. The largest city of newly established hedge funds companies achieved a new record high of $21 billion at the beginning of 2011 (Kashif, Shajar, et al., 2023; Khan et al., 2022). The percentage of developing nations in the world's adjusted GDP grew from 27% in 1960 to approximately 53% in 2013. The presence of South Korea, Poland, and sometimes Taiwan is questionable because the IMF and World Bank no longer identify them as developing countries. The phrases 'emerged markets' and 'emerged nations' describe states that are moving forward from their emergent industry but have not yet reached the degree of technological and economic progress (Ayorinde et al., 2024; Shajar, Kashif, et al., 2024).

3. Research Method

This chapter investigates how hazards related to climate change influence investment approaches and estimation of assets in developing nations through qualitative case study analysis from economic and ecological reports. The philosophical and theoretical obstacles encountered by shareholders are clarified mainly in this paradigm. Meaningful insights into the social and political implications of these threats have been gained through examining actual events like heatwave exposure in Ahmedabad, a drought in India's hydro-energy business, and Cyclone Amphan in West Bengal; a comprehensive assessment of the risk mitigation approaches employed in these fields is feasible by the immediate ramifications on the valuation of assets, infrastructural adaptability, and confidence in investors that are studied in every case. The investigation examined secondary data sources, including accounting records and assessments of environmental impact.

3.1. Real-world Case Studies: Highlighting the Impact of Climate Risks on Asset Valuation and Portfolio Management in Emerging Markets

The following are the four case studies; every single one of which has been simplified into a paragraph highlighting how climate risk in emerging markets influences investment diversification and asset evaluation.

3.1.1. Financial Consequences of Cyclone Amphan in West Bengal and Odisha

In May 2020, the states of West Bengal and Odisha were devastated by Cyclone Amphan, one of the worst hurricanes that have impacted India in recent history. Residences, infrastructures, buildings, and farming land were heavily impacted by the storm, which resulted in roughly $13 billion in revenue losses. The event caused seaside areas – especially those that rely on sectors like seafood and farming land – more exposed to major climate disasters. The tropical cyclone highlights to shareholders how important it is to incorporate climate risk into the valuation of assets. The possible damages from recurrent cyclones must be comprised of operations in these regions, especially in agriculture. Storm-resistant facilities and flood protection are instances of climate-resilient improvement projects that can help mitigate potential risks and enhance the attraction of these sectors.

3.1.2. Health Status and Heatwave Vulnerability in Ahmedabad

The impact of Global warming has led to escalating temperatures in Ahmedabad, a city renowned for its extreme summers. The city and the Natural Resources Défense Council developed a Thermal Action Plan to prepare for and minimize the damaging effects of droughts. Early alert systems, community education tasks, and simpler availability of healthcare throughout moments of high temperatures are all facets of this strategy. These programmes present shareholders option alongside protecting the humanity's health. The town's adaptability can be improved and potential earnings are accessible by engaging in urban plants, energy efficiency, and medical centres. Similar initiatives can operate as prototypes for other towns having health risks connected to global warming, particularly since heatwaves are predicted to become more common.

3.1.3. Flood Resistance and Environment Adaptation

Due to its frequent rainfall, Gujarat city chose the steps to modify its infrastructure to climate change. The initial emission trading schedule in India to reduce microscopic emissions, enhanced sewage, and disaster alert networks represent a few endeavours. The approach generates finance for municipal climate resilient measures and supports the fast response to water risks. Communities like Surat that prioritize climate change mitigation have attracted a greater number of donors since these attempts can offer predictable profits on subjects like urban development and ecological technology. The portfolios may profit from the adaptability of climate-conscious urban areas which encourage healthy development by investing in smart city projects.

3.1.4. The Southeast Asian Farming Environment Constraints and Lessons for India

The nation's crop production is equally dependent on environmental threats like inconsistent rainfall, severe droughts, and warmer temperatures, mainly located in Southeast Asia. Uncertain harvest outcomes and supply chain breakdowns present monetary difficulties to India's farming sector, particularly in regions that depend heavily on wheat and maize. Diversity of crops, modern watering techniques, and climate-tolerant seed strains are all instances of sustainable farming that are getting greater focus in investment approaches. These regulations provide stakeholders the opportunity to promote methods of farming that decrease climate risks, maintain production, and produce profits over time.

The importance of climate risk evaluation in the emergent market development, particularly in India, is proven by each of these case studies. Entrepreneurs can develop portfolios with diversity that minimize risk and encourage equitable growth by becoming mindful of the regional impacts of climate risk.

4. Understanding Climate-related Risks: Types of Climate Risks in Emerging Markets

The definition of climate risk indicates the potential adverse impacts of worldwide warming on the financial system, culture, or ecology. This refers to something from extreme weather to greater lasting shifts in the climate. This possibility can present itself in several methods, affecting facilities, purchases, distribution networks, businesses, and the economy at large. Creating efficient strategies to mitigate the effects and enhance adaptability in the context of changing climates needs a knowledge of climate risk. The realization that environmental risk is a financial one becomes more evident as the effects of worldwide warming become clearer to investors and enterprises. The monetary health of every organization is at threat from a range of variables associated with environmental crises. Risks associated with climate change can be classified into two main groups: Transition risk and Physical risk. Here, we'll discuss each of these in depth.

4.1. Physical Risks: The Tangible Impacts

The more 'evident' economic dangers linked to climate change are natural concerns. They mention the economic impacts of damage to water networks, structures, and architecture. We understand that these frameworks will be severely changed by climate change. The industry will not be able to run properly as a consequence of the increasing severity of extreme weather events, sea level rise, storms, extreme heat, water shortage, and climate movement. The physical danger of climate change is going to affect all major companies, but some areas will be more affected than others (Kashif, Kumar, et al., 2023; Khan et al., 2021). For example, oil and gas companies in the Gulf of Mexico will face more difficulties. As sea levels increase, likewise, businesses with offices in Miami will face flooding crises.

Corporations have to conduct climate risk evaluations to remain for the tangible risks related to climate change. These should reflect predicting a variety of possible eventualities for assessing how future climate, shortages, sea level rise, etc., will affect the operation of a company. Yet, there will be some unavoidable hazards. To avoid financial harm and preserve businesses' prospects of surviving, modification will be essential.

4.2. Transition Risk: The Shifting Landscape

The method of transitioning away from reliance on oil and gas and towards a low-carbon economy involves hazards referred to as transition risks. The prospective application of carbon taxes, demands on carbon openness, or the conversion to renewable energy sources are a few examples of these threats. Particular sectors will be damaged more severely than others; however, every company will suffer and must assess its transition risk. For instance, when energy sources such as petrol and diesel have been phased by environmental goals, the oil and gas industry is particularly expected to face an enormous transition threat.

Moreover, oil and gas firms are becoming more frequently challenged by non-governmental organizations and ordinary people for neglecting to fulfil their obligation to deal with the climate change. The worldwide change to powered cars also presents a transition concern to the auto sector. Massive publicly traded firms will shortly be obliged to assess their physical and transitional risk in the identical way that they examine and prepare for other feasible risk factors because of current national regulations. Businesses that work in these nations will be inspected against their assertions and may be targeted for disputes, which only adds to the transition risks for them.

5. Challenges for Investors in the Landscape of Climate-Related Risks

Climate-related risks deliver an extensive list of problems for emerging market shareholders, which can greatly affect their bottom line. Natural disasters like cyclones and floods can result in substantial economic damage by devastating facilities and affecting supply chains, which was demonstrated by the events of Cyclone Amphan; moreover, droughts and other intense weather events offer diseases that reduce worker output and increase medical costs.

Developing flood-resistant facilities in vulnerable coastlines like Mumbai requires with significant adjustment expenses for stakeholders. The farming sector is free of these issues since the distribution system and crop productivity are being affected by climate change, which also impacts the reliability of assets worldwide. The droughts can add another layer of instability by affecting the electric power, particularly for hydropower developments. The above challenges illustrate the importance for owners to include comprehensive assessments of environmental hazards into their financial strategies to minimize potential losses and ensure a consistent return.

The primary challenges that entrepreneurs and investors experience when handling climate hazards in India are monetary loss from natural disasters, coastal real estate vulnerabilities, agricultural disruption, high adaptation costs for flood resistance, health risks and productivity loss, and adverse effect of electricity generation in flooded areas. ESG adoption is very sensitive to investor behaviour and market sentiment. The demand for sustainable investments is inherently positive sentiment and this encourages ESG integration. However, scepticism or profit motives short term may prevent adoption. And where market trends, regulatory signals, and societal expectations that affect investors, ESG plays an integral part in corporate responsibility … and now the role that also plays in financial performance.

6. Climate Risk Management – Strategic Solution for Mitigating Climate Risks

Climate risk management is the procedure of determining, assessing, and decreasing any potential risks and exposures associated with climate change. It covers several strategies and procedures aimed at reducing the adverse impacts of climate change on ecological systems, human societies, and the marketplace. Following are key components of climate risk management:

- *Risk identification*: The initial phase towards controlling environmental risk is to recognize and appreciate the specific threats and weaknesses that global warming offers. This involves performing comprehensive evaluations of the hazards connected to the current and projected environment, especially severe weather, ocean level, warmth fluctuations, and changes to the pattern of precipitation. To acquire a variety of perspectives and information concerning local regional weather, community teamwork and involvement are essential.
- *Risk assessment*: To estimate their potential impacts and the likelihood of occurring, the risks associated with climate change must be assessed after they have been noticed. Risk assessments involve evaluating how susceptible organizations are impacted by climate-related risks, and their responsiveness and capacity to adjust. This method helps in classifying risks based on intensity and pressure, allowing the distribution of resources and specialized solutions.
- *Risk mitigation*: Introducing approaches that decrease the likelihood and magnitude of adverse impacts is referred to as environmental risk management. This can involve setting both non-structural and structural changes into effect to enhance adaptability and tolerance in vulnerable places. Developing shorelines, updating structures, and implementing green development concepts like greening and reclaiming wetlands into effect are instances of building measures. Community-driven adjustment initiatives, legislation regarding zoning, early alert systems, and spatial planning are examples of informal methods.
- *Strategies for adaption*: Generating changes and initiatives to prepare for and manage the adverse consequences of worldwide warming is a different component of managing climate risk. Improving the capacity to adapt at the neighbourhood stage, such as incorporating climate change into industry policies and initiatives, and including environmental issues into growth strategy are only a few of the tasks that fall within the broad category of mitigation strategy. A combination of sectors is required for a successful adaptation strategy.
- *Role of artificial intelligence*: Predictive analytics, monitoring the changes, and optimizing the use of resource make artificial intelligence improve climate risk management. Blockchain provides transparency, traceability, security on carbon credit trading. They work for sustainable finance and climate strategies with the help of data-driven decisions.
- *Evaluation and assessment*: Continuous tracking and assessment are required for the continuous method of environmental risk control to monitor advances, assess effectiveness, and implement the required approach. Information on climate-related hazards, weaknesses, and adaptation efforts is collected throughout observation to assist with policy creation and decisions. The assessment involves identifying experiences acquired, defining places for enhancement, and reviewing the outcomes and implications of adaptable approaches. The efficacy, productivity, and reactivity of worldwide risk prevention efforts are all increased by regular evaluation and tracking.

- *Global cooperation*: Funding, policy guidance, and capacity building for risk management are provided by international organizations to the emerging markets. Through such means, they promote the facilitation of climate resilience in infrastructure, green finance, and the formation risk assessment frameworks. They nurture global collaboration and transfer of technology to help the emerging economies to diversify adapt and make resilient adaptation strategies.

7. Conclusion

This is currently necessary for businesses to handle environmental hazards and manage sustainability. Companies may efficiently handle environmental hazards and contribute to developing a safer and more viable economy through preventive actions like risk evaluations, increased publications, environmentally friendly investment, and teamwork. Organizations have to develop comprehensive strategies and modify their processes on a regular schedule.

They must be compatible with outside experts to ensure credibility and transparency when dealing with environmental hazards while making towards sustainable development goals. From individuals adopting environmentally friendly techniques and advocating for changes to authorities executing laws, providing incentives, and promoting investment, everybody can help in the prevention of global warming.

Companies are now given an obligation to handle climate risk, and the private market should be in the lead of evolving, investing, and encouraging remedies for preventing global warming, particularly those businesses and enterprises that generate large pollution. Global collaboration and dissemination of technology are especially important due to the issue's global scope and complexity. The Paris Agreement, which provides as the main platform for international cooperation on environmental issues, has established several commitments and policy tools for its gatherings.

Nationally Determined Contributions (NDCs) are one of the primary resources for achieving the convention's goals. Every party will be required to develop and update these national climate changes every five years. Each nation's role in reducing emissions of greenhouse gases is stated in its NDC. Continuous low-emission plans for development are instruments of policy under the Paris Agreement which require governments to show how they plan to achieve zero carbon emissions. NDCs present immediate aims. More short-term climate goals acquire reliability and direction from these perspectives.

References

Adaobi, O. N., Olanrewaju, O. D., Gbenga, O., & Timothy Soyombo, O. (2024). Sustainable business models in satellite telecommunications. *Engineering Science & Technology Journal*, *5*(3), 1047–1059. https://doi.org/10.51594/estj/v5i3.957

Adetoyese, L., Ngozi, S. U., Munachi, C. U., & Portia, O. (2024). Strategies for corporate compliance and litigation avoidance in multinational enterprises. *World Journal of Advanced Science and Technology*, *6*(1), 073–087. https://doi.org/10.53346/wjast.2024.6.1.0048

Agbehadji, I. E., Schütte, S., Masinde, M., Botai, J., & Mabhaudhi, T. (2024). Climate risks resilience development: A bibliometric analysis of climate-related early warning systems in Southern Africa. *Climate*, *12*(1). https://doi.org/10.3390/cli12010003

Alam, M., & Akhtar, S. (2024). Introduction to green finance and technology integration. In S. H. Jafar, R. V. Rodriguez, H. Kannan, S. Akhtar, & P. Plugmann (Eds.), *Harnessing blockchain-digital twin fusion for sustainable investments* (pp. 1–19). IGI Global.

Alam, M., Akhtar, S., & Bettencourt, A. (2024). Introduction to fintech in industry 5.0: Companion or antagonist. In S. H. Jafar, H. Kannan, S. Akhtar, P. A. Khan, & H. El-Chaarani (Eds.), *The adoption of fintech* (pp. 1–16). Productivity Press.

Ayorinde, D. M., Obaigbena, A., Tega, M. M., Sunday, O. J., Winston, B. P., & Author, C. (2024). Innovative approaches to waste resource management: Implications for environmental sustainability and policy. *Engineering Science & Technology Journal*, *5*(1), 115–127. https://doi.org/10.51594/estj/v5i1.731

Cevik, S., & Miryugin, F. (2023). Rogue waves: Climate change and firm performance. *Comparative Economic Studies*, *65*(1), 29–59. https://doi.org/10.1057/s41294-022-00189-0

Contat, J., Hopkins, C., Mejia, L., & Suandi, M. (2024). When climate meets real estate: A survey of the literature. *Real Estate Economics*, *52*(3), 618–659. https://doi.org/10.1111/1540-6229.12489

Depperu, D., Galavotti, I., & Baraldi, F. (2024). Institutional distance and cross-border acquisitions into emerging markets: The moderating effect of context experience. *International Journal of Emerging Markets*, *19*(5), 1449–1472. https://doi.org/10.1108/IJOEM-12-2021-1897

Garg, H., Ike, G. N., Kashif, M., & Azam, M. S. (2024). Dynamics of sustainable and ethically responsible business practices in corporate social responsibility. In K. Singh, J. Yadav, & R. Abraham (Eds.), *Technology-driven evolution of the corporate social responsibility ecosystem* (pp. 92–113). IGI Global.

Garg, H., Kashif, M., & Sharma, P. (2024). Green investments promotions and future trends in neuromarketing and sustainable finance. In S. Taneja, B. Pal Singh Chahal, A. Johri, E. Ozen, & P. Kumar (Eds.), *Neuromarketing's role in sustainable finance* (pp. 245–284). IGI Global.

Gutiérrez-Ponce, H., & Wibowo, S. A. (2024). Do sustainability practices contribute to the financial performance of banks? An analysis of banks in Southeast Asia. *Corporate Social Responsibility and Environmental Management*, *31*(2), 1418–1432. https://doi.org/10.1002/csr.2641

Hoffman, S. A., & Maldonado, Y. A. (2024). Emerging and re-emerging pediatric viral diseases: A continuing global challenge. *Pediatric Research*, *95*(2), 480–487. Springer Nature. https://doi.org/10.1038/s41390-023-02878-7

Huang, H. H., Kerstein, J., & Wang, C. (2018). The impact of climate risk on firm performance and financing choices: An international comparison. *Journal of International Business Studies*, *49*(5), 633–656. https://doi.org/10.1057/s41267-017-0125-5

IPCC. (2021). Climate change 2021: The physical science basis. Contribution of working group i to the sixth assessment report of the intergovernmental panel on climate change. https://www.ipcc.ch/report/ar6/wg1/

Jafar, S. H., Rodriguez, R. V., Kannan, H., Akhtar, S., & Plugmann, P. (Eds.). (2024). *Harnessing blockchain-digital twin fusion for sustainable investments*. IGI Global.

Jain, P., Tambuskar, D. P., & Narwane, V. (2024). Identification of critical factors for big data analytics implementation in sustainable supply chain in emerging economies. *Journal of Engineering, Design and Technology*, *22*(3), 926–968. https://doi.org/10.1108/JEDT-12-2021-0739

Kashif, M., Garg, H., Weqar, F., & David, A. (2024). Regulatory strategies and innovative solutions for deepfake technology. In G Lakhera, S. Taneja, E. Ozen, M. Kukreti, & P. Kumar (Eds.), *Navigating the world of deepfake technology* (pp. 262–282). IGI Global. https://doi.org/10.4018/979-8-3693-5298-4.ch013

Kashif, M., Kumar, P., Ghai, S., & Kumar, S. (2023). Disruptive technologies in computational finance. In A. Singh, S. Taneja, & P. Kumar (Eds.), *Algorithmic approaches to financial technology: Forecasting, trading, and optimization* (pp. 46–60). IGI Global.

Kashif, M., Shajar, S. N., Singhal, N., & Kumar, P. (2023). Achieving sustainable investment practices through green finance: Challenges and opportunities. In S. Taneja, P. Kumar, S. Grima, E. Ozen, & K. Sood (Eds.), *Sustainable investments in green finance* (pp. 234–244). IGI Global.

Khan, P. A., Johl, S. K., & Akhtar, S. (2021). Firm sustainable development goals and firm financial performance through the lens of green innovation practices and reporting: A proactive approach. *Journal of Risk and Financial Management*, *14*(12), 605.

Khan, P. A., Johl, S. K., & Akhtar, S. (2022). Vinculum of sustainable development goal practices and firms' financial performance: A moderation role of green innovation. *Journal of Risk and Financial Management*, *15*(3), 96.

Krampe, F., & Mobjörk, M. (2018). Responding to climate-related security risks: Reviewing regional organizations in Asia and Africa. *Current Climate Change Reports*, *4*(4), 330–337. https://doi.org/10.1007/s40641-018-0118-x

Naseema, N., Akhtar, S., & Al Hinai, A. A. (2024). Disrupting financial services: A case study on Capital One's Fintech Odyssey. In S. H. Jafar, R. V. Rodriguez, H. Kannan, S. Akhtar, & P. Plugmann (Eds.), *Harnessing blockchain-digital twin fusion for sustainable investments* (pp. 363–383). IGI Global.

Omole, O., & Olatunde, P. (2024). Challenges and successes in rural electrification: A review of global policies and case studies. *Engineering Science & Technology Journal*, *5*(3), 1031–1046. https://doi.org/10.51594/estj/v5i3.956

Pinkse, J., & Kolk, A. (2012). Multinational enterprises and climate change: Exploring institutional failures and embeddedness. *Journal of International Business Studies*, *43*(3), 332–341. https://doi.org/10.1057/jibs.2011.56

Shajar, S. N., Beg, K., Kashif, M., Khan, M., Saleem, S., & Usmani, F. (2024). Enhancing firm performance through effective working capital management: A study of Indian manufacturing firms listed at S&P BSE 500. *International Research Journal of Multidisciplinary Scope*, *5*(3), 661–669.

Shajar, S. N., Kashif, M., George, J., & Nasir, S. (2024). The future of green finance: Artificial intelligence-enabled solutions for a more sustainable world. In S. H. Jafar, R. V. Rodriguez, H. Kannan, S. Akhtar, & P. Plugmann (Eds.), *Harnessing blockchain-digital twin fusion for sustainable investments* (pp. 316–328). IGI Global.

Shinbrot, X. A., Jones, K. W., Rivera-Castañeda, A., López-Báez, W., & Ojima, D. S. (2019). Smallholder farmer adoption of climate-related adaptation strategies: The importance of vulnerability context, livelihood assets, and climate perceptions. *Environmental Management*, *63*(5), 583–595. https://doi.org/10.1007/s00267-019-01152-z

Steiger, R., Demiroglu, O. C., Pons, M., & Salim, E. (2024). Climate and carbon risk of tourism in Europe. *Journal of Sustainable Tourism*, *32*(9), 1893–1923. https://doi.org/10.1080/09669582.2022.2163653

Sungkawati, E. (2024). Terms to achieve SDGs. *Revenue Journal: Management and Entrepreneurship*, *2*(1), 1–13. https://doi.org/10.61650/rjme.v1i1.333

Tanveer, M. I., Yusliza, M. Y., & Fawehinmi, O. (2024). Green HRM and hospitality industry: Challenges and barriers in adopting environmentally friendly practices. *Journal of Hospitality and Tourism Insights*, *7*(1), 121–141. https://doi.org/10.1108/JHTI-08-2022-0389

UNFCCC. (1992). United Nations framework convention on climate change. https://unfccc.int/resource/docs/convkp/conveng.pdf

Volz, U. (2022). Climate-proofing the global financial safety net. *Journal of Globalization and Development*, *13*(1), 1–30. https://doi.org/10.1515/jgd-2020-0085

Vulturius, G., Maltais, A., & Forsbacka, K. (2024). Sustainability-linked bonds – Their potential to promote issuers' transition to net-zero emissions and future research directions. *Journal of Sustainable Finance and Investment*, *14*(1), 116–127. https://doi.org/10.1080/20430795.2022.2040943

Yüksel, S., Eti, S., Dinçer, H., & Gökalp, Y. (2024). Comprehensive risk analysis and decision-making model for hydroelectricity energy investments. *Journal of Soft Computing and Decision Analytics*, *2*(1), 28–38. https://doi.org/10.31181/jscda21202321

Chapter 3

Transitioning from a Perceived Threat of Climate Change to an Established Reality: Analysing the Distinctive Susceptibilities of Developing Economies

Donkor Nawaah[a], *Leticia Bosu*[b] *and Shake Akhtar*[c]

[a]*Department of Finance and Accounting, Woxsen University, Hyderabad, India*
[b]*Department of Business and Social Sciences Education, University of Cape Coast, Cape Coast, Ghana*
[c]*College of Economics and Business Administration, University of Technology and Applied Sciences, Ibra, Oman*

Abstract

This chapter examines how climate change, once a far-off danger, is now a reality, affecting the most vulnerable, particularly developing nations facing governance issues, social inequality, and economic instability. Incorporating case studies, empirical data, and policy evaluations, it draws on multidisciplinary research conducted between 2020 and 2024, with Latin America, Africa, and South Asia serving as key examples of climate change's effects and the urgency for adaptation. Given their reliance on climate-sensitive industries and limited adaptive capacity, developing economies are disproportionately impacted. Scalable, context-specific solutions such as technology breakthroughs, nature-based approaches, and increased climate funding are essential, alongside regional collaboration and inclusive governance to mitigate risks and enhance resilience. The chapter underscores the need for further research on adaptation frameworks tailored to developing economies, particularly examining the link between socioeconomic inequality and climate change, offering valuable insights for policymakers and stakeholders.

Keywords: Climate change; climate finance; emerging economies; perceived threat; sustainable development

Climate Risk and Emerging Markets: Valuation, Volatility, and Portfolio Strategies, 41–54

Published under exclusive licence by Emerald Publishing Limited
doi:10.1108/978-1-83708-088-520261012

1. Introduction

Climate change has transitioned from being a relatively distant, hypothetical threat years ago to an inarguable global crisis that is well underway (Zolli & Healy, 2013). Originally, climate change was considered as a future problem for later generations to face, and climate scientists warning about rising greenhouse gas emissions and increasing average global temperatures were often faced with disbelief (Mintzer & Michel, 2001). Without physical evidence, many governments, industries, and citizens stayed idle and downplayed the problem. On the one hand, the climate threat had not yet been understood fully and climate policies had only been controversial. Reactions by the scientific community forewarning of the multitude of risks of climate change have only focused on future threats, but climate policies have also too often been framed reactively rather than proactively. However, towards the end of the first decade of the 21st century, the science around climate change became increasingly undeniable (Kemp et al., 2022; Moser, 2016). Unlike the scientific models which took time to validate to convince even climate change deniers, within two decades the evidence of observable trends in the natural world – changing weather patterns, rising sea levels, and increasing numbers and severity of extreme weather events left little doubt about the global climate crisis. Climate change impacts are no longer forecasts only but have developed into observable and urgent problems currently affecting the ecosystems, economies, and societies of the world (Legg, 2021).

Low- and middle-income countries have been among the most vulnerable to changes in climate due to their greater dependence on agriculture, weaker infrastructure and fall behind in financing and technology to adopt adaptive mechanisms (Lahsen et al., 2010; Saeed et al., 2023). While the wealthier countries of the world have the tools and resources to put mitigation plans in place and adapt to the new climate systems through investments in infrastructure and similar resilience preparatory phases, developing nations unfortunately do not have these same options. The poorest communities, coincidentally least able to cope with the challenges of poverty, inequality, and poor governance are those who pay the highest price for these impacts. Agriculture is one of the most climate-sensitive sectors, accounting for a significant share of national output in many developing economies. In other geographies, specifically sub-Saharan Africa, Southeast Asia and some parts of South America, agriculture tends to be the backbone of economic development and food security. But erratic rainfall, the absorption of more droughts, and the change in seasons because of climate change have destroyed local farmers. These communities have limited access to invest in modern agricultural techniques or secure climate-resilient crops and are thus subjected to direct climate impacts. Low-lying nations and coastal areas home to millions of people face the danger of rising sea levels. Countries including Bangladesh, the Maldives, and several Pacific island states are especially vulnerable; their economies being dependent on fishing, agriculture and tourism. Not only are these countries on track to lose arable land, but they are also challenged by more frequent coastal flooding, salinization of freshwater supplies, and erosion of critical infrastructure.

This economic vulnerability makes the threats of climate change more severe. Most developing countries cannot afford to build the infrastructure required to protect their citizens and companies from ever-increasing climate change challenges (Lomborg, 2020). Moreover, they are often unable to benefit from available international climate finance because global temperature limits and funding arrangements often fail to include the most vulnerable attentively. That said, in numerous developing economies, governance systems can further amplify climate vulnerabilities. The fragility of political institutions in these countries is coupled with corruption and absence of sound and effective climate policies, which prevents these countries from adapting to climate change and addressing its effects. Second issue is also the low awareness among the public about the same and the lack of political will because once it becomes very important for the political gains, such solutions would be secondary to economic growth or political stability. With climate-related disasters on the rise, the importance of focusing on the unequal burden on the economies in the Developing World will only become clearer. Climate change is no longer a looming threat; for many nations, it is a present-day reality. These vulnerable nations need effective adaptation strategies, global cooperation, and climate financing to confront the challenges ahead. This chapter examines the specific vulnerabilities that developing economies face due to climate change, and how their unique set of economic, social, and governance challenges exacerbates their risks. Recognizing these vulnerabilities along with the need for urgent climate mitigation might help to finally pave the path for better solutions that witness those affected most by climate change.

2. The Perceived Threat of Climate Change

Climate change remained largely a scientific or academic discussion for much of the 20th century (Oreskes, 2004). Greenhouse gas emissions were seen as increasingly dangerous by the scientific community, but a lot of people outside it did not appreciate the urgency. In those early years, climate change almost always played out as a 'future threat' – something that would happen to the next generation, a long way away from most people on Earth. As a result, the issue was seen too often by political leaders, policymakers, and the public as something to be dealt with later and calls for urgent action were ignored. First, everybody thought climate change was a far-off challenge, and too many people did not see the effects of climate change, of climate disruption, as being real enough to be concerned. The lack of hard, visible data at the outset was one of the major obstacles to action on climate change. Research supported the models, but like a slow-moving hurricane, it showed few signs of dramatic effects in the near term. Climate change impacts were abstract, and arguments about how real the problem was thrived. In fossil fuel-linked industries in particular, however – as well as in politics and mainstream news media – there were ongoing efforts to minimize the possibility of dangerous climate change, often muddying the waters of communications with the public. Politically and economically, this stance of accepting climate change as reality was not going to be taken lightly. In particular, governments of industrialized countries were simply not willing to adopt the wide-reaching regulatory structures that would be needed to tackle greenhouse gas emissions, in part because of the economic costs of doing so. However, by the end of the 2000s, the climate change story started to change markedly (Hansen et al., 2007). An expanding shelf of scientific papers accompanied by more frequent and severe extreme weather events soon revealed climate change to be a present and worsening problem, not merely a future projection. Increasing global temperatures, together with increasingly frequent and intense heatwaves, storms, and shifts in precipitation patterns, also started to provide powerful demonstrations that the world was already experiencing consequences of climate change. Formed in 1988 to monitor climate developments, the Intergovernmental Panel on Climate Change published reports at ever shorter intervals, giving policymakers increasingly desperate warnings (Change, 2007).

The turning point in climate change perception occurred in the early part of the 2000s, as the impacts of anthropogenic warming became harder to ignore through more visible impacts, such as those facing vulnerable communities in developing economies. The developing economies, for example, have been badly hit by climate-change-induced natural calamities and they had very limited, rather no scope to adapt as compared to the wealthier nations with better infrastructure and adaptive capacities. Low-lying coastal nations and arid-climate regions like portions of Sub-Sahara Africa, South Asia, and Southeast Asia began to manifest ever more destructive extreme weather patterns, stressing their already stretched economies and infrastructures (White, 2011). Notably, the effects of climate change on food production emerged as an area of concern for climate researchers. Yields in these regions were already under threat as developing economies become increasingly reliant on farming for both food security and economic growth, which started to suffer from erratic weather. In nations like India, Pakistan, and Ethiopia, for instance, these erratic monsoons, prolonged droughts, and unpredictable rainfall designs have attacked their agrarian areas. Over the years 2021, one of the worst heatwaves on record swept India, reaching temperatures over 50°C (122°F) in parts of the country (Hussain et al., 2023). But these heatwaves were not without consequence, as records showed that such suffering coincided with a loss of crop yield, contributing to food insecurity in a country that depends on subsistence agriculture for its people. Likewise, in 2020, extended droughts express intense impacts on the Horn of Africa, aggravating the persistent food and water shortages within the region. Gradually, as climate events increased in frequency and severity, it became evident the climate change 'bogeyman' some had imagined, was no longer an outside threat; it had come home. Once perceived as occasional events, extreme natural disasters are now common, and nations are adapting to the changing climate. The year 2020 was a major inflection point, as the COVID-19 pandemic has brought to the forefront of awareness the vulnerabilities of societies around the globe (Akhtar et al., 2020). The pandemic devastated economies worldwide, but extreme weather events, such as the Australian wildfires, Philippine typhoons, and ruinous flooding in parts of Latin America, also reminded us of the interconnected nature of global crises. This was not an isolated event, as the urgency of integrated responses to global threats reemerged as climate change emerged as one of the most urgent challenges confronting humanity.

Entering into the 2020s, the narratives around climate change only accelerated the shifts in storytelling. The flooding in China that summer and the torrid wildfires in the Amazon Rainforest highlighted the anti-climate change realities. The Yangtze River basin in China was hit by the worst floods in decades in 2020, covering extensive areas, and forcing millions to flee their homes and destroying infrastructure. These floods were aggravated by extremely heavy rain associated with climate change. While the immediate effects of such events were huge for countries like China, which have a quickly expanding city population and huge agricultural sector, for developing economies starving of resources, the effects were more devastating. Like climate change itself, the political landscape surrounding climate change has changed over recent years, highlighting the increasing urgency of the crisis, but also the challenges inherent in finding common ground. The Paris Agreement, adopted in 2015, represented a huge leap forward in global efforts to combat climate change. At the heart of the agreement was the goal of keeping global temperature rise to below 2°C above pre-industrial levels (Lawrence & Schäfer, 2019), with an aspirational effort to limit the increase to 1.5°C. However, little progress has been made in the years that have followed, with major countries failing to fulfil their pledges. In November 2024, the Paris Agreement Summit in Azerbaijan experienced a dramatic political moment (Jović-Lazić & Bošković, 2024), when net-zero leaders, including the United States and China, boycotted the summit, exposing geopolitical divides that challenge any real global climate action. It was a snapshot of a politically divided world on climate, competing economic interests and a lack of common ground in which to address the crisis.

3. The Vulnerabilities of Developing Economies to Climate Change

3.1. Economic Vulnerabilities

Climate change poses a serious development challenge, especially for developing economies who are most economically vulnerable. Highly climate-sensitive sectors like agriculture, fishing, and extraction of natural resources play a vital role in the economy of several developing nations. Climate change is leading to changes in climate events, producing more droughts, floods, and heatwaves than ever before, and compromising the capacity of these nations to sustain agricultural production. Significant economic losses have resulted from climate change in poorer nations. According to a World Meteorological Organization (WMO) assessment, weather, climate, and water-related events caused almost 12,000 disasters worldwide between 1970 and 2021, with $4.3 trillion in economic damages. Developing nations were particularly vulnerable, as evidenced by the fact that more than 90% of the related deaths took place there (WMO, 2021). Furthermore, according to a Stanford University research, since 1960, economic disparity between rich and poor countries has grown by 25% due to climate change, escalating already-existing gaps (Diffenbaugh & Burke, 2019). For example, in Bangladesh, where rice is a major crop, flooding and sea level rise have resulted in loss of agricultural land and farmers are left without food and the risk of famine increases (Alam et al., 2024; Awal & Khan, 2020). Likewise, in Africa, protracted dry periods endanger agricultural production and compound underlying poverty (Middleton & Sternberg, 2013), potentially triggering security threats in several countries, including Ethiopia and Kenya. These effects on agriculture lead to food insecurity as well as stagnation in economic growth and a rise to the poverty rate. In addition, access to financial resources and technology is also limited, deepening the economic vulnerability of these countries. Many developing economies do not have the resources required for climate adaptation measures, including constructing resilient infrastructure or developing early-warning systems for extreme weather events. International financial institutions have repeatedly withheld much-needed funds, claiming economic instability or poor governance as excuses for not assisting (Copelovitch, 2010). Consequently, these nations are susceptible to climate impacts with minimal means to alleviate climate change or acclimatize to these alterations.

3.2. Social Vulnerabilities

Just as urgent are the social vulnerabilities in developing countries, where climate change compounds existing disparities in these societies. Women are the most vulnerable to the impacts of climate change in rural areas especially in many developing economies (Yadav & Lal, 2018). The things that are directly impacted by climate change such as droughts and floods are all things that women in rural areas historically do, such as agriculture, food production, water collection. In turn, they make women more vulnerable to climate change and increase female–male disparity. Climate change can also cause people to be displaced and migrate, as there will be communities forced to leave areas that are inundated with rising sea levels or hit by extreme weather events (Nawaah et al., 2025). As an example, there is a huge and permanent population displacement from Pacific Island nations with rising sea levels – many move to neighbouring countries looking for shelter (Campbell, 2014). This movement causes urban areas to become congested, competition for limited resources, and social instability. Countries with fragile political systems, like Haiti and Yemen, can experience conflict and instability related to climate migration, making the climate crisis even harder to solve.

3.3. Political Vulnerabilities

Another aspect of climate change that requires attention is the political vulnerabilities of developing countries. The lack of institutional capacity to adequately deal with climate risks and implement adaptation strategies continues to be a problem in many developing economies. Poor governance structures, political instability, and widespread corruption frequently preclude attempts to deal with the repercussions of climate. Sometimes political realities simply will not allow governments to take on climate, with instability elsewhere on the agenda, or with reactions to economic crisis prohibiting action. The rise in international diplomatic strains over the Paris Agreement symbolizes political susceptibilities exemplified by climate change in our time. The Paris Agreement Summit in Azerbaijan in November 2024 was attended by only the poorest 50 countries, with the United States, China, and other major economies boycotting the event due to disagreements over financial commitments and national priorities (Ostovar, 2024). Such a boycott emphasized the difficulties of a united global stance on the climate response, where major powers could not agree on an action plan to tackle the catastrophe. This absence of political will from key global players endangers developing economies' efforts to procure the financing, initiatives and supports necessary for climate adaptation (Quarshie et al., 2025).

4. Pathways to Addressing Vulnerabilities: Solutions for Building Resilience

4.1. Collaboration and Financial Assistance Among Nations

Clearer steps are needed both locally and globally to combat climate change as the even harsher impacts of climate change threaten developing economies. When it comes to combating climate change, poor nations confront significant financial obstacles. In the first two decades of this century, 55 of the most climate-vulnerable nations have seen economic losses over half a trillion dollars, according to the United Nations Framework Convention on Climate Change (UNFCCC) (Oxfam, 2022). There is still a sizable financing vacuum in spite of programs like the Green Climate Fund. To strengthen its climate resilience, for example, Pakistan has applied for almost $1 billion in climate finance from the Resilience and Sustainability Trust of the International Monetary Fund (Reuters, 2025). Rich countries, the main source of greenhouse gases, have clear moral obligation to help poor countries adapt to climate change (Khan et al., 2022; Rübbelke, 2011). This assistance can include financial support, transfer of technological knowledge, and capacity-building. For example, the Green Climate Fund established under the UNFCCC supports developing countries during climate adaptation and mitigation projects. On the contrary, critics claim that it has been chronically underfunded, and many developing countries have found it difficult to access the funds they require (Conca, 2015). For developing countries, resilience under changing climatic conditions requires larger financial support accompanied by ever better governance and institutional capacity.

4.2. Road to Resilient Infrastructure

Although the idea might appear simple, putting it into practice will take a lot of work, with a focus on starting with the most challenging and demanding parts. In particular, this encompasses the vital infrastructure that supports economic operations and the infrastructure required for emerging nations to adjust to and lessen the effects of climate change. This includes constructing flood barriers, developing water control systems, and enhancing transportation systems to cope with severe weather conditions. In Dhaka, Bangladesh, investment has been made in climate-resilient infrastructure such as flood barriers and the enhancement of drainage systems, which can help the city cope with the regular flooding that has a detrimental effect on the economy (Rahman & Rahman, 2015). Moreover, these investments address climate impacts as well as create economic opportunities, including jobs and public health benefits.

4.3. Technological Innovation

Innovation in technology is a crucial instrument for helping poor nations deal with the problems caused by climate change. Integrating climate-smart technologies, including drought-resistant crops, renewable energy, and efficient irrigation systems, can lower vulnerability to climate-induced disruptions. In Kenya, mobile technology solutions have been used to disseminate climate information and early-warning systems directly to farmers to enable them to make informed decisions about planting and harvesting (Khan et al., 2021; Masinde, 2015). Technological innovations coupled with public–private partnerships can help developing nations make progress in adapting to climate change and further reduce their reliance on climate-sensitive sectors (Naseema et al., 2024).

5. Future Trends and Directions: Charting a Path Forward in the Climate Crisis

Given the ever worsening of climate change effects, developing economies should seek to implement long-term strategies that are shaped around their vulnerabilities but also provide the possibility to seize opportunities that have arisen. Over the next few decades, geopolitical relations and approaches to climate resilience and adaptation among nations, industries, and communities will evolve substantially. Here are some of the key trends and directions that will drive future climate action, especially in developing economies.

5.1. Shift to Renewable Energy Solutions

The global transition from fossil fuels to renewable sources of energy would have to be one of the most hopeful trends in our efforts to combat climate change. It is both a challenge and opportunity for developing economies. Dwindling prices and technological advancements have made solar, wind, and hydroelectric power developments easier than ever. For example, India, Kenya, and Vietnam are already getting ahead when it comes to deploying renewables (Sovacool, 2013). Kenya, on the other hand, produces upwards of 75% of its electricity renewably, largely using geothermal and wind power. Building out renewable energy infrastructure can help cut down on greenhouse gases while also tackling energy poverty, one of the biggest challenges facing many developing countries.

5.2. Advancements in Climate-resilient Agriculture

Agriculture is the backbone of many developing economies, which is why innovation around climate-resilient farming practices is vital. Looking forward, we can expect more precision agriculture practices, such as using data analytics, satellite monitoring of land usage, and AI in farms, which will lead to improved yields along with the abatement of wastage of valuable resources. Such advances will also include genetic engineering and selective breeding to create crops with greater drought tolerance, pest resistance, and heat tolerance. Examples include trials of drought-resistant maize in Sub-Saharan Africa and salt-tolerant rice varieties in South Asia, a boon especially for farmers there.

5.3. Environmental Funding and Sustainable Investment

One of the biggest obstacles still facing poor nations is the large funding gap for climate mitigation and adaptation (Biesbroek et al., 2013). Nevertheless, directions of the future show higher climate financing from public and private sectors. Tools including green bonds, carbon credits, and climate funds will be vital to assist the nations which are most vulnerable. Such international initiatives as the Green Climate Fund and new regional partnerships will provide additional support for infrastructure, renewable energy projects, and disaster management systems. There is likely to be more blended finance approaches (whereby both public and private funds are combined) become more dominant. Comparative studies show that whereas climate-related disasters cause economic losses in both affluent and developing countries, the effects are disproportionately felt in the former. For instance, while developing economies face a climate finance gap of over $300 billion annually (UNEP, 2022), developed economies have made much larger investments in climate mitigation and adaptation, with the EU allocating over €500 billion for green projects under its Green Deal (European Commission, 2023). While the majority of poor countries struggle with legislative frameworks and finance for such projects, the United States and the European Union have built extensive carbon pricing schemes (World Bank, 2023). Due to financial and technological limitations, developing countries undergo slower transitions despite initiatives like India's $90 billion renewable energy investment (IEA, 2023). This results in disproportionate climate-induced economic losses, such as Africa losing 5–15% of gross domestic product (GDP) growth as a result of climate impacts (IMF, 2022). In contrast to the catastrophic impacts on economies like Bangladesh, where climatic catastrophes account for yearly losses surpassing 2% of GDP, industrialized countries enjoy the benefits of improved infrastructure and insurance arrangements, which reduce disaster-related GDP losses to less than 1% (ADB, 2021). This discrepancy emphasizes how poor economies require more financial and technical assistance in order to achieve equal climate resilience.

5.4. Emphasis on Urban Resilience

With rising urbanization, especially within developing economies, cities are becoming epicentres of climate exposure. The future will focus more on sustainable urban planning, green infrastructure, and disaster risk management for building urban resilience. More efforts will be put in place towards smart city initiatives, as it combines technology with sustainability. Places like Curitiba in Brazil and Kigali in Rwanda are leading the way with green spaces, public transport and waste services that build greater urban resilience.

5.5. Regional and International Cooperation

Climate change, being as interconnected as it is, requires collective action. Future trends are going to focus more on the regional and global cooperation to tackle the joint fight, such as cross-border agreements over management of waters, disaster-response mechanisms on a regional level, brainstorming over sharing more technologies. Regional organizations, including the African Union, ASEAN, and the Caribbean Community, are likely to be central in orchestrating regional responses to climate impacts.

5.6. Using Technology and Innovation

The most consequential climate solutions of the future will sit at the intersection of technology and biology. For instance, new early warning systems, blockchain to give rights to transparent carbon trading, and machine learning for climate modelling, will ensure that developing countries can anticipate and respond to climate risks in a more suitable fashion (Jafar et al., 2024). The growing availability of low-cost mobile technologies also opens new ways to educate and engage communities in climate adaptation efforts. Things such as mobile apps save rural farmers by giving instant weather information and farming advice.

5.7. Emphasizing Social Equality and Engaging Policies

Marginalized communities, especially in developing countries, are most vulnerable and adversely impacted by climate change. Incorporating social justice into climate policies, climate initiatives will place a greater emphasis on human welfare and equity. Throughout the decision-making process, this method guarantees that initiatives created with equality in mind make it easier for marginalized and disadvantaged groups to access resources and technology. For example, due to the critical roles of women in agriculture and natural resource management, policies that are sensitive to gender are receiving attention. Strengthening the role of women and other marginalized groups will be imperative for fostering inclusive and community-informed climate resilience.

5.8. Local Governance and Capacity Development

Good local governance will be critical for implementing and maintaining climate adaptation. Decentralization will take centre stage, driving more local involvement in disaster preparedness, resource management, and community engagement. Capacity-building (e.g., local official and community leader training) initiatives help ensure that adaptive measures are context-specific and sustainable in the long run.

5.9. Nature-based Solutions (NbS) Integration

NbS are emerging as a sustainable and economically feasible ecosystem-based response to climate and other global changes (Stefanakis et al., 2021). These span from reforestation, wetland restoration, to protecting mangroves and coral reefs as natural shields from climate impacts. NbS present worthwhile advantages for developing economies, especially biodiverse ones. For instance, nations with large coastlines such as Indonesia and the Philippines are considering mangrove restoration initiatives that can help address rising sea level and coastal erosion as well as promote fisheries to the local communities.

6. Conclusion

Climate change is not a future risk; it is here and happening today, especially for developing economies. This chapter touched on the increasing ferocity of climate events threatening the economic, social, and political fragility of these countries. The floods in Valencia and the unravelling of diplomacy at the Paris Agreement Summit are just two examples of the latest headlines highlighting the need for meaningful climate action. But international solidarity, additional funding, and investment in resilience will create the conditions for developing countries to confront these challenges squarely. International cooperation is key to ensuring a climate-resilient future for all countries, rich and poor. Aside from the political tensions, climate change has created a global social movement revolution led by young people, activists, and marginalized communities to push for rapid change and action on climate political movements. Protests erupted all over the globe in 2021, including by youth climate activists lead by Greta Thunberg, urging governments to reduce emissions enough to promote drastic reductions and to pay enough for adaptation efforts in the Global South. Such movements also indicate the rising anger of people who believe that their leaders are not doing enough to avoid the worst effects of climate change, especially in places where we are already seeing the results.

Yet the abundance of evidence and the evolution of the climate change story are not translating into sufficient action – especially with regard to the aspirations of developing world's economies. They are the countries that continue to experience the climate crisis first, coupled with the socioeconomic fragility amplified by rising inequalities exacerbated by the impacts of environmental destruction. The effects of climate change amplify vulnerabilities, resulting in a downward spiral of poverty and environmental degradation. This chapter describes the unique challenges developing countries experience, including the necessity for immediate, targeted adaptation, and the collective responsibility developed countries have to help assure these bottom tier climates are not sidelined in the face of climate change.

References

Akhtar, S., Niazi, M. H., & Khan, M. M. (2020). Cascading effect of COVID 19 on Indian economy. *International Journal of Advanced Science and Technology*, *29*(9), 4563–4573.

Alam, M., Akhtar, S., & Bettencourt, A. (2024). Introduction to fintech in Industry 5.0: Companion or antagonist. In S. H. Jafar, H. K. (Hemachandran), S. Akhtar, P. A. Khan, & H. El-Chaarani (Eds.), *The adoption of Fintech: using technology for better security, speed, and customer experience in finance* (pp. 1–16). Productivity Press. https://doi.org/10.4324/9781032644165-1

Asian Development Bank (ADB). (2021). *Climate risk country profile: Bangladesh*. https://www.adb.org/publications/climate-risk-country-profile-bangladesh

Awal, M. A., & Khan, M. A. H. (2020). Global warming and sea level rising: Impact on agriculture and food security in southern coastal region of Bangladesh. *Asian Journal of Geographical Research*, *3*(3), 9–36.

Biesbroek, G. R., Klostermann, J. E., Termeer, C. J., & Kabat, P. (2013). On the nature of barriers to climate change adaptation. *Regional Environmental Change*, *13*, 1119–1129.

Campbell, J. R. (2014). Climate-change migration in the Pacific. *The Contemporary Pacific*, *26*(1), 1–28. https://doi.org/10.1353/cp.2014.0023

Change, O. C. (2007). Intergovernmental panel on climate change. *World Meteorological Organization*, *52*, 1–43.

Conca, K. (2015). *An unfinished foundation: The United Nations and global environmental governance*. Oxford University Press.

Copelovitch, M. S. (2010). *The International Monetary Fund in the global economy: Banks, bonds, and bailouts*. Cambridge University Press.

Diffenbaugh, N. S., & Burke, M. (2019). Global warming has increased global economic inequality. *Proceedings of the National Academy of Sciences*, *116*(20), 9808–9813. https://doi.org/10.1073/pnas.1816020116

European Commission. (2023). *The European green deal: Investment plan and funding*. https://ec.europa.eu/commission/presscorner/detail/en/ip_23_567

Hansen, J., Sato, M., Kharecha, P., Russell, G., Lea, D. W., & Siddall, M. (2007). Climate change and trace gases. *Philosophical Transactions of the Royal Society A: Mathematical, Physical and Engineering Sciences*, *365*(1856), 1925–1954.

Hussain, M. A., Shuai, Z., Moawwez, M. A., Umar, T., Iqbal, M. R., Kamran, M., & Muneer, M. (2023). A review of spatial variations of multiple natural hazards and risk management strategies in Pakistan. *Water*, *15*, 407.

International Energy Agency (IEA). (2023). *Renewable energy market update*. https://www.iea.org/reports/renewable-energy-market-update-2023

International Monetary Fund (IMF). (2022). *Climate change and economic impact in Sub-Saharan Africa*. https://www.imf.org/en/Publications/WP/Issues/2022/10/13/Climate-Change-and-Economic-Impact-in-Sub-Saharan-Africa-524310

Jafar, S. H., Hemachandran, K., Akhtar, S., Khan, P. A., & El-Chaarani, H. (Eds.). (2024). *The adoption of fintech: Using technology for better security, speed, and customer experience in finance*. CRC Press.

Jović-Lazić, A., & Bošković, S. (2024). Azerbaijan's foreign policy positioning towards Russia and its impact on the Second Nagorno-Karabakh War: A hedging strategy. *The Review of International Affairs*, *75*, 55–82.

Kemp, L., Xu, C., Depledge, J., Ebi, K. L., Gibbins, G., Kohler, T. A., Rockström, J., Scheffer, M., Schellnhuber, H. J., Steffen, W., & Lenton, T. M. (2022). Climate endgame: Exploring catastrophic climate change scenarios. *Proceedings of the National Academy of Sciences*, *119*(34), e2108146119. https://doi.org/10.1073/pnas.2108146119

Khan, P. A., Johl, S. K., & Akhtar, S. (2021). Firm sustainable development goals and firm financial performance through the lens of green innovation practices and reporting: A proactive approach. *Journal of Risk and Financial Management*, *14*(12), 605.

Khan, P. A., Johl, S. K., & Akhtar, S. (2022). Vinculum of sustainable development goal practices and firms' financial performance: A moderation role of green innovation. *Journal of Risk and Financial Management*, *15*(3), 96.

Lahsen, M., Sanchez-Rodriguez, R., Romero Lankao, P. R., Dube, P., Leemans, R., Gaffney, O., Mirza, M., Pinho, P., Osman-Elasha, B., & Stafford Smith, M. S. (2010). Impacts, adaptation and vulnerability to global environmental change: challenges and pathways for an action-oriented research agenda for middle-income and low-income countries. *Current Opinion in Environmental Sustainability*, *2*(5–6), 364–374.

Lawrence, M. G., & Schäfer, S. (2019). Promises and perils of the Paris Agreement. *Science*, *364*(6443), 829–830.

Legg, S. (2021). IPCC, 2021: Climate change 2021–the physical science basis. *Interaction*, *49*(4), 44–45.

Lomborg, B. (2020). Welfare in the 21st century: Increasing development, reducing inequality, the impact of climate change, and the cost of climate policies. *Technological Forecasting and Social Change*, *156*, 119981.

Masinde, M. (2015). An innovative drought early warning system for sub-Saharan Africa: Integrating modern and indigenous approaches. *African Journal of Science, Technology, Innovation and Development*, *7*(1), 8–25.

Middleton, N. J., & Sternberg, T. (2013). Climate hazards in drylands: A review. *Earth-Science Reviews*, *126*, 48–57.

Mintzer, I., & Michel, D. (2001). Climate change, rights of future generations and intergenerational equity: an in-expert exploration of a dark and cloudy path. *International Journal of Global Environmental Issues*, *1*(2), 203-222.

Moser, S. C. (2016). Reflections on climate change communication research and practice in the second decade of the 21st century: What more is there to say?. *Wiley Interdisciplinary Reviews: Climate Change*, *7*(3), 345–369.

Naseema, N., Akhtar, S., & Al Hinai, A. A. (2024). Disrupting financial services: A case study on capital one's Fintech odyssey. In S. H. Jafar, R. V. Rodriguez, H. Kannan, Akhtar, S., & Plugmann, P. (Eds.), *Harnessing blockchain-digital twin fusion for sustainable investments* (pp. 363–383). IGI Global. https://doi.org/10.4018/979-8-3693-1878-2.ch015

Nawaah, D., Asare, P. Y., & Quarshie, M. A. (2025). Climate finance and natural capital: Linking global initiatives with local impact. In R. Singh & W. L. Filho (Eds.), *Climate neutrality through smart eco-innovation and environmental sustainability* (pp. 317–332). Climate Change Management. Springer. https://doi.org/10.1007/978-3-031-83250-5_19

Oreskes, N. (2004). Beyond the ivory tower: The scientific consensus on climate change. *Science*, *306*(5702), 1686–1686. https://doi.org/10.1126/science.1103618

Ostovar, A. (2024). *Wars of ambition: The United States, Iran, and the struggle for the Middle East*. Oxford University Press.

Oxfam. (2022). *Footing the bill: Fair finance for loss and damage in an era of escalating climate impacts*. https://www.oxfam.org/en/press-releases/189-million-people-year-affected-extreme-weather-developing-countries-rich-countries

Quarshie, M. A., Akhtar, S., & Nawaah, D. (2025). Barriers to breakthroughs: The crucial role of support services in advancing accounting practices, financial literacy and performance in disability-led SMEs. *Quality & Quantity*, *59*(2), 955–977. https://doi.org/10.1007/s11135-024-02050-1

Rahman, S., & Rahman, M. A. (2015). Climate extremes and challenges to infrastructure development in coastal cities in Bangladesh. *Weather and Climate Extremes*, *7*, 96–108.

Reuters. (2025, February 20). *IMF, Pakistan to open $1 billion climate finance talks next week, says adviser*. https://www.reuters.com/sustainability/sustainable-finance-reporting/imf-pakistan-open-1-billion-climate-finance-talks-next-week-says-adviser-2025-02-20/

Rübbelke, D. T. (2011). International support of climate change policies in developing countries: Strategic, moral and fairness aspects. *Ecological Economics*, *70*(8), 1470–1480.

Saeed, S., Makhdum, M. S. A., Anwar, S., & Yaseen, M. R. (2023). Climate change vulnerability, adaptation, and feedback hypothesis: A comparison of lower-middle, upper-middle, and high-income countries. *Sustainability*, *15*(5), 4145.

Sovacool, B. K. (2013). A qualitative factor analysis of renewable energy and sustainable energy for all (SE4ALL) in the Asia-Pacific. *Energy Policy*, *59*, 393–403.

Stefanakis, A. I., Calheiros, C. S., & Nikolaou, I. (2021). Nature-based solutions as a tool in the new circular economic model for climate change adaptation. *Circular Economy and Sustainability*, *1*, 303–318.

United Nations Environment Programme (UNEP). (2022). *Adaptation gap report 2022*. https://www.unep.org/resources/adaptation-gap-report-2022

White, G. (2011). *Climate change and migration: Security and borders in a warming world*. OUP USA.

World Bank. (2023). *State and trends of carbon pricing 2023*. https://openknowledge.worldbank.org/handle/10986/39455

World Meteorological Organization (WMO). (2021). *Atlas of mortality and economic losses from weather, climate and water extremes (1970–2019)*. https://library.wmo.int/doc_num.php?explnum_id=10769

Yadav, S. S., & Lal, R. (2018). Vulnerability of women to climate change in arid and semi-arid regions: The case of India and South Asia. *Journal of Arid Environments*, *149*, 4–17.

Zolli, A., & Healy, A. M. (2013). *Resilience: Why things bounce back*. Simon and Schuster.

Chapter 4

Effects of Climate Changes on the Value of Emerging Markets in BRICS Nations

Dhaya M.[a], *Sundaram N.*[a], *Divya Meena S.*[b] *and Dhanuskodi Rengasamy*[c]

[a]*Department of Commerce, School of Social Science and Languages, VIT-Vellore, Tamilnadu, India*
[b]*Department of Computer Science, School of Computer Science and Engineering, VIT-AP University, Andhra Pradesh, India*
[c]*Faculty of Business, School of Accounting and Finance, Curtin University Malaysia, Sarawak, Malaysia*

Abstract

This chapter examines how market values in the Brazil, Russia, India, China, and South Africa (BRICS) economies are affected by climate change, highlighting the financial risks associated with environmental shocks. It is crucial to comprehend how climate change affects developing markets because of the growing threat it poses to economic variety and growth. After adjusting for confounding variables, the study uses panel data analysis with the fixed effects technique to analyze the relationship between gross domestic product (GDP) and temperature changes and CO_2 emissions, accounting for unobserved country-specific variability. Furthermore, the Spatial Durbin Model (SDM), which takes into account economic linking factors like inflation and foreign direct investment (FDI), is used to evaluate both direct and spillover impacts. The empirical results show that elements related to the climate have a major impact on market expansion. The findings of the ordinary least squares (OLS) regression show that temperature variations have a smaller but significant impact on GDP ($p = 0.059$), whereas CO_2 emissions have a significantly significant positive effect ($p < 0.0001$). The model highlights a substantial correlation between environmental factors and economic performance, explaining around 83%

Climate Risk and Emerging Markets: Valuation, Volatility, and Portfolio Strategies, 55–70

doi:10.1108/978-1-83708-088-520261015

of the variation in GDP (R^2 = 0.8299). Nonetheless, the residuals' significant autocorrelation (Durbin–Watson = 0.077) points to possible model improvements. The SDM results illustrate the economic effects of climate variability by highlighting the mild temperature effects and reaffirming the importance of carbon emissions. These results highlight the need for adaptable economic strategies and mitigating policies to protect market stability.

Keywords: Climate change; panel data; fixed effects; market value; BRICS; Spatial Durbin Model

1. Introduction

Changes in temperature and carbon emissions are directly connected with economic performance. Countries with economic linkages and geographical connections can have spillover effects due to climate change. Industrialization in emerging nations is typically linked to changes in growing emissions, and its aftereffects have the potential to completely destroy the nation's economic progress and development. This has made it possible for scholars, financiers, and decision-makers to focus on the economy's resilience and equilibrium sustainability. This chapter examines the detrimental impacts of temperature fluctuations and CO_2 emissions on the GDP growth of emerging economies, highlighting the significance of adaptable policies and practical steps to boost these countries' economic development. The majority of scholars are currently concentrating on the several ways that climate change affects national economies and rates of growth. Research indicates that it significantly affects the nations' natural and socioeconomic systems, and there is a good likelihood that it will persist in the future (Auffhammer, 2018; Carleton & Hsiang, 2016; Carrilho-Nunes & Catalão-Lopes, 2022; Climate Action Tracker, 2023; Fabozzi et al., 2022; Stern, 2013). Many geographical areas and different types of industries are affected by climate change. Multinational-level industries including tourism, the health sector, the agricultural sector, and energy are at risk. Natural calamities like floods, landslides, and drought have the potential to disrupt the infrastructure of the well-versed industries of the economy and affect the overall GDP growth, which will result in extreme monetary loss. The determination of top-down effects of climate change on GDP has already been done in the past literature, and macroeconomic level impacts have been identified and studied in the previous studies. According to Burke et al. (2015), Newell et al. (2021), Dell et al. (2009), Azmi and Akhtar (2023), Kalkuhl and Wenz (2020), and Colacito et al. (2021), this topic has emerged as a crucial area of research in climate econometrics. The relationship between GDP and temperature changes has been the subject of numerous analyses in the field of climate econometrics. The researchers concluded that changes in rising temperatures can have an impact on investment, which in turn can alter productivity and economic growth. Climate change may have a longer-term impact on economic productivity and may permanently eliminate the growing trend that could hurt GDP, according to emerging researchers in several studies (Burke et al., 2015; Dell et al., 2012; Hsiang & Jina, 2014; Moore & Diaz, 2015; Moyer et al., 2014; Pindyck, 2013; Stern, 2013). Since not all countries are equally affected by climate change, there is a chance that some will gain from it (Hope, 2006). The poor country people are likely to suffer due to the damage to their water resources, ecosystems, crop production, fisheries, and human health (Nordhaus, 1991; Stern et al., 2006; Tol, 2008; Yohe & Schlesinger, 2002). According to Dell et al. (2012), an empirical study from a panel of 136 countries spanning 1950–2003 captures that there are mainly three causes for why rising temperature is affecting the GDP growth. The first reason is that it drastically slows down the economic growth of emerging economies; a 1 °C change in temperature can reduce economic growth by 1.3%. Secondly, it will reduce the output levels of the economy. Thirdly, the rising temperature has an impact on political stability, agricultural production, and industrial growth. According to the scientific community, climate change is directly and significantly affecting global growth and civilizations. Economic growth, yearly income, labor productivity and supply, human capital, migration, energy consumption, food security, and demography are some examples that fall under this statement (Burke et al., 2015; Casey et al., 2019; Cattaneo et al., 2019; De Cian & Wing, 2019; Dell et al., 2012; Deryugina & Hsiang, 2014; Deschenes & Greenstone, 2007; Desmet & Rossi-Hansberg, 2015; Graff Zivin & Neidell, 2014; Graff Zivin et al., 2018; Isaac & Van Vuuren, 2009; Newell et al., 2018).

These effects may be different according to the difference in the geographical area, the difference in income and consumption, and job level also depending upon other related factors. The theoretical background of climate change and economic growth consists of mainly two popular theories that are dynamic approach and the enumerative approach. In the enumerative technique, only one sector at a time is being examined with the climate change effects, for example how it affects the tourism sector, and agriculture sector separately. To arrive at the overall change in the ecosystem of the society these separate effects are combined (Cline, 1994; De Laubier Longuet Marx, Espagne, & Ngo Duc, 2019; Nordhaus, 1991; Tol, 1995). The second strategy utilizes different growth technique specifications and takes the damage function into account. The two widely used models for assessing how climate change affects economic growth are the Solow–Swan and Ramsey–Cass–Koopmans models. The least popular growth model is Mankiw et al. (1992) (Fankhauser & Tol, 2005).

2. Literature Review and Hypothesis Development

Past pieces of literature have already found that climate change has significant effects on the agricultural sector in many emerging economies who are having agriculture productivity as their major source of income. Researchers state that for every degree Celsius rise in temperature has a 10% drop-down effect on agricultural productivity. This kind of reduction in crops will have a strong impact on the economies of developing countries whose major share is the agricultural sector (Schlenker & Roberts, 2009). In the case of CO_2 emissions and GDP growth rate, CO_2 emissions and GDP have a complex relationship. There are previous researches that state that climate change has only short-term effects on economic growth. However, the long-term consequences and after-effects of climate change will affect economic stability for a longer period (Stern, 2007). Economic growth and environmental sustainability are the most sensitive factors in the case of emerging economies (Pindyck, 2013). Not every country in the world is equally affected by climate change; low-income countries that are already facing economic stability issues and productivity issues are the most affected due to climate change challenges and they are getting into huge economic loss (Kahn et al., 2015). The reason behind this is the inability of emerging economies to overcome and withstand the hazards of climate change. According to the researchers, emerging economies will lose up to 3% of their GDP yearly by the year 2050 because of poor weather conditions and a rise in temperature levels (Hallegatte et al., 2016). Different sectors of the economy are affected differently due to climate change. For example, emerging economies in the coastal areas may be affected by climate change and their tourism sector can have negative impacts. An increase in sea levels may affect the GDP by a 2–5% loss (Becken & Hay, 2012). To overcome these issues and attain environmental resilience, effective mitigation strategies should be adopted which can promote economic growth (Akhtar et al., 2020). To stabilize the GDP in emerging economies there are measures like investing in renewable energies, and this could reduce the effects of climate change (IPCC, 2014). The cost of adapting the climate change is a crucial element while coming to developing economies. As per the future forecasts, the emerging economies' GDP might drop by as much as 10% by 2100 if proper action is not taken especially in the areas where there are climate-sensible industries (Burke et al., 2015). A better and more effective policy framework should be implemented to reduce the effects of climate change on GDP. Proper economic planning with at most importance to climate change can promote sustainable growth and development. It can increase the resilience of emerging economies (OECD, 2015). Another possible way is to improve the cooperation between developed and emerging economies so that they can transfer resources and share the knowledge which enhances the capability and also helps in implementing new ideas (Backstrand & Lovbrand, 2019). According to Kumar and Singh (2018), the case studies done in India and Brazil show the importance of localized adaptation and mitigation effects illuminating the diverse effects of climate change on GDP. Using integrated assessment models and econometric models many studies suggest that market value losses are highly linked with climate changes. Based on the world data by 2100 in tropical developing regions there is a chance of GDP losses in between 10% and 20% due to unmitigated emissions (Hsiang et al., 2017). However, as per Nordhaus's (2017) point of view he is focusing more on cost–benefit analysis to drop down climate change risk.

The motivation for choosing BRICS countries for this study is their substantial contributions to the global economy, varied climates, and differing degrees of climate change susceptibility. BRICS account for about 40% of the world's population and nearly 25% of its GDP; therefore, their climate policies and impacts are crucial (World Bank, 2023). Due to their economic and geographic variety, these nations are also more vulnerable to climate-related issues. India is particularly vulnerable to devastating heatwaves and erratic monsoons, South Africa and Brazil suffer from severe droughts and biodiversity loss, and Russia's permafrost thaws pose a hazard to infrastructure and natural ecosystems (IPCC, 2022). In addition, the BRICS nations contribute about 40% of global emissions, making them among the world's largest greenhouse gas polluters. There are cases of adverse impacts of climate change on GDP. Climate change has significant economic implications; according to a study, a 3.2 °C rise in global temperatures could cause the world's GDP to drop by as much as 18% by 2050 (World Economic Forum, 2021). The impact on the economy varies by country, with emerging nations often being more vulnerable. For instance, climate-change-related disruptions in labor productivity, infrastructure, and agriculture might result in a 25% drop in India's GDP by 2070 (Asian Development Bank, 2021).

This study focuses on identifying the lasting effects of climate changes on the market value of emerging economies, which is still a gap in the literature. On the basis of that, we have framed the hypothesis. One of the major objective of the study is to target the long-term impact of climate change on BRICS countries. Next crucial objective of the study is to find out the direct and indirect effects of climate change among countries. Then it investigates the time-invariant country-specific effects of climate change to discover the uncovered heterogeneity between countries across time. Another valuable contribution is the spatial spillover effects; by analyzing the spatial relationship of countries we can understand the level of influence between the countries due to the economic connections and linkages.

Based on the aims, we developed the following hypothesis:

H1. The level of CO_2 emissions and temperature changes negatively affect the GDP growth of BRICS countries.

H2. The level of CO_2 emissions and temperature changes in one BRICS country can lead to spillover effects on neighboring countries' GDP growth.

3. Research Design

3.1. Data and Methodology

Data have been collected for the past 24 years starting from the year 2000 through secondary sources. To assess the market value of BRICS countries "GDP" has been selected as the dependent variable for the analysis from "WORLD DEVELOPMENT INDICATORS." The independent variables are CO_2 emissions and temperature change, data for CO_2 emissions have been retrieved from "OUR WORLD IN DATA," and temperature change data have been collected from "INTERNATIONAL MONETARY FUND CLIMATE CHANGE INDICATORS." Panel data analysis, fixed effects methods, and the SDM are the methods used in this study to find out the direct, indirect, and spillover effects. Panel data is the combination of cross-section and time series in econometrics, which is one of the most widely used models. In this method, we can observe many entities over different times. Moreover, panel data permits us to account for unseen effects that may influence the independent variables. These unseen effects are time-invariant and also time-varying called individual effects. The progress of one variable over a period of time and how the change in one variable affects the other variable can be furnished with the help of panel data. Another significant advantage of panel data is its superior statistical power. Through the fixed effects method, the individual-specific intercepts are brought together into the regression model. These intercepts are useful for overlooking heterogeneity. The next tool utilized in the study is the SDM; it is a flexible spatial econometrics tool in which we can find the spatial lag dependence in the dependent variable and spatial lag dependence in independent variables. This makes it specifically effective for exploring spatial correlations stuck between variables when one unit's influence on alternatives goes beyond direct exchanges with nearby units. It will evaluate the direct, indirect, and total effects.

Given below is the model specification for the regression:

$$\text{GDP}_{it} = \beta_0 + \beta_1\text{CO2}_{it} + \beta_2\text{Tempchange}_{it} + \beta_3\text{Inflation}_{it} + \beta_4\text{FDI}_{it} + \varepsilon_{it} \quad \text{(i)}$$

GDP_{it} is the proxy for the market value of an emerging economy, i denotes for country and t represents the time. CO_{2it} is the carbon dioxide emissions of a country, and Tempchange_{it} is the amount of variation in average temperature for the country. Inflation_{it} is the rate of inflation for a country, FDI_{it} is the foreign direct speculation of the country. ε_{it} is the error term, and $\beta_0\ \beta_1\ \beta_2\ \beta_3\ \beta_4$ are the coefficients to be estimated.

4. Result Analysis

Table 4.1 shows the descriptive statistics of the dataset. The BRICS countries have an average temperature of 15.2 °C, with a minimum of 12.0 °C and a maximum of 18.5 °C. When evaluating the effects of climate change, this variation is significant. These economies differ in their industrialization and environmental policies, as evidenced by the 300–500 metric tons of CO_2 emissions. The $50 billion–$150 billion range for FDI indicates that the BRICS countries are not equally receiving capital inflows.

Fig. 4.1 shows the correlation heatmap, which depicts the connections between variables to demonstrate the substantial linkages of climate indicators and economic growth indicators. The Temperature change and CO_2 emissions have a high positive association (0.8), indicating that higher temperatures are associated with more energy use or industrial activity. The economic linkage variables, inflation, and FDI provide information about possible effects. Temperature change has a moderate negative connection with inflation (–0.2), indicating a minor negative influence, whereas CO_2 emissions have a minimum negative link with inflation (–0.1). In contrast, temperature change has a modest positive relation with FDI (0.5), and CO_2 emissions show an even higher positive correlation (0.6),

Table 4.1. Descriptive Statistics.

Variable	Mean	Std.Dev	Min	Max
Temperature	15.2	1.5	12.0	18.5
CO_2 emissions	400.5	50.2	300.0	500.0
Inflation	2.5	0.8	1.0	4.0
FDI	100.0	20.0	50.0	150.0
GDP	2,000.0	500.0	1,000.0	3,000.0

Source: Author's compilation.

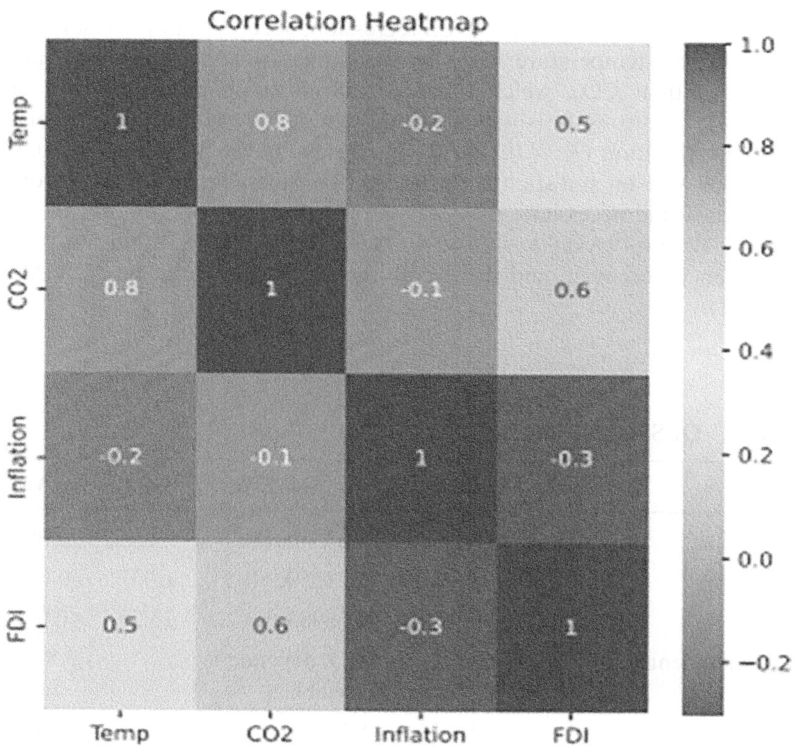

Fig. 4.1. Correlation Heatmap. *Source*: Caesar Labs, Inc. (2024).

suggesting that investment inflows may be focused on carbon-intensive industries. The inverse relationship between inflation and FDI (–0.3) indicates that rising inflation deters international investment. These relations highlight the complicated interplay between climate change indicators (temperature and CO_2 emissions) and economic indicators (inflation and FDI), providing significant insights into the indirect effects on GDP.

According to the highly substantial CO_2 coefficient, there is a considerable correlation between carbon emissions and economic activity in these markets.

This draws attention to the difficult fact that historically, carbon-intensive activities have been linked to economic progress in emerging markets. Climate change is starting to affect the economic results in these markets, according to the temperature coefficient, which is nearly significant. Infrastructure stability, labor efficiency, and agricultural yield can all be impacted by even slight temperature rises. Even before considering climate considerations, the negative constant value raises the possibility that these markets may be vulnerable to underlying economic difficulties. High predictive power ($R^2 = 0.83$): A significant amount of economic variance can be explained by climatic parameters, indicating that these emerging economies are especially susceptible to climate dynamics. The strong autocorrelation indicates that climate shocks have long-lasting, compounding economic repercussions.

Table 4.2 shows the results of OLS regression; according to the results of the OLS regression, temperature has a smaller impact on the dependent variable ($p = 0.059$) than CO_2, which has a significantly significant positive effect ($p < 0.0001$). A strong fit is indicated by the model's ability to explain around 83% of the variation ($R^2 = 0.8299$). Nonetheless, the high Rho value (0.9867) and Durbin–Watson statistic (0.077) suggest considerable positive autocorrelation, which would necessitate time-series corrections. In spite of this, the selection criteria values (Akaike = 7,089.46, Schwarz = 7,097.82) indicate that the model offers a decent fit, and the overall model is very significant ($F = 285.44$, $p < 0.0001$).

Table 4.2. OLS Regression.

	Coefficient	**Std. Error**	***t*-Ratio**	***p*-Value**
Constant	−6.69910e+011	3.46810e+011	−1.932	0.0558*
Temperature	5.17731e+011	2.71559e+011	1.907	0.0590*
CO_2	1.08333e+09	4.66983e+07	23.20	<0.0001**
Mean dependent variables	2.68e+12	S.D. dependent variables		3.87e+12
Sum squared residuals	3.04e+26	S.E. of regression		1.61e+12
R^2	0.829914	Adjusted R^2		0.827006
$F(2, 117)$	285.4435	p-value(F)		9.87e−46
Log-likelihood	−3,541.730	Akaike criterion		7,089.460
Schwarz criterion	7,097.823	Hannan–Quinn		7,092.856
Rho	0.986711	Durbin–Watson		0.077012

Source: Author's compilation.
*$p < 0.10$ (marginally significant).
**$p < 0.01$ (highly significant).

The fixed effects model is more dependable for the panel data, as demonstrated by the Hausman test's robust rejection of the random effects model ($H = 58.4252$, $p = 2.05652e{-}013$). The assumptions of the random effects model are not supported by the low *p*-value, which indicates significant differences between the two models. The fixed effects model is favored since unseen factors could be connected to the independent variables. Table 4.3 shows that CO_2 emissions and temperature variations have an impact on GDP. The beneficial effect of a 1-unit increase in temperature is substantial ($p = 0.0154$**), while the positive effect of CO_2 emissions is significantly greater ($p < 0.0001$***). The intercept, also highly significant ($p < 0.0001$***), suggests that GDP would decline if temperature and CO_2 emissions were zero. The fixed effects model provides more accurate results by accounting for hidden differences between countries, highlighting the strong impact of CO_2 emissions and temperature changes on economic growth.

Fig. 4.2 reveals the spatial impacts of climatic factors on GDP using the SDM. The direct impacts demonstrate that a temperature of 0.599 and CO_2 emissions of 0.472 have a considerable impact on GDP. Indirect effects show spillover effects, such as a temperature of 0.537 and CO_2 of 0.415, which affect the GDP of BRICS countries. The temperature of 1.136 and CO_2 of 0.887 have a significant impact on the GDP. FDI has strong and positive direct and indirect effects on GDP. It plays an important role in the growth of GDP in the country and has spillover

Table 4.3. Fixed Effects Method.

	Coefficient	**Std. Error**	***t*-Ratio**	***p*-Value**
Constant	−2.99607e+012	2.94586e+011	−10.17	<0.0001***
Temperature	5.43501e+011	2.20840e+011	2.461	0.0154**
CO_2	1.98512e+09	7.69671e+07	25.79	<0.0001***

Source: Author's compilation.

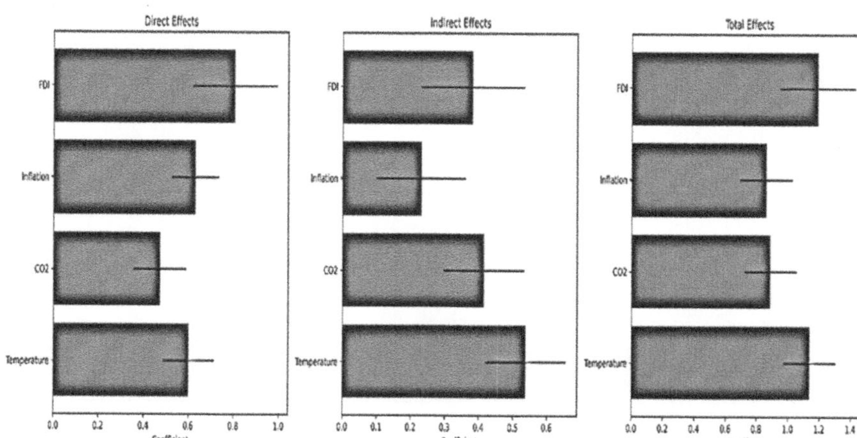

Fig. 4.2. Direct, Indirect, and Total Effects. *Source*: Caesar Labs, Inc. (2024).

effects. CO_2 emissions also show positive effects which indicates that industrial activities related to emissions can contribute to economic growth. In the case of temperature changes and inflation, they have very mild effects but temperature changes influence GDP growth both directly and indirectly, whereas inflation has very low spillover effects among the countries. The total effects which consist of direct effects and indirect effects with FDI and CO_2 emissions have played a vital role as GDP drivers. It is been acting as the factor affecting GDP concerning climate change issues.

Strong direct and indirect consequences of CO_2 emissions highlight their crucial significance in economic production. The overall effect of temperature (0.6) points to both direct and indirect advantages. While FDI may cause initial disruptions, it may also promote long-term growth, as seen by its contradictory consequences, which include both positive indirect and negative direct effects.

The existence of spatial autocorrelation is confirmed by Moran's I scatter plot, indicating that the GDP growth of one BRICS country is impacted by the economic performance of its neighbors. The Moran's *I* scatter plot in Fig. 4.3 is the autocorrelation analysis of BRICS countries defining the relationship between spatially lagged residuals and real residuals. The plot lacks visible clustering with no pattern in the spatial lag indicating that spatial autocorrelation is not a big issue. That confirms the model's residuals are mostly independent across the regions.

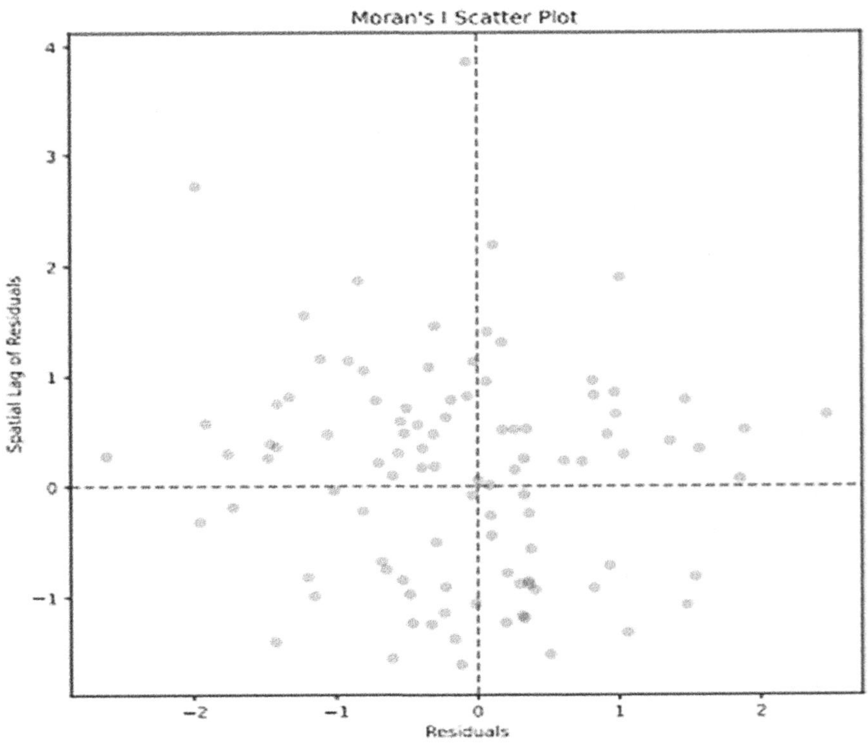

Fig. 4.3. Moran's *I* Scatter Plot. *Source*: Caesar Labs, Inc. (2024).

Fig. 4.4, the scatter plot, shows the link between temperature changes on the *X*-axis and CO_2 emissions on the *Y*-axis, the two important independent variables in SDM. Economic linkage variables here are the FDI and inflation and it has been included in the weight matrix to record the spatial dependencies. And that demonstrates how one country influences another through economic connections. The trend of the scatter plot is nonlinear; CO_2 emissions show slight changes at lower temperatures but a huge change at higher temperatures. This depicts the probable correlation between temperature and emissions. The SDM demonstrates both direct effects and indirect effects; in direct effects, we can see the immediate impact of emissions and temperature on a country's GDP. In spillover effects, it is showing how climate change indicators and economic situation in one country are affecting the other country which is having economic links. The economic linkages or interconnections can be because of trade networks, investment flows, and similar policies. The economic linkage variables show that climate change issues are not confined to one country, rather they can spread through spatial interdependence. This spatial dependence highlights the significance of global partnerships and policies.

5. Discussion

There is a significant economic output as a result of rising temperatures, particularly in the case of low-income countries (Dell et al., 2012). Burke et al. (2015) identified the fact that temperature changes affect GDP not only through direct

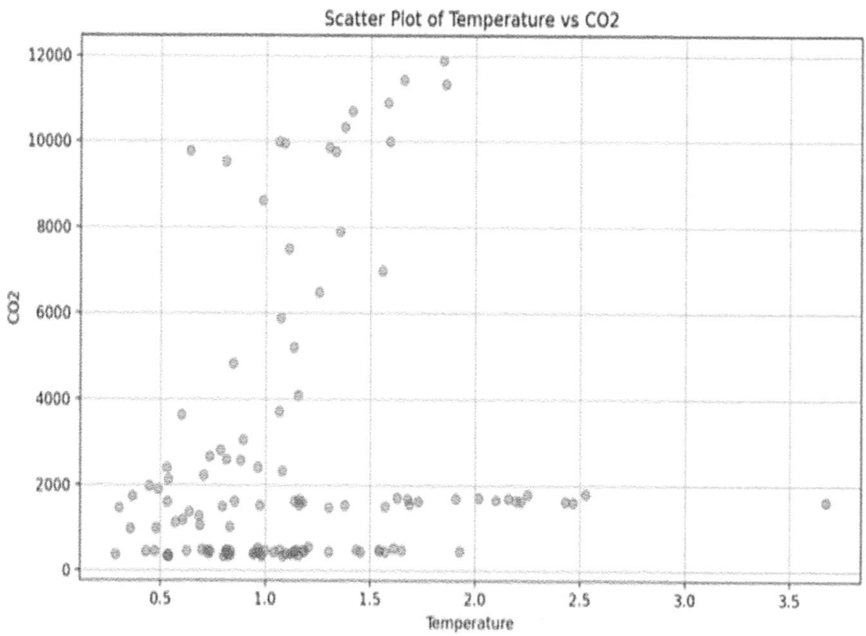

Fig. 4.4. Scatter Plot of Temperature Versus CO_2. *Source*: Caesar Labs, Inc. (2024).

economic losses but also through spillover effects from nearby regions. These spillover effects show the need for collaborative policy implications among countries to mitigate climate change issues (Elhorst, 2014). Moreover, the act of economic linkages such as FDI and inflation uncover the climate-related economic inequalities in the global investment pattern. The FDI can promote global wellness by enhancing sustainable development and same time can contribute to the deterioration of the environment if the country doesn't have accurate regulatory frameworks (Kellenberg, 2009; International Labour Organization, 2024; Naeem et al., 2024). The suggestions from the discussion strongly go with the statement that the incorporation of social, environmental, and governance factors into economic policies and investing decisions is very crucial for the long-term growth of emerging economies, especially in climate-sensitive countries (UNEP, 2021). As per academicians, banks also play a vital role in implementing green initiative projects by enhancing the integration of fintech, innovations, and IT governance into practice (Almaqtari et al., 2024; Khan et al., 2021). Also, there should be better collaboration between government and private entities for initiating entrepreneurship programs that can lead to better and sustainable economic growth (Hardi et al., 2024; Khan et al., 2022). The nationally determined contributions (NDCs) of each country detail their efforts to reduce emissions and get ready for the effects of climate change. These NDCs are at the heart of the Paris Agreement. The Russian Federation filed its NDC in 2016; Brazil and Russia submitted theirs in 2020; and China and South Africa submitted theirs in 2021. South Africa, China, India, and Russia have all pledged to reach net zero by 2050, 2060, 2070, and 2060, respectively. Because of this, only one of the BRICS countries, South Africa, meets the Paris Agreement's mid-century net-zero targets (International Labor Organization, 2021).

Here are the details of some of the successfully implemented climate adaptation strategies by BRICS countries. The BRICS nations have agreed on a Memorandum of Understanding to establish a Carbon Market Partnership at the BRICS Summit (2024). This project aims to facilitate the exchange of experiences in creating carbon markets and implementing joint climate initiatives, like issuing carbon units. The BRICS countries are pushing the "One Health" idea, which highlights the connection between human, animal, and environmental health. The relationship between climate change and public health is addressed holistically because environmental changes can directly affect human health outcomes (Observer Research Foundation, n.d).

6. Conclusion and Policy Implications

The study unravels the detangling relationship between climate change indicators and the market value of BRICS countries to find out the effects of climate change on emerging markets. The study has adopted 24 years of panel data of BRICS countries and figured out both the direct and indirect effects of CO_2 emissions and temperature changes on the GDP of the countries. The climate change indicators have a considerable impact on the GDP both within the country and spillover effects to other countries that are economically connected. The direct effects imply that rising temperatures and emissions have consequences on GDP resulting in economic stress. The spillover effects or indirect effects demonstrate the interdependence between countries as a result of similar economic conditions and policies. Cross-country trade and investments are harming the GDP among countries in BRICS. The overall result of the study highlights the emergency of coordinated climate policies and economic policies to reduce the negative impact of climate changes. As BRICS is a group of climate-vulnerable countries, following implications will be suitable to lessen the worst effects of climate issues (Brazil, World Bank, Center for Global Development, & Rockefeller Foundation, 2024; Sakharov, 2024). Implications of coordinated regional climate agreements are essential in this situation. Proper resource management, investing in renewable energy, and sustainable finance practices are some of the effective measures. When coming into the investing decisions, the policymakers should consider the environmental, social, and governance and also should pay special attention to sustainable finance and green finance. To cut emissions, the only possible way is to promote economic growth, invest in renewable energy sectors, and FDI in low-carbon. BRICS countries should give the most priority to agricultural strengthening policies, climate adaptation policies, and preparation for disasters. These steps will minimize the negative effects of weather and rising temperatures on GDP. For trade linking countries like BRICS can establish trade regulations beneficial to eco-friendly goods and services. This study analyzes the output from long-term panel data and the SDM and narrates the time-variant effects of climate change on market value.

References

Akhtar, S., Niazi, M. H., & Khan, M. M. (2020). Cascading effect of COVID-19 on Indian economy. *International Journal of Advanced Science and Technology*, *29*(9), 4563–4573.

Almaqtari, F. A., Rehman, S., Nigam, S., & Khan, M. (2024). The impact of board structure, IT governance, and fintech on green finance and sustainability: An integrated model. *Strategic Change*. https://doi.org/10.1002/jsc.2623

Asian Development Bank. (2021). *Climate risk and response: Economic implications for India*. https://www.ft.com/content/927a4c8b-db4c-4a46-af68-71c5a03452ab

Auffhammer, M. (2018). Quantifying economic damages from climate change. *Journal of Economic Perspectives*, *32*, 33–52.

Azmi, S. N., & Akhtar, S. (2023). Interactions of services export, financial development and growth: Evidence from India. *Quality & Quantity*, *57*(5), 4709–4724.

Backstrand, K., & Lovbrand, E. (2019). The road to Paris: Climate governance and the role of civil society. *Global Environmental Politics*, *19*(2), 1–22.

Becken, S., & Hay, J. E. (2012). Climate change and tourism: Impacts and adaptation. *Journal of Sustainable Tourism*, *20*(5), 705–726.

Brazil, World Bank, Center for Global Development, & Rockefeller Foundation. (2024). *The tropical forests forever facility: A proposed multilateral investment fund to reward tropical forest conservation and restoration*. https://globalfoundation.org.au/wp-content/uploads/2024/06/Brazil-Government-Tropical-Forests-Forever-Initiative.pdf

BRICS. (2024, October 23). *XVI BRICS Summit Kazan Declaration: Strengthening multilateralism for just global development and security*. https://dirco.gov.za/xvi-brics-summit-kazan-declaration-strengthening-multilateralism-for-just-global-development-and-security-kazan-russian-federation-23-october-2024/

Burke, M., Hsiang, S. M., & Miguel, E. (2015). Global non-linear effect of temperature on economic production. *Nature*, *527*, 235–239.

Caesar Labs, Inc. (2024). *Julius (April 7 version)* [Large language model]. https://julius.ai/example-url

Carleton, T. A., & Hsiang, S. M. (2016). Social and economic impacts of climate. *Science*, *353*, aad9837.

Carrilho-Nunes, I., & Catalão-Lopes, M. (2022). The effects of environmental policy and technology transfer on GHG emissions: The case of Portugal. *Structural Change and Economic Dynamics*, *61*, 255–264.

Casey, G., Shayegh, S., Moreno-Cruz, J., Bunzl, M., Galor, O., & Caldeira, K. (2019). The impact of climate change on fertility. *Environmental Research Letters*, *14*(5), 054007.

Cattaneo, C., Beine, M., Fröhlich, C. J., Kniveton, D., Martinez-Zarzoso, I., Mastrorillo, M., Millock, K., Piguet, E., & Schraven, B. (2019). Human migration in the era of climate change. *Review of Environmental Economics and Policy*, *13*(2), 189–206.

Climate Action Tracker. (2023). *Global emissions and the role of emerging economies*. https://climateactiontracker.org/global/2023-report

Cline, W. R. (1994). The costs and benefits of greenhouse gas abatement. A guide to policy analysis. In OECD (Ed.), *The economics of climate change*. (pp. 51–91) OECD.

Colacito, R., Hoffmann, B., & Phan, T. (2021). The impact of rising temperature on US economic growth. In J. B. Ritchie, H. Kunreuther, & R. Pindyck (Eds.), *World scientific encyclopedia of climate change: Case studies of climate risk, action, and opportunity* (Vol. 3; pp. 133–138). World Scientific.

De Cain, E., & Wing, I. S. (2019). Global energy consumption in a warming climate. *Environmental and Resource Economics*, *72*(2), 365–410.

De Lau bier Languet Marx, N., Sponge, E., & Ngo Duck, T. (2019). Non-linear impacts of climate change on income and inequality in Vietnam. *AD Report*, *36*, 15–42.

Dell, M., Jones, B. F., & Olsen, B. A. (2009). Temperature and income: Reconciling new cross-sectional and panel estimates. *American Economic Review*, *99*, 198–204.

Dell, M., Jones, B. F., & Olsen, B. A. (2012). Temperature shocks and economic growth: Evidence from the last half century. *American Economic Journal of Macroeconomics*, *4*, 66–95.

Deryugina, T., & Hsiang, S. M. (2014). *Does the environment still matter? Daily temperature and income in the United States* [Technical Report]. National Bureau of Economic Research.

Deschênes, O., & Greenstone, M. (2007). The economic impacts of climate change: Evidence from agricultural output and random fluctuations in weather. *American Economic Review*, *97*(1), 354–385.

Desmet, K., & Rossi-Hansberg, E. (2015). On the spatial economic impact of global warming. *Journal of Urban Economics*, *88*, 16–37.

Elhorst, J. P. (2014). *Spatial econometrics: From cross-sectional data to spatial panels*. Springer. https://doi.org/10.1007/978-3-642-40340-8

Fabozzi, F. J., Focardi, S., Ponta, L., Rivoire, M., & Mazza, D. (2022). The economic theory of qualitative green growth. *Structural Change and Economic Dynamics*, *61*, 242–254.

Fankhauser, S., & Tol, R. S. (2005). On climate change and economic growth. *Resource and Energy Economics*, *27*(1), 1–17.

Graff Zivin, J., Hsiang, S. M., & Neidell, M. (2018). Temperature and human capital in the short and long run. *Journal of the Association of Environmental and Resource Economists*, *5*(1), 77–105.

Graff Zivin, J., & Neidell, M. (2014). Temperature and the allocation of time: Implications for climate change. *Journal of Labor Economics*, *32*(1), 1–26.

Hallegatte, S., Green, C., Nicholls, R. J., & Corfee-Morlot, J. (2016). Future flood losses in major coastal cities. *Nature Climate Change*, *3*(9), 802–806.

Hardi, I., Afjal, M., Khan, M., Idroes, G. M., Noviandy, T. R., & Utami, R. T. (2024). Economic freedom and growth dynamics in Indonesia: An empirical analysis of indicators driving sustainable development. *Cogent Economics & Finance, 12*(1). https://doi.org/10.1080/23322039.2024.2433023

Hope, C. W. (2006). The marginal impact of CO2 from PAGE2002: an integrated assessment model incorporating the IPCC's ve reasons for concern. *Integrated Assessment Journal, 6*(1), 19–56.

Hsiang, S. M., & Jina, A. S. (2014). *The causal effect of environmental catastrophe on long-run economic growth: Evidence from 6,700 cyclones* [NBER Working Paper No. 20352]. National Bureau of Economic Research. https://doi.org/10.3386/w20352

Hsiang, S. M., Kopp, R. E., Jina, A., & Rising, J. (2017). Estimating economic damage from climate change in the United States. *Science*, 356(6345), 1362–1369.

Intergovernmental Panel on Climate Change (IPCC). (2014). *Climate change 2014: Impacts, adaptation, and vulnerability. Part A: Global and sectoral aspects*. Cambridge University Press.

Intergovernmental Panel on Climate Change (IPCC). (2022). *Sixth assessment report: Climate change impacts, adaptation, and vulnerability*. https://www.ipcc.ch/report/ar6/wg2

International Labour Organization. (2021). *Employment and just transition to sustainability in the BRICS countries*. https://www.ilo.org/media/280786/download

International Labour Organization. (2024, August 13). *ILO's offer on strengthening NDCs for a just transition and decent work*. https://www.ilo.org/resource/brief/ilo%E2%80%99s-offer-strengthening-ndcs-just-transition-and-decent-work

Isaac, M., & Van Vuuren, D. P. (2009). Modeling global residential sector energy demand for heating and air conditioning in the context of climate change. *Energy Policy, 37*(2), 507–521.

Kahn, M. E., Mohaddes, K., & Pesaran, M. H. (2015). Climate change, financial risk, and the economy. *The Economic Journal, 125*(583), 1–13.

Kalkuhl, M., & Wenz, L. (2020). The impact of climate conditions on economic production. Evidence from a global panel of regions. *Journal of Environmental Economics and. Management, 103*, 102360.

Kellenberg, D. K. (2009). An empirical investigation of the pollution haven effect with strategic environment and trade policy. *Journal of International Economics, 78*(2), 242–255. https://doi.org/10.1016/j.jinteco.2009.04.004

Khan, P. A., Johl, S. K., & Akhtar, S. (2021). Firm sustainable development goals and firm financial performance through the lens of green innovation practices and reporting: A proactive approach. *Journal of Risk and Financial Management, 14*(12), 605.

Khan, P. A., Johl, S. K., & Akhtar, S. (2022). Vinculum of sustainable development goal practices and firms' financial performance: A moderation role of green innovation. *Journal of Risk and Financial Management, 15*(3), 96.

Kumar, S., & Singh, R. (2018). Climate change and economic growth: Evidence from India. *Environmental Science and Policy, 88*, 1–10.

Mankiw, N. G., Romer, D., & Weil, D. N. (1992). A contribution to the empirics of economic growth. *The Quarterly Journal of Economics, 107*(2), 407–437.

Moore, F. C., & Diaz, D. B. (2015). Temperature impacts on economic growth warrant stringent mitigation policy. *Nature Climate Change, 5*, 127–131.

Moyer, E. J., Woolley, M. D., Matteson, N. J., Glotter, M. J., & Weisbach, D. A. (2014). Climate impacts on economic growth as drivers of uncertainty in the social cost of carbon. *Journal of Legal Studies, 43*, 401–425.

Naeem Azmi, S., & Akhtar, S. (2024). Does financial development and economic growth matter for services export? Cross-country evidence from OECD countries. *The Journal of International Trade & Economic Development, 33*(5), 1–22.

Newell, R. G., Prest, B. C., & Sexton, S. E. (2018). *The GDP-temperature relationship: Implications for climate change damages* [RFF Working Paper Series, p. 63]. Resources for the Future.

Newell, R. G., Prest, B. C., & Sexton, S. E. (2021). The GDP-temperature relationship: Implications for climate change damages. *Journal of Environmental Economics and Management*, *108*, 102445.

Nordhaus, W. D. (1991). To slow or not to slow: the economics of the greenhouse effect. *Economic Journal*, *101*(407), 920–937.

Nordhaus, W. D. (2017). Revisiting the social cost of carbon. *Proceedings of the National Academy of Sciences*, *114*(7), 1518–1523.

Observer Research Foundation. (n.d.). *The role of BRICS leadership in forging climate and health strategies for a One Health world.* Retrieved February 25, 2025, from https://www.orfonline.org/research/the-role-of-brics-leadership-in-forging-climate-and-health-strategies-for-a-one-health-world

Organisation for Economic Co-operation and Development (OECD). (2015). Climate change and the economic costs of climate change. *OECD Economic Outlook*, *2015*(2), 1–30.

Pindyck, R. S. (2013). Climate change policy: What do the models tell us? *Journal of Economic Literature*, *51*, 860–872.

Sakharov, A. (2024). BRICS countries' progress in achieving the climate and environmental goals of Agenda 2030. *International Organisations Research Journal*, *19*(1), 106–128. https://doi.org/10.17323/1996-7845-2024-01-05

Schlenker, W., & Roberts, M. J. (2009). Nonlinear temperature effects indicate severe damages to U.S. crop yields under climate change. *Proceedings of the National Academy of Sciences*, *106*(37), 15594–15598.

Stern, N. (2007). *The economics of climate change: The Stern review*. Cambridge University Press.

Stern, N. (2013). The structure of economic modeling of the potential impacts of climate change: Grafting gross underestimation of risk onto already narrow science models. *Journal of Economic Literature*, *51*(3), 838–859.

Stern, N., Peters, S., Bakhshi, V., Bowen, A., Cameron, C., Catovsky, S., Crane, D., Cruickshank, S., Dietz, S., Edmonson, N., Garbett, S. L., Hamid, L., Hoffman, G., Ingram, D., Jones, B., Patmore, N., Radcliffe, H., Sathiyarajah, R., Stock, M., ... Zenghelis, D. (2006). *Stern review: The economics of climate change*. HM Treasury.

Tol, R. S. J. (1995). The damage costs of climate change toward more comprehensive calculations. *Environmental and Resource Economics*, *5*(4), 353–374.

Tol, R. S. J. (2008). Why worry about climate change? A research agenda. *Environmental Values*, *17*(4), 437–470.

United Nations Environment Programme (UNEP). (2021). *Emissions gap report 2021: The heat is on – A world of climate promises not yet delivered.* UNEP. https://www.unep.org

World Bank. (2023). *BRICS nations and their economic significance*. https://www.worldbank.org/en/topic/brics

World Economic Forum. (2021). *The impact of climate change on global GDP*. https://www.weforum.org/stories/2021/06/impact-climate-change-global-gdp

Yohe, G. W., & Schlesinger, M. E. (2002). The economic geography of the impacts of climate change. *Journal of Economic Geography*, *2*(3), 311–341.

Part II

Maneuvering Through the Tempest

Chapter 5

Climate Change and Market Chaos: A Review of Methods for Assessing Stock Price Volatility

Shiva Sai Kiran Pothula[a], *Pratik More*[a] *and Nawazkhan Meeya*[b]

[a]*School of Business, Woxsen University, Hyderabad, India*
[b]*College of Economics and Business Administration, University of Technology and Applied Sciences, Ibra, Oman*

Abstract

Climate change is increasingly affecting the global economy, with extreme weather events and disasters resulting in unprecedented economic losses. Financial institutions, including the United States Financial Stability Oversight Council (US FSOC) and Reserve Bank of India (RBI), have recognized these climate change risks as major systemic threats. Apart from the imminent importance of understanding these risks, accurately quantifying climate disaster impacts on stock prices is challenging due to market noise and other exogenous factors. Hence, this chapter examines the relationship between climate change events and stock market vulnerabilities. Despite many methods to assess this relationship, there are variations in terms of assumptions, selection criteria, approaches, scalability, and generalizability, leading to an inconsistent finding, interpretations, synthesis of findings, integration of insights, validation complexities, and comparability issues. Furthermore, for non-seasoned researchers, the compounding and conflicting nature of varied methodologies across academic research poses a steep learning curve. A comparative analysis spanning across various methods appears to be sparse in the current academic literature. Hence, this chapter attempts a comparative analysis of various methods, including but not limited to, event study analysis (ESA), Generalized Autoregressive Conditional Heteroskedastic (GARCH) models, ordinary least squares (OLS) estimation methods and seemingly unrelated

Climate Risk and Emerging Markets: Valuation, Volatility, and Portfolio Strategies, 73–87

Published under exclusive licence by Emerald Publishing Limited
doi:10.1108/978-1-83708-088-520261018

regression (SUR) models, used to assess climate change impacts on stock prices, highlighting their limitations and challenges.

Keywords: Climate change events; sustainable finance; climate change risk management; events analysis; stock price vulnerability; SDG13 and SDG8

1. Introduction

It is widely acknowledged that traditional finance theory falls short in fully explaining stock market behavior (Chen et al., 2024). Between 2010 and 2019, these climate change or extreme weather events led to a staggering $1.5 trillion in losses (Emma Charlton, 2023), indicating that financial markets are vulnerable to external factors, making the impact of climate change related events on stock performance a topic of growing interest. A study found that the climate and biological disasters have a higher impact on international financial markets compared to disasters (geological, hydrological and meteorological) in 104 countries (Li et al., 2024). Hence, given the increasingly unpredictable nature of climate related disasters and a five times increase in disasters driven by climate change over the past 50 years (World Meteorological Organization, 2024), any stochastic and exogenous negative event represents a significant cause for price dynamics and volatility in both domestic and international financial markets.

These climate induced risks can be broken down into two; physical risks and transitional risks (CICERO, 2017). While physical risks refer to the extreme weather or climate change events and their consequences, transitional risks refer to the risks realized in transition toward a low-carbon economy including but not limited to policy and regulation changes, technological shifts, consumer behavior and the subsequent production-level changes. Given that the financial markets need to account for the transition risks soon, abnormal returns due to physical risks represent a significant cause of stock price dynamics in the short term. However, it is expected to have varied impacts on different sectors and impacts may also vary due to other factors such as geographical location. For instance, a study exploring the effects of climate change events in the United States and China on Chinese stock market reveals that domestic climate events have a higher effect on volatility of the Chinese market than climate events in the United States (Alam & Akhtar, 2024; Cao et al., 2015).

Recently, disruptive potential of climate change events is also emphasized by the recognition of climate-related disaster events as a systematic risk by financial institutions. The US FSOC considered climate change a major threat to financial stability (FSOC, 2021). More recently, climate change is named as the greatest source of systematic risk by RBI (RBI, 2024). Hence, it is well understood that assessing the impacts of climate-change-related events on stock market will assist financial regulatory boards, investors, and businesses in identifying and mitigating the physical risks posed by extreme events. Further, it also helps in maintaining and operating a stable financial system.

However, quantifying the impacts of climate-related disasters or any disaster is a daunting task. A fundamental challenge lies in eliminating/reducing the inherent noise due to many exogenous variables in stock market prices and identifying and assessing the impacts of climate disasters. Even though there is no single deterministic way to identify the exact impact, researchers have employed varied methods to examine the market volatility. Based on 3,209 news articles, one study conducted a sentiment analysis utilizing a pre-trained bidirectional Fin BERT neural network (Fedorova & Iasakova, 2024). The results indicated that new sentiments could influence dynamics of stock prices. In addition, the study also identified five dimensions, which showed a significant impact on the financial market. In another study, using the event study methodology on a total of 526 climate change disasters, five dimensions such as biological dimension, climatic, geological dimension, hydrological, and meteorological dimensions have been identified that have significant impacts on stock prices in US markets (Jafar, Hemachandran et al., 2024; Li et al., 2024).

In both the examples, researchers were able to arrive at similar results using varied methodological approaches. Furthermore, the application of ESA varies across similar studies, primarily in terms of event window and estimation period. Apart from sentiment analysis and event study methodology, other methods include GARCH, E-GARCH, ARMA, Pessimism Index, ARMAX-GARCH, Continuous Wavelet Transform, Paired sample *t*-tests, to name a few. All these methods vary in terms of assumptions, selection criteria, approaches, scalability, and generalizability, leading to an inconsistent finding, interpretations, inferences, integration of insights, validation complexities, and comparability issues. For non-seasoned researchers, the compounding and conflicting nature of varied methodologies across academic research poses a steep learning curve. A comparative examination spanning across various methodologies appears to be sparse in the current academic literature. In this direction, this chapter examines and compares the various methodologies used in academic research to assess the impact of climate-change-related events on stock prices. To achieve this objective, this chapter

- explores and briefly discusses how exogenous event or shocks influence stock markets and how they are identified, examined, and evaluated;
- identifies and catalogues various methodologies used in the current literature for measuring the impacts of climate-change-related events and disasters on stock prices;
- presents a comparative review on the identified methodologies; and finally
- concludes by highlighting the limitations and challenges of these methodologies.

2. Impact of Exogenous Events on Stock Market

Financial markets are susceptible to endogenous and exogenous disruptions across the globe (Alam et al., 2024; Arias-Calluari et al., 2021; Jafar, Rodriguez et al., 2024) and "descriptive" and "structural" models are used to capture these risks of market movements. Current descriptive models are modeled in microeconomic fashion, considering dynamic factors affected by flow of market orders and time scale (Puertas et al., 2020). The existing structural models, which rely on physical systems, incorporate exogenous systematic risks as a perpetual global risk factor. The impact of such external systematic risks is caused by sudden shifts at macro-level of market dynamics, usually caused by sudden events or shocks (Onnela et al., 2003), including, but not limited to extreme weather, political changes/upheavals, war, and natural disasters.

For exogenous shocks, market prices are not determined by the "rational" market participants in advance, as these events are unforeseeable in nature because of lack of detectable precursor warning signals. For instance, unlike economic downturns or mergers, which often exhibit warning signs, natural disasters like earthquakes strike without warning. A recent example of a systematic exogenous shock is the COVID-19 pandemic that led to record-high volatility across financial markets, exacerbated by soaring unemployment and business closures worldwide (Akhtar et al., 2020). Few other examples of such exogenous shocks on financial markets are the terrorist attacks (Chaudhry et al., 2018) such as the attacks on the World Trade Centre on September 11, 2001, Hurricane Katrina in 2004, and Sumatra–Andaman earthquake of Indian Ocean in 2004. From these examples, few insights can be derived:

- First, there were hardly any precursor signals or warnings for the "rational" agents to determine the market prices ahead of time.
- Second, these events exposed the vulnerabilities in foundational structures (financial systems, economic systems, and business landscapes) on which our pragmatic societies were built upon.
- Third, these events highlighted the need for resilient financial systems.
- Finally, these events are major catastrophes (not to mention rare) with unsurmountable human and economic losses.

2.1. Climate Change Events

As the Earth's getting warmer, severe floods, droughts, extreme wildfires, widespread flooding during typhoons, record breaking heat waves are all becoming more frequent and more intense (NASA, 2024). These events might not look as disastrous in terms of human or economic losses or their impact on financial markets. Still, they disrupt our economic (OXERA, 2024) and societal systems (Curtis et al., 2017) that profoundly impact financial markets. According to the existing literature, this impact on stock price can be understood through three observations:

1. Exogenous shocks like extreme weather events create a market anomaly, indicating that changes in equity prices cannot be explained by rational models.
2. They create financial uncertainty and have a negative impact on future cash flows of the company.
3. The perception of risk in financial markets is sensitive to climate change events and investors might be cautious about their investments in companies that are not resilient to climate risks (Altin, 2024).

Hence, when under pressure due to exogenous shocks and events, stock markets tend to exhibit state transitions, see Fig. 5.1. First, the stock price is expected to thrive in the original state (S_0), where the returns are reliable, and expectation of returns can be based on market models. More resilient industries are expected to be much reliable. This state is disrupted by an exogenous shock and the stock is pushed into vulnerability state (S_v). In this state, the stock price is expected to fall and lead to negative returns. This vulnerability is measured by the decline in performance following the event, until a stable state is reached. The vulnerability state reflects the measurable indicator – *abnormal returns.*

Abnormal return is a deviation from an investment's expected returns over a certain period based on an asset pricing model (Investopedia, 2024). This deviation is usually described as an unusually large profits or losses generated by a given investment or portfolio. Abnormal returns are usually produced by bad actors, chance and exogenous shocks or extreme weather events. Hence, almost all the methods in assessing the impact of these exogenous shocks on stock volatility employ abnormal returns as an indicator in many forms such as cumulative abnormal returns (CAR) and cumulative average abnormal returns.

This vulnerability state can last from a day to couple of days depending on several factors, until a stable state of disruption (S_d) is achieved, followed by a recovery state (S_r), and stable recovered state (S_s). One can measure recoverability from an exogenous stock by the time when a disrupted state (S_d) is reached to the time a recovery state (S_r) is completed, and a post recovery stable state is achieved.

The findings from literature reflect this fundamental understanding that abnormal returns are expected from climate change events. For instance, one study examining the stock yield observed that biological and hydrological dimensions of climate change, in general, have a significant negative impact (Li et al., 2024). Findings from another study reveal a significant negative impact of extreme weather on stock returns (Chen et al., 2024). Another study, from emerging markets, indicates that companies exposed to climate risks are associated with a higher level of stock price crash (Zhao et al., 2024). To better interpret these findings, it is fundamental to understand the methodological approach for assessing stock price volatility.

3. Methodology for Assessing Stock Price Volatility

Despite extensive research on stock price volatility, quantifying the impacts of climate-related disasters or any disaster is a daunting task, and researchers have employed varied methods to examine the volatility and derive insights form it. However, this chapter proposes a four objective-conceptual understanding of the broad methodology for assessing these impacts. These objectives include:

1. to define, identify, and operationalize climate change/extreme weather events and classify them (O1);
2. to identify any abnormal returns (O2);
3. to examine the historical trends to adjust for any seasonal noise in stock market data (O3); and
4. to estimate the effect of each type of event (O4).

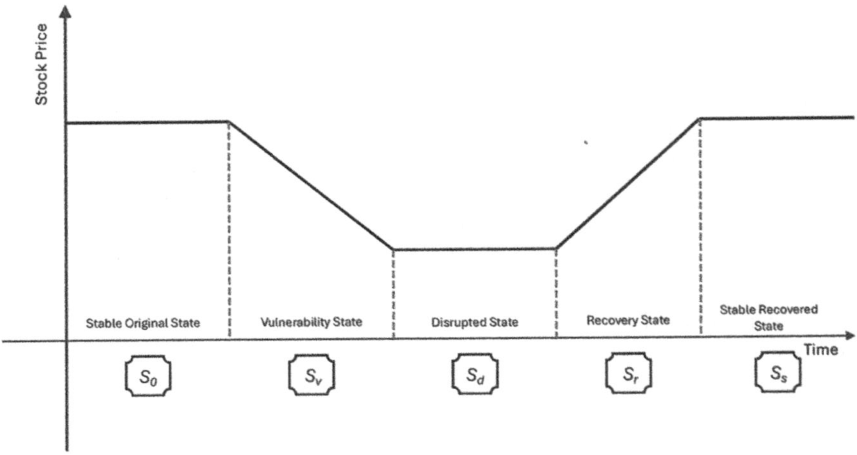

Fig. 5.1. Transition of Stock Price Through an Exogenous Shock. *Source*: Authors' compilation.

These objectives explicitly address the "vulnerability state," discussed in Fig. 5.1. By tackling all the objectives, ideally, studies attempt to explain the holistic influence of climate/weather events on stock price. One of the instances in research exploring all four objectives is Hong et al. (2023). First, one-sample *t*-test was used to examine significant weather anomalies for pre, during and after the COVID-19 lockdown and identified five types of anomalies. Then, ESA method was used to estimate the CAR of the sample traded stocks in the study period, using a Capital Asset Pricing Model (CAPM). A paired-sample *t*-test was performed to examine the effects of COVID-19 lockdown on the Vietnamese stock market. In other words, paired-sample *t*-test was performed to see if the CAR values "During – After" the COVID-19 lockdown are significantly different from the "Before – During" the COVID-19 lockdown. Then the researchers employed "Seasonal Holt-Winters smoothing method" to identify the trend and seasonality and then implemented forecasting models on the historical weather data and performed predictions for the study period in 2020. Finally, the association between meteorological anomalies and stock market performance throughout the research period is assessed using the OLS estimation method.

4. A Comparison of Methods

However, not all studies aim for addressing all the four objectives; see Table 5.1, which examines the methods employed in the literature from the lens of the objectives the study is aiming to achieve. It is also important to highlight that researcher, depending on the study, employ a single method for fulfill each objective or multiple objectives. For instance, ESA method can be used to identify abnormal returns (Robinson & Bangwayo-Skeete, 2016) or Autoregressive moving average (ARMA) model can be used to identify abnormal returns and to

Table 5.1. Objectives and Methods Employed in Literature.

Reference, Climate Event(s), Impact	Method(s) for O1	Method(s) for O2	Method(s) for O3	Method(s) for O4
Hong et al. (2023), temperature, negative	One-sample *t*-test	CAMP and two-sample paired *t*-test	Seasonal Holt-Winters smoothing method	OLS estimation method
Lanfear et al. (2019), hurricanes, negative	Identified from NOAA	Event Study Analysis with single-factor CAMP	NA	NA
Robinson & Bangwayo-Skeete (2016), hurricanes, negative	Identified from unspecified database	Event Study Analysis with adjusted market model and *t*-tests.	NA	NA
Pagnottoni et al. (2022), various, negligible	EM-DAT and CRED	SUR models		
Worthington (2008), various, no significant impact	Identified from Emergency Management Australia	GARCH-Mean model		
Bourdeau-Brien & Kryzanowski (2017), various, negative	Identified from FEMA's major disasters database and NCDC's storm events dataset	Intervention analysis framework with a GARCH model	ARMA	NA
Worthington and Valadkhani (2004), various, negligible	Identified from Emergency Management Australia	ARMA model with augmented dummy variables	ARMA	NA
Wang and Kutan (2013), negligible	Identified from the JAXA/EORC Tropical Cyclone Database and The National Geophysical Data Center	Exponential GARCH (E-GARCH)		

(*Continued*)

Table 5.1. (*Continued*)

Reference, Climate Event(s), Impact	Method(s) for O1	Method(s) for O2	Method(s) for O3	Method(s) for O4
Altin (2024), various, negative	Identified from Foreks FXPlus internet platform	E-GARCH	Seasonally adjusted time series	E-GARCH
Chen et al. (2024), temperature and humidity, negative	Identifies extreme hot days and extreme humid days, weather trend changes over time and geographies using the China Meteorological Administration data	NA	NA	Multivariate OLS regression model
Ahmed et al. (2024), temperature, varied results	21 day moving average and moving standard deviation method	GARCH	21 day moving average and moving standard deviation method	Logit model analysis

Source: Authors' compilation.

examine the historical trends to adjust for any seasonal noise (Bourdeau-Brien & Kryzanowski, 2017). Hence, this section examines the methods employed in the study from the perspective of the objectives the study is aiming to achieve.

4.1. O1: To Define, Identify and Operationalize Climate Change/ Extreme Weather Events

Climate change and extreme weather events require a multi-faceted approach to define, identify, and operationalize. Anthropogenic climate change is characterized by long-term temperature, precipitation, and wind patterns increase, as well as more frequent and severe extreme weather events like hurricanes, heatwaves, floods, and droughts. Hence, "climate change" encapsulates two distinct types of exogenous shocks that can be measured:

1. Climate change indicators – primarily increase in temperature.
2. Climate change induced extreme weather events – hurricanes, heatwaves, floods, and droughts.

For the later, "Climate change induced extreme weather events," most studies sourced the information from national and international databases such as National Oceanic Atmospheric Administration (NOAA), International Emergency Events Database (EM-DAT), Federal Emergency Management (FEMA) databases. However, these events are further classified based on their intensity, damage and location. Utilizing reputable national and international databases such as NOAA, EM-DAT, and FEMA ensures the reliability and accuracy of data on extreme weather events.

However, "indicators of climate change" is subjected to varied interpretations. For instance, Hong et al. (2023) interpreted "significant weather anomalies" as statistically significant deviations of air pressure, temperature, rainfall, humidity, and wind speed from the forecasted values. In justification to this interpretation, the researcher used one-sample *t*-test. On the other hand, Chen et al. (2024) identified extreme hot days and extreme humid days, weather trend changes over time and geographies using the China Meteorological Administration data. Ahmed et al. (2024), in their study, considered for several indicators including temperature (temp), humidity, cloud cover, and visibility as indicators of climate change and a full spectrum of severe weather conditions.

Researchers interpret climate change indicators in varied ways. This diversity in interpretation highlights the importance of context-specific analysis and the need for multiple methodological approaches to capture the complexity of climate change. Employing statistical tests like the one-sample *t*-test to identify significant weather anomalies provides a rigorous approach to impact analysis. Using moving averages and moving standard deviations helps in identifying long-term trends (Ahmed et al., 2024). By integrating these insights, researchers can develop a nuanced understanding of climate change and its impacts, leading to more effective methodological approaches.

4.2. O2: To Identify Any Abnormal Returns

Abnormal return, in simplest terms, is usually described as an unusually large profits or losses generated over time, which cannot be explained by the behavior of rational agents. The simplest method to achieve this objective is to perform a two-sample paired *t*-test. A paired *t*-test will help us understanding if the returns after an event are significantly different from before the event.

In a study, discussed earlier (Hong et al., 2023), the researchers first employed ESA to calculate abnormal returns and then, used paired *t*-test to see if the abnormal returns are significantly different from stock prices before COVID-19. Here, paired *t*-test is used as a confirmatory analysis for the findings from ESA. A similar approach was also employed by Robinson & Bangwayo-Skeete (2016) and Lanfear et al. (2019). ESA examines the impact of specific events on the value of financial instruments. It focuses on the abnormal returns related to the event, rather than just comparing means.

4.2.1. Event Study Analysis

ESA usually involves four steps. First step is to identify the period during which the event is expected to impact stock prices – event window. Second step is to calculate the expected returns during the event window using a model. Third step is to determine the difference between actual and expected returns during the event window. Final and fourth step is to use statistical tests to determine if the abnormal returns are significantly different.

For the first step, identifying the period during which the event is expected to impact stock prices is culmination of three distinct windows. These windows, in chronological order, include specific number of days before the event, specific number of days during which the event occurs and specific number of days after the event. Hong et al. (2023) considered 10 days for each window and 3 days gap between each window for the information of extreme weather events to propagate. Lanfear et al. (2019) defined windows as: before the event, from storm formation to landfall; during the event, a 2-day period; and after the event, up to 31 days. However, Robinson & Bangwayo-Skeete (2016) used five overlapping windows, ranging from 30 days before and after the event to 10 days on either side, for robust results, see Table 5.2.

Extreme weather events such as hurricanes, heatwaves, and floods have different durations and impact timelines. For instance, hurricanes can have prolonged effects from formation to landfall and aftermath, requiring variable windows to capture the full impact. A contextually flexible event window allows to capture significant impacts when it aligns with the event's timeline. As evident in the study by Lanfear et al. (2019), a variable period starting from the formation date of the storm to landfall date is considered while choosing the event window.

Hong et al. (2023), in their study, accommodated for information propagation delays, as climate events' impact on stock prices may not be immediate. Flexible event windows allow researchers to account for this lag, ensuring that the analysis captures the accurate abnormal returns. Furthermore, employing multiple overlapping windows, as considered by Robinson & Bangwayo-Skeete (2016)

Table 5.2. Event Windows and Market Models Used in Event Study Analysis.

Reference, Climate Event(s), Impact	Event Window (in days)			Estimation Window (in days)	Market Model
	Before	During	After		
Hong et al. (2023), temperature, negative	10	10	10	365	Capital Asset Pricing Model (CAPM)
Lanfear et al. (2019), hurricanes, negative	Variable	2	Up to 31	180	Single factor Capital Asset Pricing Model (CAPM)
Robinson & Bangwayo-Skeete (2016), hurricanes, negative	30	1	30	120	Adjusted Market Model

Source: Authors' compilation.

and Lanfear et al. (2019), helps in achieving robust results. This approach ensures that the volatility is not entirely dependent on a single window definition and can capture different phases of the impact.

The second step in ESA is to calculate the expected returns during the event window using a market model. These expected returns are usually calculated using "estimation window" and modeled using a market model. Estimation window is the specific number of days before the event window. As seen in Table 5.2, the estimation windows vary across studies. As the estimation window increases, the accuracy of the expected predictions increases. However, it also introduces the seasonal patterns observed in stock prices. Usually, market models are developed based on existing indicators that reliably predict market behavior.

The CAPM employed by Hong et al. (2023) and Lanfear et al. (2019), is used to determine the expected return on an asset based on its systematic risk relative to the overall market. However, it relies on unrealistic assumptions and only accounts for systematic risk. The adjusted market model provides a more accurate estimation of expected returns by considering leads, current, and lagged market returns. Unlike CAPM, this model can incorporate multiple factors affecting returns.

4.3. O3: To Examine the Historical Trends to Adjust for Any Seasonal Noise in Stock Market Data

Other methods observed in the literature include SUR model, GARCH model, and few variations of GARCH model. These models with varying capacity also address this objective. For instance, Pagnottoni et al. (2022) used SUR models, which allowed them to express the abnormal returns as regression coefficients. It also overcome the dependency of abnormal return on means comparison, accounts for eventual heteroskedasticity across equations and contemporaneous correlation among the error terms and can also be adjusted for seasonal noise/patterns with modifications to base model.

Similarly, variations of GARCH model can also be employed to identify the abnormal returns and used to eliminate the seasonal noise/patterns. The asymmetric terms are considered by both the TARCH and E-GARCH models. The ARMAX-GARCH model effectively describes shocks from new market information, trends, and mean-reversion, characteristic of asset returns. However, ARMAX models assume constant volatility over time and conditional heteroskedasticity. Bourdeau-Brien & Kryzanowski (2017), augment the classic intervention analysis framework with a GARCH model to work around these assumptions.

There are many methods to get rid of the seasonal effect. The most used methods include logarithm, square root, and mean seasonal factor transformations. These methods include Average Seasonal Factor Method, 21 days moving average and moving standard deviation method, ARMA model, Seasonal Holt-Winters smoothing method, and seasonally adjusted time series. An important constraint is that each series transformation weakens the model's predictive power.

4.4. O4: To Estimate the Effect of Each Type of Event

ESA method is effective at identifying and quantifying the abnormal return; however, one limitation is that it cannot specifically estimate the effect of each type of event. Hence, researchers usually employ different methods to achieve this objective. SUR models allowed researchers to express the abnormal returns as regression coefficients to measure the effect of each type of extreme weather event using dummy variables (Pagnottoni et al., 2022). Other researchers performed Logit Model Analysis and OLS estimation methods, which again utilizes dummy variables (Ahmed et al., 2024; Chen et al., 2024; Hong et al., 2023; Khan et al., 2022).

5. Discussion

In this section, we have looked at various methods to achieve the objectives to assess the impact of climate change/extreme weather events. From the discussions made above, a few insights can be made to further future research:

- Emphasis should be placed on context-specific analysis and the need for multiple methodological approaches to capture the complexity of climate change/extreme weather events.
- By utilizing robust research designs, researchers can develop a nuanced understanding of climate change and its impacts, leading to more effective methodological approaches.
- A contextually flexible event window allows to capture significant impacts when it aligns with the event's timeline. This approach ensures that the volatility is not entirely dependent on a single window definition and can capture different phases of the impact.

Table 5.3. Potential Utility of Methods Across Four Objectives.

Method	O1	O2	O3	O4
One sample *t*-test	*			
Paired *t*-test	*	*		
Event Study Analysis with market models		*		
GARCH and its variations		*	*	*
Logit Model Analysis				*
Autoregressive moving average (ARMA)			*	
Autoregressive moving average (ARMA) model with augmented dummy variables		*	*	
Seasonally adjusted time series			*	
OLS estimation method				*
21 day moving average and moving standard deviation method	*			*
Intervention analysis framework with a GARCH model		*	*	

Source: Authors' compilation.
*Indicates the applicability of a method for a given objective.

- In identifying abnormal returns, ESA appears to be simple and robust enough in most cases, if adjusted for seasonal effects.
- There should be balance between eliminating seasonal effects and sacrificing predictive power.
- Regression analysis with dummy variables is likely the most suitable approach to estimate the effect of each type of climate change/extreme weather event.
- Fundamentally, there is no one-method-fits-all solution here. Each method offers a potential utility to address one or more objectives, see Table 5.3.

6. Conclusion

In this chapter, first, a fundamental understanding of impacts of exogenous events on stock market is established by adopting resilience concepts to state transitions of an equity experiencing exogenous shocks. Then the conceptual methodology for assessing stock price volatility in the context of climate change/extreme weather events is discussed in terms of four objectives. Then the chapter examines the methods employed in the studies from literature from the perspective of the objectives the study is aiming to achieve, leading to a much-nuanced understanding of the utility of the methods and the context in which it was used and to fulfill which objective. Finally, we briefly presented the utility of all the methods discussed and their potential contributions to the four objectives were discussed.

References

Ahmed, R., Chen, X. H., Hoang, Y. H., & Do-Linh, C. (2024). Climate change effects and their implications for the financial markets: Evidence from the United Kingdom. *Journal of Environmental Management*, *366*, 121782. https://doi.org/10.1016/j.jenvman.2024.121782

Akhtar, S., Niazi, M. H., & Khan, M. M. (2020). Cascading effect of COVID 19 on Indian economy. *International Journal of Advanced Science and Technology*, *29*(9), 4563–4573.

Alam, M., & Akhtar, S. (2024). Harnessing blockchain-digital twin fusion for sustainable investments. In S. H. Jafar, R. V. Rodriguez, H. Kannan, S. Akhtar, & P. Plugmann (Eds.), *Harnessing Blockchain-digital twin fusion for sustainable investments* (pp. 1–9). IGI Global. https://doi.org/10.4018/979-8-3693-1878-2

Alam, M., Akhtar, S., & Bettencourt, A. (2024). Introduction to Fintech in Industry 5.0: Companion or Antagonist. In S. Hasan Jafar, H. K, S. Akhtar, P. Alam Khan, & H. El-Chaarani (Eds.), *The Adoption of Fintech* (pp. 1–16). Productivity Press. https://doi.org/10.4324/9781032644165

Altin, H. (2024). The impact of extreme weather events on the S&P 500 return index. *International Journal of Sustainable Engineering*, *17*(1), 642–649. https://doi.org/10.1080/19397038.2024.2393577

Arias-Calluari, K., Alonso-Marroquin, F., Najafi, M. N., & Harré, M. (2021). Methods for forecasting the effect of exogenous risks on stock markets. *Physica A: Statistical Mechanics and Its Applications*, *568*, 125587. https://doi.org/10.1016/j.physa.2020.125587

Bourdeau-Brien, M., & Kryzanowski, L. (2017). The impact of natural disasters on the stock returns and volatilities of local firms. *The Quarterly Review of Economics and Finance*, *63*, 259–270. https://doi.org/10.1016/j.qref.2016.05.003

Cao, G., Xu, W., & Guo, Y. (2015). Effects of climatic events on the Chinese stock market: Applying event analysis. *Natural Hazards*, *77*(3), 1979–1992. https://doi.org/10.1007/s11069-015-1687-9

Chaudhry, N., Roubaud, D., Akhter, W., & Shahbaz, M. (2018). Impact of terrorism on stock markets: Empirical evidence from the SAARC region. *Finance Research Letters*, *26*, 230–234. https://doi.org/10.1016/j.frl.2018.02.024

Chen, X., Luo, Y., & Yan, Q. (2024). Does extreme weather impact performance in capital markets? Evidence from China. *Sustainability*, *16*(16), 6802. https://doi.org/10.3390/su16166802

CICERO. (2017). *Shades of climate risk: Categorizing climate risk for investors*. CICERO.

Curtis, S., Fair, A., Wistow, J., Val, D. V., & Oven, K. (2017). Impact of extreme weather events and climate change for health and social care systems. *Environmental Health*, *16*(S1), 128. https://doi.org/10.1186/s12940-017-0324-3

Emma Charlton. (2023, November 29). *This is what the climate crisis is costing economies around the world*. World Economic Forum.

Fedorova, E., & Iasakova, P. (2024). The impact of climate change news on the US stock market. *The Journal of Risk Finance*, *25*(2), 293–320. https://doi.org/10.1108/JRF-06-2023-0133

Financial Stability Oversight Council. (2021). *FSOC Annual Report*. https://home.treasury.gov/system/files/261/FSOC2021AnnualReport.pdf

Hong, N. T. H., Huong, P. T. M., & Linh, N. Y. (2023). Does weather anomaly still affect the emerging stock market under the unexpected event? New evidence from the COVID-19 pandemic. *Heliyon*, *9*(8), e18665. https://doi.org/10.1016/j.heliyon.2023.e18665

Investopedia. (2024, August 26). *Abnormal return: Definition, causes, example*. https://www.investopedia.com/terms/a/abnormalreturn.asp

Jafar, S. H., Hemachandran, K., Akhtar, S., Khan, P. A., & El-Chaarani, H. (Eds.). (2024). *The adoption of fintech: Using technology for better security, speed, and customer experience in finance*. CRC Press.

Jafar, S. H., Rodriguez, R. V., Kannan, H., Akhtar, S., & Plugmann, P. (Eds.). (2024). *Harnessing blockchain-digital twin fusion for sustainable investments*. IGI Global.

Khan, P. A., Johl, S. K., & Akhtar, S. (2022). Vinculum of sustainable development goal practices and firms' financial performance: A moderation role of green innovation. *Journal of Risk and Financial Management*, *15*(3), 96.

Lanfear, M. G., Lioui, A., & Siebert, M. G. (2019). Market anomalies and disaster risk: Evidence from extreme weather events. *Journal of Financial Markets*, *46*, 100477. https://doi.org/10.1016/j.finmar.2018.10.003

Li, C., Liu, Y., & Pan, L. (2024). A study of impact of climate change on the U.S. stock market as exemplified by the NASDAQ 100 index constituents. *Scientific Reports*, *14*(1), 15468. https://doi.org/10.1038/s41598-024-66109-7

NASA. (2024). *Extreme weather and climate change*. https://science.nasa.gov/climate-change/extreme-weather/

Onnela, J.-P., Chakraborti, A., Kaski, K., & Kertész, J. (2003). Dynamic asset trees and Black Monday. *Physica A: Statistical Mechanics and Its Applications*, *324*(1–2), 247–252. https://doi.org/10.1016/S0378-4371(02)01882-4

OXERA. (2024). *The economic cost of extreme weather events*. OXERA.

Pagnottoni, P., Spelta, A., Flori, A., & Pammolli, F. (2022). Climate change and financial stability: Natural disaster impacts on global stock markets. *Physica A: Statistical Mechanics and Its Applications*, *599*, 127514. https://doi.org/10.1016/j.physa.2022.127514

Puertas, A. M., Sánchez-Granero, M. A., Clara-Rahola, J., Trinidad-Segovia, J. E., & de las Nieves, F. J. (2020). Stock markets: A view from soft matter. *Physical Review E*, *101*(3), 032307. https://doi.org/10.1103/PhysRevE.101.032307

RBI. (2024). *Financial stability report*. RBI.

Robinson, C. J., & Bangwayo-Skeete, P. (2016). The financial impact of natural disasters: Assessing the effect of hurricanes & tropical storms on stock markets in the Caribbean. *SSRN Electronic Journal*. https://doi.org/10.2139/ssrn.2845429

Wang, L., & Kutan, A. M. (2013). The impact of natural disasters on stock markets: Evidence from Japan and the US. *Comparative Economic Studies*, *55*(4), 672–686. https://doi.org/10.1057/ces.2013.16

World Meteorological Organization. (2024). *Extreme weather*. https://wmo.int/topics/extreme-weather

Worthington, A. (2008). The impact of natural events and disasters on the Australian stock market: A GARCH-M analysis of storms, floods, cyclones, earthquakes and bushfires. *Global Business and Economics Review*, *10*(1), 1. https://doi.org/10.1504/GBER.2008.016824

Worthington, A., & Valadkhani, A. (2004). Measuring the impact of natural disasters on capital markets: An empirical application using intervention analysis. *Applied Economics*, *36*(19), 2177–2186. https://doi.org/10.1080/0003684042000282489

Zhao, R., Zhang, D., & Guo, M. (2024). Do natural disasters affect stock price crash risk? Evidence from emerging markets. *Journal of International Financial Markets, Institutions and Money*, *93*, 102001. https://doi.org/10.1016/j.intfin.2024.102001

Chapter 6

Building Resilient Portfolios: Integrating Climate and Environmental Risks into Portfolio Diversification Strategies in the Modern Era

K. Balaji[a], *Shakeb Akhtar*[b] *and Mahfooz Alam*[c]

[a]*School of Business and Management, Christ University, Bengaluru, India*
[b]*College of Economics and Business Administration, University of Technology and Applied Sciences, Ibra, Oman*
[c]*Department of Business Administration, University of the People, CA, USA*

Abstract

In the modern era, integrating climate and environmental risks into portfolio diversification is crucial for building resilient investment strategies. This chapter explores strategies for building resilient investment portfolios by integrating climate and environmental risks into portfolio diversification strategies. It aims to provide a comprehensive framework for balancing financial returns with sustainable, long-term environmental goals in the context of the modern investment landscape. The chapter reviews innovative financial instruments, such as green bonds and environmental, social, and governance (ESG) strategies, and examines case studies of successful integration within both developed and emerging markets. The chapter finds that incorporating climate and environmental risks into portfolio strategies not only enhances resilience but also presents new opportunities for sustainable growth. Successful approaches include active engagement with ESG criteria, the use of environmental risk assessments, and the adoption of climate-aware investment products. The chapter faces limitations in the availability of ESG data across markets, which affects the generalization of research outcomes. Future studies need to establish advanced mathematical models for better assessing environmental hazards

Climate Risk and Emerging Markets: Valuation, Volatility, and Portfolio Strategies, 89–102

doi:10.1108/978-1-83708-088-520261019

during portfolio spread assessment. For investors and portfolio managers, the research provides actionable insights into integrating climate and environmental considerations into their strategies. It recommends adopting robust risk management tools, enhancing transparency in ESG reporting, and fostering collaboration with policymakers to create a more climate-resilient financial ecosystem. It is valuable for investors, financial institutions, and policymakers seeking to adapt to the challenges of a rapidly changing climate while ensuring sustainable economic growth.

Keywords: Climate risk; environmental sustainability; portfolio diversification; resilient investments; ESG integration

1. Introduction

The contemporary financial world is experiencing a shift towards a new type of financial model, based on ESG factors. Given the current state of ecological issues in the world climate finance and ESG principles have been merged into portfolio diversification imperatives. This shift is a drastic revolution from the stereotype of the pure profit-benefit model of investment to an ethicist-proper-value model of investment that stimulates long and sustainable value creation.

It began with the United Nations Earth Summit, held in Rio de Janeiro in 1992, the need for climate finance, as the essential element of countering climate change, was recognized. Later success, including the Kyoto Protocol in 1997 and the Paris Agreement in 2015, intensified global action to mobilize financial resources for low carbon along with climate change resilience. Likewise, the idea of ESG investing has transformed from socially responsible investing that started in the 1960s starting from the civil rights movement and during the Anti-Apartheid that took root in the 1980s. Newer to the specific type of investing, ESG principles developed throughout the decades from as simple as excluding the industries with unethical activities to the active approach of selecting the companies with high ESG scores. ESG and climate finance integration into portfolios has been rapidly accelerating in investors' plans and action plans in the past decade. Investments for sustainable development increased to 35 trillion USD in 2020 from 13 trillion USD in 2018 and account for over one-third of all professionally managed assets globally. Investment bankers, interested in pursuing and promoting that type of portfolio, are aware that institutional investors, sovereign wealth funds, and individual retail investors are quickly appreciating the compelling financial argument for ESG-compliant assets – including the reduction of potential risk in portfolios, and evidence that during recent turbulence they outperformed standard benchmarks for greater levels of sustained returns.

1.1. Objectives of the Study

The present chapter aims to explore the modern concepts that have been applied in diversification by incorporating climate and environmental factors in portfolio management. Incorporating green bonds and ESG into the study, the chapter discusses emerging techniques for running financial markets in developed and emerging economies, including practical cases of integration. The discussed policy frameworks and investment strategies are also analysed to identify their ability to manage environmental threats.

2. Review of Literature

The permanent income hypothesis was originally introduced by Milton Friedman in 1957, while (Arellano & Bond, 1991) introduced the equity premium puzzle which called for more on average history returns of equities to risk-free securities. Following this argument Arslan-Ayaydin et al. (2014) proposed that it might be explained by rare disaster risk; Arellano and Bover (1995) proposed that the observed risk justified a premium. Balaji (2024b) further developed the rare disaster framework, covering economic justifications for failure and how these affected asset markets. Analysing time-varying disaster risks, Balaji (2024b) also focused on the relationship of these risks with the overall stock market fluctuations. This line of research was further developed by Balaji (2024c) who added disaster risk as a variable to the asset pricing framework and thereby provided a new look at how climatic risks influence market actions. Barney (1991) looked at the effect of temperature shocks on the cost of equity and the financial effects of climate change perceptions. Similarly, Barney (1995) examined the effects of tornado shocks on home value indicators and equity values arguing that regional weather hazards had implications for the stock market (Barney et al., 2021).

Contemporary studies, including the works of Barry et al. (2022), investigated climatic risks for a century, concentrating on the ability of the climate index to explain the stock market returns. To support this research, Bates et al. (2009) extended the analysis of state-level climatic risks for stock market volatility, highlighting the regional variation in exposure to climate risks (Berkhout et al., 2006). Pioneered works on stock market volatility and the efficiency of the market have given ideas about the impact of non-financial indicators on the price of the asset. Strengthening this, Billett and Garfinkel (2004) have given an understanding of climate finance and how ESG metrics affect long-term portfolio performance. Bilyay-Erdogan (2020) looked at climate finance from an investor perspective, focusing on the desire for ESG-aligned investment products (Blundell & Bond, 1998). Also, some analysis of the relations between the financial markets and the firms in climate risk environment specifically the energy companies are highly focusing on climate and environmental risk based investments (Hao et al., 2022). Recently, Balaji (2023b) gave a macroeconomic view, describing how economic disasters affected aggregate investment returns, finding that localized climate risks had broader economic repercussions.

Recent works, such as those by Balaji (2023b), analysed climate risks over a century, focusing on their predictive power for stock market returns. Using advanced econometric techniques, they revealed that climate risks were not only significant predictors of market performance but also key determinants of portfolio resilience. Balaji (2023a) complemented this research by exploring the relationship between climate risks and state-level stock market volatility, emphasizing regional disparities in climate risk exposure. Seminal works on stock market volatility and market efficiency laid the groundwork for understanding the role of non-financial factors in asset pricing (Balaji & Rao, 2024). His insights are foundational for integrating ESG considerations into financial models. Building on this, Kabir et al. (2021) provided a comprehensive review of climate finance, linking ESG metrics to long-term portfolio performance.

Mackay and Moeller (2007) explored investor perceptions of climate finance, emphasizing the growing demand for ESG-compliant investment products. Roodman (2009) examined the interactions between financial markets and energy companies under climate risk conditions. Sautner et al. (2023) provided a macroeconomic perspective, analysing how economic disasters influenced aggregate investment behaviour. Similarly, Shea et al. (2020) provided evidence that climatic risks affected US stock market tail risks with some useful instruments for prediction and control. In his work, Siddique et al. (2021) underlined this heterogeneity of climate risks and stressed that an adequate diversification plan should consider regional threats. The argument for climate risks as systemic is advanced higher integration of ESG metrics to improve investment decision-making.

The price volatility of long-run temperature shifts in capital markets for understanding climate risks as a determinant of price determination. Likewise, used growth risks arising from climate change to explain the relationship between climate change risks and economic growth. Starks (2023) used quantile regression to analyse the effect of global integration on BRICS stock markets. These weaknesses point to the fact that these markets have different levels of vulnerability to global risks and are thus important in climate finance approaches for emerging economies. In another study, Sudhakara Reddy and Assenza (2009) employed dynamic panel threshold models to evaluate the brute and direction of the relations between the BRICS stock return and country risk ratings and highlighted the country-specific risks in ESG integration. They offered a landscape of techniques for forecasting financial market volatility to provide the necessary background in the potential of ESG metrics in predicting performance. This study took volatility forecasting within structural breaks an area that has a clear application to today's portfolio risk management in light of climate finance disruption.

Hao et al. (2022) having estimated the distributional loss of temperature shocks investigated welfare and macroeconomic consequences. Following this, Kabir et al. (2021) studied the impact of global temperature variability on spending on R&D with a focus on economic growth patterns, discussing the role of climate advancements for sustainable investments. Mackay and Moeller (2007) discussed the persistence of state-level uncertainty in the United States and mapping climate risks as factors influencing the economic environment at various levels of disaggregation. Building on this, Kabir et al. (2021) investigated the global temperature volatility's influence on research and development expenditures and economic growth, showcasing the importance of climate innovation for sustainable investment strategies. Mackay and Moeller (2007) examined the persistence of state-level uncertainty in the United States, revealing that climate risks play a critical role in shaping economic conditions at granular levels.

In a study by Roodman (2009), the focus was laid on the internet of commodity prices involved in the empirical analysis of international stock returns and; the interactions between fundamentals and sentiment. The authors' observations are especially useful in assessing the impact of the energy market on climate finance possible approaches. Similarly, Balaji (2024c) investigated linkages between oil prices and the stock market, a building block of integrating energy transition risk on portfolio diversification. Sautner et al. (2023) analysed the link between gold, platinum, and expected stock returns, grossing out the capabilities of hedging portfolios for climate risks. Shea et al. (2020) investigated the macroeconomic uncertainty that affects the conditional stock market volatility in South Africa. This work enriches more extensive literature, for instance, Siddique et al. (2021), which focuses on risk-return. They have identified the difficulties and possibilities of putting ESG factors into practice. Balaji and Rao (2024) used the regime-switching generalized autoregressive conditional heteroskedasticity (GARCH) models to predict stock market volatility in the presence of geopolitical risks. Balaji (2023a) in particular samples the stock market volatility systematically, offering an overall view of the dynamic interaction between climate finance and market fluctuation.

Assessing the Starks (2023) for implications of climate risks to the volatility of emerging markets in South Africa, what they find out is that incorporating risk-related factors in diversification increases the mitigation of portfolios in climates that are characterized by high risks. Balaji (2023b) presented fractionally integrated time-varying GARCH models pose interesting consequences for climate finance. This approach exposes the characteristics of volatility dynamics and ESG-focused portfolios. Sudhakara Reddy and Assenza (2009) revealed that the levels of volatility of cryptocurrencies are higher than those of traditional stock markets. Based on these results, investors adopting ESG factors to the crypto investment thesis could reduce risks while enhancing sustainability.

3. Research Methodology

Therefore, this research utilizes a quantitative approach in addition to qualitative analysis. Secondary research data were collected from financial databases, ESG performance reports, and climate finance indices to analyse the relationship between climate risks and asset return. It utilizes case-based analysis to determine the effectiveness of a climate-adjusted diversification strategy on risk-adjusted returns. Empirical data were collected from academic journals, business reports, and best practices used by companies adopting ESG factors into the investment management system. Lastly, documentary interviews with financial analysts, sustainability consultants, and institutional investors were conducted to triangulate data and identify new trends.

3.1. Climate Change and Financial Markets

Climate change is a danger and an opportunity as it impacts and transforms the structure of the financial system, investment, risk evaluation, and economic systems. Main physical climate change risks include the operational disruption of industries through things such as increased extremity of the natural environment or climatic change affecting structures and impairing asset value, resulting in operation losses and higher risk and return volatility. Transition risks refer to risks that stem from changes towards low-emissions economies affecting sectors that have carbon exposure by regulations, market switches, or having asset value. Many financial institutions are considering ESG factors and climate risk models, among other problems, when developing investment solutions. Carbon pricing and climate risk management instruments are now available in the markets because this is an emerging field and people have started managing these risks and opportunities.

3.2. Climate Finance and ESG

Climate finance plays a key role in promoting ESG in the world. It is an emerging field and people have started managing these risks and opportunities. The detailed explanation of climate finance and its relation to ESG in investment alternatives has been discussed as follows.

3.2.1. Environmental Criteria

The ESG criteria help point organizations in the right direction, as they assess the risks and possibilities with a vision towards sustainable development, with respect to financial impacts. Regulatory, management, and financial risks, which are among ESG factors, encompass physical risks such as floods and repetitive climate changes affecting assets and operations. Transition risks involve changes towards a low carbon economy such as policy, technologies, and market transition. Using policies, geopolitics, regulations, and laws impacts the cash flows and credit ratings where variance in climate policies arises (Khan et al., 2022).

3.2.2. Social Criteria

Based on social criteria, a company has various responsibilities to society such as the responsibility of its employees, the responsibility towards the shareholders, the responsibility to its customers, the responsibility towards its suppliers, and the responsibility towards the community. These standards evaluate the company in terms of its commitment to human rights and other societal issues, health and safety in the workplace, customer product responsibility, diversity as well as ethical stewardship of consumer relationships (Khan et al., 2021).

3.2.3. Governance Criteria

Governance criteria deal with the proper management and system of an organization to ensure the right ethical standard is followed. Such principles include the board of directors' responsibility, executives' pay, shareholders' entitlements, and adherence to existing governance standards. These policies compel organizations to incorporate CSR strategies and set sustainability goals and risk declarations.

3.3. Climate Change and ESG Financial Instruments to Support Climate Finance

- *Green bonds:* A green bond is a bond that is designed to finance projects with environmental or climate co-benefits on the capital markets. These bonds fund renewable energy, energy efficiency, or sustainable agriculture – in other words, they tie rewards to eco-friendly outcomes (Alam & Akhtar, 2024).
- *Sustainability-linked loans:* Such loans offer an opportunity for certain targeted measurable ESG performance, which will grant otherwise more favourable loan terms. For instance, the attainment of a target to cut carbon emissions or increase the deployment of renewable energy resources attracts low interest rates.
- *Carbon credits and offsetting market:* These markets help firms sell carbon credits within the capacity of cap-and-trade systems or voluntary offset programmes. It has been on sale for companies to procure credits for cutting out greenhouse gas emissions around the world.
- *Blended finance:* This money is pooled from both the public and private entities, to finance initiatives which may not attract conventional private capital. Blended finance removes risks from investments in sustainable infrastructure, renewable energy or other ESG-related projects (Naseema et al., 2024).
- *ESG-linked derivatives:* Futures and options are derived from ESG indices or certain ESG figures so that investors can protect themselves against certain risks or invest sustainably.

These instruments also represent exactly how it is possible to use the power of finance to support both the sustainability and the resilience of global economies with inclusion being at the core of investment processes that embrace the ESG standards.

3.4. Case Studies

3.4.1. The Case of In-climate Finance Mobilization: Glasgow City Region

In June 2021, the Glasgow City Region presented the first Adaptation Strategy and the Action Plan within Climate Ready Clyde51. This considered the overall goal of the strategy is not only to make the region's economy, society, and environment resistant to the effects of climate change but rather, to be able to compete in the future created by climate change. The climate finance mobilization strategy of the Glasgow city region is in Fig. 6.1.

Fig. 6.1 reflects the plan that identifies key activities and early actions that are prerequisites to addressing climate risks and realizing climate opportunities and is designed to serve as a high-level, strategic framework that can coexist with and support other plans, policies, or activities. This new tactic included a

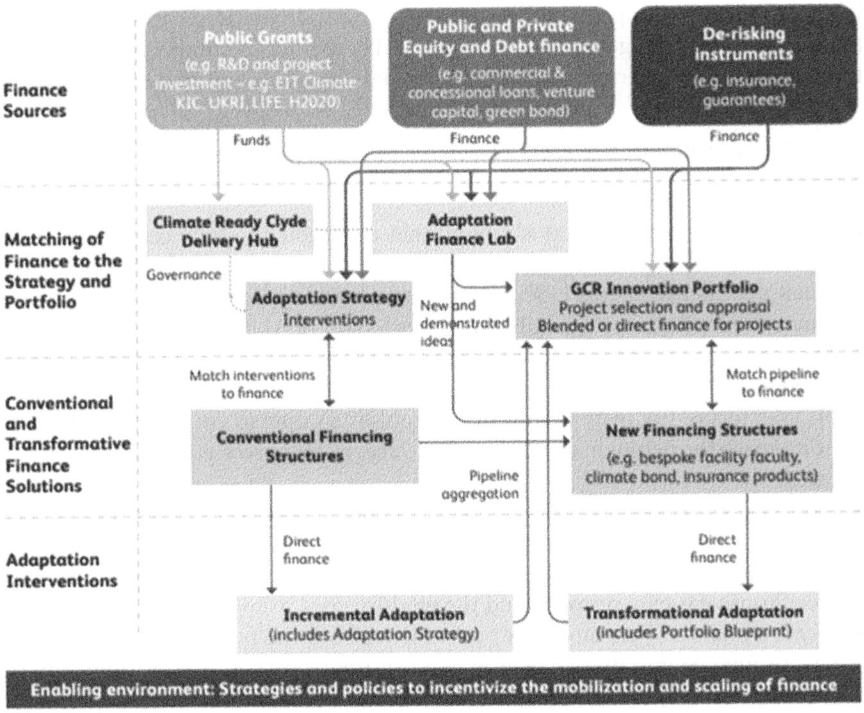

Fig. 6.1. Climate Finance Mobilization: Glasgow City Region. *Source*: Authors Compilation.

vision-orientated framework which focused on the communication of new opportunities, and the so-called co-benefits of adaptation. To examine the context for policy reform it adopted systems thinking, political economy analysis, and social network analysis. Along the same line, the strategy encompassed multiple interventions with low to high levels of disruption. One of the key activities within the strategy was the search for finance opportunities. In support of this, an economic and financial assessment and resource mobilization plan were conducted to evaluate the efficiency of adaptation mechanisms and financing avenues.

3.4.2. Portfolio Climate Risk Management: AP2 Case Study

The specific example of the Second Swedish National Pension Fund known as AP2 is an example of an industry leader that embedded climate risk management into investment processes for a global sustainable future. The university has operated AP2 since 2015 and as a result, it has lowered the overall carbon intensity of the equity portfolio more than by half, has tripled the green bonds share from 1% to 3% has invested in sustainable infrastructure and forestry. Further, it exited 80 energy and utility companies that pose risks to its own finances due to climate change. The above efforts are proceeded in line with AP2's promotion of ESG standards.

Set up in 2001 as a buffer fund in Sweden and currently one of four AP2's portfolio comprises assets amounting to about SEK 381 billion (USD 40 billion). The Fund applies sustainability throughout its operational strategies affordability by using some governance characteristics such as compulsory ESG training of the board, and engagement. Based on the spirit of the Paris Agreement, AP2 integrates climate review into its ALM programme and assesses fossil fuel-linked risks to inform divestments. AP2 increases transparency and collaboration through the utilization of tools such as Morgan Stanley Capital International emissions data as well as through participation in the Climate Action 100+ campaign. In the future, the fund aims to enlarge the climate risk evaluation, adhere to the EU Paris-aligned benchmark, and enhance the scenario analysis once again proving the fund's role as a leading sustainable investor.

3.4.3. Brunel Pension Partnership

Brunel Pension Partnership was formed in 2017 as a dedicated manager for UK Local Government Pension Scheme funds. It oversees more than £30bn ($40bn USD) in assets and has 24 portfolios. Every local authority has its own management, investment policy, and portfolio, while Brunel aligns its climate risk with the investment management overall portfolio. Brunel has demanded that all external asset managers evaluate and mitigate climate risks and bring their portfolios in line with a low-carbon world. It engages in the Climate Action 100+ and the Transition Pathway Initiative to ensure corporate climate change accountability.

Brunel's Climate Change Policy was initiated in early 2020 and intends to shift financial systems towards adaptation to CC and uptake of positive climate impact investment. The policy outlines five strategic areas: policy action, product control, portfolio administration, value creation, and influence. The partnership engages specifically with asset managers, to minimize climate risk exposure and advance alignment with a 2 °C future.

3.5. Artificial Intelligence (AI) and Blockchain to Improve ESG Integration and Climate Risk Management

Organizations can achieve better transparency and precise climate risk management and enhanced ESG sustainability decision-making through AI and blockchain integration in sustainable finance (Jafar et al., 2023). AI coupled with analytics technologies permits users to search large ESG databases for climate risks while achieving optimal portfolio spread in real-time. Blockchain technology enables both exact data quality management and full transparency for origin tracking through responsible systems that boost investor security levels in their investments. Financial institutions should create sustainable investment frameworks that use blockchain and AI predictive functions to generate resilient profit-focused strategies. Financial institutions which implement these technologies can support investor decision-making and complete regulatory requirements before reaching substantial sustainability progress in worldwide financial markets (Alam et al., 2024).

3.6. Investor Behaviour and Market Sentiment Impact the Adoption of ESG

The way investors behave along with their sentiment determines the rate at which ESG principles gain acceptance. The increasing perception of sustainability issues together with investor need for responsible investments is pushing capital towards ESG-aligned assets. The positive sentiment in the market regarding ESG implementation leads organizations to expand their involvement with these principles thus affecting both corporate decision-making and financial outcomes (Ladeira et al., 2024). The widespread integration of ESG principles suffers from doubts among investors and short-term profit orientation as well as from unreliable ESG metrics assessment systems. ESG investments receive greater investor trust through favourable market patterns together with regulatory backing and stakeholder advocacy activities. The enhanced transparency of ESG metrics combined with standardized reporting measures will maintain investor confidence in ESG investments which supports long-term value creation and sustainable financial market growth (Jafar et al., 2024).

3.7. Impact of Global Partnerships and Financial Tools on the Integration of ESG Principles in Emerging Markets

The role of global partnerships combined with financial tools becomes crucial for introducing ESG principles into emerging markets because they bring funding along with advisory services and governance mechanisms. The United Nations together with multilateral banks run sustainability-linked initiatives which help markets adopt ESG principles through the implementation of policies and funding structures. Green bonds together with ESG-focused private equity and blended finance instruments serve as financial resources which connect funding gaps to sustainably motivate investment initiatives. These initiatives drive market trust which makes companies follow ESG standards while speeding up the development of sustainable economies. Emerging markets achieve sustainability standards alongside escalating economic resistance through international partnerships which use creative financial resources.

3.8. Challenges in Integrating Climate and Environmental Risks into Portfolio Diversification Strategies

Several hurdles exist when modern investors attempt to include climate and environmental risks in their portfolio diversification strategies due to multiple factors including non-standard ESG criteria and insufficient data as well as inconsistent regulations. The inconsistency in global standard implementation between the Global Reporting Initiative, the Sustainability Accounting Standards Board, and the Task Force on Climate-Related Financial Disclosures produces confusion about climate-related risk evaluation.

Specific data gaps prevent the successful implementation of ESG principles into financial investment models. The lack of environmental data infrastructure exists among numerous businesses that operate mainly in developing markets. The ESG adoption faces significant difficulties because countries have different rules about these standards. Environmental reporting practices differ between nations since some use mandatory requirements but others have merely optional guidelines which creates ambiguities regarding compliance. Standard sustainability assessment models remain out of reach for global investors because international and national standards do not agree on the same requirements.

3.9. Policy Frameworks Supporting ESG Integration

Governments and regulatory bodies across the globe have put policies in place to push ESG integration into the financial world. The European Union's Sustainable Finance Action Plan, for instance, brought in the Taxonomy Regulation. This regulation offers a system to classify economic activities that are good for the environment. The EU also brought in the Non-Financial Reporting Directive. This directive makes big companies share their ESG performance helping investors make better choices. In the same way, the Task Force on Climate-Related Financial Disclosures has become a global benchmark for companies to share climate-related risks. This encourages openness in how businesses handle their impact on the environment. In the United States, the Securities and Exchange Commission has started to include climate and ESG disclosures in the reporting rules for public companies.

4. Findings of the Study

The study shows that portfolios with climate-adjusted diversification hold up better than traditional ones when the economy takes a hit. Companies with high ESG scores tend to be less volatile and give better returns over time. Green financial products, like green bonds, have done well and caught the eye of many investors. This points to a change in where money is flowing, with more going to sustainable assets. The study also points out that while ESG integration helps manage risks, the big problem is still the lack of standard ESG measures and data that don't match up. Also, areas like clean energy, eco-friendly infrastructure, and electric cars stand out as good bets for investors looking to grow their money.

5. Financial and Non-financial Implications

Green governance, equity, and social governance metrics and other principles of climate finance integrate well with modern portfolio theory not only from the perspective of financial implications but also from the view of non-financial implications for investors and portfolio managers. Such integration has strength in financial terms by improving risk-adjusted returns on those factors since they develop and improve the identification and risk management of environmental and social risks which may be detrimental to long-term performance. In non-financial terms too, ESG criteria outwardly reflect changes in responsible investment, which is investment strategies that are aligned with the value ideas of society and contribute to sustainable development. Such an approach would translate, for investors, into better corporate governance, social responsibility, and, indeed, environmental stewardship.

6. Future Research Directions

Emerging studies could focus on what would normally be considered challenges in ESG standardization and assess the role of further technology such as AI and blockchain in enhancing ESG reporting and climate risk assessments. Longitudinal studies could investigate how portfolio performance over time and across several markets is affected by staying with ESG integration for a long time. Furthermore, research can look into how social equity and climate finance intersect and how investments in marginalized communities can create joint value for them.

7. Conclusion

Nowadays, it is not an option instead; it has become an important necessity to consider climate and environmental risks for diversification in portfolios in modern-day investment strategies. This study showcases how ESG investments can impart resilient portfolios with financial returns while meeting society at large by embracing that larger meta-narrative. There might be discrepancies and pinches like the earlier ones, but the benefits of including principles of sustainable finance far outnumber these petty drawbacks. As the financial ecosystem moves into a new phase, it is vital for cooperation among all different parties-including investors, institutions, and policymakers to advance the kinds of assimilation of climate and environmental risk into financial investment practices. Such an effort will not merely reinforce portfolio risk but help enhance a more sustainable and equitable global economy.

References

Alam, M. & Akhtar, S. (2024). Introduction to green finance and technology integration. In S. Jafar, R. Rodriguez, H. Kannan, S. Akhtar, & P. Plugmann (Eds.), *Harnessing blockchain-digital twin fusion for sustainable investments* (pp. 1–19). IGI Global Scientific Publishing. https://doi.org/10.4018/979-8-3693-1878-2.ch001.

Alam, M., Akhtar, S., & Bettencourt, A. (2024). Introduction to fintech in industry 5.0: Companion or antagonist. In S. H. Jafar, H. Kannan, S. Akhtar, P. Alam Khan, & H. El-Chaarani (Eds.), *The adoption of fintech* (pp. 1–16). Productivity Press. https://doi.org/10.4324/9781032644165

Arellano, M., & Bond, S. (1991). Some tests of specification for panel data: Monte Carlo evidence and an application to employment equations. *The Review of Economic Studies*, *58*(2), 277–297. https://doi.org/10.2307/2297968

Arellano, M., & Bover, O. (1995). Another look at the instrumental variable estimation of error-components models. *Journal of Econometrics*, *68*(1), 29–51. https://doi.org/10.1016/0304-4076(94)01642-D

Arslan-Ayaydin, ¨O., Florackis, C., & Ozkan, A. (2014). Financial flexibility, corporate investment and performance: Evidence from financial crises. *Review of Quantitative Finance and Accounting*, *42*(2), 211–250. https://doi.org/10.1007/s11156-012-0340-x

Balaji, K. (2023a). Blockchain based banking transactions enabled by big data. In *2023 5th International conference on energy, power and environment: Towards flexible green energy technologies (ICEPE), Shillong, India*, IEEE *2023* (pp. 1–6). https://doi.org/10.1109/ICEPE57949.2023.10201613

Balaji, K. (2023b). Unlocking the potential of BI-enhancing banking transactions through AI&ML Tools. In *2023 International conference on applied intelligence and sustainable computing (ICAISC), Dharwad, India*, IEEE *2023* (pp. 1–6). https://doi.org/10.1109/ICAISC58445.2023.10200018

Balaji, K. (2024a). Harnessing AI for financial innovations: Pioneering the future of financial services. In K. Jermsittiparsert, N. Phongkraphan, & N. Lekhavichit (Eds.), *Modern management science practices in the age of AI* (pp. 91–122). IGI Global. https://doi.org/10.4018/979-8-3693-6720-9.ch004

Balaji, K. (2024b). Charting the path to global prosperity: Unveiling the impact and promise of sustainable development. In P. Ordóñez de Pablos, M. Anshari, & M. Almunawar (Eds.), *Harnessing green and circular skills for digital transformation* (pp. 1–22). IGI Global. https://doi.org/10.4018/979-8-3693-2865-1.ch001

Balaji, K. (2024c). The nexus of smart contracts and digital twins transforming green finance with automated transactions in investment agreements: Leveraging smart contracts for green investment agreements and automated transactions. In S. Jafar, R. Rodriguez, H. Kannan, S. Akhtar, & P. Plugmann (Eds.), *Harnessing blockchain-digital twin fusion for sustainable investments* (pp. 287–315). IGI Global. https://doi.org/10.4018/979-8-3693-1878-2.ch012

Balaji, K., & Rao, P. S. (2024). Artificial intelligence and Chatbots: Transforming user experience in E-tailing. In *2024 9th International conference on communication and electronics systems (ICCES), Coimbatore, India*, IEEE *2024* (pp. 1375–1379). https://doi.org/10.1109/ICCES63552.2024.10859474

Barney, J. (1991). Firm resources and sustained competitive advantage. *Journal of Management*, *17*(1), 99–120. https://doi.org/10.1177/014920639101700108

Barney, J. B. (1995). Looking inside for competitive advantage. *Academy of Management Perspectives*, *9*(4), 49–61. https://doi.org/10.5465/ame.1995.9512032192

Barney, J. B., Ketchen, D. J., & Wright, M. (2021). Resource-based theory and the value creation framework. *Journal of Management*, *47*(7), 1936–1955. https://doi.org/10.1177/01492063211021655

Barry, J. W., Campello, M., Graham, J. R., & Ma, Y. (2022). Corporate flexibility in a time of crisis. *Journal of Financial Economics*, *144*(3), 780–806. https://doi.org/10.1016/j.jfineco.2022.03.003

Bates, T. W., Kahle, K. M., & Stulz, R. M. (2009). Why do U.S. firms hold so much more cash than they used to? *The Journal of Finance*, *64*(5), 1985–2021. https://doi.org/10.1111/j.1540-6261.2009.01492.x

Berkhout, F., Hertin, J., & Gann, D. M. (2006). Learning to adapt: Organisational adaptation to climate change impacts. *Climatic Change*, *78*(1), 135–156. https://doi.org/10.1007/s10584-006-9089-3

Billett, M. T., & Garfinkel, J. A. (2004). Financial flexibility and the cost of external finance for US bank holding companies. *Journal of Money, Credit, and Banking*, *36*(5), 827–852. https://doi.org/10.1353/mcb.2004.0071

Bilyay-Erdogan, S. (2020). Does financial flexibility enhance firm value? A comparative study between developed and emerging countries. *Verslas: Teorija Ir Praktika*, *21*(2), 723–736. https://doi.org/10.3846/btp.2020.12680

Blundell, R., & Bond, S. (1998). Initial conditions and moment restrictions in dynamic panel data models. *Journal of Econometrics*, *87*(1), 115–143. https://doi.org/10.1016/S0304-4076(98)00009-8

Hao, Z., Zhang, X., & Wei, J. (2022). Research on the effect of enterprise finance for US bank holding companies. *Journal of Money, Credit, and Banking, International Review of Financial Analysis, 75*, Article 101734.

Jafar, S. H., Akhtar, S., & Johl, S. K. (2023). AI in insurance. In S. H. Jafar, S. Akhtar, & S. K. Johl (Eds.), *Artificial intelligence for business* (pp. 164–173). Productivity Press.

Jafar, S. H., Hemachandran, K., Akhtar, S., Khan, P. A., & El-Chaarani, H. (Eds.). (2024). *The adoption of fintech: Using technology for better security, speed, and customer experience in finance* (pp. 1–328). CRC Press.

Kabir, M. N., Rahman, S., Rahman, M. A., & Anwar, M. (2021). Carbon emissions and default risk: International evidence from firm-level data. *Economic Modelling, 103*, Article 105617. https://doi.org/10.1016/j.econmod.2021.105617

Khan, P. A., Johl, S. K., & Akhtar, S. (2021). Firm sustainable development goals and firm financial performance through the lens of green innovation practices and reporting: A proactive approach. *Journal of Risk and Financial Management, 14*(12), 605.

Khan, P. A., Johl, S. K., & Akhtar, S. (2022). Vinculum of sustainable development goal practices and firms' financial performance: A moderation role of green innovation. *Journal of Risk and Financial Management, 15*(3), 96.

Ladeira, W. J., Santini, F. D. O., Rasul, T., Cheah, I., Elhajjar, S., Yasin, N., & Akhtar, S. (2024). Big data analytics and the use of artificial intelligence in the services industry: A meta-analysis. *The Service Industries Journal, 44*(15–16), 1117–1144.

Mackay, P., & Moeller, S. B. (2007). The value of corporate risk management. The *Journal of Finance, 62*(3), 1379–1419. https://doi.org/10.1111/j.1540-6261.2007.01239.x

Naseema, N., Akhtar, S., & Al Hinai, A. A. (2024). Disrupting financial services: A case study on Capital One's Fintech Odyssey. In S. Jafar, R. Rodriguez, H. Kannan, S. Akhtar, & P. Plugmann (Eds.), *Harnessing blockchain-digital twin fusion for sustainable investments* (pp. 363–383). IGI Global.

Roodman, D. (2009). How to do Xtabond2: An introduction to difference and system GMM in Stata. *STATA Journal, 9*(1), 86–136. https://doi.org/10.1177/1536867X0900900106

Sautner, Z., Van Lent, L., Vilkov, G., & Zhang, R. (2023). Firm-level climate change exposure. *The Journal of Finance, 78*(3), 1449–1498. https://doi.org/10.1111/jofi.13219

Shea, M. M., Painter, J., & Osaka, S. (2020). Representations of Pacific Islands and climate change in US, UK, and Australian newspaper reporting. *Climatic Change, 161*(1), 89–108. https://doi.org/10.1007/s10584-020-02674-w

Siddique, M. A., Akhtaruzzaman, M., Rashid, A., & Hammami, H. (2021). Carbon disclosure, carbon performance and financial performance: International evidence. *International Review of Financial Analysis, 75*, Article 101734. https://doi.org/10.1016/j.irfa.2021.101734

Starks, L. T. (2023). Presidential address: Sustainable finance and ESG issues – value versus values. *The Journal of Finance, 78*(4), 1837–1872. https://doi.org/10.1111/jofi.13255

Sudhakara Reddy, B., & Assenza, G. B. (2009). The great climate debate. *Energy Policy, 37*(8), 2997–3008. https://doi.org/10.1016/j.enpol.2009.03.064

Chapter 7

Understanding Dynamics of Environmental Sustainability and Financial Inclusion: Evidence from BRICS Countries

Boishali Das[a], Gaurav Kumar[a] and Parvez Alam Khan[b]

[a]Department of Humanities and Management, Dr. B.R. Ambedkar National Institute of Technology, Jalandhar, India
[b]Department of Management and Humanities, Universiti Teknologi PETRONAS, Perak, Malaysia

Abstract

This chapter investigates the association between financial inclusion (FI) and Environmental Sustainability (ES). Moreover, the study also explores the reciprocal impact of ES on FI. Data is collected for BRICS nations for the time period of 2008–2020. The major sources for data collection are the International Monetary Fund and World Bank for all the indicators of FI and ES. Principal component analysis (PCA) is used to create separate indexes for FI and ES. Pooled OLS is used to identify the association among the variables, i.e. FI and ES and vice versa. The results reflect a negative relation between the variables, i.e. FI and ES, indicating that increased FI causes environmental quality to decline. The percentage of the population availing clean fuels and technologies for cooking and forest areas shows a significant but negative impact on FI, while access to electricity indicates a positive impact on FI. Carbon intensity also revealed a negative impact on FI. The study also checked for a reverse causality test where ES is the dependent variable, where the number of commercial bank branches (per 100,000 adults) and outstanding deposits with commercial banks (% of gross domestic product (GDP)) have a positive and significant impact on ES. Outstanding loans from commercial banks (% of GDP) have a negative and significant impact on ES. The study is limited only to Brazil, Russia, India, China, and South Africa (BRICS) nations

Climate Risk and Emerging Markets: Valuation, Volatility, and Portfolio Strategies, 103–115

Published under exclusive licence by Emerald Publishing Limited
doi:10.1108/978-1-83708-088-520261021

which can be further extended to other emerging countries and groups like South Asian Association for Regional Cooperation (SAARC), Association of Southeast Asian Nations (ASEAN), etc., to derive a more comprehensive finding.

Keywords: FI; ES; BRICS; World Bank; principal component analysis

1. Introduction

A well-known climate pact, also known as the Paris Agreement, was signed in 2015 to address environmental concerns and limit increasing temperatures United Nations (2015). Despite the presence of such agreement, CO_2 emissions are rapidly growing over a period of time, endangering human life on a continual basis. Several measures are implemented by countries to provide affordable access to clean and green energy. Renewable energy sources is considered as an essential tool to accomplish the targeted goal of diminishing global greenhouse gas (GHG) emissions, which further helps in shifting to a less carbon usage system easier (Ji et al., 2021). Global warming is a severe threat to human beings and all other species, which has influenced academicians and policymakers to identify measures to control and prevent uncertainties associated with it. Human activities have marked for continuous deterioration of the environment because there is absence of proper solution that can lead to creation of a proper balance between economic activity and environmental concerns (Le & Quah, 2018). Due to lesser financial resources and more economic output, developing countries have witnessed significant environmental deterioration over the years. The effects of droughts and floods have severely damaged the environment in developing countries, which has a negative influence on their economic production and raises their health care costs (Jafar, Hemachandran et al., 2024; Sitorus, 2018).

FI and sustainable development are considered major development blueprint that has significant implication towards the society and environment. The primary concern of this study is to establish an association between these two development plans. FI helps in generation of capital for investment and also acts as a power source to boost the economy. Further, it is the procedure to set up financial instruments and services easily accessible to individuals and businesses (World Bank, 2022). Over the period of time, FI is recognized as an efficient driver of both global and national economic growth. Its major byproducts are capital creation, better insight of investment activities and effective resource distribution (Fareed et al., 2022; Naseema et al., 2024). Financial development is effective in reduction of carbon emissions and enhances the quality of environment by increasing affordability to adopt technologies that are efficient for the environment (Jafar, Rodriguez et al., 2024; Le et al., 2020). The major goal of ES is to meet the needs of the present generation while ensuring that no compromise is made on the requirements of future generation (Keeble, 1988).

Le et al. (2020) stated the association between FI and environment can be either positive or negative. It is assumed that FI will lead to a major shift for environment friendly products, for example, as lack of finance acts as a drawback in using solar systems (Baulch et al., 2018). Green technologies can be used for investments and domestic purposes by businesses and individuals, to afford such technologies it is mandatory to have easy and affordable access to financial services. The report by IPA (2017) emphasizes that FI has a great contribution in mitigating harm towards the environment as it allows the populations to follow green practices.

As per the reports of World Economic Forum (2024), BRICS group's results are 40% of global population and an estimate of 37.3% of GDP of the world. The study focused on BRICS nation as they have the largest share in the world's output. Wilson and Purushothaman (2003) assumed that by the end of 2041, the major mergers of Russia, Brazil, and South Africa and the upcoming global powered nations like China and India are capable to build an economy size that will be larger than G-6 countries. Also, BRICS countries fall under the category of greatest contributors in carbon emissions and are victims of severe climate change. The level of energy usage of BRICS countries has increased over the period of time as a result of increase in investments in infrastructure and industries (Razzaq et al., 2021). Massive environmental challenges in BRICS countries are the outcomes of severe energy consumption, rapid urbanization and increased inflow and outflow of trade that leads to increase in GHG emissions.

The exploration of the association between FI and ES is a recent area of inquiry that warrants further attention, particularly in the context of emerging and developing countries. Our study is inspired by the significant environmental challenges such as climate change, deforestation, energy crisis, etc., experienced by the countries in recent period (Du et al., 2022; Rehman et al., 2023).

The study is focused on exploring the link between FI and ES using PCA and explores the effect of carbon emissions and foreign direct investment (FDI) on FI.

2. Literature Review

A systematic literature review presented in this section exhibits mixed and inconclusive findings about the nexus between FI and ES. Understanding this association can support efforts under frameworks like the Paris Agreement, where financing plays a central role in climate mitigation and adaptation.

2.1. Financial Inclusion

Chibba (2009) mentioned the idea of FI in his study that considered financial exclusion as one of the major poverty alleviation programme. In the contemporary era, FI is the top priority policy for nations (Dabla-Norris et al., 2021). A study of the BRICS group exhibits positive findings of FI except for China from 2005 to 2014 (Khandare, 2019). Literature provides strong evidence that

FI is crucial driver for women's empowerment, economy, and mitigating poverty (Alam et al., 2024; Aziz et al., 2022; Omar et al., 2020; Van et al., 2019). Zaidi et al. (2021) investigated that energy consumption, CO_2 emissions, and FI have positive relation in 23 OECD nations. Findings from literature emphasized FI as crucial tool for eradicating poverty (Churchill & Marisetty, 2019; Koomson et al., 2020; Xu et al., 2024). Sujhalana and Kiran (2018) suggested that in India, overall inclusive growth needs to be considered with proper implementation of initiatives that can fulfil the purpose of overall development of the people residing in rural sector of the nation as FI is in nascent stage.

2.2. *Environmental Sustainability*

The process of preserving natural capital is regarded as ES (Goodland, 1995). The determinants of environmental degradation are identified as deforestation, population, industrialization, etc. (Hasanov et al., 2018; Khan et al., 2022; Zhang et al., 2017). A study conducted by Voica (2017) defined that a major role is being played by FI in driving social inclusion and further revealed that social inclusion plays a dominant role to drive sustainable development, they concluded that FI is a driver for sustainable development. The study also proposed that to achieve overall growth of the economy, FI should be promoted using international initiatives. Zhang et al. (2022) revealed that one of the major problem that the world is facing is extreme reliance on fossil fuels and the increased concentration of GHGs which are results of human activities leading to environmental disaster. As a result, measures are adapted by the International organizations to encourage nations to rely more on renewable energy sources in order to lower their carbon emissions. Attempts are being made by countries to reduce the factors that are major contributors of GHG emissions which can further help in achievement of sustainable development (Khan et al., 2021; Yu et al., 2023).

2.3. *FI and ES*

Shoaib et al. (2020) analysed between developed and developing countries to understand their association, specifically the G8 and D8 nations. The results showed financial development positively affects CO_2 emissions for both the nations. Wan et al. (2023) revealed that financial sustainability through digital finance leads to reduction in pollution through innovations, structural adjustments, etc. The results are in line with Cao (2023) that stated green financing initiatives can encourage financial sustainability where ASEAN-5 countries were analysed using dynamic ordinary least squares and fully modified OLS methods. Financial development increases CO_2 emissions (Nasir et al., 2019). The conclusion derived by Khan et al. (2019) for a panel of 193 countries revealed positive impact of financial development on CO_2 emissions which contributes to higher pollution levels. Pooled OLS, 2SLS, and generalized method of moments approaches were implemented by Ozturk and Ullah (2022) across 42 OBRI countries to identify the impact of FI on economic growth and ES. The analysis demonstrated that though digital FI encourages economic growth, it also leads in reduction of ES due to higher CO_2 emissions. It was identified that development in finance has a positive association with carbon emissions which implies that it significantly contributes to environmental degradation. Le et al. (2020) stated that an inclusive financial system improves the environment tremendously, whereas, Wang et al. (2022) commented that increase in financial development calls for increased CO_2 emissions, as accessibility to financial services promotes industries and manufacturing units. A study was performed on a panel time series data for the period 2004–2018 where Ahmad et al. (2022) concluded that in BRICS group FI leads to degradation of environment. Further study was conducted by Mukalayi and Inglesi-Lotz (2023) to investigate the development of FI and innovation of digital services considering environmental and energy consumption for various nations based on their geographic locations. A comprehensive dataset was curated using Global FI Database, World Bank providing insights into how individuals across the globe save, borrow, make payments, and manage their risks. The results concluded that when the proxies for FI are higher, they further increase energy consumption and CO_2 emissions.

3. Data and Methodology

3.1. Sample and Data

A sample of the BRICS group is considered to unveil the nexus between FI and ES from 2008 to 2020. Data for FI and ES variables are collected from World Bank and IMF databases.

3.2. Principal Component Analysis

PCA is a technique that reduces a dispersed multivariate data collection's dimensions while maintaining the information in a smaller set of uncorrelated data (Bartholomew, 2010).

Table 7.1 explains the results of PCA of the variables representing FI. Component refers to the variables, i.e. Number of commercial bank branches, Automated teller machines (ATMs) (per 100,000 adults), and outstanding deposits with commercial banks (% of GDP) and outstanding loans with commercial banks (% of GDP). Eigenvalue for each component represents the amount of variance that component explains. Larger eigenvalue indicates that the component explains more variance in the dataset. Comp1 has an eigenvalue of 2.227 which is highest among the other components, thus explains more variance in the dataset. The percentage that each component accounts for in explaining the overall variance in the table, i.e. Comp1 explains 55.6% of the variance in the data, which makes it the most significant component. Comp2 adds another 28.0%, so together, Comp1 and Comp2 explain 83.6% of the total variance. Comp3 contributes 13.9%, bringing the cumulative variance explained to 97.6%. Comp4 explains only 2.4% of the variance, and adding it brings the total variance explained to 100%

Table 7.1. FI.

Component	Eigenvalue	Proportion	Cumulative
Comp1	2.227	0.556	0.556
Comp2	1.119	0.280	0.836
Comp3	0.556	0.139	0.976
Comp4	0.095	0.024	1.000

Source: Author's own analysis.

Table 7.2. ES.

Component	Eigenvalue	Proportion	Cumulative
Comp1	2.220	0.740	0.740
Comp2	0.418	0.139	0.879
Comp3	0.360	0.120	1.000

Source: Author's own analysis.

Table 7.2 represents the results of PCA of the variables representing ES. The component refers to access to clean fuels and technologies for cooking (% of population), Access to electricity (% of population) and forest area (% of land area). Comp1 has an eigenvalue of 2.220 which explains 74% of the variance in the dataset. This component captures majority of the variance in the dataset, making it the most significant component. Comp2 explains 13.9% of the variance in the dataset and together with Comp1 it explains 87.9% of the variance. Comp3 explains 12.0% of the variance. Adding this component brings the total variance explained to 100%, accounting for all the variability in the dataset.

3.3. Methodology and Variables

To explore the nexus among FI and ES, pooled OLS method is utilized. In model 1, the FI index is dependent variable and ES variables are explanatory variables. In model 2, the ES index is dependent variables and FI variables are explanatory variables. Total GHG emission, carbon intensity, FDI are the control variables. Description of variables used in study is provided in Table 7.3.

$$\begin{aligned}\mathrm{FI}_{i,t} = \alpha_{i,t} + \beta 1\mathrm{cleanfuel}_{i,t} + \beta 2\mathrm{electricity}_{i,t} + \beta 3\mathrm{forestarea}_{i,t} \\ + \beta 4\mathrm{totalghgemissions}_{i,t} + \beta 5\mathrm{carbonintensity}_{i,t} + \beta 6\mathrm{fdi}_{i,t} + \epsilon_{i,t}\end{aligned} \quad (1)$$

$$\begin{aligned}\mathrm{ES}_{i,t} = \alpha_{i,t} + \beta 1\mathrm{noofcb}_{i,t} + \beta 2\mathrm{atm}_{i,t} + \beta 3\mathrm{oslaoan}_{i,t} + \beta 4\mathrm{osdeposits}_{i,t} \\ + \beta 5\mathrm{totalghgemissions}_{i,t} + \beta 6\mathrm{carbonintensity}_{i,t} + \beta 7\mathrm{fdi}_{i,t} + \epsilon_{i,t}\end{aligned} \quad (2)$$

Table 7.3. Description of Variables.

Variables	Definition
FI index variables	
noofcb	Number of commercial bank branches (per 100,000 adults)
atm	Automated teller machines (ATMs) (per 100,000 adults)
osloan	Outstanding loans from commercial banks (% of GDP)
osdeposits	Outstanding deposits with commercial banks (% of GDP)
ES index variables	
cleanfuel	Access to clean fuels and technologies for cooking (% of population)
electricity	Access to electricity (% of population)
forestarea	Forest area (% of land area)
Control variables	
totalghgemissions	Total greenhouse gas emissions per capita excluding LULUCF (t CO_2e/capita)
carboninten~10000000	Carbon intensity of GDP (kg CO_2e per constant 2021 US$ of GDP)
FDI	Foreign direct investment, net inflows (% of GDP)

Source: Author's own analysis.

4. Results and Discussion

4.1. Descriptive Statistics

The descriptive statistics reveal the variables involved in the study, shown in Table 7.4. Mean of noofcb is 248.32 with a minimum value of 30 and maximum of 1,058. The average of number of Atm is 77.05 with a standard deviation of 49.90. The mean value of osloan and osdeposits is 55.80 and 64.11, respectively, and the standard deviation is 21.87 and 40.67, respectively. The variables that represent ES are cleanfuel, electricity, and forest area. The mean value for cleanfuel is 78.31 and the minimum value is 31.90 and the maximum value is 99.7. The average of electricity is 93.70 with a standard deviation of 8.02 and a maximum value of 100. Forest area has a mean value of 34.09 with a standard deviation of 17.96. Total GHG emissions have an average of 9.01 with a minimum of 2.124

Table 7.4. Summary Statistics.

Variables	Mean	Stand. Dev.	Min	Max
Noofcb	248.32	269.35	30.00	1,058.00
Atm	77.05	49.90	4.27	185.41
osloan	55.80	21.87	29.11	119.70
osdeposits	64.11	40.63	22.59	158.08
cleanfuel	78.31	20.66	31.90	99.70
electricity	93.70	8.02	74.10	100.00
forestarea	34.09	17.96	14.05	62.15
totalghgemissions	9.01	4.66	2.12	17.39
carboninten~10000000	14.34	4.25	6.85	19.90
FDI	2.25	1.08	0.43	4.50
FI	0.00	1.49	−2.35	3.10
ES	0.00	1.49	−3.04	1.76

Source: Author's own analysis.

and a maximum of 17.39. The average of carbon intensity of GDP is 14.34 with a minimum value of 6.85 and a maximum value of 19.90. FDI depicts a mean value of 2.25 with a minimum value of 0.43 and a maximum of 4.50.

4.2. Regression

Table 7.5 represents the Pooled OLS results for two models, the dependent variable for Model 1 is FI and the dependent variable for Model 2 is ES.

The results for access to cleanfuel in Model 1 depict a negative association with FI. The coefficient is –0.075 significant at 1% level which indicates that increased dependency on clean fuel decreases the FI. Access to electricity indicates a positive impact on FI and significant (0.017) at 5% level of significance. Forest area is negative and significant (−0.074) indicating that an increase in forest area will result in decrease of FI. The results of total GHG emissions show a positive and highly significant coefficient (0.262) which exhibits positive impact of total GHG emissions on FI. Carbon Intensity of GDP has a negative but significant coefficient (−0.388) resulting significant impact on FI. FDI has a positive but insignificant (0.039) relationship with FI. The adjusted R-square value is 0.975, which indicates that 97.5% of the variation in FI is explained by Model 1.

This model checks the reverse causality of the study. Noofcb has a positive and highly significant coefficient (−0.001) suggesting that more banks positively impact ES. The results are consistent with the conclusion drawn by Ozili (2022). Number of atms has a negative and insignificant coefficient (−0.000) indicating that the number of atms has no impact on ES. Both osloan and osdeposits have positive and significant impact on ES at 1% level of significance.

Table 7.5. Pooled OLS Results.

	(1)	(2)
Variables	**FI**	**ES**
noofcb		0.001***
		(0.000)
atm		−0.000
		(0.001)
osloan		−0.034***
		(0.005)
osdeposits		0.009***
		(0.002)
totalghgemissions	0.262***	0.211***
	(0.021)	(0.022)
carbonintensity	−0.388***	−0.284***
	(0.020)	(0.017)
FDI	0.039	0.004
	(0.0362)	(0.041)
cleanfuel	−0.075***	
	(0.004)	
electricity	0.017**	
	(0.007)	
forestarea	−0.074***	
	(0.003)	
Constant	9.922***	3.243***
	(1.030)	(0.409)
R-squared	0.975	0.976

Source: Author's own analysis.

Notes: ***$p < 0.01$; **$p < 0.05$.

Total GHG emissions shows a positive and significant (0.211) which has a high impact on ES. A highly significant negative coefficient (−0.284) is derived for carbon Intensity of GDP indicating that greater carbon intensity strongly reduces ES. FDI has a positive but insignificant (0.004) relationship with FI. The adjusted *R*-squared value is 0.976, which exhibits that 97.6% variations of ES are explained by Model 2.

5. Conclusion

This study explored the connection between ES and FI. In this chapter, the link between FI (in terms of noofcb, Atms, osdeposits, osloan) and several indicators of sustainable development was investigated. The data for the study was extracted from World Bank Database for BRICS countries from 2008 to 2020.

The analysis concluded that FI is negatively impacted by ES. The findings align with Ozturk and Ullah (2022) who found that FI increased economic growth but had a detrimental effect on the quality of environment. The control variable carbon intensity also has a significantly negative association on FI. This suggests that increased FI causes environmental quality to decline in tandem with a rise in the environment's carbon intensity. The robustness of the study also revealed negative interconnection between FI and ES. Environmental quality was negatively impacted by the FI metrics. The analysis can be useful for the policymakers and authorities of the BRICS nations for policy implications. The authorities should make FI policy in consideration of the linkage to environmental quality, carbon emissions, and energy consumption.

The study considered only the BRICS nation which can further consider the extended BRICS countries for future research. Apart from the unavailability of data, similar research can be conducted by future researchers for other developing nations like SAARC, ASEAN, OBRI, etc.

References

Ahmad, M., Ahmed, Z., Bai, Y., Qiao, G., Popp, J., & Olah, J. (2022). FI, technological innovations, and environmental quality: Analyzing the role of green openness. *Frontiers in Environmental Science*, *10*, 851263.

Alam, M., Akhtar, S., & Bettencourt, A. (2024). Introduction to fintech in industry 5.0: Companion or antagonist. In *The adoption of fintech* (pp. 1–16). Productivity Press. https://www.taylorfrancis.com/chapters/edit/10.4324/9781032644165-1/introduction-fintech-industry-5-0-companion-antagonist-mahfooz-alam-shakeb-akhtar-alberto-bettencourt

Aziz, F., Sheikh, S. M., & Shah, I. H. (2022). FI for women empowerment in South Asian countries. *Journal of Financial Regulation and Compliance*, *30*(4), 489–502.

Bartholomew, D. J. (2010). Principal components analysis. In *International Encyclopaedia of Education* (3rd ed., pp. 374–377). Elsevier. https://doi.org/10.1016/B978-0-08-044894-7.01358-0.

Baulch, B., Do, T. D., & Le, T. H. (2018). Constraints to the uptake of solar home systems in Ho chi Minh city and some proposals for improvement. *Renewable Energy*, *118*, 245–256.

Cao, L. (2023). How green finance reduces CO_2 emissions for green economic recovery: Empirical evidence from E7 economies. *Environmental Science and Pollution Research*, *30*(2), 3307–3320.

Chibba, M. (2009). FI, poverty reduction and the millennium development goals. *The European Journal of Development Research*, *21*, 213–230.

Churchill, S. A., & Marisetty, V. B. (2019). FI and poverty: A tale of forty-five thousand households. *Applied Economics*, *52*(16), 1777–1788. https://doi.org/10.1080/00036846.2019.1678732

Dabla-Norris, E., Ji, Y., Townsend, R. M., & Unsal, D. F. (2021), Distinguishing constraints on FI and their impact on GDP, TFP, and the distribution of income. *Journal of Monetary Economics*, *117*, 1–18.

Du, Q., Wu, N., Zhang, F., Lei, Y., & Saeed, A. (2022). Impact of FI and human capital on environmental quality: Evidence from emerging economies. *Environmental Science and Pollution Research*, *29*(22), 33033–33045. https://doi.org/10.1007/s11356-021-17945-x

Fareed, Z., Rehman, M. A., Adebayo, T., S., Wang, Y., Ahmad, M., & Shahzad, F. (2022). FI and the environmental deterioration in Eurozone: The moderating role of innovation activity. *Technology in Society*, *69*(2), 101961.

Feingold, S. (2024). BRICS: Here's what to know about the international bloc. In *World economic forum*. https://www.weforum.org/stories/2024/11/brics-summit-geopolitics-bloc-international/

Goodland, R. (1995). The concept of ES. *Annual Review of Ecology and Systematics*, *26*, 1–24. http://www.jstor.org/stable/2097196

Hasanov, F. J., Liddle, B., & Mikayilov, J. I. (2018). The impact of international trade on CO_2 emissions in oil exporting countries: Territory vs consumption emissions accounting. *Energy Economics*, *74*, 343–350. https://doi.org/10.1016/j.eneco.2018.06.004

IPA. (2017). *Climate change and FI*. www.poverty-action.org/sites/default/files/publications/Climate-Change-FinancialInclusion_Final.pdf

Jafar, S. H., Hemachandran, K., Akhtar, S., Khan, P. A., & El-Chaarani, H. (Eds.). (2024). *The adoption of fintech: Using technology for better security, speed, and customer experience in finance*. CRC Press.

Jafar, S. H., Rodriguez, R. V., Kannan, H., Akhtar, S., & Plugmann, P. (Eds.). (2024). *Harnessing blockchain-digital twin fusion for sustainable investments*. IGI Global.

Ji, X., Zhang, Y., Mirza, N., Umar, M., & Rizvi, S. K. A. (2021). The impact of carbon neutrality on the investment performance: Evidence from the equity mutual funds in BRICS. *Journal of Environmental Management*, *297*, 113228. https://doi.org/10.1016/j.jenvman.2021.113228

Keeble, B. R. (1988). The Brundtland report: 'Our common future.' *Medicine and War*, *4*(1), 17–25. https://doi.org/10.1080/07488008808408783

Khan, P. A., Johl, S. K., & Akhtar, S. (2021). Firm sustainable development goals and firm financial performance through the lens of green innovation practices and reporting: A proactive approach. *Journal of Risk and Financial Management*, *14*(12), 605.

Khan, P. A., Johl, S. K., & Akhtar, S. (2022). Vinculum of sustainable development goal practices and firms' financial performance: A moderation role of green innovation. *Journal of Risk and Financial Management*, *15*(3), 96.

Khan, S., Peng, Z., & Li, Y. (2019). Energy consumption, environmental degradation, economic growth and financial development in globe: Dynamic simultaneous equations panel analysis. *Energy Reports*, *5*, 1089–1102. https://doi.org/10.1016/j.egyr.2019.08.004

Khandare, V. B. (2019). FI: Empirical study of BRICS countries. *International Journal of Social Science and Economic Research*, *4*(5), 3319–3334.

Koomson, I., Villano, R. A. & Hadley, D. (2020). Effect of FI on poverty and vulnerability to poverty: Evidence using a multidimensional measure of FI. *Social Indicators Research*, *149*, 613–639. https://doi.org/10.1007/s11205-019-02263-0

Le, T. H., & Le, H-C., & Taghizadeh-Hesary, F. (2020). Does FI impact CO2 emissions? Evidence from Asia. *Finance Research Letters, Elsevier*, *34*(C). https://doi.org/10.1016/j.frl.2020.101451

Le, T. H., & Quah, E. (2018). Income level and the emissions, energy, and growth nexus: evidence from Asia and the pacific. *International Economics*, *156*, 193–205.

Mukalayi, N. M., & Inglesi-Lotz, R. (2023). Digital FI and energy and environment: Global positioning of Sub-Saharan African countries. *Renewable and Sustainable Energy Reviews*, *173*, 113069.

Naseema, N., Akhtar, S., & Al Hinai, A. A. (2024). Disrupting financial services: A case study on Capital One's Fintech Odyssey. In *Harnessing blockchain-digital twin fusion for sustainable investments* (pp. 363–383). IGI Global. https://doi.org/10.4018/979-8-3693-1878-2.ch015

Nasir, M. A., Huynh, T. L. D., & Tram, H. T. X. (2019). Role of financial development, economic growth and foreign direct investment in driving climate change: A case of emerging ASEAN. *Journal of Environmental Management*, *242*, 131–141. https://doi.org/10.1016/j.jenvman.2019.03.112

Omar, M. A., & Inaba, K. (2020). Does FI reduce poverty and income inequality in developing countries? A panel data analysis. *Economic Structures*, *9*, 37. https://doi.org/10.1186/s40008-020-00214-4

Ozili, P. K. (2022). Financial inclusion and sustainable development: an empirical association. *Journal of Money and Business*, *2*(2), 186–198. https://doi.org/10.1108/JMB-03-2022-0019

Ozturk, I., & Ullah, S. (2022). Does digital FI matter for economic growth and ES in OBRI economies? An empirical analysis. *Resources, Conservation and Recycling*, *185*, 106489.

Razzaq, A., Wang, Y., Chupradit, S., Suksatan, W., & Shahzad, F. (2021). Asymmetric interlinkages between green technology innovation and consumption-based carbon emissions in BRICS countries using quantile-on-quantile framework. *Technology in Society*, *66*, 101656. https://doi.org/10.1016/j.techsoc.2021.101656

Rehman, A. U., Malik, A. H., Md Isa, A. H. b., & Jais, M. b. (2023). Dynamic impact of FI and industrialization on ES. *Social Responsibility Journal*, *19*(5), 906–929. https://doi.org/10.1108/SRJ-07-2021-0275

Shoaib, H. M., Rafique, M. Z., Nadeem, A. M., & Huang, S. (2020). Impact of financial development on CO_2 emissions: A comparative analysis of developing countries (D8) and developed countries (G 8). *Environmental Science and Pollution Research*, *27*(12461–12475), 1–15. https://doi.org/10.1007/s11356-019-06680-z

Sitorus, R. R. (2018). Does e-commerce effect on total tax paid through taxpayer's compliance? *Journal of Accounting, Business and Finance Research*, *4*(2), 40–48

Sujhalana, P, & Kiran, C. (2018). A study on status of FI in India. *International Journal of Management Studies*, *2*(3), 96–104. http://dx.doi.org/10.18843/ijms/v5i2(3)/12

United Nations. (2015). *Paris agreement*. https://www.un.org/en/climatechange/paris-agreement

Van, L. T. H., Vo, A. T., Nguyen, N. T., & Vo, D. H. (2019). FI and economic GROWTH: An international evidence. *Emerging Markets Finance and Trade*, *57*(1), 239–263. https://doi.org/10.1080/1540496X.2019.1697672

Voica. (2017). Financial inclusion as a tool for sustainable development. *Romanian Journal of Economics, Institute of National Economy*, *44*(1(53), 121–129.

Wan, J., Pu, Z., & Tavera, C. (2023). The impact of digital finance on pollutants emission: Evidence from Chinese cities. *Environmental Science and Pollution Research*, *30*(15), 42923–42942. https://doi.org/10.1007/s11356-021-18465-4

Wang, L., Wang, Y., Sun, Y., Han, K., & Chen, Y. (2022). FI and green economic efficiency: Evidence from China. *Journal of Environmental Planning and Management*, *65*(2), 240–271.

Wilson, D., & Purushothaman, R. (2003). Dreaming with BRICs: The path to 2050. *Goldman Sachs Global Economics Paper*, *99*, 1–24

World Bank. (2022). *World Bank overview on FI*. https://www.worldbank.org/en/topic/financialinclusion/overview

Xu, F., Zhang, X., & Zhou, D. (2024). Does digital FI reduce the risk of returning to poverty? Evidence from China. *International Journal of Finance & Economics*, *29*(3), 2927–2949.

Yu, M., Jin, H., Zhang, H., & Chong, A. Y. L. (2023). ICT, financial development and renewable energy consumption. *Journal of Computer Information Systems*, *63*(1), 190–203.

Zaidi, S. A. H., Hussain, M., & Zaman, Q. U. (2021). Dynamic linkages between FI and carbon emissions: Evidence from selected OECD countries. *Resources, Environment and Sustainability*, *4*, 100022.

Zhang, Y. J., Peng, Y. L., Ma, C. Q., & Shen, B. (2017). Can environmental innovation facilitate carbon emissions reduction? Evidence from China. *Energy Policy*, *100*, 18–28. https://doi.org/10.1016/j.enpol.2016.10.005

Zhang, C., Zhai, H., Cao, L., Li, X., Cheng, F., Peng, L., ... & Wang, X. (2022). Understanding the complexity of existing fossil fuel power plant decarbonization. *Iscience*, *25*(8). https://doi.org/10.1016/j.isci.2022.104758

Chapter 8

Riding the Waves of Uncertainty: Unveiling the Interaction Among Global Uncertainties and Sustainable Stocks in India Through Wavelet Coherence and TVP-VAR

Neenu Chalissery[a], *Rufsha Melath*[a] *and Tanveer Bagh*[b, c]

[a]*Assistant Professor, Department of Commerce and Professional Studies, Rajagiri College of Social Science, Kochi, Kerala, India*
[b]*Research Department of Commerce, Farook College (Autonomous) Kozhikode, University of Calicut, Kerala, India*
[c]*Department of Finance, School of Economics and Wang Yanan Institute for Studies in Economics, Xiamen University, China*

Abstract

Green investment is essential for advancing sustainable economic growth, reducing climate risks, and facilitating the transition to low-carbon economies. Nonetheless, uncertainties, including economic instability, climate risk, and geopolitical conflicts, may influence asset prices and the general appeal of sustainable investments. This chapter looks at how different global uncertainties, like changes in economic policies, oil prices, and climate policies, affect the performance of sustainable stock investments in the Indian stock market, using wavelet coherence and time-varying parameter vector autoregression (TVP-VAR) methodologies, from January 2013 to July 2024. Among the uncertainty indicators, we find that oil price uncertainty (OPU) significantly influences the returns of green stocks, exhibiting a moderate relationship with both economic and climate shocks. Further, climate policy uncertainty (CPU) emerges as the primary contributor of risk to sustainable indices, highlighting the vulnerability of green investments to energy market variations. Thus, investors should consider the effects of climate and oil price shocks, along with economic policy changes

Climate Risk and Emerging Markets: Valuation, Volatility, and Portfolio Strategies, 117–132

Published under exclusive licence by Emerald Publishing Limited
doi:10.1108/978-1-83708-088-520261023

while investing in sustainable stocks. Policymakers need to develop more transparent and uniform regulatory frameworks to mitigate uncertainty and enhance the resilience of green investments in India.

Keywords: Climate policy uncertainty; oil price uncertainty; economic policy uncertainty; sustainable stock indices; wavelet coherence; TVP-VAR

1. Introduction

The past two years have been marked by exceedingly high levels of uncertainty globally. This elevated market uncertainty induces heightened risk aversion among investors, thereby driving the pursuit of alternate portfolio strategies to mitigate losses. Investors are transitioning to green investments by constructing portfolios that include environmentally sustainable enterprises. Such companies are increasing in prominence as they manufacture and endorse eco-friendly products and services (Dutta et al., 2020). The primary root causes have been recognised in the literature as essential for enhancing the acceptance of sustainability (Jafar, Hemachandran, et al., 2024; Khan et al., 2021; Shang et al., 2022), including the ongoing climate change crisis, technological advancements, and fluctuations in oil prices (Awosusi et al., 2022). Climate change is ascribed with regard to greenhouse gas (GHG) emissions, with fossil fuels and conventional energy sources accounting for approximately three-fourths of global CO_2 emissions (Piris-Cabezas et al., 2023). Reducing the global carbon footprint is considered the sole solution to this issue (Shang et al., 2022). Oil is a crucial raw commodity that facilitates industrialisation, although it also raises worries regarding environmental difficulties (Chen et al., 2015; Jia et al., 2021). This is because when the oil market goes down, investors who care about the environment will have fewer reasons to invest, which could cause the prices of environmental assets to go down. Conversely, when oil costs rise, incentives increase, resulting in the appreciation of equity prices for environmentally friendly companies (Dutta et al., 2020). A different but similar important type of uncertainty arises from alterations in economic fundamentals and policies, prospective economic development, and geopolitical shifts (Baker et al., 2016). The EPU index quantifies the degree to which internal and external political, social, legal, and financial disruptions impact policy uncertainty (Alam et al., 2024; Gartia et al., 2024; Jafar, Rodriguez, et al., 2024). These kinds of uncertainties might undermine the economic feasibility of a green portfolio; substantial adverse fluctuations would diminish the incentives for green investments (Kanamura, 2020).

At this outset, this study examines the dynamic return co-movement and risk spillover among CPU, economic policy uncertainty (EPU), OPU, and green stocks, represented by BSE GREENEX and BSE CARBONEX, while also incorporating conventional stocks, such as the BSE Oil and Gas index. Employing wavelet coherence and TVP-VAR methods, we unveil the dynamic nature of the connection between uncertainty indicators and green stocks. By doing so, we address the following key questions:

> *Q1*. How do uncertainties stemming from climate policy, economic policy, and oil price influence the returns on green investments in the Indian stock market?
>
> *Q2*. To what extent do oil price shocks, climate, and economic policy uncertainties contribute to the volatility of green investment in the Indian stock market?
>
> *Q3*. Do green stocks exhibit a different response compared to conventional stocks in relation to policy and energy uncertainties?

By answering these questions, the study advances the scholarly discussion on green investment as outlined. Firstly, considering the importance of uncertainties around oil prices, climate, and economic policies, our study develops a dynamic model of uncertainty and sustainable investment. Second, our study takes into account the Indian stock market, which is an emerging economy that prioritises sustainable investments. The Indian government has set goals to achieve carbon neutrality by 2070, reduce the country's projected total carbon emissions by 1 billion metric tons by 2030, and increase installed capacity for clean energy to 500 GW by the same year. It has also set goals to reduce the country's economic carbon intensity by less than 45%. Lastly, with the application of wavelet coherence and TVP-VAR, we uncover the temporal and spatial relationship among uncertainties and green stocks.

Our findings underscore the role of global uncertainties, particularly CPU, in estimating the risk of sustainable stocks in India. The study finds negligible co-movement between global uncertainties and the return of renewable and non-renewable stocks (except in the case of OPU, where it has strong low-frequency co-movement). Furthermore, uncertainty surrounding oil prices, climate, and economic policies significantly influences the volatility of green stocks. These findings offer valuable insights to policymakers to enhance climate risk management, formulate appropriate policies on climate action and economic regulations, and minimise the impact of fluctuations on these uncertainties. Further, by defining the risk transmission paths, it will help investors to mitigate the effect of uncertainty.

The subsequent section covers the theory and literature in pertinent study domains. Section 3 outlines the data and empirical procedures employed. Section 4 highlights the empirical findings and their discussions, while the last section concludes the study with implications.

2. Literature Background

Incorporating environmental, social, and governance factors in the asset allocation and decision-making (Avramov et al., 2022; Khan et al., 2022), sustainable investing has grown rapidly on the global financial market over the past few decades. This growth has led to an increasing interest from corporations and investors in incorporating sustainable aspects into their investment (Urom & Ndubuisi, 2023). Sustainable investment is crucial for promoting long-term economic and environmental resilience, although it frequently encounters uncertainties arising from changing regulations, market dynamics, and the unforeseen effects of climate change. For instance, Nittayakamolphun et al. (2024) look at how EPU, India Implied Volatility Index (VIX), and geopolitical risk affect green equities across seven emerging markets. They find a positive interplay between EPU and sustainable stock return in Thailand. Similarly, Youssef et al. (2021) investigate the dynamic association between stock indices and EPU using a time-varying VAR connectedness approach. With the exception of Italy, they identify European markets that transmit more spillovers than they receive. Further, Li et al. (2023) discovered that ambiguity about policy has a detrimental effect on sustainable investment in US companies, and uncertainty around presidential elections has a detrimental effect on sustainable return. Additionally, Rehman et al. (2023) used the quantile VAR to look at the relationship between global uncertainties and the top seven global renewable energy indices. They found a strong link among the uncertainty indices and green energy. Using a TVP-QVAR-DY paradigm, Du and Xu (2024) find that rising EPU and geopolitical turbulence raise market volatility in energy. Jiang et al. (2024) also utilised the Diebold and Yilmaz models to analyse volatility spillovers among EPU, energy, and carbon markets.

The magnitude of research on carbon prices has been growing dramatically in the last few decades, particularly concerning carbon risk, sustainable finance, and investment, driven by a worldwide push against climate change (Ha et al., 2024). Researchers have shown that climate change risks and uncertainties might impact different aspects of the global economy (Shang et al., 2022). Huang et al. (2023) proposed that the GHG emissions are greatly impacted by EPU, gross domestic product (GDP) per capita, and foreign direct investment, all of which contribute to climate change. Addressing climate change requires green assets, which include climate risk reduction, sustainable development, and public health enhancement. Due to the increasing significance of responsible investments supporting the targets for mitigating climate change (Iqbal et al., 2022), empirical research on sustainable bonds and the connection between carbon prices and stocks and commodities of sustainable and conventional energy has emerged as a key area of study in finance (Alam & Akhtar, 2024; Bajo & Rodríguez, 2023; Gabriel & Pinho, 2024; Pinto-Gutiérrez, 2024).

Emerging economies prioritise sustainable economic growth by reconciling industrial development with environmental conservation and promoting innovations in green technologies. India's focus on sustainable development and finance underscores its dedication to an environmentally sustainable future; yet, few studies have examined the complex interplay between economic uncertainty, climate issues, and sustainable investment within the Indian context. For instance, Dutta, Kanjilal, et al. (2023) investigate how oil price volatility spikes affect the realised variability of clean and dirty stocks in India. They discovered that dirty and green equities respond to changes in crude oil volatility in a similar way, suggesting that these assets are interchangeable. Ayad et al. (2023) investigate the connection among CO_2 emissions, energy consumption, GDP per capita, population clustering, and the globalisation and global uncertainty indices using a variety of cointegration techniques. They discover that while globalisation lowers long-term environmental degradation by encouraging green technologies and international cooperation, uncertainty worsens it by preventing sustainable actions. Dutta et al. (2021) also look into whether information in commodity market implied volatility indexes can be used to guess how volatile the stocks of Indian green businesses will be using a generalized autoregressive conditional heteroskedasticity (GARCH)-based quantile regression model. They end up with the fact that, during moments of significant uncertainty, the energy and precious metals markets are more likely to cause volatility in green stocks.

Even though the above-mentioned studies provide valuable insight into the literature, they lack conclusive evidence on the relation between different forms of uncertainties (economic, climate, and energy) and sustainable investment. Moreover, only a few studies focused on the Indian stock market. In this background, this study looks into the dynamic co-movement and volatility spillover among Climate Policy Uncertainty (CPU), EPU, OPU, and green stock investments (BSE GREENEX, BSE CARBONEX) in India, utilising advanced methodologies, namely wavelet and TVP-VAR.

3. Data and Methodology

3.1. Data

The study utilises a monthly dataset of CPU, OPU, EPU, and stock price data of green indices (BSE GREENEX and BSE CARBONEX) and conventional indices (BSE Sensex, BSE 100, and BSE Oil and Gas) from January 2013 to July 2024. We sourced the data of uncertainties around oil price, climate, and economic policy from https://www.policyuncertainty.com/. The stock price data is collected from the BSE website https://www.bseindia.com/. The stock returns are calculated as the change in the logarithm percentage of stock prices, represented as:

$$rt = \ln\left(\frac{P_t}{P_{t-1}}\right) \times 100 \tag{1}$$

The GARCH process is applied to estimate the volatility of stock indices. The univariate GARCH (1,1) process are as follows:

$$h_{i,t}^2 = \omega + \alpha\varepsilon_{i,t-1}^2 + \beta h_{i,t-1}^2 \tag{2}$$

The summary statistics indicate that uncertainty indices have the highest average, while BSE Sensex has the lowest average daily return. The standard deviation was relatively higher for BSE oil and gas, indicating higher variability in return compared to green stocks. The skewness is negative for all stock indices, whereas uncertainty indices report a positive skewness. This implies a low central tendency and asymmetric features in the variables. For all the time series returns, excess kurtosis is excessively elevated, signifying peakedness and heavy tails. Furthermore, the results of the JB test show that most time series do not follow a normal distribution. The negative values of the ERS unit root suggest potential stationarity.

3.2. Methodology

3.2.1. Wavelet Coherence

The study employs the wavelet coherence to analyse the dynamic relation between uncertainty indices and return of stocks indices. A specific characteristic of wavelet analysis is its ability to divide a data into more fundamental functions that capture temporal and frequency information about the series (Yang et al., 2016).

In accordance with the methodology established by Torrence and Compo (1998), the cross wavelet transformation (CWT) of two series $x(t)$ and $y(t)$ is determined utilising their respective CWT, $W_n^x(u,s)$ and $W_n^y(u,s)$ as follows:

$$W_{xy}(u,s) = W_x(u,s)W_y^*(u,s) \tag{3}$$

where "u" indicates to the location and "s" to the scale. The * represents the complex conjugate. The CWT identifies regions in the temporal and frequency domain where time series have significant shared power.

Following the methodology of Torrence and Webster (1999), the wavelet coherence between uncertainty indices and stock return can be represented as:

$$R^2(u,s) = \frac{\left|S\left(s^{-1}W_{x,y}(u,s)\right)\right|^2}{S\left(s^{-1}\left|W_x(u,s)\right|^2\right)S\left(s^{-1}\left|W_y(u,s)\right|^2\right)} \tag{4}$$

where s is the smoothing operator (Rua & Nunes, 2009). The term $R^2(u, s)$ is the wavelet squared coherence (ranges from 0 to 1), where a greater value indicates a stronger connection.

Furthermore, the graphical representation of wavelet-squared coherence can elucidate the causal linkages between the series, which can be defined as:

$$\Phi_{xy}(u,s) = \tan^{-1}\left(\frac{\operatorname{Im}\left\{S\left(s^{-1}W^{xy}(u,s)\right)\right\}}{\operatorname{Re}\left\{S\left(s^{-1}W^{xy}(u,s)\right)\right\}}\right) \tag{5}$$

where the phases are denoted by black arrows. A phase difference of 0 represents that the time series are moving in tandem. Arrows directed to the right (left) signify series that are in-phase (out of phase) or exhibit positive (negative) correlation.

3.2.2. Time-Varying Parameter VAR

To analyse the spillover among uncertainty measures and volatility of green and dirty stocks, we utilised the TVP-VAR connectivity methodology by Antonakakis et al. (2020). The TVP-VAR (1) in accordance with the BIC is as follows:

$$v_t = \phi_t v_{t-1} + \varepsilon_t \varepsilon_t \sim N(0, F_t) \tag{6}$$

$$\text{vec}(\phi_t) = \text{vec}(\phi_{t-1}) + \varepsilon_t \varepsilon_t \sim N(0, G_t) \tag{7}$$

In this case, the $N\times1$ dimensional vectors v_t, v_{t-1}, and εt, respectively, indicate all risk series in (t, t–1) and the corresponding error term. The $N\times N$ dimensional matrices ϕ_t and F_t, vec(ϕ_t) respect the TVP-VAR coefficients and the time-varying variance–covariance, whereas G_t is a $N^2 \times N^2$ dimensional matrix and εt and vec(ϕ_t) are $N^2 \times 1$ dimensional vectors.

We need to employ the following equality to identify the vectoral moving-average process of the estimated model:

$$v_t = \sum_{i=1}^{p} \phi_t v_{t-1} + \varepsilon_t = \sum_{j=0}^{\infty} \Delta_{jt} \varepsilon_{i-j} \tag{8}$$

This is also applicable for the unscaled generalised forecast error variance decomposition (GFEVD):

$$\theta_{ij,t}^{g}(H) = \frac{F_{ij,t}^{-1} \sum_{t-1}^{H-1} (e_i' \Delta_t F_t e_j) 2}{\sum_{j=1}^{k} \sum_{t=1}^{H-1} (e_i \Delta_t F_t \Delta_t' e_i)} \tag{9}$$

In this instance, H stands for the prediction horizon, while e_i is a vector that has 1 on the ith element and 0 otherwise. To guarantee that each row's sum equals one. The scaled GFEVD $\left(\theta_{ij,t}^{-g}(H)\right)$ is computed.

$$\theta_{ij,t}^{-g}(H) = \frac{\theta_{ij,t}^{g}(H)}{\sum_{j=1}^{N} \theta_{ij,t}^{g}(H)} \tag{10}$$

where $\sum_{j=1}^{k} \theta_{ij,t}^{g}(H) = 1$, $\sum_{j=1}^{k} \theta_{ij,t}^{-g}(H) = k, \theta_{ij,t}^{-g}(H)$ signify the degree of pairwise directional connectivity.

In accordance with Diebold and Yılmaz (2014), we used GFEVD to calculate the different connectivity measures:

The Total Connectedness Index (TCI_t):

$$\text{TCI}_t = \frac{\sum_{i,j=1(i\neq j)}^{N} \theta_{ij,t}^{-g}(H)}{\sum_{i,j=1}^{N} \theta_{ij,t}^{-g}(H)} \tag{11}$$

The total directional connectedness of market i to all the other markets 'TO':

$$C_{\blacksquare \leftarrow i,t}(H) = \frac{\sum_{j=1(j\neq i)}^{N} \theta_{ji,t}^{-g}(H)}{\sum_{i,j=1}^{N} \theta_{ji,t}^{-g}(H)} \times 100 \tag{12}$$

The total directional connectedness of all markets to market i 'FROM':

$$C_{i \leftarrow \blacksquare,t}(H) = \frac{\sum_{j=1(i\neq j)}^{N} \theta_{ji,t}^{-g}(H)}{\sum_{i,j=1}^{N} \theta_{ij,t}^{-g}(H)} \times 100 \tag{13}$$

The net direction connectedness 'NET':

$$C_{i,t}(H) = C_{\blacksquare \leftarrow i,t}(H) - C_{i \leftarrow \blacksquare,t}(H) \tag{14}$$

4. Empirical Results and Discussions

4.1. Wavelet Coherence Analysis of Return Co-Movement

In the preliminary part of our analysis, we investigate the wavelet coherence between uncertainty measures and the return of both green and conventional stocks. The wavelet coherence map in Fig. 8.1 demonstrates the relation between CPU, OPU, EPU, and the return of green stocks. This indicates that variations in economic and CPU exert negligible direct influence on the returns of green stocks. In contrast, the findings underscore a notable and robust connection among OPU and green stock return at low-frequency bands. This observation indicates that the performance of green equities, including those in the BSE GREENEX and BSE CARBONEX indices, is affected by long-term fluctuations in OPU. This relationship highlights the susceptibility of green investments to energy market fluctuations, especially oil prices, which significantly influence the cost and competitiveness of renewable energy technologies and alternative investments. Upon examining the co-movement between policy uncertainties and investments in traditional or polluting stocks, a comparable trend emerges. The correlation between dirty stock indices and uncertainty pertaining to CPU, EPU, and OPU reflects the results observed for green stocks. This suggests that the reactions of dirty and conventional equities to policy uncertainty are similar to those of green stocks.

4.2. Static Volatility Connectedness

We use the TVP-VAR-based connectedness method to figure out how volatility (risk) of green and conventional stocks is affected by uncertainties. Table 8.1 shows a TCI of 50.40%, which suggests that, on average, the overall connectivity among uncertainty indicators and volatility of stocks is moderate over the research period. The BSE CARBONEX and BSE 100 experienced the most risk spillovers from the system, with respective percentages of 74.37 and 74.25, followed by BSE GREENEX (73.25%), BSE Sensex (70.52%), and BSE Oil and Gas (70.51%). It was found that BSE 100 (78.38%) and BSE CARBONEX (78.17%) are the two biggest risk spillovers to the system. BSE GREENEX (64.97%) and BSE Sensex (51.13%) are very close behind. All uncertainty indices are the net transmitter of risk, with the highest risk transmission from CPU (25.95%), followed by EPU (19.22%) and OPU (10.09%). On the contrary, BSE GREENEX, BSE Sensex, and BSE Oil and Gas are net absorbers of static risk spillover. Further, the BSE CARBONEX also functioned as the transmitter of risk with 3.80%. This indicates that, compared to BSE GREENEX, the BSE CARBONEX is least vulnerable to uncertainty.

Analysing the dynamic nature of connectedness, we observed a significant fluctuation in the total connectedness among uncertainties and risk associated with

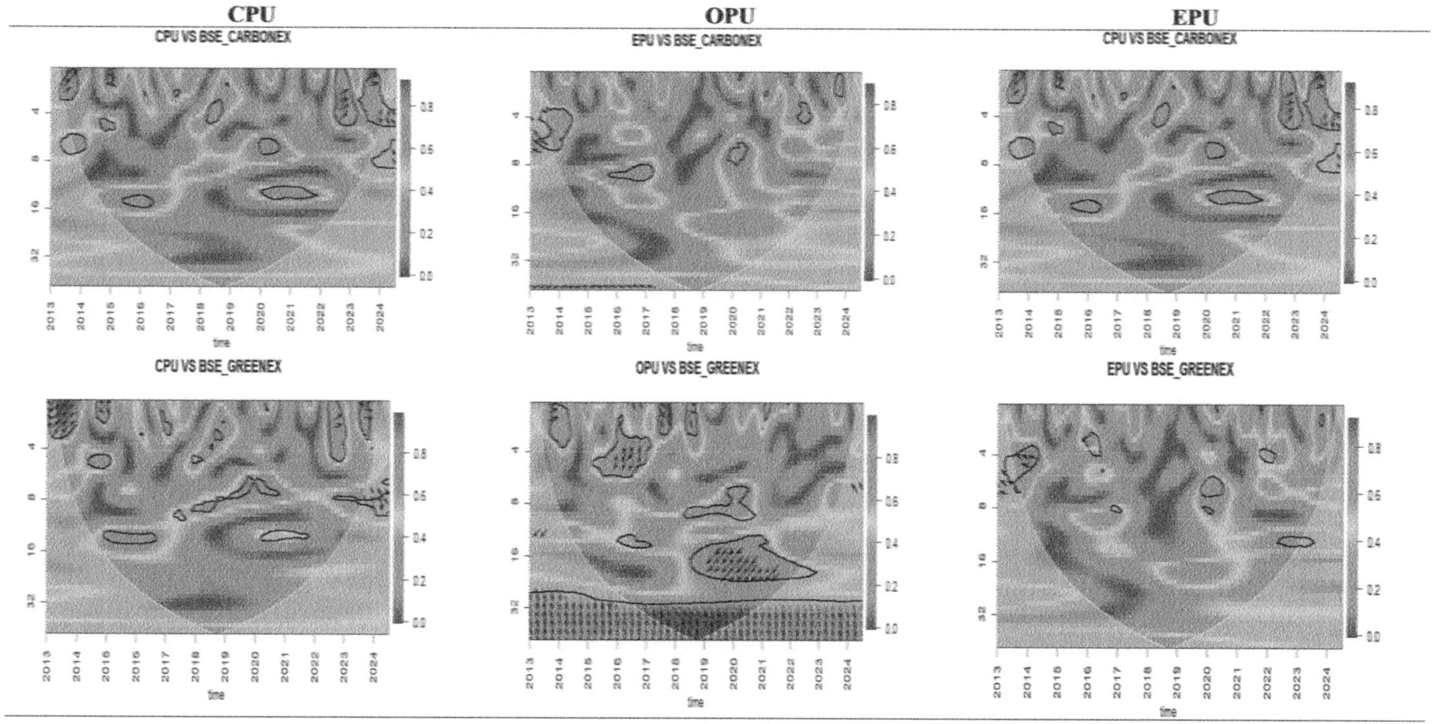

Fig. 8.1. Wavelet Coherence Analysis of Co-movement Between Policy Uncertainty and Return of Sustainable Stocks, BSE Sensex, BSE 100, and BSE Oil and Gas. *Source*: Authors' calculation.

(*Continued*)

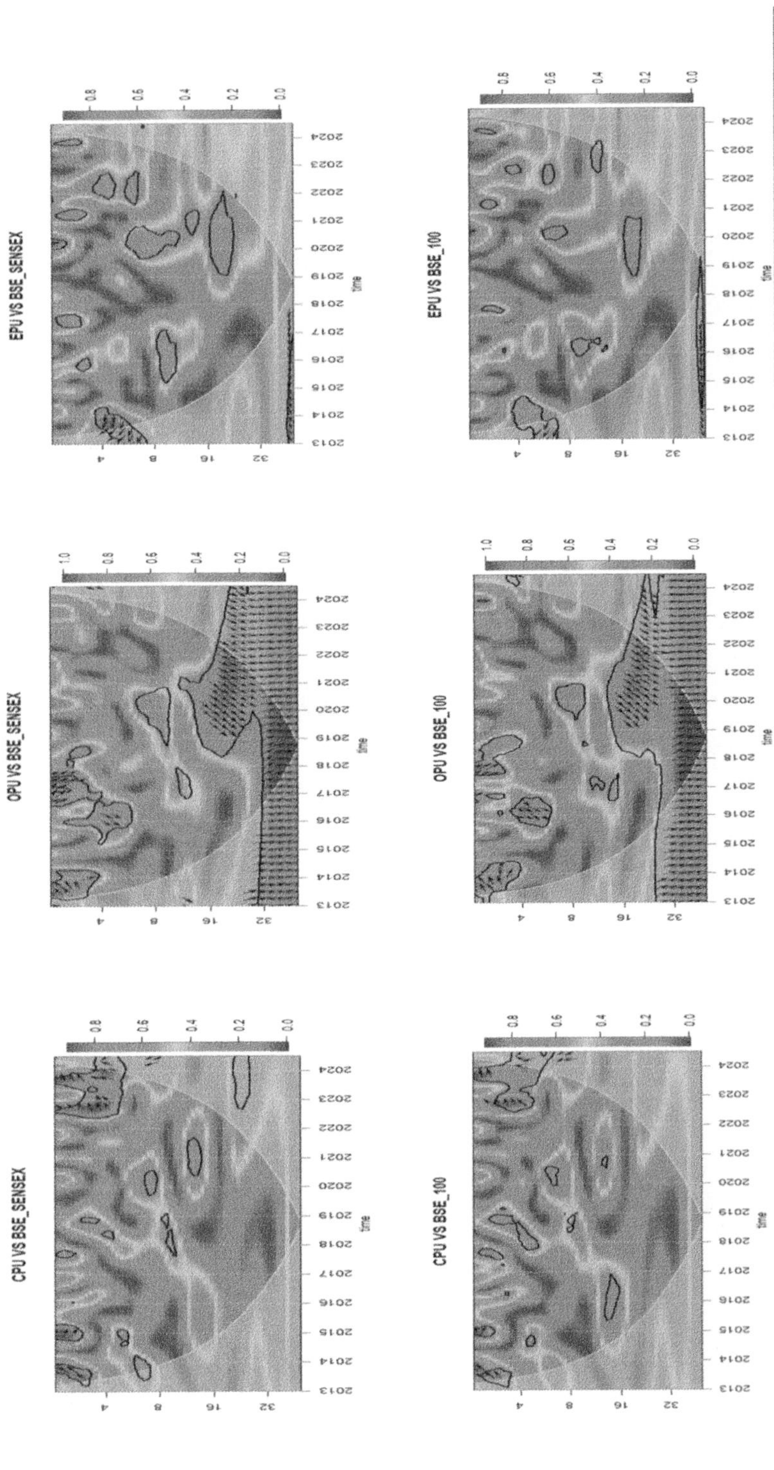
EPU VS BSE_SENSEX
OPU VS BSE_SENSEX
CPU VS BSE_SENSEX
EPU VS BSE_100
OPU VS BSE_100
CPU VS BSE_100

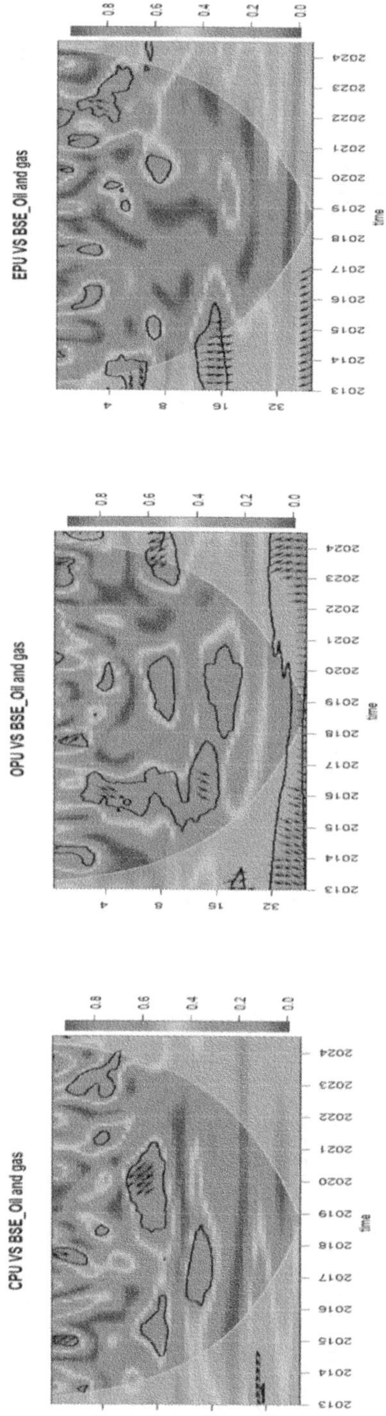

Fig. 8.1. *(Continued)*

Table 8.1. Static Connectedness Among Policy Uncertainty and Volatility of Stock Indices.

	CPU	EPU	OPU	BSE CARBONEX	BSE GREENEX	BSE Sensex	BSE 100	BSE Oil & Gas	FROM
CPU	89.86	5.02	4.67	0.06	0.07	0.17	0.08	0.06	10.14
EPU	4.45	78.79	7.01	1.84	1.79	2.63	2.01	1.47	21.21
OPU	5.06	2.96	91.06	0.15	0.09	0.28	0.27	0.11	8.94
BSE CARBONEX	0.77	1.26	0.59	25.63	20.48	15.88	25.03	10.37	74.37
BSE GREENEX	7.85	2.20	0.70	21.16	26.75	10.62	20.33	10.39	73.25
BSE Sensex	12.29	4.71	0.83	18.00	11.29	29.48	20.12	3.29	70.52
BSE 100	0.52	1.18	0.61	25.14	19.79	17.73	25.75	9.30	74.25
BSE OG	5.15	23.10	4.61	11.82	11.48	3.83	10.52	29.49	70.51
TO	36.09	40.42	19.02	78.17	64.97	51.13	78.38	34.98	403.18
Inc.Own	125.95	119.22	110.09	103.80	91.73	80.61	104.13	64.48	TCI
NET	25.95	19.22	10.09	3.80	−8.27	−19.39	4.13	−35.52	50.40

Source: Authors' calculation.

Note: The table depicts the results of TVP-VAR of the static connectedness among the uncertainty indices, green and conventional stocks with a lag length of order of 1 (BIC) and a 10-step ahead forecast, window size is 100.

green stocks. The total connectedness reached its peak during the initial years, after which it began to diminish. Further, there is a short break in connectedness in 2020; it may be due to the outbreak of COVID-19. But immediately, the overall connectedness rose dramatically. Throughout the sample period, BSE Sensex and BSE Oil and Gas were primarily net recipients of spillovers. It should be noted that the net receipt by these conventional stocks was at its peak during 2020. However, the magnitude of the receipt decreases thereafter. The green stocks also functioned as shock receivers, but the behaviour of BSE CARBONEX and BSE GREENEX was different. On the contrary, BSE CARBONEX shifted its position from net receiver to transmitter, notably after 2020. Moreover, the transmission patterns of the CPU and EPU are nearly identical. Their contribution to shock is prominent until 2020. After 2020, the shock transmission's magnitude decreases while the transmitter's position remains unchanged. In the case of OPU, the transmission of shock is almost in the same magnitude throughout the period.

5. Discussion

The study's result demonstrates that there is strong spillover of oil price shock to the return of green stocks in India. However, EPU and CPU demonstrate no impact on the return of green stocks. This is consistent with finding of Rehman et al. (2023), who state that the return of the renewable energy sector is least affected by CPU. This may be due to the fact that these investments are directly connected with the long-term global transition towards sustainability and regulatory frameworks that promote green energy and technologies. In contradiction, Dutta, Bouri, et al. (2023) provide evidence that the returns of green energy investments are positively impacted by climate risk, but their volatility is negatively impacted. Conversely, the returns on green equities are sensitive to oil price volatility, as variations in oil prices can directly influence the competitiveness of renewable energy and green technologies. Low oil prices enhance the cost-competitiveness of fossil fuels, potentially diminishing the demand for renewable energy alternatives. In contrast, elevated oil costs enhance the appeal of renewable alternatives, fostering increased interest and investment in green equities. Further, we find moderate connectedness among uncertainties and green stocks. This supports the findings of Wang et al. (2023), who indicate that oil price volatility beneficially influences green investment. Further, it is observed that BSE CARBONEX was the primary net transmitter of shocks, which is corroborated by Attarzadeh et al. (2024). This increased significance for investments in clean energy, motivated by heightened environmental awareness, as indicated by Attarzadeh et al. (2024), signifies a change in investor preferences.

6. Conclusion

This chapter looks into the intricate interplay between oil price shocks, CPU and EPU, and green stock investments in the Indian stock market, alongside traditional stocks. By utilising wavelet coherence and TVP-VAR techniques, we find that uncertainty indexes exhibit weak return co-movement and modest volatility connectivity with green stocks. Specifically, we find that the returns of green stocks are unaffected by uncertainty arising from CPU and EPU. Conversely, uncertainty regarding oil prices exhibits a significant low-frequency co-movement with green stock returns. Furthermore, responses of green and conventional equities to fluctuations in CPU, EPU, and OPU are identical. Moreover, the time-varying interconnectedness of uncertainty indices and the volatility of green and conventional stocks suggest a moderate overall connectivity. Moreover, for net spillovers, all uncertainty indices function as net transmitters, whereas green stocks serve as the primary risk recipients. In summary, the chapter indicates that the returns on green stocks are influenced by uncertainties in oil prices only, whereas volatility is impacted by uncertainties related to climate action, economic policy, and fluctuations in oil prices.

Due to the robust interconnections between uncertainty indicators and the volatility of green stocks, policymakers must develop a comprehensive governance framework to mitigate their vulnerability. In this context, uncertainty around climate policy garners increased attention. The Indian government must be cautious about climate actions, strengthen the stability of climate policy, progressively establish a prudential regulatory framework for climate change risks, and optimise the allocation of market resources. Further, investors should consider these uncertainties while constructing portfolios consisting of green and conventional stocks.

References

Alam, M., & Akhtar, S. (2024). Introduction to green finance and technology integration. In *Harnessing blockchain-digital twin fusion for sustainable investments* (pp. 1–19). IGI Global.

Alam, M., Akhtar, S., & Bettencourt, A. (2024). Introduction to fintech in industry 5.0: Companion or antagonist. In *The adoption of fintech* (pp. 1–16). Productivity Press.

Antonakakis, N., Chatziantoniou, I., & Gabauer, D. (2020). Refined measures of dynamic connectedness based on time-varying parameter vector autoregressions. *Journal of Risk and Financial Management*, *13*(4), 84. https://doi.org/10.3390/jrfm13040084

Attarzadeh, A., Isayev, M., & Irani, F. (2024). Dynamic interconnectedness and portfolio implications among cryptocurrency, gold, energy, and stock markets: A TVP-VAR approach. *Sustainable Futures*, *8*, 100375. https://doi.org/10.1016/j.sftr.2024.100375

Avramov, D., Cheng, S., Lioui, A., & Tarelli, A. (2022). Sustainable investing with ESG rating uncertainty. *Journal of Financial Economics*, *145*(2), 642–664. https://doi.org/10.1016/j.jfineco.2021.09.009

Awosusi, A. A., Rjoub, H., Dördüncü, H., & Kirikkaleli, D. (2022). Does the potency of economic globalization and political instability reshape renewable energy usage in the face of environmental degradation? *Environmental Science and Pollution Research*, *30*(9), 22686–22701. https://doi.org/10.1007/s11356-022-23665-7

Ayad, H., Mishra, P., Kumari, B., Ray, S., Nuţă, F. M., Gautam, R., Balsalobre-Lorente, D., Nuţă, A. C., & Zamfir, C. G. (2023). The spillover effects of uncertainty and globalization on environmental quality in India: Evidence from combined cointegration test and augmented ARDL model. *Frontiers in Environmental Science*, *11*, 1144201. https://doi.org/10.3389/fenvs.2023.1144201

Bajo, M., & Rodríguez, E. (2023). Green parity and the decarbonization of corporate bond portfolios. *Financial Analysts Journal*, *79*(4), 118–137. https://doi.org/10.1080/0015198X.2023.2246579

Baker, S. R., Bloom, N., & Davis, S. J. (2016). Measuring economic policy uncertainty. *The Quarterly Journal of Economics*, *131*(4), 1593–1636. https://doi.org/10.1093/qje/qjw024

Chen, W., Huang, Z., & Yi, Y. (2015). Is there a structural change in the persistence of WTI–Brent oil price spreads in the post-2010 period? *Economic Modelling*, *50*, 64–71. https://doi.org/10.1016/j.econmod.2015.06.007

Diebold, F. X., & Yılmaz, K. (2014). On the network topology of variance decompositions: Measuring the connectedness of financial firms. *Journal of Econometrics*, *182*(1), 119–134. https://doi.org/10.1016/j.jeconom.2014.04.012

Du, R., & Xu, P. (2024). Time-varying spillover effects between clean and traditional energy under multiple uncertainty risk: Evidence from the U.S. market. *Sustainability*, *16*(21), 9164. https://doi.org/10.3390/su16219164

Dutta, A., Bouri, E., Dutta, P., & Saeed, T. (2021). Commodity market risks and green investments: Evidence from India. *Journal of Cleaner Production*, *318*, 128523. https://doi.org/10.1016/j.jclepro.2021.128523

Dutta, A., Bouri, E., Rothovius, T., & Uddin, G. S. (2023). Climate risk and green investments: New evidence. *Energy*, *265*, 126376. https://doi.org/10.1016/j.energy.2022.126376

Dutta, A., Jana, R. K., & Das, D. (2020). Do green investments react to oil price shocks? Implications for sustainable development. *Journal of Cleaner Production*, *266*, 121956. https://doi.org/10.1016/j.jclepro.2020.121956

Dutta, A., Kanjilal, K., Ghosh, S., Park, D., & Uddin, G. S. (2023). Impact of crude oil volatility jumps on sustainable investments: Evidence from India. *Journal of Futures Markets*, *43*(10), 1450–1468. https://doi.org/10.1002/fut.22442

Gabriel, V., & Pinho, C. (2024). Are clean and black energy exchange-traded funds driven by climate risk? *Journal of Sustainable Finance & Investment*, 1–27. https://doi.org/10.1080/20430795.2024.2303501

Gartia, U., Bhue, R., & Panda, A. K. (2024). Unlocking the dynamic linkages between sustainable equity investment and economic policy uncertainty: An empirical analysis for G-20 countries. *Business Strategy & Development*, *7*(2), e359. https://doi.org/10.1002/bsd2.359

Ha, L. T., Bouteska, A., Sharif, T., & Abedin, M. Z. (2024). Dynamic interlinkages between carbon risk and volatility of green and renewable energy: A TVP-VAR analysis. *Research in International Business and Finance*, *69*, 102278. https://doi.org/10.1016/j.ribaf.2024.102278

Huang, H., Ali, S., & Solangi, Y. A. (2023). Analysis of the impact of economic policy uncertainty on environmental sustainability in developed and developing economies. *Sustainability*, *15*(7), 5860. https://doi.org/10.3390/su15075860

Iqbal, N., Naeem, M. A., & Suleman, M. T. (2022). Quantifying the asymmetric spillovers in sustainable investments. *Journal of International Financial Markets, Institutions and Money*, *77*, 101480. https://doi.org/10.1016/j.intfin.2021.101480

Jafar, S. H., Hemachandran, K., Akhtar, S., Khan, P. A., & El-Chaarani, H. (Eds.). (2024). *The adoption of fintech: Using technology for better security, speed, and customer experience in finance*. CRC Press.

Jafar, S. H., Rodriguez, R. V., Kannan, H., Akhtar, S., & Plugmann, P. (Eds.). (2024). *Harnessing blockchain-digital twin fusion for sustainable investments*. IGI Global.

Jia, Z., Wen, S., & Lin, B. (2021). The effects and reacts of COVID-19 pandemic and international oil price on energy, economy, and environment in China. *Applied Energy*, *302*, 117612. https://doi.org/10.1016/j.apenergy.2021.117612

Jiang, W., Dong, L., Liu, X., & Zou, L., (2024). Volatility spillovers among economic policy uncertainty, energy and carbon markets—The quantile time-frequency perspective. *Energy*, *307*, 132683.

Kanamura, T. (2020). Are green bonds environmentally friendly and good performing assets? *Energy Economics*, *88*, 104767. https://doi.org/10.1016/j.eneco.2020.104767

Khan, P. A., Johl, S. K., & Akhtar, S. (2021). Firm sustainable development goals and firm financial performance through the lens of green innovation practices and reporting: A proactive approach. *Journal of Risk and Financial Management*, *14*(12), 605.

Khan, P. A., Johl, S. K., & Akhtar, S. (2022). Vinculum of sustainable development goal practices and firms' financial performance: A moderation role of green innovation. *Journal of Risk and Financial Management*, *15*(3), 96.

Li, J., Umar, M., & Huo, J. (2023). The spillover effect between Chinese crude oil futures market and Chinese green energy stock market. *Energy Economics*, *119*, 106568. https://doi.org/10.1016/j.eneco.2023.106568

Nittayakamolphun, P., Bejrananda, T., & Pholkerd, P. (2024). Asymmetric effects of uncertainty and commodity markets on sustainable stock in seven emerging markets. *Journal of Risk and Financial Management*, *17*(4), 155. https://doi.org/10.3390/jrfm17040155

Pinto-Gutiérrez, C. (2024). The impact of business group affiliation on CO2 emissions: Evidence from Chile. *Academia Revista Latinoamericana de Administración*, *37*(1), 57–77. https://doi.org/10.1108/ARLA-06-2023-0102

Piris-Cabezas, P., Lubowski, R. N., & Leslie, G. (2023). Estimating the potential of international carbon markets to increase global climate ambition. *World Development*, *167*, 106257. https://doi.org/10.1016/j.worlddev.2023.106257

Rehman, M. Z., Khan, S., Khan, U. A., Alonazi, W. B., & Noman, A. A. (2023). How do global uncertainties spillovers affect leading renewable energy indices? Evidence from the network connectedness approach. *Sustainability*, *15*(18), 13630. https://doi.org/10.3390/su151813630

Rua, A., & Nunes, L. C. (2009). International comovement of stock market returns: A wavelet analysis. *Journal of Empirical Finance*, *16*(4), 632–639. https://doi.org/10.1016/j.jempfin.2009.02.002

Shang, Y., Han, D., Gozgor, G., Mahalik, M. K., & Sahoo, B. K. (2022). The impact of climate policy uncertainty on renewable and non-renewable energy demand in the United States. *Renewable Energy*, *197*, 654–667. https://doi.org/10.1016/j.renene.2022.07.159

Torrence, C., & Compo, G. P. (1998). A practical guide to wavelet analysis. *Bulletin of the American Meteorological Society*, *79*(1), 61–78. https://doi.org/10.1175/1520-0477(1998)079<0061:APGTWA>2.0.CO;2

Torrence, C., & Webster, P. J. (1999). Interdecadal changes in the ENSO–Monsoon system. *Journal of Climate*, *12*(8), 2679–2690. https://doi.org/10.1175/1520-0442(1999)012<2679:ICITEM>2.0.CO;2

Urom, C., & Ndubuisi, G. (2023). Do geopolitical risks and global market factors influence the dynamic dependence among regional sustainable investments and major commodities? *The Quarterly Review of Economics and Finance*, *91*, 94–111. https://doi.org/10.1016/j.qref.2023.07.007

Wang, F., Ma, W., Mirza, N., & Altuntaş, M. (2023). Green financing, financial uncertainty, geopolitical risk, and oil prices volatility. *Resources Policy*, *83*, 103716. https://doi.org/10.1016/j.resourpol.2023.103716

Yang, L., Cai, X. J., Zhang, H., & Hamori, S. (2016). Interdependence of foreign exchange markets: A wavelet coherence analysis. *Economic Modelling*, *55*, 6–14. https://doi.org/10.1016/j.econmod.2016.01.022

Youssef, M., Mokni, K., & Ajmi, A. N. (2021). Dynamic connectedness between stock markets in the presence of the COVID-19 pandemic: Does economic policy uncertainty matter? *Financial Innovation*, *7*(1), 13. https://doi.org/10.1186/s40854-021-00227-3

Chapter 9

Toward a Low-carbon Economy: Exploring the Asymmetric Linkages Between Green Bonds and Non-renewable Energy Resources

Sreekha Pullaykkodi[a] and Sreekanth Peringanam Veluthedan[b]

[a]Manipal School of Commerce and Economics, Manipal Academy of Higher Education (MAHE), Manipal, India
[b]School of Banking and Finance, Management Development Institute of Singapore in Tashkent (MDIS), Tashkent, Uzbekistan

Abstract

Growing concerns over economic distress and ecological degradation have demanded framing those policies that will accelerate economic growth by least hurting the environment. The 2030 agenda of sustainable development has made the world more alert to the actions that mitigate negative impacts on the environment. Green finance has become an essential instrument for tackling the twin demands of economic expansion and environmental preservation. Green bonds (GB) are one of the most prevalent ways to fund green projects and eventually build a low-carbon economy. However, the impacts of growing investment in GB on non-renewable energy (NRE) resources were not examined well. This study examines the asymmetric linkages between GB, crude oil (CO), natural gas (NG), and heating oil (HO) using global data spanning over a decade from 2013 to 2023. The long- and short-term asymmetric connectedness between the variables is examined using a Non-linear Auto Regressive Distributed Lag (NARDL) model. The study reveals an asymmetric linkage between the variables. The results have implications for investors, especially those who wish to create portfolios using GB and other NRE resources. The study becomes novel in terms of the methodology and data. The study has insinuations on

Climate Risk and Emerging Markets: Valuation, Volatility, and Portfolio Strategies, 133–145

doi:10.1108/978-1-83708-088-520261025

government and policymakers. Furthermore, the study alerts the portfolio investors about the asymmetric association between GB and other NRE resources.

Keywords: Green bonds; non-renewable energy resources; low-carbon economy; sustainable development goals; NARDL

1. Introduction

The 2030 agenda of sustainable development has made the world more alert to the actions that mitigate adverse impacts on the environment. The concept of sustainable development goals (SDGs), which contains 17 goals and 169 targets on social, economic, and ecological issues, emerged in 2015 (Khan et al., 2022; Mustafa et al., 2024). The world has vigorously affianced those activities that might reduce the adverse effects of increasing pollution and carbon emissions on the environment so that the SDG goals can be attained. However, despite these ongoing efforts, the ecological condition worsened (Fan et al., 2024; Khan et al., 2021). The Industrial Revolution, along with the growth of other sectors such as services and agriculture, has enriched the quality of life (Du & Wang, 2023); nevertheless, the same acted as a double-edged sword. As the standard of life is augmented, the exploitation of nature has increased, further accelerating environmental degradation. Patti et al. (2021) stated that the exploitation of the environment has amplified because of the intense supply and demand of renewable and non-renewable means, nitrogen-based fertilizers, forestry fires, usage and wastage of chemicals, and excessive carbon dioxide emissions.

Intensifying environmental deterioration compels officials to focus on framing sustainability in the fiscal growth outlines. The SDG has been attributed to the global universal growth design of being accountable for the issue of amplifying climatic catastrophes across the globe (United Nations, 2019). The 2030 Agenda of Sustainable Development has proposed SDGs as a crucial goal for steering global development toward a sustainable path (Alam et al., 2024; Naseema et al., 2024; Q. Zhang et al., 2024). As the magnitude of universal climate variations and ecological dilapidation rises, the importance of SDGs has augmented. It is revealed that the SDGs can only be attained through the constant efforts of the government, business organizations, and other multi-stakeholder contributions, which also matter a lot (Robert et al., 2005). Growing concerns over economic distress and ecological degradation have demanded framing those policies that will accelerate economic growth by least hurting the environment. Here comes the importance of green financing (GF). Green finance has been developed globally to incorporate sustainable development in financial decision-making; it has emerged as a vital tool in addressing the twin demands of environmental preservation and economic expansion (Alam & Akhtar, 2024; Jafar et al., 2024; Zhang, Bawuerjiang et al., 2024). Green finance is an investment funding that promotes sustainability and helps safeguard the environment. It covers all financial goods and services that help achieve environmental sustainability and integrates a variety of financial instruments targeted at sinking greenhouse gas emanations and extenuating the upshots of climate variations (Falcone et al., 2018).

Xiang and Cao (2023) advocate for a little-carbon and climate-adaptable market to be demanded by the government and environmental scientists. Disinvesting in fossil fuels and financing green projects is one of the specific measures taken to achieve this goal. Ran and Minhai (2021) and Naeem, Adekoya, et al. (2021) imply that among the best methods for funding environment-friendly initiatives in this area is through GB. Additionally, they stated that the GB assists local and international environmental organizations in raising money by selling fixed-income securities that may be used to finance environmentally friendly and sustainable projects.

The first ever GB was released in 2007 by the European Investment Bank. Like a standard bond, GB also helps raise money from the debt market; however, unlike standard bonds, GB is used to finance "green" or eco-friendly activities such as energy-efficient, low-carbon (Flammer, 2020). GB is crucial in fostering renewable energy (RE) development (Dong et al., 2023). The RE investment is significant for triumphing carbon neutrality aims (Erdogan et al., 2023; Wang, 2023). Due to the overwhelming importance of GB on RE resources, the topic has attained the interest of scholars, policymakers, and business people. However, what kind of relation exists between GB and NRE resources? Green finance or GB investments aim to reduce carbon emissions and mitigate environmental degradation. However, what are the results of such classic approaches? Did the boost in the RE sector affect the prices of the NRE resources? This chapter's significant objective is to investigate the short- and extended-run nexus between GB and NRE resources, such as CO, HO, and NG.

This chapter examines the nexuses between GB and the pricing of NRE resources, such as CO, NG, and HO. Since the investment in green projects is measured using GB and intended to reduce the carbon emissions from NRE resources, it is essential to discuss the effects of NRE resource prices on GB. This chapter uses the daily global data from 2013 to 2023 for 10 years. The inspiration for this work stems from the following reasons: First, various studies examined the association between energy costs and the financial market. Second, the influence of GB on NRE resources is less discussed. However, this chapter noticed that few studies examined the brief-term and extended-term nexus between the GB and the prices of ecological commodities, such as Naeem, Adekoya, et al. (2021) and Xiang and Cao (2023). Nevertheless, this work is unique because of the following reasons.

This chapter becomes novel in terms of methodology and data. Most of the studies used the Quantile Autoregressive Distributed Lag (QARDL) model – Xiang and Cao (2023) and Li et al. (2024) – whereas this chapter uses NARDL to examine the association. Since this work is interested in exploring the non-linear nexus between GB and NRE resources, and most previous studies examine the direct association between GB energy, employing a model that captures asymmetric association is essential. NARDL adapts the ARDL model, which senses short-run and long-run non-linearities (Tsunga et al., 2020). Further, Kumar (2017) claims that the NARDL model has the advantage of handling asymmetries and various cointegration patterns among series simultaneously compared to other models.

Furthermore, since this chapter uses global daily data and the data are not limited to a specific country, it is free from geographical constraints. Moreover, the author observed that earlier studies examined the linkages between the GB and NRE markets in the context of COVID-19 (Li et al., 2024; Naeem, Farid, et al., 2021). However, this chapter collected data for a decade to understand the behavior of GB and NRE resources during that period. The chapter found an asymmetric relationship between GB and NRE resources. Policymakers and investors can benefit from the chapter. The asymmetric relationships between these variables can be recognized by the investor who wants to build a portfolio employing GB and NRE resources. Furthermore, the insights about the energy fluctuations and their impacts on GB may help policy framers develop policies supporting green finance growth.

The remaining section of this chapter is organized in the following ways: Section 2 provides a brief literature; Section 3 provides the model specifications and methodologies, followed by Section 4 data. Results and empirical estimation are presented in Section 5, followed by an explanation in Section 6, and finally, the conclusion is presented in Section 7.

2. Literature Review

The SDGs have attained the attention of scholars, governments, and other multi-stakeholders due to their overwhelming importance in reducing carbon emissions and environmental protection. Pham (2016) discussed the nexus between GB and other financial markets. The past 10 years have witnessed GB's popularity amplifying when the economy becomes more climate-friendly and less carbonized (Zhang et al., 2019). Flaherty et al. (2017) reveal that GBs effectively finance climate alteration costs, thereby signifying the importance of GBs in mitigating emissions and environmental effects. Reboredo and Ugolini (2018) observe the association among energy prices and neat energy using quantile dependence.

Naeem, Adekoya, et al. (2021) observed the uneven linkages of GBs and commodities using Diebold and Yilmaz's (2012) method; the chapter observed asymmetric spillover in the assets across periods and different cycles. The role of geothermal energy usage in attaining carbon neutrality is discussed by Idroes et al. (2024), and a unidirectional nexus among variables is revealed. Xiang and Cao (2023) explored the small and elongated-term nexus between GBs and prices of commodity markets using a QARDL model in the context of COVID-19. The chapter revealed significant associations among commodity prices and GBs in the low-quantiles. A QARDL approach was employed by Li et al. (2024) to examine the uneven interconnections between natural resources, fintech, and green innovations. This chapter found that natural resources are negatively linked with carbon emanations at all quantiles in the extended run. Naeem, Nguyen, et al. (2021) examined the irregular nexus between GBs and commodities using a quantile regression method, and this chapter observed a negative correlation between GBs and particular commodities. The performance efficiency of GBs and standard bonds was compared by Naeem, Nguyen, et al. (2021) in the context of COVID-19. The chapter confirms the presence of irregular multifractality in the eco-friendly and standard bonds.

Wang and Liu (2024) analyzed the connection between GBs and corporate environmental investment; this chapter reveals a positive connection between GBs and corporate environmental investments. Furthermore, they identified that environmental concern is a moderating variable in this relationship. A direct approach was used by Zhang, Bawuerjiang et al. (2024) to inspect the impacts of green finance investment on environmental impurity in China. This chapter observed that green finance is crucial in mitigating pollution by altering the energy mix and elevating green technology.

Apart from the discussions about the association between GBs and energy products, the prices of natural commodities are a diverged attempt made by Mustafa et al. (2024) to explore the environmental implications of cryptocurrencies. The empirical examination revealed that bitcoin trading substantially and positively influences progress toward SDGs. Sinha et al. (2021) estimated the role of eco-friendly financing in augmenting ecological and social responsibility. The output revealed that eco-friendly financing mechanisms might negatively affect the environment and social responsibility. Cao et al. (2024) examine linkages between US monetary policy ambiguity and GB using the bootstrap rolling-window GC test. The chapter found a substantial rapport between the variables.

From the above-discussed studies, GF has been widely discussed in recent decades. However, most studies address the association between GF and environmental contamination. Specific works focused on the linkages between GB and financial markets, and a few studies explore the connectedness between GB and NRE in the context of COVID-19. Thus, the chapter observed a shortage of studies on the association between GB and NRE for a longer duration. This research divulges the nexus between GB and NRE resources using the NARDL method to address the existing gap in this field.

3. Data and Methodology

3.1. Data

The research plans to inspect the effects of NRE resource prices on GB in 2013–2023 using global daily data. The work retrieved data on GB, CO, NG, and HO. This chapter uses GB, represented by the S&P green bond index, as a dependent variable. Whereas HO, NG, and CO represent NRE resources; these are the independent variables for this chapter. All the data are retrieved from investing.com.

The data analysis is carried out with the help of the NARDL model. To begin with, all the basic assumptions of the NARDL model are tested first. The chapter converted all prices into a log form and then tested the unit root to ensure the stationarity of the variables. After confirming the stationarity, the chapter developed the model for NARDL analysis. Then, we tested the association of variables using NARDL.

3.2. Log Conversion

To begin with the analysis, the chapter first converted all the prices (GB, CO, NG, HO) into the log form for further analysis,

$$\ln \text{GB}_t = \log(\text{GB}_t) \tag{1}$$

$$\ln \text{CO}_t = \log(\text{CO}_t) \tag{2}$$

$$\ln NG_t = \log(NG_t) \tag{3}$$

$$\ln \text{HO}_t = \log(\text{HO}_t) \tag{4}$$

3.3. Unit Root Testing

To conduct NARDL, it is essential to test the stationarity of these variables, and the model expects that the data will follow the stationarity of either $I(0)$ or $I(1)$. A unit root test is essential to establish the order of integration between variables. In the first stage, a unit root test will be conducted at the level, and then, to attain stationarity, data can be differentiated. Both level and first difference unit root tests are conducted using the Augmented Dicky Fuller (ADF) test. The chapter ensured that all the variables were stationary in I (1) order. The structural break of the periods is determined by employing the Zivot and Andrews (1992) unit root test.

3.4. Model Specification

The nexus among the dependent and independent variables is established in the following way:

$$\text{GB} = \alpha + \beta_1 \text{CO} + \beta_1 \text{NG} + \beta_1 \text{HO} + \varepsilon i \tag{5}$$

GB stands for Green Bond, CO stands for Crude oil, NG stands for Natural Gas, and HO stands for Heating Oil.

3.5. Non-linear Auto Regressive Distributed Lag

This work employed a NARDL introduced by Shin et al. (2014). The nonlinearity of numerous macroeconomic factors and processes has long been documented (Shin et al., 2014). Since this work emphasizes the link between GB and non-green bond markets, it is essential to address the features of macroeconomic variables. Broadstock and Cheng (2019) suggested that macroeconomic variables such as economic activity, ambiguous policy decisions, and market instability affect the linkages between GB and non-GB markets. Xiang and Cao (2023) suggest that these macroeconomic variables can also influence the functioning of the commodity market. Thus, addressing the non-linear nature of these variables is also important. According to Salem et al. (2022), like the ARDL model, the NARDL model is also supple because this method does not entail that all the factors have the same order of integration. This model helps the researcher explore the short-run and extended-run uneven impacts of the variables involved.

To begin with the NARDL approach, first, this chapter defines the ARDL equation.

$$GB_t = \beta_0 + \sum_{i=1}^{p} \beta_i GB_{t=i} + \sum_{i=0}^{k1} \gamma_i CO_{t=i} + \sum_{i=0}^{k2} \delta_i NG_{t=i} + \sum_{i=0}^{k3} \rho_i HO_{t=0} + \varepsilon_t \quad (6)$$

Defining the proper lags for each independent and dependent variable is a must for a linear ARDL model. The lags of the dependent variable are denoted using *p*, whereas the independent variables are denoted using *k*. Equation (6) can be rewritten in the following way to meet the requisites of the ARDL bound test.

$$\begin{aligned} \Delta \ln GB_t = {} & \beta_0 + \sum_{i=1}^{p} \beta_i \Delta \ln GB_{t-1} + \sum_{i=0}^{k} \gamma_i \Delta \ln CO_{t-1} + \\ & \sum_{i=0}^{k} \delta_i \Delta \ln NG_{t-1} + \sum_{i=0}^{k} \rho_i \Delta \ln HO_{t=0} + \lambda_1 \ln GB_{t-1} + \\ & \lambda_2 \ln CO_{t-1} + \lambda_3 \ln NG_{t-1} + \lambda_4 \ln HO_{t-1} + \varepsilon_t \end{aligned} \quad (7)$$

Δ is the difference operator and the natural log of the variables denoted using ln. To capture the short-run dynamics λ, is used. The long-run dynamics can be captured using. β_i, γ_i, δ_i, ρ_i. Equation (7) is rewritten using a shorter and error correction model in the following way:

$$\begin{aligned} \Delta \ln GB_t = {} & \beta_0 + \sum_{i=1}^{p} \beta_i \Delta \ln GB_{t-1} + \sum_{i=1}^{p} \gamma_i \Delta \ln CO_{t-1} + \\ & \sum_{i=0}^{k} \delta_i \Delta \ln NG_{t-1} + \sum_{i=0}^{k} \rho_i \Delta \ln HO_{t=0} + \lambda_1 \ln GB_{t-1} + \\ & \lambda_2 \ln CO_{t-1} + \lambda_3 \ln NG_{t-1} + \lambda_4 \ln HO_{t-1} + \lambda ECT_{t-1} \varepsilon_t \end{aligned} \quad (8)$$

Error correction term represented using ECT, which seizures the extended-run linkages among the variables and their coefficient, λ measures the speed of price alteration to extended-run symmetry given any shock to the system.

To develop the NARDL model, the chapter decomposes the explanatory variables into their positive and negative shocks. As explained earlier, this chapter uses three independent variables: CO, NG, and HO.

$$NEG\ CO_t = \sum_{i=1}^{t} \ln CO_t^- = \sum_{i=1}^{t} Max(\Delta \ln CO_t, 0) \quad (9)$$

$$POS\ CO_t = \sum_{i=1}^{t} \ln CO_t^+ = \sum_{i=1}^{t} Max(\Delta \ln CO_t, 0) \quad (10)$$

$$NEG\ NG_t = \sum_{i=1}^{t} \ln NG_t^- = \sum_{i=1}^{t} Max(\Delta \ln NG_t, 0) \quad (11)$$

$$POS\ NG_t = \sum_{i=1}^{t} \ln NG_t^+ = \sum_{i=1}^{t} Max(\Delta \ln NG_t, 0) \quad (12)$$

$$NEG\ HO_t = \sum_{i=1}^{t} \ln HO_t^- = \sum_{i=1}^{t} Max(\Delta \ln HO_t, 0) \quad (13)$$

$$POS\ HO_t = \sum_{i=1}^{t} \ln HO_t^+ = \sum_{i=1}^{t} Max(\Delta \ln HO_t, 0) \quad (14)$$

The partial sum of each independent variable is considered to frame the NARDL model equation. Thus, equations (9)–(14), included in equation (7), to frame the following equation:

$$\begin{aligned}\Delta \ln \mathrm{GB}_t &= \alpha_0 + \sum_{i=1}^{p} \alpha_i \Delta \ln \mathrm{GB}_{t-i} + \sum_{i=0}^{p} \alpha_i^- \Delta \ln \mathrm{NEG(CO)}_{t-i} + \\ &\sum_{i=0}^{p} \alpha_i^+ \Delta \ln \mathrm{POS(CO)}_{t-i} + \sum_{i=0}^{p} \delta_i^- \Delta \ln \mathrm{NEG(NG)}_{t-i} + \\ &\sum_{i=0}^{p} \delta_i^+ \Delta \ln \mathrm{POS(NG)}_{t-i} + \sum_{i=0}^{p} \rho_i^- \Delta \ln \mathrm{NEG(HO)}_{t-i} + \\ &\sum_{i=0}^{p} \rho_i^- \Delta \ln \mathrm{POS(HO)}_{t-i} + \lambda_1 \ln \mathrm{GB}_{t-1} + \lambda_2^- \ln \mathrm{NEGCO}_{t-1} + \\ &\lambda_2^+ \ln \mathrm{POSCO}_{t-1} + \lambda_3^- \ln \mathrm{NG}_{t-1} + \lambda_2^+ \ln \mathrm{NG}_{t-1} + \lambda_4^- \ln \mathrm{HO}_{t-1} + \lambda_5^- \ln \mathrm{HO}_{t-1}\end{aligned} \tag{15}$$

Equation (14) helps test various asymmetric hypotheses. The EViews software is used for the analysis and automatically fixes the optimal lag.

4. Empirical Results

Table 9.1 shows the descriptive statistics for all the variables. The table shows that HO has a lower average return, whereas CO has the highest average return among the NRE resources. GB exhibited less volatility, whereas all other commodities exhibited high volatility. The normality assumption of the data is tested using the Jarque–Bera (J–B) test. However, J–B statistics showed that all the variables are significant. Thus, the normality assumptions are rejected for all the variables. Thus, it qualifies for non-linear analysis.

Table 9.2 represents the results of unit root analysis and structural break. The outcome of the stationarity test shows that all the factors are stationary at level 1. ZA analysis explores the structural break in the time series data.

Except for NG, all other commodities displayed a structural break in 2020. The structural break and stationary analysis use Zivot and Andrews (ZA) (1992). ZA analysis shows that variables are stationary at level one.

The uneven nexus between GB and other NRE resources is examined using NARDL analysis. Table 9.3 represents the long-run estimation of NARDL output. The long-run estimation shows that positive or negative variables carry a

Table 9.1. The Descriptive Statistics of Variables.

Variables	Mean	Min	Max	Std. dev.	J–B Status
Green Bond (GB)	4.89	4.69	5.06	0.07	77.38**
Heating Oil (HO)	0.67	0.49	1.63	0.33	84.13**
Crude Oil (CO)	4.08	2.18	4.81	0.31	49.6**
Natural Gas (NG)	1.12	0.39	2.26	0.35	46.5**

Source: Author's calculation.

Note: * shows significance at 5%, ** shows significance at 10%.

Table 9.2. Outcome of ADF and ZA Test at Level and First Difference.

Variables	ADF (Level)	ADF (First Difference)	ZA	Structural Break	ZA (First Difference)	Structural Break
Green Bond (GB)	−1.45	−45.09***	−5.41	6/5/2020	−2.49***	14/1/2022
Heating Oil (HO)	−1.73	−49.60***	−3.50	2/8/2020	−2.71***	28/2/2023
Crude Oil (CO)	−2.05	−9.96***	−5.90	17/11/2020	−5.78***	31/8/2021
Natural Gas (NG)	−2.60	−53.90***	−3.41	25/5/2021	−2.67***	28/2/2023

Source: Author's calculation.

Note: *** shows significance at 10%.

meaningful coefficient. HO (+), NG (−), and CO (+) show a significant association between GB. Thus, a 1% change in HO prices leads to a 0.023% upsurge in green bond prices. In the same way, 1% change in CO prices may decrease green bond prices by 0.35%.

Table 9.4 includes the short-run asymmetry estimation and diagnostics of the NARDL model. In the short-run asymmetric association, HO (+), NG (−), and CO (+) show a significant and meaningful relationship. This chapter observes that, among the two compositions of each explanatory variable, at least one partial sum substantially impacts the dependent variable.

The model test diagnostic is conducted to determine whether the NARDL models lack autocorrelation and heteroskedasticity. The post-estimation of the method shows that residuals are free from return predictability and heteroskedasticity effects. Furthermore, the chapter conducted the Ramsey RESET test to certify that the model's functional form is correctly specified, and the results of the Ramsey RESET test show that the method specifications are correct.

Table 9.3. Long Run Estimation.

Variable	Coefficient	*T*-statistic	*P*-value
HO_POS	0.023	−0.20	0.03
HO_NEG	−0.01	−0.14	0.88
NG_POS	−0.05	−0.66	0.50
NG_NEG	−0.03	−0.44	0.01
CO_POS	−0.35	−1.68	0.02
CO_NEG	−0.42	−1.69	0.09
Constant	4.67	36.33	0.00

Source: Author's calculation.

Table 9.4. Short Run Estimation.

Variable	Coefficient	*T*-statistic	*P*-value
HO_POS	−0.003	−0.64	0.01
HO_NEG	0.006	1.35	0.21
NG_POS	0.002	0.67	0.51
NG_NEG	0.001	0.48	0.02
CO_POS	0.002	0.84	0.03
CO_NEG	−0.007	−1.75	0.07
ECM (−1)	−0.003	−2.25	0.024
Model test diagnosis *F*-statistics probability			
Breusch–Godfrey serial correlation LM test: 1.260.26			
Heteroskedasticity test: Breusch–Pagan–Godfrey: 9.380.01			
Ramsey RESET test 7.130.22			

Source: Author's calculation.

5. Discussion

This chapter examines the asymmetric association between eco-friendly bonds and NRE resources, such as heating, crude, and NG. The increased concern over climate change and ecological issues has made the world focus more on those activities that mitigate the undesirable environmental impact. As a part of these initiatives, SDG goals gained worldwide attention. The augmented growth of SDGs promoted the progress of eco-friendly bonds.

The chapter used NARDL analysis to explore the asymmetric association between the variables. Short-run and extended-run nexus are estimated, and an asymmetric relationship between the variables is also found.

This chapter is in line with Xiang and Cao (2023). However, they estimated the asymmetric price relationship among eco-friendly bonds, coal, CO, and NG and used the QARDL method. This chapter confirms that GB have a significant nexus between the oil prices. This chapter also found that oil prices are positively associated with GB, confirming that green bond prices increase as oil prices increase. Furthermore, this chapter notices that, in the long run, both HO and NG influence GB. Naeem, Farid, et al. (2021) examined the uneven node among eco-friendly bonds and commodities. This chapter also found that the low returns of energy markets follow the small returns of the GB market. The returns of CO and HO especially show a steep decay followed by a decrease in green bond returns. This chapter revealed a positive and significant node between GB, CO, and HO. The result also aligns with the results of this chapter.

The outcome of this chapter also aligns with the results of Naeem, Adekoya, et al. (2021), who investigated the uneven spillover between GB and commodity prices. They found that CO has the most substantial nexus with GB in the long run, which is also explored in the present chapter. This chapter also ensures the short-run uneven connectedness between the variables, which aligns with the results of the present chapter.

6. Conclusion and Policy Implications

The globe has had to reconsider its actions due to the increased frequency of natural disasters, unfavorable weather patterns, and climate change. The adverse effects of nature on human life have started to gain the attention of policymakers, governments, academicians, and even researchers. Furthermore, these incidents demanded specific actions that mitigate the impacts of human actions on ecology. As a result, one of the SDG goals is given importance for climate action. The high demand for eco-friendly projects amplified the investment in GB.

This chapter investigated the uneven linkages between GB and other NRE resources, such as CO, HO, and NG, using a NARDL model. The irregular node between GB and other NRE resources is evident from this chapter. The chapter has insinuations for investors, policymakers, and government. Investors should exercise caution while building a portfolio of NG, HO, and CO since the analysis shows an unbalanced connection between these commodities and GB. Since this chapter covered the commodities that come under non-renewable resources, the government and policymakers can better understand the association with these commodities and promote the growth of green finance. This chapter provides insight into how changes in energy prices impact GF, allowing regulatory bodies to formulate policies that promote green funding and, eventually, a low-carbon economy.

References

Alam, M., & Akhtar, S. (2024). Introduction to green finance and technology integration. In S. Jafar, R. Rodriguez, H. Kannan, S. Akhtar, & P. Plugmann (Eds.), *Harnessing blockchain-digital twin fusion for sustainable investments* (pp. 1–19). IGI Global.

Alam, M., Akhtar, S., & Bettencourt, A. (2024). Introduction to fintech in Industry 5.0: Companion or antagonist. In S. H. Jafar, K. Hemachandran, S. Akhtar, P. Alam Khan, & H. El-Chaarani (Eds.), *The adoption of fintech* (pp. 1–16). Productivity Press.

Broadstock, D. C., & Cheng, L. T. (2019). Time-varying relation between black and green bond price benchmarks: Macroeconomic determinants for the first decade. *Finance Research Letters*, *29*, 17–22.

Cao, F., Su, C. W., Qin, M., & Moldovan, N. C. (2024). The investment of renewable energy: Is green bond a safe-haven to hedge US monetary policy uncertainty? *Energy*, *307*, 132651.

Diebold, F. X., & Yilmaz, K. (2012). Better to give than to receive: Predictive directional measurement of volatility spillovers. *International Journal of Forecasting*, *28*(1), 57–66.

Dong, W., Li, Y., Gao, P., & Sun, Y. (2023). Role of trade and green bond market in renewable energy deployment in Southeast Asia. *Renewable Energy*, *204*, 313–319.

Du, Y., & Wang, W. (2023). The role of green financing, agriculture development, geopolitical risk, and natural resources on environmental pollution in China. *Resources Policy*, *82*, 103440.

Erdogan, S., Pata, U. K., & Solarin, S. A. (2023). Towards carbon-neutral world: The effect of renewable energy investments and technologies in G7 countries. *Renewable and Sustainable Energy Reviews*, *186*, 113683.

Falcone, P. M., Morone, P., & Sica, E. (2018). Greening of the financial system and fueling a sustainability transition: A discursive approach to assess landscape pressures on the Italian financial system. *Technological Forecasting and Social Change*, *127*, 23–37.

Fan, L., Peng, B., Lin, Z., Zou, H., & Du, H. (2024). The effects of green finance on pollution and carbon reduction: Evidence from China's industrial firms. *International Review of Economics and Finance*, *95*, 103490.

Flaherty, M., Gevorkyan, A., Radpour, S., & Semmler, W. (2017). Financing climate policies through climate bonds – A three-stage model and empirics. *Research in International Business and Finance*, *42*, 468–479.

Flammer, C., (2020). Green bonds: effectiveness and implications for public policy. *Environmental and Energy Policy and. Economy*, *1*(1), 95–128.

Idroes, G. M., Afjal, M., Khan, M., Haseeb, M., Hardi, I., Noviandy, T. R., & Idroes, R. (2024). Exploring the role of geothermal energy consumption in achieving carbon neutrality and environmental sustainability. *Heliyon*, *10*(23).

Jafar, S. H., Rodriguez, R. V., Kannan, H., Akhtar, S., & Plugmann, P. (Eds.). (2024). *Harnessing blockchain-digital twin fusion for sustainable investments*. IGI Global.

Khan, P. A., Johl, S. K., & Akhtar, S. (2021). Firm sustainable development goals and firm financial performance through the lens of green innovation practices and reporting: A proactive approach. *Journal of Risk and Financial Management*, *14*(12), 605.

Khan, P. A., Johl, S. K., & Akhtar, S. (2022). Vinculum of sustainable development goal practices and firms' financial performance: A moderation role of green innovation. *Journal of Risk and Financial Management*, *15*(3), 96.

Kumar, S. (2017). On the nonlinear relation between crude oil and gold. *Resources Policy*, *51*, 219–224.

Li, X., Jiang, Y., Xin, X., Nassani, A. A., & Yang, C (2024). The asymmetric role of natural resources, fintech, and green innovations in the Chinese economy. Evidence from QARDL approach. *Resources Policy*, *90*, 104731.

Mustafa, F., Mordi, C., & Elamer, A. A. (2024). Green gold or carbon beast? Assessing the environmental implications of cryptocurrency trading on clean water management and carbon emission SDGs. *Journal of Environmental Management*, *367*, 122059.

Naeem, M. A., Adekoya, O. B., & Oliyide, J. A. (2021). Asymmetric spillovers between green bonds and commodities. *Journal of Cleaner Production*, *314*, 128100.

Naeem, M. A., Farid, S., Ferrer, R., Shahzad, & S. J. H. (2021). Comparative efficiency of green and conventional bonds pre-and during COVID-19: An asymmetric multifractal detrended fluctuation analysis. *Energy Policy*, *153*, 112285.

Naeem, M. A., Nguyen, T. T. H., Nepal, R., Ngo, Q. T., & Taghizadeh–Hesary, F. (2021). Asymmetric relationship between green bonds and commodities: Evidence from extreme quantile approach. *Finance Research. Letters*, *43*, 101983.

Naseema, N., Akhtar, S., & Al Hinai, A. A. (2024). Disrupting financial services: A case chapter on Capital One's Fintech Odyssey. In S. Jafar, R. Rodriguez, H. Kannan, S. Akhtar, & P. Plugmann (Eds.), *Harnessing blockchain-digital twin fusion for sustainable investments* (pp. 363–383). IGI Global.

Patti, A., Cicala. G., & Acierno. D., (2021). Eco-sustainability of the textile production: Waste recovery and current recycling in the composites world. *Polymers*, *13*(1), 134. https://doi.org/10.3390/polym13010134

Pham, L. (2016). Is it risky to go green? A volatility analysis of the green bond market. *Journal of Sustainable Finance Investment*, *6*(4), 263–291.

Ran, R., & Minhai, M., (2021). Analysis of consumers' purchase behavior preference in e-commerce platform based on biotechnology and light algorithm. *Journal of Commercial Biotechnology*, *26*(4). https://doi.org/10.5912/jcb1039

Reboredo, J. C., & Ugolini, A. (2018). The impact of energy prices on clean energy stock prices. A multivariate quantile dependence approach. *Energy Economics*, *76*, 136–152.

Robert, K. W., Parris, T. M., & Leiserowitz, A. A. (2005). What is sustainable development? Goals, indicators, values, and practice. *Environment: Science and Policy for Sustainable Development*, *47*(3), 8–21.

Salem, L. B., Nouira, R., Jeguirim, K., & Rault, C. (2022). The determinants of crude oil prices: Evidence from ARDL and nonlinear ARDL approaches. *Resources Policy*, *79*, 103085.

Shin, Y., Yu, B., & Greenwood. N. M. (2014). Modelling asymmetric cointegration and dynamic multipliers in a nonlinear ARDL framework. Festschrift in honor of Peter Schmidt: *Econometric methods and applications* (pp. 281–314). Springer.

Sinha, A., Mishra, S., Sharif, A., & Yarovaya, L., (2021). Does green financing help to improve environmental & social responsibility? Designing SDG framework through advanced quantile modelling. *Journal of Environmental Management*, *292*, 112751.

Tsunga, K. R., Moores-Pitt, P., & Mccullough, K. (2020). A non-linear analysis of South African exports and selected macroeconomic variables. *International Journal of Economics and Finance*, *12*(2), 436–452.

United Nations Global Compact. (2019). *Scaling finance for the sustainable development goals*. https://unglobalcompact.org/library/5721

Wang, F., & Liu, J. (2024). Green bond and corporate environmental investment: The moderating effect of environmental concern. *Finance Research Letters*, *65*, 105607.

Wang, H. (2023). Does the financial investment preference of renewable energy firms promote their advance towards sustainable development goals? *Renewable Energy*, *218*, 119326.

Xiang, S., & Cao, Y. 2023. Green finance and natural resources commodities prices: Evidence from COVID-19 period. *Resources Policy*, *80*, 103200.

Zhang, D., Zhang, Z., & Managi, S. (2019). A bibliometric analysis on green finance: Current status, development, and future directions. *Finance Research Letters*, *29*, 425–430.

Zhang, Q., Guan, T., & Liao, Y. (2024). Knowledge of and policy support for the SDGs: An inverted U-shaped relationship. *Journal of Environmental Management*, *368*, 122117.

Zhang, Y., Bawuerjiang, R., Lu, M., Li, Y., & Wang, K., (2024). Green finance and environmental pollution: Evidence from China. *Economic Analysis and Policy*, *84*, 94–110.

Zivot, E., & Andrews, D. W. K. (1992) Further evidence on the great crash, the oil price shock, and the unit root hypothesis. *Journal of Business and Economic Statistics*, *10*(3), 251–270.

Chapter 10

Can Greenhouse Gas Emissions Be a Driving Factor for Economic Stability? An In-depth Study of D8 Nations

Mohammad Irfan[a], *Manas Khemka*[b], *Sakshi Kumari*[b] *and Rui Manuel Teixeira Santos Dias*[c]

[a]*School of Business and Management, Christ University, Bangalore, India*
[b]*School of Business and Management, Christ University, Pune, India*
[c]*Instituto Superior de Gestão (ISG), Business & Economics School, CIGEST, Lisbon, Portugal*

Abstract

This chapter examines the relationship between greenhouse gas (GHG) emissions and economic stability in D8 countries – Bangladesh, Egypt, Indonesia, Iran, Malaysia, Nigeria, Pakistan, and Turkey. It aims to assess whether emissions, particularly methane (CH_4), nitrous oxide (N_2O), and carbon dioxide (CO_2), serve as economic indicators and how transitioning to renewable energy influences economic growth and environmental sustainability. The chapter employs statistical analysis using regression models to evaluate the impact of GHG emissions on key economic indicators such as gross domestic product (GDP), gross national income (GNI), inflation, and energy consumption. Data from the World Development Indicators (WDI) spanning 2001–2023 are utilized. The Environmental Kuznets Curve (EKC) and Stochastic Impacts by Regression on Population, Affluence, and Technology (STIRPAT) models are applied to examine the interplay between emissions and economic growth. Additionally, sectoral analysis is conducted to highlight the role of renewable energy and policy measures in mitigating emissions. The results indicate a complex relationship between emissions and economic stability. Methane and nitrous oxide emissions exhibit a significant correlation with economic performance, whereas CO_2 emissions show mixed effects. Countries

Climate Risk and Emerging Markets: Valuation, Volatility, and Portfolio Strategies, 147–160

Published under exclusive licence by Emerald Publishing Limited
doi:10.1108/978-1-83708-088-520261029

investing in renewable energy, such as Indonesia and Malaysia, demonstrate improved economic resilience while reducing emissions. The chapter highlights the need for energy efficiency measures, investment in clean energy, and regional cooperation to balance economic growth with environmental sustainability. This chapter provides a comprehensive analysis of the economic impact of GHG emissions in D8 nations, offering policy recommendations to achieve sustainable development while maintaining economic stability.

Keywords: D8 nations; greenhouse gas emissions; renewable energy transition; economic growth; environmental sustainability

1. Introduction

The D8 countries or Developing-8 comprise Bangladesh, Egypt, Indonesia, Iran, Malaysia, Nigeria, Pakistan, and Turkey. It is majorly due to the energy needs and economic issues in such countries that require extra effort to achieve industrial development through sustainable environmental means (IRENA, 2022). The D8 countries are huge consumers of fossil fuel, making it tough to limit energy emissions and thus resulting in an enormous carbon footprint (UNCTAD, 2021). Shifts in their economies towards reductions in emissions and adoption of renewable energy sources have made strides. The most important steps to be taken to successfully address the climate crisis, catalyse sustainable development, and create space for the clean energy sector are the three main steps: invest in renewable energy, adopt better energy efficiency, and phase out fossil fuel subsidies (Agency, 2021). The D8 countries: the differentiated resource, new sectors, and strategic trading networks make them significant actors in the global marketplace. Bangladesh and Pakistan have strong bases of exports in textiles; Malaysia and Indonesia are the world's largest producers of palm oil. The regional economic integration between Europe and Asia can be seen in the case of Turkey (Agency, 2021). Oil and gas exportation can also be seen in the powerhouse energy sectors of Iran and Nigeria. In addition to promoting trade, investment, and technological cooperation among themselves, the D8 countries represent the growing form of South-South cooperation as newly emerging global economic superpowers (Akram et al., 2022). The D8 countries have specific states of energy resource, defining their sustainability and status. Bangladesh is blessed with natural gas, while Egypt is the major energy player in Africa, and it is also the largest developer of renewable solar power (World Bank, 2022). Indonesia is the world's largest developer of renewable geothermal energy. Iran and Malaysia have significant oil and gas reserves, and Nigeria, a major African oil producer, has huge potential in terms of solar energy (World Bank, 2021). The aforementioned resources contribute to fulfilling national energy requirements and assist the international energy markets that further accelerate economic growth (Batoukhteh & Darzi-Naftchali, 2024). The D8 countries are highly important for global trade, investments, and economic growth. Strategically located with natural wealth in plenty, they have made a niche for themselves in the global supply chain (Borsha et al., 2024). Their industrial sectors bubbling with activity attract foreign investments into manufacturing, infrastructure, and renewable energy projects. They advance the cause of renewable energy initiatives thereby working for sustainability while strengthening their positions in this fight against climate change (Bunnag, 2023). Objective: This chapter tracks the trend of methane, nitrous oxide, and CO_2 emissions in D8 countries, determines the associated key factors with emissions, and discusses how renewable energy could reduce them in order to further sustainable development. It analyses the green-gas emissions and their relationship to GDP, GNI, and energy consumption in the D8 countries from 2001 to 2023. This study is scrutinizing the impact of renewable energy, energy efficiency, and macroeconomic factors on environmental sustainability in D8 countries.

2. Literature Review

Methane (CH_4) has a stronger climate impact than CO_2. Study on OECD nations shows GDP and energy use increase emissions, while human progress and renewable energy reduce them. Policies should support sustainable growth and renewable energy (Chen et al., 2023). Study on 30 low- and middle-income countries (LMICs) and 10 high-income countries (HICs) (2000–2014) shows GDP raises emissions in LMICs; university education reduces them. In HICs, tertiary education increases emissions. Rule of law has minimal impact (Chovancova et al., 2024). Study on Thailand (1971–2014) finds GDP, energy use, CO_2, and foreign direct investment (FDI) have causative links. Renewable energy and controlled FDI are recommended (Furkan et al., 2023).

Study on Bangladesh (1992–2021) confirms EKC. Renewable energy reduces CO_2, while industrialization increases it. Sustainable energy and stricter regulations are recommended (Gao et al., 2023). Study on India's life expectancy (2000–2020) finds economic growth improves life expectancy, while carbon emissions harm it. Suggests sustainable energy policy (Jaiswal et al., 2022). Study on Indonesia (1990–2021) finds GDP and population growth increase CO_2 emissions. EKC not supported; income inequality has minimal impact (Kanwal et al., 2022).

Building sector study examines carbon emission accounting methods. Top-down methods used for urban assessments; bottom-up for individual buildings. Recommends more research on emissions across building stages (Khan et al., 2024). Study on EU27 (1990–2018) using EKC framework finds economic growth reduces environmental impact in some countries. Service sector emissions are high in countries with poor energy efficiency (Liu et al., 2022). Agricultural development study (1961–2017) shows GHG emissions doubled in developing nations. Calls for environmentally sustainable food security programmes (Martín-Ortega & González-Sánchez, 2025).

Study on China's CETEs (2006–2019) finds improved carbon emission efficiency post-launch. Investments in pollution control and innovation drove efficiency gains (Mohsin et al., 2022). Study on renewable energy and growth in OECD nations (1997–2015) finds risks impact the growth benefit. Only first threshold crossing is favourable; double crossing has negative impact (UNEP Programme, 2021). Study on China's provinces (2012–2019) finds digital economy growth raises emissions due to reduced energy efficiency. Emissions increase with population growth and coal-based energy (Tutak & Brodny, 2022).

Study integrates renewable energy sources with grid-connected energy hubs. Flexible energy hubs lower costs and increase efficiency (Wanga et al., 2023). Study on EU (2000–2019) shows increased renewable energy usage. Positive impact on economic growth and reduced GHG emissions, especially in 'old' EU countries (Yunita et al., 2023). Study on top 10 CO_2-emitting nations (1990–2016) finds renewable energy supports growth but risks environmental quality. Policymakers should promote innovation for sustainability (Zhang et al., 2022).

Study assesses renewable energy's economic, social, and environmental benefits. Biofuel production from lignocellulosic biomass suggested (Zhang et al., 2023). Study on Pakistan's energy security finds coal reserves key for electricity needs. Suggests syngas production as a solution (Zhao et al., 2022). Study on renewable hydrogen in Pakistan finds wind energy most efficient. Wind projects help meet energy needs and reduce fossil fuel dependency (IRENA, 2022). Study on renewable energy and green growth in ECOWAS (1990–2018) finds R&D and renewable energy improve sustainable performance. Recommends increased government spending (UNCTAD, 2021). Study on Mexico, Indonesia, Nigeria, and Turkey countries (1990–2014) finds renewable energy and efficiency reduce emissions. Emphasizes energy efficiency in emission reduction policies (Agency, 2021).

3. Research Methodology

This chapter analyses the interaction of GHGs with microeconomic variables utilizing statistical methods such as linear regression analysis and data visualization. Then, data are collected based on multiple observations of time periods of GHGs along with significant microeconomic variables. Independent variables are CH_4 (methane), N_2O (nitrous oxide), CO_2 (carbon dioxide), CO_2 from gaseous fuel consumption (gfc), and total GHG emissions, and the dependent variable is the average of microeconomic indicators like production costs, energy prices, and consumption levels. In this case, a regression model would be applied to correlate the chosen GHGs with the dependent variable, defined as:

$$Y = \beta_0 + \beta_1 X_1 + \beta_2 X_2 + \beta_3 X_3 + \beta_4 X_4 + \beta_5 X_5 + \varepsilon \tag{1}$$

where Y is the dependent variable; X_1, X_2, X_3, X_4, X_5 are independent variables (CH_4, N_2O, CO_2, CO_2 gfc, GHG); β_0 is the intercept; β_1, β_2, β_3, β_4, β_5 are coefficients; ε is the error term.

The detail description of variables is shown in Table 10.1.

To show how the variations in GHG emissions influence the dependent variable over time, the author has plotted line graphs to enable visual representations of data. Contribution levels of each gas to the microeconomic fluctuations are also drawn out. The rationale for the research paper on the effects of GHGs

Table 10.1. Description of Variables.

Variable	Type	Description
Y	Dependent variable	Average of microeconomic indicators (production costs, energy prices, and consumption levels)
X_1 (CH_4)	Independent variable	Methane emissions (CH_4) measured in metric tons
X_2 (N_2O)	Independent variable	Nitrous oxide emissions (N_2O) measured in metric tons
X_3 (CO_2)	Independent variable	Carbon dioxide emissions (CO_2) per capita
X_4 (CO_2 gfc)	Independent variable	CO_2 emissions from gaseous fuel consumption (gfc) measured in kilotons
X_5 (GHG)	Independent variable	Total greenhouse gas (GHG) emissions measured in kilotons

Source: Authors' estimation.

for microeconomic conditions will offer a reflection of the interaction between environmental-economic variables.

This includes continuing with the residual analysis to check if the assumptions of the model are satisfied: normality, homoscedasticity, and diagnostic tests for multicollinearity, autocorrelation, and outliers. From all the gases taken into consideration, two major ones seemed to be N_2O and CO_2.

4. Data Analysis

Interpretation for Table 10.2: For this model, the R Square is 0.8048, indicating that this model describes 80.48% of the variation in the dependent variable with an excellent fit. Adjusted R Square: 0.7474 retains the number of predictors and still indicates a good fit but loses a little explanatory power. Significance of the F value as low as 1.6E−05 with a very, very high statistical significance, meaning that the predictors in aggregate explain a significant part of the variance of the outcome. The intercept has a coefficient value of 9.39 (p = 8.24E−07), meaning that when all predictors are zero, then at base is 9.39. Methane (CH_4) has a strong positive effect on the dependent variable with a coefficient of 1.4198 and a p-value of 0.000152, indicating to be significant. Therefore, wherever there's methylene, the quantity of NO increased. Nitrous oxide (N_2O) also has a positive effect but with a smaller coefficient of 0.1476 and a p-value of 0.0368. CO_2 coefficient is −0.108. Its p-value, however, is a little greater than the accepted limit of 0.05 so it is only insignificantly small. CO_2 from gfc is not statistical at $p = 0.1278$ with a negative coefficient of −0.3537. GHG correlates negatively with the dependent

Table 10.2. Bangladesh and Egypt (Regression Analysis).

Multiple *R*		0.897		Multiple *R*			0.566	
R Square		0.805		*R* Square			0.320	
Adjusted *R* Square		0.747		Adjusted *R* Square			0.120	
Standard Error		0.834		Standard Error			6.287	
Observations		23.000		Observations			23.000	
	F	**Sig. *F***				***F***	**Sig. *F***	
Regression	14.02	0.00		Regression		1.60	0.21	
Residual				Residual				
Total				Total				
		Bangladesh				**Egypt**		
Variable	**COEFF**	**SE**	***T***	***P***	**COEFF**	**SE**	***T***	***P***
Intercept	9.39	1.25	7.53	0.00	7.70	2.33	3.31	0.00
CH_4	1.42	0.29	4.84	0.00	0.77	0.31	2.46	0.02
N_2O	0.15	0.07	2.27	0.04	0.03	0.28	0.10	0.92
CO_2	−0.11	0.06	−1.79	0.09	−0.45	0.75	−0.60	0.56
CO_2 (gfc)	−0.35	0.22	−1.60	0.13	0.12	0.39	0.32	0.76
GHG	−0.43	0.15	−2.92	0.01	0.11	0.68	0.16	0.88

Source: Authors' calculation.

variable, as its coefficient shows –0.4296 and *p*-value shows 0.00965, meaning that there is a probable decline in the predicted outcome.

Key observations: The model has an *R* Square value of 0.3201, which means it can explain only 32% of the variability in the dependent variable, which is extremely low in explanatory power. Adjusted *R* Square comes down to 0.1201 as well, adjusting it with the number of predictors as well reflects the weakness of the model. Standard error is 6.2867 and is pretty high, meaning there was much variability around the predicted values. A *p*-value of 0.2133 indicates that the overall model is not statistically significant, meaning that, in aggregate, the independent variables do not explain a statistically significant portion of the variation in the dependent variable.

The intercept is statistically significant at 7.7020 with a *p*-value equal to 0.0041, suggesting that when all predictors are set to zero, the dependent variable would be approximately 7.70. Methane (CH_4) is the only predictor whose coefficient is significantly different from zero: It was 0.7716 and has a *p*-value of 0.0248, meaning positive impact. The coefficient for nitrous oxide (N_2O) is close to zero at 0.0274 with a *p*-value as high as 0.9236; hence it's statistically insignificant. Carbon dioxide (CO_2) had a coefficient of –0.4465 but wasn't statistically significant at a *p*-value of 0.5589. In the consumption of gaseous consumption,

Table 10.3. Indonesia and Iran (Regression Analysis).

Multiple *R*		0.566		Multiple *R*			0.736	
R Square		0.320		*R* Square			0.541	
Adjusted *R* Square		0.120		Adjusted *R* Square			0.406	
Standard error		6.287		Standard error			7.256	
Observations		23.000		Observations			23.000	
	F	**Sig. *F***				***F***	**Sig. *F***	
Regression	1.60	0.21		Regression		4.01	0.01	
Residual				Residual				
Total				Total				
		Indonesia				**Iran**		
Variable	**COEFF**	**SE**	***T***	***P***	**COEFF**	**SE**	***T***	***P***
Intercept	7.70	2.33	3.31	0.00	8.20	2.84	2.89	0.01
CH_4	0.77	0.31	2.46	0.02	0.18	0.27	0.67	0.51
N_2O	0.03	0.28	0.10	0.92	−0.77	0.33	−2.35	0.03
CO_2	−0.45	0.75	−0.60	0.56	0.95	0.70	1.36	0.19
CO_2 (gfc)	0.12	0.39	0.32	0.76	0.11	0.46	0.23	0.82
GHG	0.11	0.68	0.16	0.88	0.44	1.01	0.43	0.67

Source: Authors' calculation.

the coefficient is at 0.1227 with a *p*-value at 0.7551, while GHG variable does not have any significant effect with a coefficient of 0.1069 and high *p*-value at 0.8774.

Interpretation for Table 10.3: The *R* Square value of the model is 0.4458, meaning that it explains about 44.58% variability in the dependent variable; this is moderate but not very strong. Adjusted *R* Square is 0.2828, which suggests that the effectiveness of the model reduces considerably while adjusting for the number of predictors. Standard error comes out to be 4.6162 lesser as compared to the previous model, and thus the variability around the predicted values comes out to be lesser. The significance *F*-value with a value of 0.0545 means that the overall regression was close to the threshold of having a meaningful level of statistical significance because it was slightly more than 0.05, thus implying that the set of independent variables together was somewhat meaningful in explaining the variation in the outcome. The intercept is extremely highly significant with coefficients and *p*-values, indicating that the dependent variable should be 7.94 if all predictors were zero. Methane (CH_4) was also a statistically significant predictor with a coefficient of 0.9662 and a *p*-value of 0.0485, positive for the dependent variable. N_2O has a negative coefficient of –0.3814, although statistically insignificant at *p*-value 0.2631. The most significant of them is positively biased CO_2, having a coefficient of 0.0655, very high in p-value with 0.8493, statistically insignificant. The coefficient of gaseous consumption equation was 0.1927 and p-value 0.2820, but coefficient of the GHG variable was negative at –0.1139 with p-value of 0.7474 showing no effect of any significance.

Key observations: R Square for the model is 0.5412, which means it explains around 54.12% variance in the dependent variable, showing to be a moderate explained variance. The Adjusted R Square is significantly lower at 0.4063, and that means though the model is pretty stronger compared to this, maybe some of the predictors do not add much value to it. The standard error is still relatively high at 7.2562, which means that there exists large variance of predictions. The Significance F value is 0.0138, which states that the model is statistically significant as a whole, $p < 0.05$. This means that, taken as a whole, the independent variables contribute meaningfully to explaining the variance in the dependent variable. The intercept is statistical at 8.1992, $p = 0.0103$ which implies if all the predictors are zero, the dependent variable is at a baseline of 8.20. Methane (CH_4) has a coefficient of 0.1804 but since its p-value is greater than 0.05, it is not significant in this model and its impact on the dependent variable is minimal. In contrast, N_2O has high-negative impact on the dependent variable with coefficient –0.7730, $p = 0.0310$, which in turn points to the fact that when the levels of N_2O will be greater, the dependent variable will show a decrease. On the other hand, CO_2 has a positive coefficient of 0.9502, and the value of $p = 0.1919$, that indicates the relationship is positive but not valid because $p > 0.05$. The other variable is the CO_2 (gfc), which has a coefficient of 0.1054 with a p-value of 0.8204, thus also non-significant. Lastly, the GHG variable has a coefficient of 0.4356 with a p-value of 0.6704, which is non-significant.

Interpretation for Table 10.4: This model has an R Square value of 0.5861, meaning that this model explains approximately 58.61% of the variance in the dependent variable and demonstrates relatively good explanatory power. Adjusted R Square is lower at 46.43% so some predictors probably are not adding worthwhile value to the model; however, by overall summary, this model is stronger than previous versions. Standard error of 3.4609 represents a drop that would imply predictions are getting closer and closer to the real values. A significant F value of 0.0063 is obtained, meaning that the model, as an aggregate, is statistically significant, because together, the predictors explain a meaningful part of the variance within the dependent variable. The p-values and coefficients indicate that the intercept is 2.3969, which is not statistically significant with a p-value of 0.1395. This means that the level of the dependent variable at baseline thus that when all predictors are zero-is not significantly different from zero. Methane (CH_4) has a coefficient of –0.0616 with a p-value of 0.8385, meaning that it's not a significant predictor and its inconsiderable implications on the dependent variable. Nitrous oxide has a coefficient of 0.1887 ($p = 0.0771$), approaching significance and suggesting it could have an interesting positive impact though barely misses the traditional 0.05 threshold. Carbon dioxide has a coefficient of 0.0932 ($p = 0.8918$), so it is not statistically significant, and its contribution to the model is minimal. The coefficient of CO_2 (gfc) stands at 0.1802 ($p = 0.2362$) hence, not statistically significant but fairly positively influential. Finally, GHG

Table 10.4. Malaysia and Pakistan (Regression Analysis).

Multiple *R*			0.766	Multiple *R*			0.546	
R Square			0.586	*R* Square			0.299	
Adjusted *R* Square			0.464	Adjusted *R* Square			0.092	
Standard error			3.461	Standard error			3.965	
Observations			23.000	Observations			23.000	
	F		**Sig. *F***			*F*		**Sig. *F***
Regression	4.814		0.006	Regression		1.448		0.258
Residual				Residual				
Total				Total				
	Malaysia				**Pakistan**			
Variable	**COEFF**	**SE**	***T***	***P***	**COEFF**	**SE**	***T***	***P***
Intercept	2.40	1.55	1.55	0.14	7.78	2.54	3.07	0.01
CH_4	−0.06	0.30	−0.21	0.84	1.45	1.06	1.36	0.19
N_2O	0.19	0.10	1.88	0.08	−0.25	0.46	−0.55	0.59
CO_2	0.09	0.68	0.14	0.89	1.37	1.00	1.37	0.19
CO_2 (gfc)	0.18	0.15	1.23	0.24	0.14	0.15	0.97	0.35
GHG	0.25	0.78	0.31	0.76	−2.44	2.31	−1.06	0.30

Source: Authors' calculation.

shows a coefficient of 0.2468 with a *p*-value of 0.7567. Again, it is shown to be an insignificant predictor in this model with a high *p*-value and little influence on the dependent variable.

Key observations: The *R* Square value of this model is 0.2986, that is, it explains only 29.86% of the variance in the dependent variable. This means the fit is quite poor. So, less than a third of the variability in the dependent variable is explained by the predictors. The Adjusted *R* Square is much lower at 0.0923 (9.23%). This means that the model is not performing well and most predictors do not seem to contribute significantly to this model. The standard error is at 3.9651, up a little from previous models, indicating that predictions are less accurate. The significant *F* value of 0.2581 is not statistically significant, *p*-value = 0.258. This means that the predictors together could not explain the dependent variable in a statistically meaningful way. Looking at coefficients and *p*-values, we find that the intercept is 7.7774 ($p = 0.0070$). This is a statistically significant coefficient – it means that, when holding all the predictors constant, the baseline level of the dependent variable is meaningfully different from zero. Methane (CH_4) has positive coefficient 1.4452 but is not statistically significant since $p > 0.05$. Nitrous oxide (N_2O) has negative coefficient of –0.2532 ($p = 0.5920$). It is not significant and adds little to the model. The CO_2 has a coefficient of +1.3729, $p = 0.1876$

with weak effects while CO_2 (gfc) has a coefficient of 0.1425, $p = 0.3458$, therefore not statically significant and has the lowest effect. Lastly, the GHG have a negative coefficient of –2.4422, $p = 0.3050$ with negative effects on the dependent variable. The high p-value indicates that it is not statically significant.

Interpretation for Table 10.5: R Square for the model is 0.3674, meaning it actually explains about 36.74% of the variance in the dependent variable and thus displays improvement over the previous versions but is still relatively weak. The Adjusted R Square is appreciably lower at 0.1814 (18.14%), which suggests that there may exist some predictors in this model that are not having significant contribution to the actual model. The Standard Error is fairly large at 10.6783, so predictions are not very precise. An F value of 0.1344 in a test for significance means that the overall model is not statistically significant ($p = 0.134$), or in other words, the predictors taken together don't explain the dependent variable in a statistically meaningful way. On coefficients and p-values, the intercept is 13.8867 with a p-value of 0.0115, which means it's statistically significant at a very strong baseline effect. The coefficient on methane is 0.8312, with a negative effect on the dependent variable but not statistically significant at $p > 0.05$. Nitrous oxide has a positive coefficient of 0.5565, though not statistically significant. Carbon

Table 10.5. Nigeria and Türkiye (Regression Analysis).

Multiple R			0.606	Multiple R			0.420	
R Square			0.367	R Square			0.176	
Adjusted R Square			0.181	Adjusted R Square			−0.066	
Standard error			10.678	Standard error			7.629	
Observations			23.000	Observations			23.000	
		F	**Sig. *F***			***F***		**Sig. *F***
Regression		1.975	0.134	Regression		0.728		0.612
Residual				Residual				
Total				Total				
		Nigeria				**Turkiye**		
Variable	**COEFF**	**SE**	***T***	***P***	**COEFF**	**SE**	***T***	***P***
Intercept	13.89	4.91	2.83	0.01	9.47	3.16	3.00	0.01
CH_4	−0.83	0.54	−1.54	0.14	−0.37	0.67	−0.55	0.59
N_2O	0.56	0.57	0.98	0.34	0.51	0.98	0.53	0.60
CO_2	2.16	3.70	0.58	0.57	0.72	0.70	1.03	0.32
CO_2 (gfc)	0.92	0.40	2.29	0.04	0.12	0.12	1.02	0.32
GHG	−3.31	4.57	−0.72	0.48	−1.02	1.39	−0.74	0.47

Source: Authors' calculation.

dioxide has a positive effect of 2.1611, though its high p-value points to it as well not of significance. The variable CO_2 (gfc) has a coefficient of 0.9202 (p-value of 0.0354), and hence is statistically significant, implying that GHG concentrations in gas-fired combustion make a meaningful contribution to the model. Lastly, GHG is at –3.3070 with a p-value of 0.4793, meaning this is not a statistically significant variable.

Key observations: This model has an R Square of 0.1764, meaning it explains only 17.64% of variance in the dependent variable. As such, the model is a bad fit. The Adjusted R Square is also highly negative at –0.0658, showing that there may be overfitting of the model or that the predictors do not add up much to the explanation of the dependent variable. The Standard Error is at 7.6289, relatively high meaning that the predictions are imprecise. The Significance F of 0.6119 indicates that the overall model is statistically insignificant as the overall impact of predictors is not meaningful ($p > 0.05$). In terms of coefficients and p-values, the intercept is 9.4706 with a value of 0.0081, indicating that it's highly statistically significant and shows a very strong baseline effect. Methane (CH_4) has a coefficient of –0.3650 ($p = 0.5905$), but it is not significant at all. So, the impact of this methane is negligible. Nitrous oxide (N_2O) has a positive coefficient of 0.5147 ($p = 0.6047$). It is also insignificant. Carbon dioxide (CO_2) has a plus effect of 0.7212 with $p = 0.3155$, which also is insignificant. The variable on CO_2 (gfc) shows weak positive 0.1208 effect with a p-value of 0.3216, which is non-significant. Finally, the GHG show that GHG have a negative coefficient of –1.0224. It has potential for negative influences also, but again that one also is not significant.

5. Conclusion

The D8 countries are Bangladesh, Egypt, Indonesia, Iran, Malaysia, Nigeria, Pakistan, and Turkey. These are giants in the new world economy at a time when industrial development must be pursued in a sustainable manner; these countries also need to overcome the challenges of managing fossil fuels. A transition towards renewable energy and the phasing out of fossil fuel subsidy is a step to combat climate change and promote the growth of clean energy. The D8 economies have diversified energy resources. Bangladesh has the highest reserves in natural gas, while Egypt boasts natural gas as well as solar energy, and Indonesia has developed geothermal energy. Nigeria and Iran have major dependence on oil and gas. These countries – important ones for international trade and investment with growing population and an increasingly large middle class – foster renewable energy for economic development and foreign investments. Renewable initiatives are at the core of D8's energy security, de-carbonizing energy, creating jobs, and enhancing their role in global climate discussions.

6. Limitations of the Study

Even though the study offers valuable insights into the interaction between energy resources, greenhouse emissions, and economic stability in D8 countries, it has several limitations. First, the reliance on secondary data from WDI can provide inconsistencies that stem from variations in reporting requirements and data collection procedures among nations. Furthermore, the analysis is predominantly based on macroeconomic factors and fails to consider differences in sectors at the micro level that can influence trends in emissions. The impact of informal economies, which are highly significant in some D8 countries, on the environment is not also well represented through this analysis. The role of technological innovation, policy measures, and energy efficiency in cutting emissions is not also covered in the analysis. The application of the EKC and STIRPAT models, while useful, is perhaps not able to capture the complex socio-political and institutional determinants of the pattern of emissions. Lastly, the paper does not even try to estimate the long-run sustainability of the take-up of renewable energy due to lack of data, and nor does it carry out a serious cost-benefit analysis of a shift to cleaner forms of energy. The study may eliminate such gaps in the future by being more sectoral in approach, targeted, and even involving other determinants such as trade policies, technological advancements, and government policies.

7. Recommendations and Suggestions

Countries such as Bangladesh and Iran would need to make reductions in methane emissions with increased investment in technology targeting the agriculture, waste, and energy sectors. Policymakers can further encourage industries to switch to cleaner sources of energy. For a country like Egypt and Pakistan that has minimal impact from GHGs, strengthened environmental policies and increased monitoring of GHGs could be a pre-emptive measure to obviate future economic shocks as they move into industrious scales of development. Adding the variables of energy use, technological change, and regulatory regimes helps to tailor the strategies to the economic context that each country faces. Carbon pricing, technology transfers, and capacity building will enable developing countries to achieve balancing of reduced emissions with their growing economies. Public campaigns should relate the economic costs of environmental degradation and benefits from green activities that foster sustainable practices. These may minimize the damage by GHG while at the same time promoting robust economic structures.

8. Policy Solutions for All D8 Countries

- *Bangladesh:* Strengthen investments in solar and wind power as policies, scale up waste-to-energy activities in a bid to eliminate methane emissions, and incentivize industry in the adoption of cleaner technology through tax credits and subsidies.
- *Egypt:* Increase large-scale renewable energy projects, particularly solar energy, and introduce bold carbon-reducing policies in industrial processes while developing public transportation systems to reduce fuel-based emissions.
- *Indonesia:* Encourage sustainable forest management to reduce deforestation-related emissions, develop clean coal technology, and adopt stricter emission standards in manufacturing and palm oil sectors.

- *Iran:* Increase nuclear and renewable energy production to diversify the energy mix, invest in energy efficiency programmes in the industrial sector, and eliminate fossil fuel subsidies to favour cleaner alternatives.
- *Malaysia:* Implement stronger carbon pricing mechanisms to facilitate industrial emission abatement, induce electrification of the transport sector, and accelerate research and development in biofuels to take advantage of the palm oil industry in the country.
- *Nigeria:* Design a national, unified plan to develop solar and hydropower, exert tougher controls over emission in the petroleum and natural gas sectors, and promote cleaner-burning cooking fuel in an attempt to end indoor air pollution.
- *Pakistan:* Ramp up hydro and wind energy capacity, encourage public–private collaboration on clean energy investments, and devise policies for pro-environmental urbanization in handling rising urbanization-driven emissions.
- *Turkey:* Reinforce incentives for renewable energy production, implement energy efficiency in industry and building sectors, and implement carbon taxation to accelerate the phasing out of fossil fuels.

References

Agency, T. I. (2021). *Net zero by 2050: A roadmap for the global energy sector*. International Energy Agency (IEA).

Akram, R., Umar, M., Xiaoli, G., & Chen, F. (2022). Dynamic linkages between energy efficiency, renewable energy along with economic growth and carbon emission. A case of MINT countries an asymmetric analysis. *Energy Reports*, *8*, 2119–2130.

Batoukhteh, F., & Darzi-Naftchali, A. (2024). A global study on decoupling greenhouse gas emissions from agricultural development. *Environment, Development and Sustainability*, *26*, 13159–13183.

Borsha, F. H., Voumik, L. C., Rashid, M., & Das, M. K. (2024). An empirical investigation of GDP, industrialization, population, renewable energy and CO_2 emission in Bangladesh: Bridging EKC-STIRPAT models. *International Journal of Energy Economics and Policy*, *14*(3), 560–571.

Bunnag, T. (2023). Analyzing short-run and long-run causality relationship among CO_2 emission, energy consumption, GDP, square of GDP, and foreign direct investment in environmental Kuznets curve for Thailand. *International Journal of Energy Economics and Policy*, *13*(2), 341–348.

Chen, J., Gui, W., & Huang, Y. (2023). The impact of the establishment of carbon emission trade exchange on carbon emission efficiency. *Environmental Science and Pollution Research*, *30*, 19845–19859.

Chovancova, J., Bergougui, B., Zambrano-Monserrate, M., Ahakwa, I., & Dam, M. M. (2024). Global determinants of methane emissions in OECD countries: A dynamic panel approach. *Research in Globalization*, *9*, 100232.

Furkan, H. B., Md, K. R., & Md, J. U. (2023). Greenhouse gas emission, GDP, tertiary education, and rule of law: A comparative st. *Heliyon*, *9*, e16265.

Gao, H., Wang, X., Wu, K., & Zheng, Y. (2023). A review of building carbon emission accounting and prediction models. *Buildings*, *13*, 1617.

IRENA. (2022). *Renewable energy market analysis: Africa and its regions*. IRENA.

Jaiswal, K. K., Chowdhury, C. R., Yadav, D., & Verma, R. (2022). Renewable and sustainable clean energy development and impact on social, economic, and environmental health. *Energy Nexus*, *7*, 100118.

Kanwal, S., Mehran, M. T., & Hassan, M. (2022). An integrated future approach for the energy security of Pakistan: Replacement of fossil fuels with syngas for better environment and socio-economic development. *Renewable and Sustainable Energy Reviews*, *156*, 111978.

Khan, A., Khan, M. A., & Asif, M. (2024). Assessing the impact of carbon emission, health expenditure, IMR and GDP on life expectancy in India: Using cointegration approach. *Journal of Environmental and Energy Economics*, *3*(1), 54–62. https://doi.org/10.56946/jeee.v3i1.398.

Liu, H., Khan, I., Zakari, A., & Alharthi, M. (2022). Roles of trilemma in the world energy sector and transition towards sustainable energy: A study of economic growth and the environment. *Energy Policy*, *170*, 113238.

Martín-Ortega, J. L., & González-Sánchez, M. (2025). Sectoral composition of GDP and greenhouse gas emissions: An empirical analysis in EU27. *Environment, Development and Sustainability*, *27*(2), 3899–3926.

Mohsin, M., Taghizadeh-Hesary, F., Iqbal, N., & Saydaliev, H. B. (2022). The role of technological progress and renewable energy deployment in green economic growth. *Renewable Energy*, *190*, 777–787.

Tutak, M., & Brodny, J. (2022). Renewable energy consumption in economic sectors in the EU-27. The impact on economics, environment and conventional energy sources. A 20-year perspective. *Journal of Cleaner Production*, *345*, 131076.

UNCTAD. (2021). *South-south cooperation in a digital world*. United Nations.

UNEP Programme. (2021). *Emissions gap report 2021*. United Nations Environment Programme (UNEP).

Wanga, Q., Dong, Z., Lia, R., & Wanga, L. (2023). Renewable energy and economic growth: New insight from country risks. *Energy*, *238*, 122018.

World Bank. (2021). *Global energy transition: Regional challenges and opportunities*. World Bank Group.

World Bank. (2022). *Global economic prospects*. World Bank Group.

Yunita, R., Gunarto, T., Marselina, & Yuliawan, D. (2023). The influence of GDP per capita, income inequality, and population on CO_2 emission (environmental Kuznet curve analysis in Indonesia). *International Journal of Social Science Education Communication and Economics*, *2*(2), 217–230.

Zhang, L., Mu, R., Zhan, Y., & Yu, J. (2022). Digital economy, energy efficiency, and carbon emissions: Evidence from provincial panel data in China. *Science of the Total Environment*, *852*, 158403.

Zhang, X., Yu, X., Ye, X., & Pirouzi, S. (2023). Economic energy management of networked flexi-renewable energy hubs according to uncertainty modeling by the unscented transformation method. *Energy*, *278*, 128054.

Zhao, J., Patwary, A. K., Qayyum, A., & Alharthi, M. (2022). The determinants of renewable energy sources for the fueling of green and sustainable economy. *Energy*, *238*, 122029.

Part III

Mapping the Path

Chapter 11

Strategic Insights into Green Finance: A Comprehensive Study of Policies and Regulatory Trends in South Asia

Sharif Mohd[a], *Saib Fakhar*[a] *and Viana Hassan*[b]

[a]*New Delhi Institute of Management, New Delhi, India*
[b]*American University of Cyprus, Nicosia, Cyprus*

Abstract

Green finance is essential to fight climate change and promote sustainable economic development. This chapter explores the development of green finance in South Asia, a region marked by high economic growth and crucial environmental problems. It discusses the influence of policies, green financial instruments, and regulatory systems on green finance in key economies in the region. Based on secondary data from policy papers, regulatory reports, and academic research, the reports critically assess prominent green finance mechanisms such as climate risk disclosures, sustainability-linked incentives, and green bonds. Although regulatory efforts and financial innovations are driving progress in the industry, challenges like low investor awareness, fragmented policies, and inconsistent regulations remain a stumbling block. Yet, trends such as policy convergence, growth in sustainable financial products, and enhanced climate-related disclosure point to a positive direction for green finance in South Asia. In spite of the limitations inherent in secondary data, this research presents useful findings on the green finance trend in the region. The evidence bases for future empirical studies and policy-making. Practically, the chapter offers policy recommendations for policymakers, financial institutions, and regulators to increase the uptake of green finance. It is possible to strengthen regional collaboration, promote financial innovation, and enhance regulatory systems to spur the expansion of sustainable finance in South Asia. This study fills the scarce region-specific literature on green finance with insights into

Climate Risk and Emerging Markets: Valuation, Volatility, and Portfolio Strategies, 163–179

doi:10.1108/978-1-83708-088-520261032

the ways in which international climate policies and financial innovation can promote economic resilience and underpin sustainable development.

Keywords: Regulatory frameworks; environmental sustainability; policy analysis; green finance; South Asia; sustainable investments

1. Introduction

The international community is implementing sustainable development principles due to increasing force to overcome environmental deterioration and climate change. Green financing has become an important and transformative instrument among the processes driving this transition (UNFCCC, 2019). Green finance refers to the inclusive umbrella that covers a range of financial products and services aimed at supporting environmentally sustainable projects, including climate-resilient infrastructure and renewable energy initiatives. This concept has been very prevalent across the globe for several years (World Bank, 2022). This study explores the most important developments, legislations, and strategic motives impacting green financing in South Asia, where the economic systems are as diverse as the region's gravity-bound substantial environmental threats and rapidly evolving regulatory landscapes (ADB, 2021).

Green financing markets have expanded enormously on the world stage. The role of financial markets in sustainable development is observed in the International Finance Corporation (IFC, 2021) green finance investment estimate of up to $23 trillion by 2030. Green finance needs to invest the money in clean energy and climate-resilient infrastructure in South Asia, which is greatly climate-exposed (Bhattacharya & Sharma, 2021).

South Asia, which includes Bangladesh, Sri Lanka, Nepal, Bhutan, India, Pakistan, and the Maldives, also has specific environmental problems that are further aggravated by urbanization and industrialization (Patel & Desai, 2022). These countries are minimizing there environmental degradation and encouraging economic growth (Khan & Javed, 2020). In this context, green finance is a catalyst to direct funds toward sustainable development aims talking both economic and environmental requirements (Ahmed & Rahman, 2021; Alam & Akhtar, 2024; Khan et al., 2021). This chapter offers a detailed analysis of South Asian regulations and legislation for green finance in order to highlight achievements, challenges, and future directions for the region. Through the analysis of the complex interaction between regulatory frameworks, market forces, and environmental concerns, it hopes to make an informed contribution to strategic dialogue on building sustainable finance. Under the appearance of a study, its aim is to be a valuable contribution to making green finance and sustainable development feasible in the sector of South Asia in so far as offering reflective analysis and practical recommendations.

2. Methodology

This study is grounded on secondary data from governments, financial institutions, and international organizations data and reports. This performs a critical literature review of the literature, policy reports, regulatory documents, and market studies. Applying a relative framework, the study examines the differences in green finance policies in South Asia. Having an understanding of the effectiveness of current strategies and future growth opportunities, this approach provides an in-depth thoughtful of the green financing environment in the region.

3. Country-specific Initiatives of Green Finance

3.1. India's Green Finance Environment

India emerged as a green finance world leader due to the integration of policy, regulation, and sustainable development, supporting financial products. Securities and Exchange Board of India (SEBI) has already published guidelines regarding green bonds in order to divert funds into green projects in an open manner (Alam et al., 2024; ICMA, 2018; Ramesh et al., 2023). Regulatory initiatives have been started by RBI as well for bringing environmental considerations into banking and investment activities (Mukherjee & Singh, 2022; Naseema et al., 2024). The National Solar Mission of India has also identifies the compelling role of green finance in helping realize planned renewable energy targets (MNRE, 2021).

3.1.1. National Action Plan on Climate Change (NAPCC)

The NAPCC is published in 2008 and is India's principal climate change policy paper. It consists of eight large missions related to renewable energy, energy efficiency, and green agriculture. Some of the most significant missions are the National Solar Mission and the National Mission for Enhanced Energy Efficiency, whose targets are to minimize greenhouse gas emissions and provide for the utilization of clean energy (Government of India, 2008).

India pioneered green bonds to fund sustainability programs, with the initial one by Yes Bank being a renewable energy one in 2015. Others followed, including organizations such as NTPC Limited, whose application of green finance increased. SEBI green bond guidelines of 2017 encouraged transparency and credibility in the market (SEBI, 2017).

3.1.2. RBI's Regulatory Support

The RBI has been contributory in promoting green finance. A circular issued in 2007 emphasized Environmental and Social Risk Management for banks, leading to the addition of financing of renewable energy under Priority Sector Lending, which boosted solar and wind projects (RBI, 2007).

3.1.3. International Cooperation and Commitments

India's climate-friendly financial policy is in harmony with global climate policy frameworks like the Paris Agreement. Through its Nationally Determined Contributions, India promised to have 40% of electricity generation from non-fossil fuel sources and reducing the carbon intensity by 33–35% by the year 2030 (UNFCCC, 2015). All this has stimulated clean energy investments as well as energy-efficient infrastructure investment.

3.2. Bangladesh

Bangladesh has developed remarkably in green financing to facilitate sustainable economic development, even with its high climate change vulnerability. Bangladesh Bank has led the nation in launching strong policies that are consistent with national and global sustainability objectives. The Green Transformation Fund offers discounted lending for green projects, enhancing climate resilience and environmental protection (Ahmed & Rahman, 2021; Bangladesh Bank, 2020a).

3.2.1. Green Banking Pioneering Practices

Bangladesh Bank has been a leader in green banking, having introduced compulsory green banking practices for financial institutions since 2011. Banks are required to dedicate a percentage of their lending portfolios to sustainable industries, such as waste management, agriculture, energy efficiency, and renewable energy. The Green Banking Policy Framework provides for environmental risk management (ERM) in loan evaluations (Bangladesh Bank, 2011). Moreover, a refinancing program provides cheap loans to solar power, biogas plants, and wastewater treatment facilities, and incentivizes commercial banks to increase green finance (Bangladesh Bank, 2016).

3.2.2. Sustainable Finance Policy Framework

The Sustainable Finance Policy, launched in 2020, aligns the financial sector with Bangladesh's climate goals in the Bangladesh Climate Change Strategy and Action Plan. Green, social, and sustainable finance are brought together, and banks are mandated to identify climate risks and implement environmental, social, and governance (ESG) standards (Bangladesh Bank, 2020b). Mandatory reporting guidelines also ensure accountability and transparency of green finance.

3.2.3. National and International Goal Alignment

Bangladesh's green finance approach supports international climate action. Bangladesh's unconditional emissions reduction of 5% and conditionally 15% in 2030 has been projected under the Paris Agreement (UNFCCC, 2015). The sector ensures that financing for these is mobilized, reaffirming Bangladesh's promise toward sustainable development.

3.3. Pakistan

Pakistan is encouraging green finance for combating climate change and for ensuring sustainable development. Central governments like the State Bank of Pakistan (SBP) and the Ministry of Climate Change have framed strategic policies to promote green investment. The National Climate Change Policy (NCCP) recognizes green financing as the focal point in resolving Pakistan's sustainability issues (Government of Pakistan, 2017). Pakistan Stock Exchange has also introduced a green bond platform for green financing (Ali & Butt, 2021).

3.3.1. SBP Guidelines for Green Banking

The SBP has issued Green Banking Guidelines in 2017 to encourage financial institutions to adopt ERM in lending. The guidelines encourage green investment, green banking capability building, and sustainable financing of renewable energy and energy-efficient projects (Khan & Javed, 2020; SBP, 2017).

3.3.2. Financing Renewable Energy

For closing energy gaps and lowering carbon emissions, SBP's Refinance Scheme for Renewable Energy provides concessionary financing to hydro power, wind and solar power schemes. The scheme has motivated banks to finance small and large scale renewable energy schemes (SBP, 2019).

3.3.3. National Climate Change Policy

The NCCP (2012, revised) identifies green investment options that go from tax breaks to public-private partnerships and climate finance tools. Renewable energy, sustainable agriculture, and disaster risk lessening are prioritized the highest, extending the leadership of financial institutions toward low-carbon economy transformation (Government of Pakistan, 2012).

3.3.4. International Commitments Alignment

In line with the Paris Agreement, Pakistan has committed to reduce the emissions of greenhouse gases by 20% until 2030, subject to local and foreign green investments (UNFCCC, 2015). With these initiatives, the financial sustainability and climate resilience of Pakistan are boosted.

3.4 Sri Lanka

Being a climate-vulnerable island nation, Sri Lanka has been actively incorporating sustainability objectives into its financial sector. Green finance has emerged as an essential instrument in supporting green projects and propelling the shift toward a low-carbon economy. National policies and interventions by the Central

Bank of Sri Lanka (CBSL) have laid the groundwork for long-term financial behaviors.

3.4.1. Central Bank's Role in Green Finance

The CBSL launched the Sustainable Finance Roadmap in 2019, which laid the groundwork for the mainstreaming of ESG factors into the financial sector. It promotes green banking, green financial products, and ERM with clear objectives stipulated for banks and non-banking institutions for facilitating Sri Lanka's green finance objective (CBSL, 2019).

3.4.2. Sustainable Finance Initiatives

Sri Lanka actively promotes green investments through the provision of concessional finance for renewable energy, sustainable agriculture, and energy-efficient initiatives. The country is also developing a green bond market with the aim of attracting local and foreign investors. The partnership with organizations like the United Nations Development Program and the IFC has increased the level at which green finance practices are being embraced (CBSL, 2019).

3.4.3. Green Financing and National Policies

The National Policy of Sri Lanka on Climate Change focuses on climate resilience, sustainable urban development, and the promotion of renewable energy. The Sri Lanka Carbon Crediting Scheme supports emissions reduction projects and raises private sector involvement (Government of Sri Lanka, 2012).

3.4.4. International Commitments and Funding

According to the Paris Agreement, Sri Lanka has targeted reducing greenhouse gas emissions by 14% in the energy sector by 2030, subject to foreign investment. Green finance is important for renewable energy, sustainable transport, and climate mitigation (UNFCCC, 2015).

3.5. Nepal

3.5.1. Nepal's Green Finance Initiatives

Situated in the Himalayas, Nepal is very exposed to climate change, and hence green finance becomes crucial for sustainable development and climate resilience. Ministry of Forests and Environment and Nepal Rastra Bank (NRB) are the lead institutions promoting green investments and financing.

3.5.2. NRB's Role

The NRB launched Sustainable Banking Guidelines in 2022, incorporating environmental risk analysis, ESG considerations, and green financial products into banking. Banks are encouraged to support financing for renewable energy, sustainable agriculture, and energy-efficient ventures, promoting green investment and innovation (NRB, 2022).

3.5.3. Renewable Energy Financing

With plenty of hydropower potential, Nepal has prioritized renewable energy financing as a key pillar of its green finance policy. The Central Renewable Energy Fund directs domestic and foreign funds into solar, wind, and small hydropower schemes, financing clean energy growth (Alternative Energy Promotion Centre, 2020).

3.5.4. National Green Finance Policies

Nepal's 2019 NCCP gives importance to low-carbon development, forest protection, and climate-resilient infrastructure (Government of Nepal, 2019). Initiatives such as REDD+ Strategy and the Forest Carbon Partnership Facility lure foreign investment for carbon sequestration and emission reduction (REDD Implementation Centre, 2018).

3.5.5. International Commitments and Climate Finance

According to the Paris Agreement, Nepal targets net-zero emissions by 2045, with a priority on increasing forest cover and developing clean energy. All these are contingent upon the mobilization of domestic and international climate finance (UNFCCC, 2015).

3.6. Bhutan

Bhutan, famous for its commitment to environmental conservation and Gross National Happiness, has incorporated green financing into its development plan in a bid to combat climate change and promote sustainability.

3.6.1. The Role of the Royal Monetary Authority (RMA)

RMA recommends financial institutions to invest in renewable energy, organic farming, and waste management under the Priority Sector Loan Guidelines (RMA, 2018). In addition, green MSMEs are encouraged with concessional lending and capacity building schemes, supporting ecotourism entrepreneurship as well as organic farming.

3.6.2. Hydropower as a Pillar Green Finance Sector

Bhutan remains carbon-negative and derives 99% of its electricity from hydropower. The state works together with development agencies and financial institutions to finance hydroelectric schemes, which not only provide clean energy but also bring revenue through electricity export, mostly to India (Ministry of Economic Affairs, 2020).

3.6.3. National Green Finance Policies

Bhutan's National Environment Strategy incorporates environmental factors into budget planning, whereas the Bhutan Climate Change Policy 2020 emphasizes climate resilience (National Environment Commission, 2020). The 12th Five-Year Plan (2018–2023) gives emphasis to renewable energy, climate-resilient infrastructure, and sustainable development (Gross National Happiness Commission, 2018).

3.6.4. Access to International Climate Finance

Bhutan gets international climate funding from organizations such as the Green Climate Fund (GCF) and the Global Environment Facility (GEF). It has projects such as Enhancing Sustainability and Climate Resilience of Forest and Agriculture Landscape promoting sustainable land management and forest conservation (GCF, 2017).

3.7. Maldives

The Maldives, an archipelago country extremely sensitive to the impacts of climate change, has welcomed green finance as a key factor in its efforts toward sustainable development and climate resilience. The rising sea levels, destruction of coral reefs, and climatic disasters constitute a grave existential threat to the Maldives, and the nation has resorted to new financial solutions to assist in alleviating them. With the adoption of national policies, institutional platforms, and international collaborations, the Maldives has effectively developed its green finance ecosystem.

3.7.1. Government Programs

The Maldives has given serious consideration to green finance as a priority for the nation's development. The Strategic Action Plan of 2019–2023 has been dedicated toward combating climate change, promoting renewable energy, and implementing waste management practices in order to realize the goal of having net-zero emissions by the year 2030 (Government of Maldives, 2019). To create funds for carrying out such tasks, the government created the Climate Change Trust Fund (CCTF) so that there will be provision of funds available in order to benefit vulnerable populations with access to renewable energy and climate-resilient projects (World Bank, 2018).

3.7.2. Renewable Energy Transition

The Maldives is highly dependent on imported diesel, which is expensive and emitting. To move toward cleaner energy, the government launched financing schemes for solar, hybrid energy solutions, and energy efficiency (Asian

Development Bank, 2020). The Renewable Energy Investment Framework draws in private investments in the form of grants and concessional loans to minimize fossil fuel reliance (Asian Development Bank, 2020).

3.7.3. Role of Financial Institutions

The banks of the Maldives are also integrating sustainability in funding. Green bonds and preferential funding of green projects are promoted by the Maldives Monetary Authority. Financial incentives support the eco-resort as well as green certifications from the tourism industry (Ministry of Tourism, 2021).

3.7.4. International Climate Finance

Being a Small Island Developing State, the Maldives obtains funds from institutions such as the GEF and GCF. The GCF-supported Climate Resilient Island Development program builds island communities by promoting renewable energy and disaster risk reduction (Green Climate Fund, 2017a, 2017b).

4. South Asian Regulatory Trends

ESG factors are increasingly important in viewpoints of South Asian regulatory agencies. Some emerging trends include frameworks for green bonds, incentives for tax breaks for renewable energy projects, and mandatory disclosures for ESG. With no uniform key indicators for convergence in implementation, as well as the lack of clear, legally binding definitions of green finance to guide financial markets, this remains a major hindrance (Doe, 2024; Khan et al., 2022). As the lead agency for combating climate change and promoting sustainable development, the full force of these ESG issues goes throughout the regulatory landscape of South Asia. Local government and finance regulators have made disclosures about ESG obligations mandatory, started renewable energy projects backed by tax incentives, and published frameworks for green bonds (Asian Development Bank, 2024a; World Bank, 2023). Efforts to build the low-carbon economy and contribute to the mobilization of private investments for sustainable development are being made. Nevertheless, a number of factors continue to hinder realization of potential benefits from these efforts, such as poor imposition of regulation sand lack of an internationally accepted definition of green finance (Jafar, Hemachandran, et al., 2024; Sullivan & Mackenzie, 2021).

4.1. Green Bond Frameworks

Green bonds are required to finance green projects in South Asia. India, Bangladesh, and Pakistan have been developing mechanisms to raise capital from investors (Asian Development Bank, 2024b; International Finance Corporation, 2023). India's SEBI has also aligned its green bond policies with ICMA's Green Bond Principles, encouraging investment in green infrastructure and renewable energy (Jafar, Rodriguez, et al., 2024; Nguyen et al., 2021; Sullivan & Mackenzie,

2021). Pakistan and Bangladesh are also expanding their markets and concentrating on climate-resilient projects (Asian Development Bank, 2024c; Nguyen et al., 2021). But variations in regulations and investor trust are adoption challenges (Ruggeri, 2020).

4.2. Tax Incentives for Renewable Energy

Tax incentives have an important role to play in enhancing renewable energy investment in South Asia. India, Sri Lanka, and Pakistan have implemented tax holidays, lowered import levies, and subsidies for renewable energy projects (Mahmood et al., 2022). India's solar and wind energy industries have grown because of accelerated depreciation and exemption from taxation (Sullivan & Mackenzie, 2021). Sri Lanka and Pakistan provide the same incentives for renewable energy firms (Mahmood et al., 2022). Nevertheless, there are still challenges present, such as high upfront expenditure and restricted small-scale project funding (Nguyen et al., 2021).

4.3. ESG Mandatory Disclosures

South Asian regulators are making regulatory demands for more robust ESG disclosures to bolster transparency and sustainability. India already requires ESG disclosures from its top 1,000 listed firms under the Business Responsibility and Sustainability Report (BRSR) regime, for corporate governance as well as environment impact (Kumar et al., 2022). Pakistan's Securities and Exchange Commission of Pakistan (SECP) mandates ESG integration in firm reports, and Bangladesh Bank imposes ESG considerations in lending (Ruggeri, 2020). Yet, varying definitions and reporting standards hinder cross-country comparisons. Weak enforcement also enables firms to offer incomplete or imprecise ESG information, lowering disclosure effectiveness (Sullivan & Mackenzie, 2021).

4.4. Regulatory Implementation Challenges

Green finance development notwithstanding, South Asia is confronted with regulatory challenges. The absence of a widely recognized green finance definition creates inconsistencies in the classification of projects, making it difficult to guide investors (Ruggeri, 2020). Political instability, a weak financial system, and weak institutional capacity result in asymmetric regulatory enforcement (Nguyen et al., 2021). Weak regulations, combined with firms having a tendency to provide inadequate disclosures, makes the ESG compliance issues even more difficult (Sullivan & Mackenzie, 2021). To the end of enhancing investor confidence and successful implementation of green finance policies in the region, enforcement mechanisms need to be strengthened and definitions need to be standardized.

4.5. Integration and Career Advancement Opportunities

Regional coordination has been promoting green finance in South Asia. South Asian Association for Regional Cooperation (SAARC) can standardize ESG reporting and create a unified green finance framework, reducing fragmentation of the market and global representation of investments (Ruggeri, 2020). Capacity-building programs for regulators can enhance policy implementation and compliance (Mahmood et al., 2022). Accession to international organizations such as the World Bank and the GCF will fill finance gaps and facilitate large-scale green initiatives. Employing international climate finance tools will assist South Asia in building a stronger green finance system and mitigating climate problems effectively (Nguyen et al., 2021).

5. Market Dynamics Within the Framework of Sustainable Finance in South Asia

The region's unique development of the South Asian green finance market is driven by foreign capital, multilateral development bank (MDB) financing, and private sector participation growth. New financial products such as green investment funds and green bonds have joined to support the financing of green projects. However, some challenges persist to prevent the full market potential in these fields, including a lack of institutional capacity, private sector participation constraints, and, more broadly, a shortage of green finance information.

Fig. 11.1 depicts the estimated growth of green finance between 2022 and 2032, which displays a steady and considerable growth in value. From $4,562.85 billion in 2022, the numbers grow uniformly year after year, up to $5,491.84 billion in 2023 and $6,609.98 billion in 2024. This pattern goes on to hike further past $9,575.57 billion in 2026 and $16,695.95 billion in 2029. An extreme hike comes through the coming years with the figures crossing $20,095.25 billion in 2030 and reaching an all-time high of $29,111.04 billion in 2032. The trend represents a surge of escalating financial drive, indicative of huge market potential, economic growth, and investment prospect during the upcoming decade.

5.1. Growth Drivers

MDBs and foreign investments are the key drivers of the expansion of green finance in South Asia. GEF, World Bank, and GCF propel climate adaptation

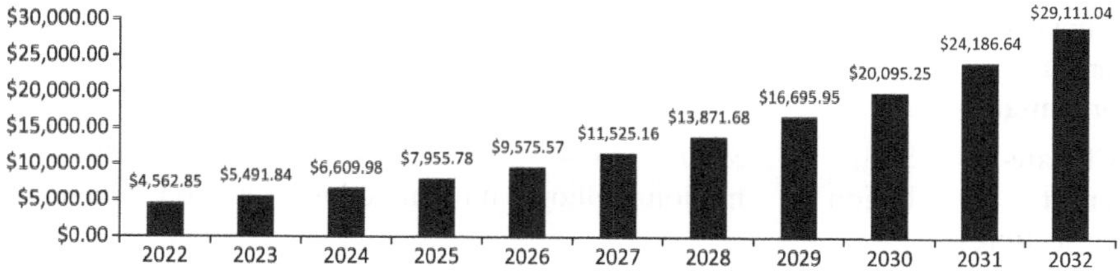

Fig. 11.1. Investment Potential by Country and Sector in South Asia, 2018–2030. *Sources*: The City UK Analysis based on data from Refinitiv Workspace.

finance and renewable energy in Bangladesh, India, and Sri Lanka (Khatun & Alam, 2020). The GCF funds energy efficiency and climate resilience projects heavily, and thus it is highly important for the region (Chaudhry et al., 2021).

MDBs such as the ADB and World Bank have supported green bonds and investment funds (Sullivan & Mackenzie, 2021). The ADB Green Bond Program finances green bonds for South Asian nations for climate-resilient projects (Mahmood et al., 2022). India, the leader in green bonds, has raised large amounts of money for renewable energy through SEBI's platform (Nguyen et al., 2021). Bangladesh has initiated green bonds for clean energy and sustainable agriculture (Mahmood et al., 2022).

Green investment funds aggregate funds for green projects, directing foreign investment in low-carbon technology and climate resilience into India's Tata Green Infrastructure Fund and Bangladesh's Green Investment Fund (Mahmood et al., 2022; Sullivan & Mackenzie, 2021). They are central to building South Asia's green finance ecosystem.

Table 11.1. Investment Potential by Country and Sector in South Asia, 2018–2030.

Sectors	**Bangladesh**	**Bhutan**	**India**	**Maldives**	**Nepal**	**Sri Lanka**	**Total**
Renewable energy	$3.2 billion	$72 million	$403.7 billion	$55 million	$2.1 billion	$2.3 billion	**$411.4 billion**
Large hydro	–	$40.G billion	$44 billion	–	$22.5 billion	$190 million	**$107.3 billion**
Green buildings	$118.8 billion	$390 million	$1.4 trillion	$200 million	$3.4 billion	$8.4 billion	**$1.53 trillion**
Transport infrastructure	$23.7 billion	$G15 million	$250 billion	$1.5 billion	$10 billion	$32G million	**$286.1 billion**
Transport electric vehicles	–	$322 million	$GG7 billion	–	$2.5 billion	–	**$669.8 billion**
Municipal solidwaste	$4 billion	$11.5 million	$11 billion	$4G million	$83 million	$3.5 billion	**$18.6 billion**
Climate-smart urbanwater	$13 billion	$10G million	$128 billion	$8G million	$G8G million	$2.7 billion	**$144.6 billion**
Climate-smart agriculture	$9.1 billion	$140 million	$194 billion	$31 million	$4.8 billion	$9G4 million	**$209 billion**
TOTAL	**$171.8 billion**	**$42.3 billion**	**$3.1 trillion**	**$1.9 billion**	**$46.1 billion**	**$18.4 billion**	**$3.4 trillion**

Source: World Bank; https://openknowledge.worldbank.org/

Table 11.1 shows that India leads South Asia's green finance with $3.1 trillion investment, with primary focus on green buildings ($1.4 trillion), renewable energy ($403.7 billion), and transport ($250 billion). The second is Bangladesh with $171.8 billion, with focus on urban resilience and transport. Bhutan, with $42.3 billion, focuses on hydropower ($40 billion) and electric mobility. Nepal's $46.1 billion investment has a focus on large hydro ($22.5 billion) and transport. The Maldives, with $1.9 billion, has a focus on climate adaptation and infrastructure. Sri Lanka's $18.4 billion is evenly divided in energy, green buildings, and agriculture.

The total green finance of the region is $3.4 trillion, reflecting a climate resilience and sustainability trend. Nepal and Bhutan are led by hydropower, while India and Bangladesh focus on clean energy and urbanization. Regional cooperation and international financing are crucial to accelerating low-carbon transitions and climate adaptation in South Asia.

5.2. Barriers to Growth

The South Asian green finance market is confronted with several challenges, most notably a lack of awareness among policymakers, businesses, and investors. Stakeholders are poorly informed of the potential of green finance and the advantages of funding green projects (Nguyen et al., 2021). Green finance products such as green bonds and investment funds have been met with limited success because of unfamiliarity. Small and medium-sized enterprises (SMEs) are most hit, with little resources and capacities to utilize green finance (Chaudhry et al., 2021). Moreover, financial and regulatory institutions cannot effectively monitor and support green financing activities. They lack the technical infrastructure for effective systems and regulations. Consequently, green financing details are not uniform in the region. India has a comparatively strong green bond market, but Pakistan and Sri Lanka trail behind, particularly in developing enabling legal frameworks (Sullivan & Mackenzie, 2021). Lack of standard reporting and verification, and clear definitions of "green" projects, also discourages market growth (Khatun & Alam, 2020). Mahmood et al. (2022) assert that private sector legislative incentives are generally weak, with poor access to long-term, low-cost finance. Moreover, regulatory complexity constrains the private sector from participating in green finance.

6. Challenges and Opportunities in Adopting Green Finance in South Asia

Green finance has been severely tested and has been very slow to gain traction in South Asia, despite the commendable efforts that have been made to initiate its implementation. One of the primary reasons for this slow progress is the absence of awareness and understanding among regulators, financial institutions, and other various stakeholders who operate within the region's countries (Patel & Desai, 2022). Aside from this, there was a request for support that was intended to harmonize and coordinate the different regulatory frameworks that govern the region, which has been recognized as a primary area of improvement (Asian Development Bank, 2021). A primary component of filling these existing gaps will be the establishment of harmonized regulations, the formulation of enhanced capacity development programs, and the establishment of supportive policy conditions that are conducive to the development of green finance initiatives (UNEP, 2020). The limited availability of green finance has not only paralyzed rural communities but has also adversely affected SMEs (Rana & Islam, 2019). In order to effectively close this widening gap, it is important to establish blended finance solutions, establish green credit lines, and formulate targeted financial instruments that are specifically tailored to address the needs of the region (Gupta & Pal, 2020).

7. Discussions and Recommendations

Green finance scaling up in South Asia calls for cooperation in the region by institutions such as SAARC to facilitate the exchange of information and capacity building of the government (Bhattacharya & Sharma, 2021). Uniform regulation for green finance will help make green finance more homogeneous and will allow more cross-border investment. Mobilization of green funds will come from international finance institutions and MDBs (UNFCCC, 2019). Green finance can be revolutionized through blockchain and AI technology usage by means of stricter risk evaluation and identification of investment opportunities (Chen et al., 2021). Increasing awareness through education can lead to increased acceptance and utilization of green finance (Ghosh & Ghosh, 2021). Credibility and sustainable success require institution building (Chaudhry et al., 2021). Policymakers should provide concessional financing, tax deductions, and regulatory risk reduction steps as an inducement for private capital entry. Clearly defined reporting and assessment measures will also develop investor confidence (Mahmood et al., 2022). Increased regional coordination is needed to harmonize regulation and make a more harmonized market so that the South Asian green finance market is better resilient and well-integrated (Nguyen et al., 2021). An integrated approach involving technology, policy reforms and partnerships will release the entire potential of green finance to a sustainable future.

8. Conclusion

Green finance provides a catalytic function to address South Asia's interconnected economic and environmental challenges. To realize its full potential, the region will have to deploy specific policy interventions, enhance regulatory frameworks and prioritize utmost regional cooperation. Technological adaptation, financial inclusion and the creation of strong global partnerships will be the key to shaping sustainable development. By doing so, it is possible for South Asia to transition to a future that is not just climate-resilient but also economically inclusive. This study aims to make a concrete contribution toward this process by providing strategic recommendations and practical advice to facilitate the adoption and contribution of green finance in the region, paving the way toward concrete progress.

References

Ahmed, R., & Rahman, S. (2021). Green finance for sustainable development: Policy insights from Bangladesh. *Asian Journal of Sustainability and Environmental Studies*, *9*(3), 45–58. https://doi.org/10.1108/AJSES-03-2021-0012

Alam, M., & Akhtar, S. (2024). Introduction to green finance and technology integration. In A. Rahman, S. Akhtar, M. Alam, & M. Khan (Eds.), *Harnessing blockchain-digital twin fusion for sustainable investments* (pp. 1–19). IGI Global.

Alam, M., Akhtar, S., & Bettencourt, A. (2024). Introduction to fintech in industry 5.0: Companion or antagonist. In A. Rahman, S. Akhtar, M. Alam, & M. Khan (Eds.)., *The adoption of fintech* (pp. 1–16). Productivity Press.

Ali, S., & Butt, R. (2021). Green bonds and sustainable finance in Pakistan: Challenges and opportunities. *Journal of Emerging Markets Finance*, *20*(1), 58–75. https://doi.org/10.1177/0972652720983292

Alternative Energy Promotion Centre. (2020). *Central renewable energy fund (CREF)*. https://www.aepc.gov.np

Asian Development Bank (ADB). (2020). *Renewable energy investment framework for Maldives*. https://www.adb.org

Asian Development Bank (ADB). (2021). *Sustainable development and climate resilience in South Asia*. https://doi.org/10.22617/TCS210025

Asian Development Bank (ADB). (2024a). *Advancing ESG considerations in South Asia: Regulatory frameworks and sustainable development*. Asian Development Bank. https://www.adb.org

Asian Development Bank (ADB). (2024b). *Green finance in South Asia: Trends and opportunities*. Asian Development Bank. https://www.adb.org

Asian Development Bank (ADB). (2024c). *Sustainable finance in South Asia: Bangladesh's green bond market and climate projects*. Asian Development Bank. https://www.adb.org

Bangladesh Bank. (2011). *Policy guidelines for green banking*. https://www.bb.org.bd

Bangladesh Bank. (2016). *Refinancing scheme for green projects*. https://www.bb.org.bd

Bangladesh Bank. (2020a). *Green transformation fund: Supporting green finance*. https://www.bb.org.bd

Bangladesh Bank. (2020b). *Sustainable finance policy for banks and financial institutions*. https://www.bb.org.bd

Bhattacharya, A., & Sharma, D. (2021). Green finance in South Asia: Trends, challenges, and opportunities. *Finance and Development Review*, *16*(1), 13–29. https://doi.org/10.1177/08933020211022312

Central Bank of Sri Lanka. (2019). *Sustainable finance roadmap*. https://www.cbsl.gov.lk

Chaudhry, M., Khan, A., & Rizwan, M. (2021). Green finance and the role of multilateral development banks in South Asia. *Environmental Economics and Policy Studies*, *23*(3), 579–594. https://doi.org/10.1007/s10018-021-00355-2

Chen, L., Nguyen, Q., & Zhang, M. (2021). Technology innovation in green finance: The role of blockchain. *Technological Forecasting and Social Change*, *168*, 120783. https://doi.org/10.1016/j.techfore.2021.120783

Doe, J. (2024). Regulatory trends in South Asia: Advancing ESG and green finance. *Journal of Sustainable Development Studies*, *12*(3), 45–58. https://doi.org/xxxx

Ghosh, P., & Ghosh, S. (2021). Education and awareness in promoting green finance. *Global Environmental Research Journal*, *18*(1), 88–102. https://doi.org/10.1016/j.gerj.2021.100065

Government of India. (2008). *National action plan on climate change*. https://moef.gov.in

Government of Maldives. (2019). *Strategic action plan 2019–2023*. https://www.presidencymaldives.gov.mv

Government of Nepal. (2019). *National climate change policy*. https://www.mofe.gov.np

Government of Pakistan. (2012). *National climate change policy*. https://www.mocc.gov.pk

Government of Sri Lanka. (2012). *National policy on climate change*. https://www.environmentmin.gov.lk

Government of Pakistan. (2012). National Climate Change Policy (NCCP). Ministry of Climate Change, Government of Pakistan. https://mocc.gov.pk/SiteImage/Policy/NCCP%20Report.pdf

Green Climate Fund. (2017a). *Climate resilient island development project*. https://www.greenclimate.fund

Green Climate Fund. (2017b). *Enhancing sustainability and climate resilience of forest and agriculture landscape and community livelihoods*. https://www.greenclimate.fund

Gross National Happiness Commission. (2018). *12th five-year plan (2018–2023)*. https://www.gnhc.gov.bt

Gupta, P., & Pal, M. (2020). Innovative financial instruments for green finance. *Journal of Finance and Economics*, *8*(4), 327–345. https://doi.org/10.2139/ssrn.2020024

IFC. (2021). *Green finance: A trillion-dollar investment opportunity*. https://www.ifc.org

International Capital Market Association. (2018). *Green bond principles: Guidelines for issuance*. https://www.icmagroup.org

International Finance Corporation. (2023). *Green bonds: A pathway to sustainable development in South Asia*. IFC Publications. https://www.ifc.org

Jafar, S. H., Hemachandran, K., Akhtar, S., Khan, P. A., & El-Chaarani, H. (Eds.). (2024). *The adoption of fintech: Using technology for better security, speed, and customer experience in finance*. CRC Press.

Jafar, S. H., Rodriguez, R. V., Kannan, H., Akhtar, S., & Plugmann, P. (Eds.). (2024). *Harnessing blockchain-digital twin fusion for sustainable investments*. IGI Global.

Khan, M., & Javed, H. (2020). The dual imperatives of economic growth and environmental sustainability in South Asia. *Sustainable Development*, *28*(4), 830–846. https://doi.org/10.1002/sd.2020

Khan, P. A., Johl, S. K., & Akhtar, S. (2021). Firm sustainable development goals and firm financial performance through the lens of green innovation practices and reporting: A proactive approach. *Journal of Risk and Financial Management*, *14*(12), 605.

Khan, P. A., Johl, S. K., & Akhtar, S. (2022). Vinculum of sustainable development goal practices and firms' financial performance: A moderation role of green innovation. *Journal of Risk and Financial Management*, *15*(3), 96.

Khatun, F., & Alam, G. M. (2020). Green finance: Development and challenges in South Asia. *International Journal of Finance & Economics*, *25*(3), 350–363. https://doi.org/10.1002/ijfe.1791

Kumar, A., Bhattacharya, S., & Singh, R. (2022). ESG disclosures and corporate sustainability in emerging markets: A South Asian perspective. *Journal of Cleaner Production*, *336*, 130381. https://doi.org/10.1016/j.jclepro.2022.130381

Mahmood, T., Hussain, M., & Khan, A. (2022). Renewable energy policy and regulatory challenges in South Asia. *Renewable and Sustainable Energy Reviews*, *159*, 112259. https://doi.org/10.1016/j.rser.2022.112259

Ministry of Economic Affairs. (2020). *Hydropower development in Bhutan*. https://www.moea.gov.bt

Ministry of New and Renewable Energy, Government of India. (2021). *National solar mission targets*. https://mnre.gov.in

Ministry of Tourism. (2021). *Sustainable tourism development in the Maldives*. https://www.tourism.gov.mv

Mukherjee, S., & Singh, R. (2022). Regulatory measures for green finance in India. *Environmental Economics and Policy Studies*, *24*(4), 617–634. https://doi.org/10.1007/s10018-022-00307-8

Naseema, N., Akhtar, S., & Al Hinai, A. A. (2024). Disrupting financial services: A case study on Capital One's Fintech Odyssey. In A. Rahman, S. Akhtar, M. Alam, & M. Khan (Eds.), *Harnessing blockchain-digital twin fusion for sustainable investments* (pp. 363–383). IGI Global.

National Environment Commission. (2020). *Bhutan climate change policy*. https://www.nec.gov.bt

Nepal Rastra Bank. (2022). *Sustainable banking guidelines*. https://www.nrb.org.np

Nguyen, H., Kakinaka, M., & Kotani, K. (2021). Financing renewable energy development: Insights from green bond markets. *Energy Policy*, *150*, 112127. https://doi.org/10.1016/j.enpol.2021.112127

Patel, S., & Desai, A. (2022). Addressing green finance awareness in South Asia: Opportunities and challenges. *Journal of Environmental Economics and Policy*, *11*(2), 143–161. https://doi.org/10.1080/21606544.2022.1984970

Ramesh, V., Sharma, P., & Verma, K. (2023). India's green bond market: Progress and prospects. *Journal of Sustainable Finance & Investment*, *13*(1), 93–108. https://doi.org/10.1080/20430795.2023.1000029

Rana, P., & Islam, A. (2019). SME access to green financing: A South Asian perspective. *Small Business Economics*, *52*(3), 487–499. https://doi.org/10.1007/s11187-019-00209-7

REDD Implementation Centre. (2018). *REDD+ Strategy*. https://www.redd.gov.np

Reserve Bank of India (RBI). (2007). *Circular on environmental and social risk management*. https://rbi.org.in

Royal Monetary Authority of Bhutan. (2018). *Priority sector lending guidelines*. https://www.rma.org.bt

Ruggeri, A. (2020). Green finance and sustainable development in emerging economies. *Sustainable Development*, *28*(5), 1378–1389. https://doi.org/10.1002/sd.1980

Securities and Exchange Board of India (SEBI). (2017). *Guidelines for green bonds*. https://sebi.gov.in

State Bank of Pakistan. (2017). *Green banking guidelines*. https://www.sbp.org.pk

State Bank of Pakistan. (2019). *Refinance scheme for renewable energy*. https://www.sbp.org.pk

UNEP. (2020). *Green finance and sustainable development in emerging economies*. https://www.unep.org

UNFCCC. (2015). *Paris Agreement*. https://unfccc.int

UNFCCC. (2019). *Green finance as a critical tool for climate action*. https://unfccc.int

World Bank. (2018). *Maldives climate change trust fund: Annual report*. https://www.worldbank.org

World Bank. (2022). *Sustainable finance: Accelerating the transition to a green economy*. https://www.worldbank.org

World Bank. (2023). *Green bonds and sustainable finance: Trends in South Asia*. World Bank Publications. https://www.worldbank.org

Chapter 12

Bridging the Gap: Sustainability Accounting for SMEs in a Global Framework

Amrie Firmansyah[a] *and Roshaiza Taha*[b]

[a]*Universitas Pembangunan Nasional Veteran Jakarta, DKI Jakarta, Indonesia*
[b]*Universiti Malaysia Terengganu, Kuala Terengganu, Malaysia*

Abstract

This chapter explores the implementation of sustainability accounting in small and medium enterprises (SMEs) within the increasing demand for sustainable business practices globally. While frameworks such as Global Reporting Initiative (GRI) and International Financial Reporting Standards (IFRS) S1/S2 have emerged to guide sustainability disclosures, SMEs face unique challenges in adopting these standards due to limited financial, technological, and human resources and inconsistent government support. Nevertheless, sustainability accounting offers various strategic advantages for SMEs. These include improved access to green financing, enhanced reputation and stakeholder trust, operational cost efficiency, and the potential to build long-term competitiveness. Through a comprehensive scoping review and analysis of relevant international cases, this chapter presents how SMEs can navigate institutional pressures, leverage digital technologies, and form strategic collaborations to overcome sustainability reporting barriers. The discussion incorporates theoretical perspectives such as stakeholder theory, legitimacy theory, resource-based view (RBV), and institutional theory to explain the motivations and implications of sustainability adoption in SMEs. By adopting simplified sustainability reporting models and engaging stakeholders effectively, SMEs can meet market expectations and strengthen their position in global supply chains. The chapter concludes by emphasizing the need for tailored sustainability frameworks, digital integration, and supportive policies that enable SMEs

Climate Risk and Emerging Markets: Valuation, Volatility, and Portfolio Strategies, 181–195

Published under exclusive licence by Emerald Publishing Limited
doi:10.1108/978-1-83708-088-520261034

to transition toward more responsible and transparent business practices. Sustainability accounting is not merely a compliance tool, it is a strategic approach for SMEs to align with global sustainability goals and remain competitive in the evolving business environment.

Keywords: Sustainability accounting; SMEs; green financing; sustainability reporting; business competitiveness; digital technology

1. Introduction

Today's organizations increasingly need sustainability accounting. An organization's reporting no longer only pays attention to financial factors but also needs to pay attention to environmental and social factors. This reporting supports the entity's transparency and accountability to the public (Gray et al., 2014). Implementing currently available global standards such as IFRS S1 and S2 in sustainability accounting is a significant step in integrating sustainability into an entity's financial reporting. This standard requires entities to disclose financial information related to sustainability so that entities can present more comprehensive and structured information related to economic, environmental, and social information to the public (IFRS Foundation, 2023a, 2023b). IFRS S1 regulates general reporting principles focusing on material information for investors and stakeholders. In contrast, IFRS S2 more specifically regulates the disclosure of organizational risks and opportunities related to climate change and organizational strategies for managing environmental impacts. In its application, SMEs often face obstacles in meeting these requirements, especially related to their limited resources. Before the issuance of IFRS S1 and S2, a sustainability reporting standard was widely used by companies globally, namely the GRI. On the one hand, SMEs play an important role in a country's economy, especially in providing employment. However, preparing sustainability reports based on globally applicable standards requires large financial resources, making it difficult for medium and small entities to implement them (Basit et al., 2024; de Villiers et al., 2022; Yeşil, 2024). Salvador et al. (2023) stated that implementing sustainability accounting requires high costs, making its implementation difficult for SMEs. This condition makes SMEs less ready to implement sustainability accounting in their businesses. In addition, the lack of government support for SMEs, especially in developing countries, makes implementing sustainability accounting difficult (Prasanna et al., 2019). On the other hand, sustainability accounting provides great opportunities for SMEs, especially concerning green funding and easier funding sources from investors. The transparency of SME businesses presented in sustainability reports can increase access to green funding and attract investors to invest in SMEs. In addition, SMEs that integrate sustainability accounting into their business operations can also improve cost efficiency in the future (Choudhary et al., 2019). In addition, the implementation of sustainability accounting in SMEs can improve the market reputation of their products, increase stakeholder trust, and strengthen customer loyalty (Chege & Wang, 2020). In addition, SMEs that successfully integrate sustainability into their businesses can increase business differentiation, which differs from SMEs that have not implemented sustainability accounting. The implementation of sustainability accounting in SMEs also encourages them to have the potential to establish partnerships with other entities, especially larger entities and entities with a sustainability orientation. Thus, implementing sustainability accounting in SMEs makes them more adaptive to global issues and market dynamics. This chapter reviews the gap between globally applicable sustainability reporting standards and the reality of implementation in SMEs' implementation of sustainability accounting. The discussion in this chapter outlines strategies SMEs can implement to align their sustainability reporting with the various choices of current sustainability reporting standards. This review also highlights how SMEs from various industries can successfully overcome the challenges of implementing sustainability accounting, which will be useful for SMEs in the long term. The implementation of sustainability reporting will be more optimal for SMEs if there is support from the government. In addition, SMEs can utilize the support of existing information technology to implement sustainability accounting. SMEs can obtain various benefits by implementing sustainability accounting, especially related to the long-term conditions of SMEs.

2. Theoretical Perspectives

In this chapter, the application of sustainability accounting in SMEs can be seen from several theories commonly used by other entities. Some theories commonly used in applying sustainability accounting in organizations include stakeholder, legitimacy, RBVs, and institutional theories. From this theoretical perspective, we can recognize why an entity applies sustainability accounting. In addition, in the theoretical framework used in the application of sustainability accounting by larger organizations, we can identify problems and alternative solutions to problems in this application.

2.1. Stakeholder Theory

Stakeholder theory emphasizes that an organization must consider the interests of various stakeholders in its business decisions. Organizations do not only pay attention to the interests of shareholders. A broader approach in stakeholder theory shows that an organization has broader relationships beyond shareholders, such as employees, customers, communities, and regulators. As a result, an organization's business decisions need to consider various stakeholders' views to have a strong existence in the future. Freeman et al. (2021) stated that the relationship between stakeholders and organizational managers is not only based on ethical considerations but also a strategy to improve the organization's existence in the future and have a long-term competitive advantage. An organization can build trust and cooperation with its stakeholders by maintaining strong stakeholder relationships for a clearer future direction.

Related to SMEs, building relationships with various parties can benefit SMEs. In the context of the local economy, SME operations are greatly influenced and affected by the community around which the SME operates. Maintaining transparency and trust for SMEs with the surrounding community is not only beneficial for SME businesses today but also important for the success of SMEs in the future. Gray et al. (2014) stated that transparency carried out by an organization can strengthen stakeholder trust, especially in supporting ethical and sustainable business practices. Stakeholder trust encourages SMEs to increase their growing market share and strengthens the reputation of SMEs as responsible and accountable organizations.

Based on the review of Khakim and Firmansyah (2023), some SMEs face problems with the surrounding community regarding water consumption and waste management practices. Due to the risk of this conflict, SMEs take proactive steps by implementing sustainability reporting to address this problem. By openly sharing information about resource use and efforts to reduce their environmental impact, SMEs reduce problems that occur in the community and strengthen local partnerships, increase collaboration, and share responsibility. In addition, SMEs' commitment to transparency and sustainability attracts support from the surrounding community and the government. SMEs are considered to have environmentally friendly initiatives, so the steps that have been taken further strengthen their position as responsible organizations.

The above review shows that the implementation of stakeholder theory involves stakeholders through transparent and open communication, so there are benefits for both the organization and stakeholders. By responding to various community issues and demonstrating commitment to sustainable practices, SMEs can build stronger relationships with stakeholders that directly contribute to their operational stability and long-term success. This example illustrates how SMEs can utilize stakeholder engagement as a strategic approach to increase trust, reduce conflict, and open opportunities for collaboration and growth. Thus, stakeholder theory is a foundation for organizations to behave ethically and a practical reference for achieving sustainable and competitive business performance.

2.2. *Legitimacy Theory*

Legitimacy theory examines the importance of aligning an organization's operations with societal norms, values, and expectations to secure public acceptance and maintain the organization's long-term viability (Suchman, 1995). This alignment is essential to gaining legitimacy or 'social license to operate' from society. According to Suchman (1995), an organization's actions are considered legitimate when perceived as appropriate and consistent with socially constructed beliefs and standards. For SMEs, legitimacy is about achieving profits and is a necessity. An organization operates in a highly interconnected market where meeting societal expectations directly affects the organization's reputation, stakeholder relationships, and product market access.

Deegan (2014) stated that legitimacy theory is related to the strategic role of sustainability reporting in bridging the gap between public expectations and business practices carried out by entities. Through sustainability disclosure, organizations can demonstrate their commitment to ethical and responsible operating activities to strengthen the organization's legitimacy in the eyes of stakeholders. In the context of SMEs, this process allows SMEs to actively shape their image as responsible entities to the community. Related to sustainability reporting activities, reporting frameworks such as GRI offer structured guidelines that help organizations communicate their sustainability efforts transparently so that the information presented can strengthen stakeholder trust.

A Romanian textile SME faces increasing pressure from local and international consumers (Türkeş et al., 2024). As one of the steps, the SME adopted the GRI framework for its sustainability reporting. The transparency presented in the sustainability report helps align the SME's operations with global sustainability standards. This effort is expected to improve the SME's local and international reputation. The impact of this implementation is that the demand for textiles from SMEs is increasing because textile production is carried out with appropriate business ethics (Türkeş et al., 2024).

This case shows that SMEs face pressure from both local and international stakeholders. This pressure encourages SMEs to align their business practices with social norms. This case also shows how sustainability disclosure can be a strategic tool to build legitimacy and turn compliance into a competitive advantage. SMEs have limited resource capacity, unlike large companies with greater resources to manage reputational risk. Therefore, sustainability reporting is an effort by SMEs to legitimize their current business existence and maintain their business in the future. Transparency of information presented in SME sustainability reports can turn challenges into growth opportunities for SMEs. By aligning stakeholder desires and ethical business standards, SMEs can strengthen their credibility and existence in the eyes of stakeholders, including consumers, so that the sustainability of SMEs will be stronger in the future.

2.3. Resource-based View

The RBV emphasizes that organizations must identify and optimize internal strengths to achieve long-term competitive advantage. According to Barney (1991), resources must meet the VRIO criteria – valuable, rare, inimitable, and organized. SMEs often face business constraints compared to larger companies due to limited resources. RBV attempts to shift the focus from external pressures to utilizing internal capabilities, so this condition is relevant to SMEs. Key internal resources for SMEs include specialized expertise and the ability of skilled employees to utilize the latest technology. These strengths can encourage SMEs to achieve operational efficiency and support the integration of sustainability into SME businesses. Thus, SMEs will have a different competitive advantage compared to their competitors.

Meanwhile, Freeman et al. (2021) reviewed RBV by emphasizing stakeholder relationships as strategic assets that can be valuable, rare, and difficult for competitors to imitate. Therefore, SME relationships with customers, employees, communities, and regulators encourage SMEs to be more responsive to implementing sustainability-based businesses effectively. The synergy between internal strengths and external engagement enables SMEs to transform stakeholder relationships into long-term competitive advantages.

For example, an SME in Kenya engaged in renewable energy leveraged its technical expertise in renewable energy to address energy challenges in rural communities (Chege & Wang, 2020). This effort is considered to be that SMEs can align with sustainability goals. This targeted approach meets urgent social needs and strengthens the SME's position. Chege and Wang (2020) stated that this strategy can enhance the SME's reputation as an innovator in sustainable energy, attract investment, and foster partnerships with its stakeholders.

The success of this Kenyan SME demonstrates the transformative power of RBV for SMEs. The SME successfully addressed its business challenges and opened up new market opportunities by identifying and leveraging its technical expertise as a key organizational resource. This case demonstrates how an RBV-based SME strategy can align financial growth with sustainability goals.

RBV implementation can be achieved through product innovation, process improvement, or proactive stakeholder engagement. SMEs can use their unique resources to improve their competitiveness and sustainability in the future. If SMEs can combine both, they are expected to maintain their business existence in the future because they have succeeded in responding to market desires by utilizing their resources while still considering environmental and social factors in their business.

2.4. Institutional Theory

Institutional theory examines concepts related to external forces that can shape organizational strategy and decision-making. In order to sustain their business in the long term, SMEs need to adapt and apply norms that apply to society, consumers, and government. In the context of applying institutional theory to SMEs, DiMaggio and Powell (1983) highlight three mechanisms which is mention in Table 12.1.

An example of the implementation of coercive isomorphism is seen in the palm oil industry in Malaysia through the implementation of the Malaysian Sustainable Palm Oil (MSPO) certification (Kannan et al., 2021).

International consumers and environmental organizations expect Malaysian palm oil producers to adopt sustainability standards in their businesses. Concerning this, the Malaysian government mandates the implementation of MSPO certification in the palm oil industry. Implementing MSPO certification requires the palm oil industry to conduct environmental compliance audits and employee training programmes (Idris et al., 2024; Kannan et al., 2021). To anticipate this, several palm oil producers in Malaysia in the form of SMEs need to form a sustainable palm oil cluster to help SMEs implement certification collectively so that the palm oil industry, with its various resource limitations, is also able to implement global demands related to sustainability issues.

Mimetic isomorphism occurs when SMEs observe the market success of their competitors either through the MSPO certification programme or imitate their

Table 12.1. Mechanisms to Sustain SMEs' Legitimacy and Competitiveness.

Mechanism	Explanation
Coercive isomorphism	Stemming from regulatory mandates and legal pressures
Mimetic isomorphism	Inspired by emulating successful competitors
Normative isomorphism	Shaped by professional and cultural expectations

Source: Authors' elaboration based on DiMaggio and Powell (2000).

competitors' business practices to be applied in their businesses. These steps are considered to reduce uncertainty and encourage implementing sustainability practices in the palm oil industry. As sustainability reporting continues to grow, this practice helps align the palm oil industry in Malaysia to adopt international sustainability standards in its business so that the philosophy of sustainability can be implemented in the business activities of the palm oil industry (Idris et al., 2024; Kannan et al., 2021).

Furthermore, normative isomorphism is important in strengthening the transition to implementing sustainability accounting. These implementation steps are driven by global sustainability practices, employee recruitment standards with sustainability knowledge, and employee education programmes to increase knowledge of sustainability issues in the industry (Idris et al., 2024; Kannan et al., 2021). These efforts encourage realizing global sustainability compliance that can meet industry expectations and ethical business practices.

The MSPO certification process illustrates how regulatory, mimetic, and normative forces interact to change the activities carried out within an organization. On the one hand, these pressures can pose challenges, but on the other hand, they also provide the potential for SMEs to grow, innovate, and carry out competitive differentiation. The Malaysian palm oil industry case is relevant to institutional theory, where SMEs can adapt to sustainability issues to indirectly strengthen their legitimacy and position themselves competitively in the global market.

3. Challenges in Implementing Sustainability Accounting for SMEs

Although sustainability accounting is supported by fairly comprehensive guidance today, SMEs often have difficulty translating the guiding principles into their business implementation. Several challenges and obstacles faced by SMEs result in ineffective implementation of sustainability. Governance issues, regulations that do not always support SMEs, technological constraints, and limited resources are some problems SMEs face in implementing sustainability reporting.

The main obstacle for SMEs is weak governance, which is often associated with limited managerial expertise and a lack of awareness of SME leaders in responding to sustainability issues in their business activities. Poor decision-making and inadequate resource allocation can cause sustainability activity initiatives to not be a priority in SME business operations. SMEs fail to implement sustainability in their business practices and prioritize long-term environmental and social goals (Khakim & Firmansyah, 2023). SMEs focus more on short-term goals and immediate business operation issues. This condition occurs in sectors that traditionally do not respond to sustainability issues. In this regard, constructive steps must be taken to address the governance gap. One thing that can be done is a leadership capacity development programme to foster a culture of sustainability-oriented decision-making (Johnson & Schaltegger, 2016).

Weak regulation on support for SMEs adds to the complexity of the problem of implementing sustainability in SMEs. Different regulatory priorities in each country can confuse and hinder the adoption of sustainability accounting standards, such as IFRS S1 and S2. Khakim and Firmansyah (2023) highlight the urgent need for policy harmonization to simplify compliance requirements in sustainability reporting for SMEs and clearer and more consistent guidance for SME-level organizations. An integrated regulatory approach will reduce the problems for SMEs in aligning themselves with global sustainability initiatives. Without such support, SMEs may struggle to meet the demands of participating in implementing sustainability accounting effectively (Türkeş et al., 2024).

Due to limited resources, SMEs find implementing information technology in their businesses difficult. The latest technologies, such as blockchain and artificial intelligence, can help SMEs in sustainability reporting related to transparency and accuracy of data and information presented. SMEs consider implementing this technology to require significant financial investment and technical expertise. SMEs that still run their businesses in traditional ways have difficulty adopting digital technology related to financial problems and the expertise they have (Kurniasari et al., 2023). Kurniasari et al. (2023) explain that SMEs can overcome this obstacle by collaborating with various stakeholders, such as local technology providers so that SMEs can prepare sustainability reports more easily. This condition shows that strategic partnerships can help SMEs to help with problems that can be solved with technology even though SMEs have limited resources (Chege & Wang, 2020). In addition, Johnson and Schaltegger (2016) stated that SMEs need to have partnerships with non-governmental organizations (NGOs) related to the implementation of sustainability in their businesses. For example, SMEs in the agricultural sector that collaborate with relevant NGOs can be assisted in increasing financial support and employee training, including implementing sustainable business practices (Arshad et al., 2023). This collaboration can address resource gaps in SMEs and facilitate knowledge transfer, allowing SMEs to incorporate sustainability concepts into their businesses (Alam et al., 2024; Arshad et al., 2023).

From the review above, SMEs still have limitations in implementing sustainability accounting in their businesses. Governance issues, weak government support, and low technology implementation discourage SMEs from implementing sustainability concepts in their businesses. Limited resources owned by SMEs also limit activities that align with sustainability. Some steps to overcome these problems include government support, capacity-building programmes, collaborative partnerships, and affordable technology solutions. Support for SMEs in sustainability reporting is currently necessary because SMEs' active participation in sustainable business practices is important in contributing to local and international economic development based on sustainability.

4. Opportunities for SMEs

Sustainability accounting offers SMEs strategic steps to strengthen their position in the global economy associated with environmental and social issues. Although adopting sustainability practices may require a significant initial investment, the long-term benefits can help SMEs achieve their competitive business in the future. This advantage allows SMEs to respond to evolving market expectations and strengthens the foundation of SMEs in an industry currently associated with sustainability issues.

One of the main opportunities for SMEs is green finance, which provides loans and investments linked to specific environmental and social performance indicators. Unlike conventional finance, green finance funds sustainability-based projects and is considered low-risk. de Andrade et al. (2025) highlight that SMEs that focus on carbon reduction, using renewable energy, or good waste management are very attractive to investors who care about environmental and social issues. For example, SMEs in Indonesia are increasingly encouraged to adopt sustainable business practices, including green financing, that can help them switch to renewable energy and reduce operational costs. (Khakim & Firmansyah, 2023).

Governments and international organizations also play an important role in supporting SMEs in sustainability reporting, regulatory support, financial assistance, and mentoring for SMEs. In addition to financial support, green financing encourages SMEs to have long-term relationships with stakeholders committed to sustainable issues. Funds provided by SMEs with a focus on sustainability not only offer additional capital for SME business development but also provide training and technical assistance to SMEs to increase their capacity. This condition drives demands from stakeholders so that SMEs have the potential to increase their market credibility and competitive advantage (Yeşil, 2024). Implementing sustainability in SMEs positions SMEs as responsible and ethical business entities and builds trust with consumers, investors, and business partners.

Operational efficiency is another key benefit of sustainability accounting. By optimizing their resources but instilling environmental and social responsibility into their businesses, SMEs can reduce operational costs in the long run, thereby increasing the productivity of their business operations. SMEs in the Kenyan agricultural sector have begun to adopt technological innovations in sustainability practices, such as the use of renewable energy and resource efficiency (Chege & Wang, 2020). The implementation of sustainability activities in their businesses has contributed to improving their performance and competitiveness (Chege & Wang, 2020). Similarly, SMEs in Romania increasingly adopt sustainability principles in their supply chains, including efficient use of resources and better waste management (Türkeş et al., 2024). The impact of this implementation is that SMEs can improve business performance and reduce environmental impacts (Türkeş et al., 2024). Sustainability accounting also plays an important role in enhancing the reputation of SMEs. Transparency and ethical business practices demonstrated in sustainability reports can enhance the credibility of SMEs in the eyes of consumers, investors, and regulators. Consumers today tend to prefer products and services that are environmentally friendly and comply with ethical businesses. This condition presents both challenges and opportunities for SMEs that prioritize their sustainability activities. Despite having limited resources, SMEs must also implement sustainability-based operational activities to gain a competitive advantage. In addition, SMEs willing to implement sustainable innovations tend to experience increased business performance, especially those with relationships with stakeholders who support sustainability (Arshad et al., 2023).

The proactive involvement of SMEs in implementing sustainability reporting with currently applicable global standards provides another opportunity to strengthen their market position. The implementation of sustainability reporting supports responsible business practices and minimizes regulatory risks. For example, SMEs in Malaysia are increasingly encouraged to implement sustainable practices through green financing policies that indirectly help SMEs improve compliance with environmental regulations (Idris et al., 2024). In addition, implementing sustainability reporting can strengthen the business reputation of SMEs (Idris et al., 2024). These proactive efforts position SMEs as environmentally and socially responsible business actors so that SMEs can gain legitimacy and competitiveness locally and globally.

Based on the above review, implementing sustainability accounting in SMEs can improve their reputation, access to green financing, operational efficiency, and compliance with sustainability issues globally. These benefits contribute to SMEs' financial performance and long-term existence because SMEs have implemented ethical business practices. Therefore, implementing sustainability accounting allows SMEs to play a broader role in local and global economies.

5. Toward a Tailored Framework for SMEs

Efforts to address the gap between implementing sustainability accounting and the problems SMEs face require a specific approach. SMEs have problems that are not easy to solve, but the involvement of SMEs in the local and global economy based on sustainability issues has great potential. In this regard, several steps can be proposed to implement sustainability accounting at the SME level.

5.1. Simple Standards for Sustainability Reporting

For SMEs, accessibility and feasibility are the main considerations when adopting sustainability accounting practices. The choice of current sustainability reporting standards still requires adequate resources, making it difficult for smaller entities, including SMEs, to meet. Implementing sustainability accounting for SMEs is possible for core sustainability accounting standards such as carbon emissions, water use, and energy efficiency. The impact of implementing sustainability accounting on SMEs can contribute to implementing sustainability-based business practices, especially related to environmental and social impacts.

Gray et al. (2014) suggest an implementation model that is carried out in stages with basic reporting requirements to implement sustainability accounting. This implementation can be expanded along with the growth of an organization's resource capabilities (Gray et al., 2014). This suggestion is relevant for SMEs to implement. Thus, SMEs prepare sustainability reports in a simple context with current global accounting standards such as GRI standards. In addition, government support also plays an important role in encouraging sustainability reporting among SMEs. For example, Malaysia's Green Technology Financing Scheme, which provides subsidized funding for sustainability projects, encourages SMEs to get involved (Idris et al., 2024). As a result, SMEs will indirectly be involved in sustainable business practices whose impacts SMEs can prepare their sustainability reports.

5.2. Digital Integration for Efficiency and Accountability

Advances in digital technology help SMEs prepare sustainability reports. Cloud-based digital technology, blockchain, and mobile applications simplify data management and minimize manual activities. It can improve decision-making. Blockchain technology can improve security and traceability, especially in supply chain management. Agribusiness SMEs in Kenya are starting to adopt technological innovations to improve sustainability and certification compliance, resulting in improved competitiveness and business performance (Chege & Wang, 2020).

SMEs in Romania have leveraged digital technologies to improve sustainability and operational efficiency (Türkeş et al., 2024). One manufacturer integrated blockchain technology to increase supply chain transparency, ensure traceability of recycled materials, and minimize risks associated with certification fraud (Türkeş et al., 2024). This approach resulted in measurable reductions in operational costs. Similarly, SMEs in Malaysia are starting to leverage collaboration with local technology providers to address digital transformation challenges, including adopting technology-based solutions that contribute to operational efficiency and business sustainability (Ern, 2024). These innovations make sustainability accounting easier for SMEs to implement, thus helping SMEs align environmental and social responsibilities in their business. Implementing digital tools that support sustainability reporting helps them achieve a competitive advantage, drive future business growth, and improve the existence of SMEs.

5.3. Stakeholder Engagement

Stakeholder engagement is very effective in aligning sustainability-based SME business activities. Organizations need to build strong relationships with stakeholders to build trust, increase credibility, and create long-term collaborations (Leeson & Kuszewski, 2023). Community engagement plays an important role in supporting the sustainability of SMEs in the future. For example, SMEs in Indonesia collaborate with the community to manage waste (Khakim & Firmansyah, 2023). This activity not only has an impact on reducing environmental impacts but can also improve the image of SMEs that they support sustainability (Khakim & Firmansyah, 2023).

In facing global demands related to sustainability, the implementation of sustainability reporting is currently important for organizations. Several global standards, such as GRI standards, can be an alternative for SMEs to implement sustainability reports even though they are still presented simply. The existence of resource problems makes it difficult for SMEs to implement sustainability reporting. One way that SMEs can use this is by collaborating with stakeholders. de Villiers et al. (2022) stated that collaboration with various stakeholders allows an entity to understand better and adopt sustainability practices effectively. For example, Kenyan SMEs that build partnerships with local NGOs can support SMEs by providing additional resources to address the social and environmental impacts of SME businesses (Chege & Wang, 2020)\.

5.4. Toward a Sustainable Future for SMEs

Sustainability reporting implemented by SMEs needs to consider the current characteristics of SMEs. The potential of SMEs to contribute to local and global economic growth makes the implementation of sustainability reporting crucial today. Simplified sustainability reporting standards that apply to SMEs can create an appropriate approach for SMEs in sustainability reporting. In addition, digital tools can be an alternative for SMEs to implement sustainability reporting. In addition, the involvement of stakeholders at the local SME level can also encourage SME efforts by integrating business and sustainability issues so that the existence of SMEs in the future is maintained. SMEs also need to ensure that society and consumers are currently paying attention to sustainability issues in their decisions, so SMEs need to consider sustainability issues in their business as an important decision. Thus, implementing sustainability accounting is also a strategy for SMEs to show their existence in the future and start the current sustainability issue that has been widely implemented by various organizations globally.

6. Conclusion

Implementing sustainability accounting provides a competitive opportunity for SMEs to meet today's global sustainability issues. In addition, implementing sustainability accounting in SMEs is expected to increase the entity's growth in the long term. In a global economy that is increasingly moving toward a sustainability basis, SMEs' efforts to integrate sustainability practices into their businesses are something that needs to be started immediately. Various findings show that SMEs implementing sustainability issues in their operational businesses can increase competitiveness and position SMEs as major contributors to the local and global economies.

The sustainability accounting framework or standard in sustainability reporting for SMEs does need to be adjusted because the current framework is quite complex for SMEs to implement. However, SMEs can initiate sustainability reporting in a simple way and adjust it to SME conditions. Some of the benefits of implementing sustainability reporting include access to green financing. Implementing sustainability accounting can also increase operational efficiency by improving financial performance while minimizing environmental and social impacts. This implementation will be more optimal if it is encouraged by utilizing resources and information technology accessible to SMEs. In addition, in implementing sustainability accounting, SMEs can foster collaboration with the government, industry associations, and NGOs, especially related to employee assistance and training related to sustainability issues. Thus, SMEs can increase cost efficiency in implementing sustainability practices in their businesses.

Although still simple, implementing sustainability accounting for SMEs is a necessity and a strategic tool for long-term SMEs, especially by continuing to encourage local and global economic growth. Through sustainability accounting, SMEs are expected to be able to overcome various problems that occur with their operational businesses. Although not easy to implement, sustainability accounting for SMEs shows a positive response to sustainability issues applied in SME businesses that can be of concern to various stakeholders.

References

Arshad, M. Z., Arshad, D., Lamsali, H., Ibrahim Alshuaibi, A. S., Ibrahim Alshuaibi, M. S., Albashar, G., Shakoor, A., & Chuah, L. F. (2023). Strategic resources alignment for sustainability: The impact of innovation capability and intellectual capital on SME's performance. Moderating role of external environment. *Journal of Cleaner Production*, *417*(January), 137884. https://doi.org/10.1016/j.jclepro.2023.137884

Barney, J. (1991). Resources and sustained competitive advantage. *Journal of Management*, *17*(1), 99–120. https://doi.org/10.1177/014920639101700108

Basit, S. A., Gharleghi, B., Batool, K., Hassan, S. S., Jahanshahi, A. A., & Kliem, M. E. (2024). Review of enablers and barriers of sustainable business practices in SMEs. *Journal of Economy and Technology*, *2*(February), 79–94. https://doi.org/10.1016/j.ject.2024.03.005

Chege, S. M., & Wang, D. (2020). The influence of technology innovation on SME performance through environmental sustainability practices in Kenya. *Technology in Society*, *60*(September 2019), 101210. https://doi.org/10.1016/j.techsoc.2019.101210

Choudhary, S., Nayak, R., Dora, M., Mishra, N., & Ghadge, A. (2019). An integrated lean and green approach for improving sustainability performance: A case study of a packaging manufacturing SME in the U.K. *Production Planning and Control*, *30*(5–6), 353–368. https://doi.org/10.1080/09537287.2018.1501811

de Andrade, R. D., Benfica, V. C., de Oliveira, H. V. E., & Suchek, N. (2025). Investigating green jobs and sustainability in SMEs: Beyond business operations. *Journal of Cleaner Production*, *486*(November 2024), 144477. https://doi.org/10.1016/j.jclepro.2024.144477

Deegan, C. (2014). *Financial accounting theory*. McGraw-Hill Education (Australia) Pty Ltd.

de Villiers, C., La Torre, M., & Molinari, M. (2022). The Global Reporting Initiative's (GRI) past, present and future: Critical reflections and a research agenda on sustainability reporting (standard-setting). *Pacific Accounting Review*, *34*(5), 728–747. https://doi.org/10.1108/PAR-02-2022-0034

DiMaggio, P. J., & Powell, W. W. (1983). The iron cage revisited: Institutional isomorphism and collective rationality in organizational fields. *Advances in Strategic Management*, *17*, 143–166. https://doi.org/10.1016/S0742-3322(00)17011-1

Ern, O. H. (2024). *Greening the SME landscape in Malaysia*. https://www.thestar.com.my/news/nation/2024/01/26/greening-the-sme-landscape-in-malaysia#goog_rewarded

Freeman, R. E., Dmytriyev, S. D., & Phillips, R. A. (2021). Stakeholder theory and the resource-based view of the firm. *Journal of Management*, *47*(7), 1757–1770. https://doi.org/10.1177/0149206321993576

Gray, R., Adams, C. A., & Owen, D. (2014). *Accountability, social responsibility and sustainability*. Pearson Education Limited. https://www.pearson.com/store/p/accountability-social-responsibility-and-sustainability-accounting-for-society-and-the-environment/GPROG_A100060879194_learnerau-availability/9780273681380

Idris, S. H., Chang, L. W., Prihandono, I., & Rasidi, S. A. (2024). Green financing and climate change: Challenges and regulatory mechanisms in Malaysia and Indonesia. *Clean Technologies and Environmental Policy*, *26*, 4471–4482. https://doi.org/10.1007/s10098-024-02829-8

IFRS Foundation. (2023a). *IFRS S1 sustainability disclosure standard: General requirements for disclosure of sustainability-related financial information*. https://www.ifrs.org/issued-standards/ifrs-sustainability-standards-navigator/ifrs-s1-general-requirements/

IFRS Foundation. (2023b). *IFRS S2 sustainability disclosure standard: Climate-related disclosure*. https://www.ifrs.org/issued-standards/ifrs-sustainability-standards-navigator/ifrs-s2-climate-related-disclosures/

Johnson, M. P., & Schaltegger, S. (2016). Two decades of sustainability management tools for SMEs: How far have we come? *Journal of Small Business Management*, *54*(2), 481–505. https://doi.org/10.1111/jsbm.12154

Kannan, P., Mansor, N. H., Rahman, N. K., Peng, T. S., & Mazlan, S. M. (2021). A review on the Malaysian sustainable palm oil certification process among independent oil palm smallholders. *Journal of Oil Palm Research*, *33*(1), 171–180. https://doi.org/10.21894/jopr.2020.0056

Khakim, L. A., & Firmansyah, A. (2023). Strengthening the existing Indonesian government policies related to MSMEs to be sustainable. *Inclusive Society and Sustainability Studies*, *3*(2), 17–28. https://doi.org/10.31098/issues.v3i2.1965

Kurniasari, F., Lestari, E. D., & Tannady, H. (2023). Pursuing long-term business performance: investigating the effects of financial and technological factors on digital adoption to leverage SME performance and business sustainability—Evidence from Indonesian SMEs in the traditional market. *Sustainability (Switzerland)*, *15*(16), 1–20. https://doi.org/10.3390/su151612668

Leeson, R., & Kuszewski, J. (2023). GRI and stakeholder engagement: Setting standards in the public interest. *Sustainability Accounting, Management and Policy Journal*, *14*(4), 877–883. https://doi.org/10.1108/SAMPJ-06-2022-0329

Prasanna, R. P. I. R., Jayasundara, J. M. S. B., Gamage, S. K. N., Ekanayake, E. M. S., Rajapakshe, P. S. K., & Abeyrathne, G. A. K. N. J. (2019). Sustainability of SMEs in the competition: A systemic review on technological challenges and SME performance. *Journal of Open Innovation: Technology, Market, and Complexity*, *5*(4), 100. https://doi.org/10.3390/joitmc5040100

Salvador, R., Søberg, P. V., Jørgensen, M. S., Schmidt-Kallesøe, L. L., & Larsen, S. B. (2023). Explaining sustainability performance and maturity in SMEs – Learnings from a 100-participant sustainability innovation project. *Journal of Cleaner Production*, *419*(June). https://doi.org/10.1016/j.jclepro.2023.138248

Suchman, M. C. (1995). Managing legitimacy: Strategic and institutional approaches. *Academy of Management Review*, *20*(3), 571–610. https://doi.org/10.5465/amr.1995.9508080331

Türkeş, M. C., Bănacu, C. S., & Stoenică, L. (2024). The effect of supply chain sustainability practices on Romanian SME performance. *Sustainability (Switzerland)*, *16*(7), 1–27. https://doi.org/10.3390/su16072887

Yeşil, T. (2024). Analysis of sustainability accounting standards: A review. *Entrepreneurship and Sustainability Issues*, *12*(1), 303–324. https://doi.org/10.9770/jesi.2024.12.1(21)

Chapter 13

Green Banking with AI: Cutting Edge Innovations for Sustainable Financial Solutions

Nikita Singhal[a], *Prabha Garg*[b], *Shikha Goyal*[c] *and Nandita Mishra*[d]

[a,b]*School of Commerce and Management, IIMT University, Meerut, India*
[c]*Amity Law School, Amity University, Noida, India*
[d]*Linköping University, Linköping, Sweden*

Abstract

This chapter explores the relationship between artificial intelligence (AI) and green banking, techniques of AI used in green banking, current trends, and new strategies used to support sustainable financial services in emerging markets. This chapter begins with a discussion of the concept of green banking and the basic principles that it is based on, which are designed to support the development of environmentally friendly financial products and services. Theoretical and exploratory study is mainly based on a literature review. Financial institutions in emerging markets can leverage the strengths of sophisticated technologies for several purposes, such as AI-enabled risk assessment and environmental, social, and governance (ESG) reporting, to make sound decisions and adhere to the set sustainability standards. Machine learning (ML)-based analysis assists in the identification of eco-friendly investments, thus helping investors to make the right decisions. In addition, AI has changed how customers are engaged by promoting sustainable behaviors and efficiency in business by reducing paper usage and energy consumption. The lack of data on ESG reporting and assessment standardization made applying AI difficult in financial institutions in emerging markets. The chapter highlighted AI's potential in evaluating environmental risks, building sustainable investment

Climate Risk and Emerging Markets: Valuation, Volatility, and Portfolio Strategies, 197–211

doi:10.1108/978-1-83708-088-520261037

portfolios, and implementing paperless and energy-efficient operations in green banking in emerging markets. The chapter explains AI's role in driving environmental responsibility and operational efficiency in the banking sector. In future research, an in-depth analysis can be conducted with the help of data that focuses on particular types of banking institutions.

Keywords: Artificial intelligence; green banking; sustainability; innovation; environmental impact

1. Introduction

Green banking activities directly impact quantitative indicators of the economy since these have great potential to foster environmentally friendly and socially responsible practices (Sharma & Choubey, 2022). While the banks may not be direct polluters, they affect polluting activities, investments, or projects. Promoting green banking is a good opportunity for banks to adopt strategic positioning that would help them gain a competitive market advantage. In emerging markets, green banking practices are crucial since rapid growth and industrialization in these markets challenge their environmental and social sustainability. Banks, regulators, and the government should also launch an aggressive marketing campaign to promote green banking practices. One such instance of an aggressive campaign is China's introduction of Guidelines for Establishing the Green Financial System in 2016. These guidelines promote green credit policies by providing several financial incentives to banks adopting green credit portfolios. The People's Bank of China (PBoC) offers green incentives for banks under its re-lending policy, where green loans and AA-rated green bonds are accepted under the standing lending facility and medium-term lending facility, respectively. Moreover, banks' green performance has been included in the PBoC macro-prudential assessment framework that provides green banks incentives to expand and report about green banking activities. Similarly, in India, the State Bank of India (SBI) has been the first green bank and has encouraged many green energy projects. Punjab National Bank and Bank of Baroda have undertaken many green banking initiatives, including funding windmills, biomass, and solar electricity projects to reduce emissions and energy use.

In generic terms, green banking is the recognized procedure aimed at protecting the environment. The main benefit of the approach is the preservation of natural resources and environmental compensation. Concerning sustainability, green banking discourages using paper. It promotes using some electronic methods like ATMs, mobile money, online money, etc. Using such means of transacting benefits not only the customers and the banks but also the environment (Alam et al., 2024; Mir & Bhat, 2022; Rahman et al., 2023). In broader terms, green banking includes environmental, economic, and social considerations. It is environmentally conscious by restraining its climate footprint, avoiding paper usage, supporting e-communication, and not offering high-carbon subsidies (Jafar et al., 2023;

Mir & Bhat, 2022). Green banks include funding renewable energy, promoting energy efficiency, and selling sustainability credits, where sound environmental finance hampers the shift toward a low-carbon future. Green banks motivate firms to embrace environmentally friendly practices and systems by levying penalties. From an economic perspective, the green bank plays a central role in enhancing the overall economy by supporting sustainable assets; this reduces risk factors like climate change, scarce resources, and environmental laws (Gunawan et al., 2022; Naseema et al., 2024). It, therefore, brings about efficiency concerning the use of certain technologies, such as energy-efficient ones, and the minimization of wastage. Other economic benefits include meeting and selling guaranteed green clients and investors since green banking eliminates dirty banking systems from the market (Global Business Outlook, 2022; Jafar, Rodriguez, et al., 2024; Zhang et al., 2022).

Green banks also play an essential role in promoting legal compliance and abiding by regulatory measures. Well-regulated green banks in the existing scenario will be better positioned to respond even more to new environmental standards and associated costs and risks. Green banking further supports the United Nations Sustainable Development Goals (SDGs) concept and vision by promoting responsible consumption and production, climate change, and sustainable economic growth (Green Banking Sustainability, 2023; McKinsey Sustainability, 2023). Green banks support international initiatives to address climate change and achieve sustainable development through partnerships with counterparts globally. These initiatives can be a broad category of engagements that involves association and investment in global ventures, for instance, partnerships or financial involvement with other banks or economic organizations, governments, and non-governmental organizations. A significant reason why participation in international development is required is that these institutions possess the knowledge and capital to make a substantial contribution. SDGs involve the consideration of ESG factors in investment choices, disclosure, and reporting, governance, and sustainability, focus on the creation of long-term value, customer understanding, value creation and adaptation, and improvement image (Guang-Wen & Siddik, 2022; Siddik et al., 2024). The incorporation of these factors guarantees that practices of economic activities not only aim at making a profit but also at providing solutions to environmental and social issues.

2. Principles and Practices of Green Banking

Green banking considers the environmental consequences of the investment to support sustainable development. The principles of green banking provide direction to banks and financial institutions to focus on both financial and non-financial returns. There are several principles and practices of green banking, as depicted in Fig. 13.1. One of the fundamental principles is incorporating ESG factors in investment analysis and decision-making. This approach requires investment decisions focusing on corporate profit, climate change, human rights, and corporate governance factors. For instance, the UN Principles for Responsible Investment is an example of a guideline for improving investment management

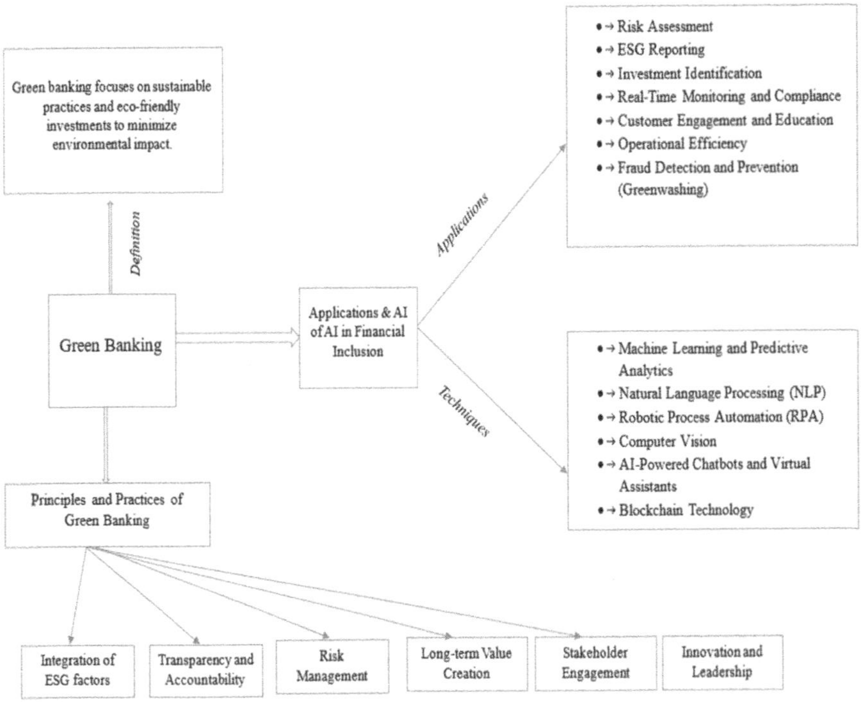

Fig. 13.1. Principles and Practice of Green Banking. *Source*: Developed by authors.

concerning ESG factors to attain sustainable investment results (Park & Kim, 2020). Green banking protects the environment by carrying out activities and framing policies that minimize environmental impacts, such as green funds and loans, environmental checks and policies, incentives for environment-oriented businesses, and the use of technology (Putri et al., 2022). Another important principle that requires financial institutions to report ESG information to their customers is transparency and accountability. This encompasses reporting the effects of investment on the environment and social impact and complying with standards and frameworks. An example of such a framework is the Global Reporting Initiative standard, through which organizations are encouraged to report, in a structured manner, how they manage their sustainability impacts, which will build stakeholders' trust.

Risk management is a principle of green banking that is concerned with identifying and managing environmental and social risks. This encompasses evaluating how climate change, resource scarcity, and social issues impact institutions' financial and risk management approaches. This principle aims to help financial institutions introduce the concept of environmental and social risks in the project costs. Building sustainable returns centered on sustainable economic revenues would bring revenues to all the stakeholders in the long run instead of concentrating on short-term returns. With this approach, only such investment projects that would help achieve sustainable development objectives and bring positive returns to the financial system are promoted. Green banks can contribute to achieving other sustainability-related objectives because their existing policies work following the overall goals of the SDGs (Gunawan et al., 2022; Khan et al., 2021).

The principle of stakeholder management entails that the various stakeholders must be involved in making the decisions so that multiple aspects of the stakeholder and its interests are considered. It aims to integrate economic activities with other societal demands into one single framework. Sustainable innovation in the banking industry empowers innovation in financial and banking activities (Khan et al., 2022; Sharma & Choubey, 2022). One example of a sustainable initiative is the Climate Bond Initiative, which is actively involved in establishing certifications for green bonds, which is helpful in innovation. Instead of focusing on market trapping, green banks should attempt to meet new sustainable development challenges and build new financial products and practices.

The principles and practices of green banking provide the blueprint through which financial institutions will achieve economic returns and respond to key environmental and social challenges. Following green banking principles, organizations support the global economy and help attain sustainability objectives (Alam & Akhtar, 2024; Kumar, 2024).

3. Trends and Initiatives in Green Banking in Emerging Markets

The green banking landscape in emerging markets is rapidly evolving as AI drives innovation to increase environmental sustainability in the financial sector. One of the most critical areas is the advanced ecological risk assessment and management enabled by AI (Abdulla et al., 2020; Jafar, Hemachandran, et al., 2024). Financial institutions are now using sophisticated ML and big data analytics to analyze vast amounts of environmental data, including satellite imagery and weather models, to help them measure risk and the impact on their investments. For example, Google Environmental Insights Explorer uses AI to provide detailed environmental data, which banks can use to make sustainable investment decisions. In commercial banks, China's Industrial and Commercial Bank assessed environmental risk through AI and data analytics and made more investments in green projects. Similarly, Standard Bank in South Africa has adopted the latest technologies, such as AI and predictive analytics, to analyze environmental data for climate risk mitigation and management.

Another major trend is AI-powered green financial products, which include green bonds, micro-lending, and sustainable investment. Banks use predictive analytics, AI, and other emerging technologies to meet environmental goals. In Brazil, several financial institutions contributed to the Brazilian green market by providing advisory services in structuring and issuing green bonds. In 2019, Banco do Brasil and ING assisted in issuing 13 green bonds with a total value of USD 1.5 billion. Similarly, Itaú Unibanco (ETF It Now ISE fund) and Banco do Brasil (BB Actions Carbono Sustentabilidade FIA fund) contribute to the management of sustainable investment funds. Further, Banco do Brasil and the

Inter-American Development Bank made a financing partnership under the Conditional Loan for Investment Projects (CCLIP) facility. CCLIP focuses on bioeconomy and sustainable infrastructure while working on connectivity and renewable energy sources for the Legal Amazon.

Automation of green financial processes is also a significant trend with AI and robotic process automation (RPA), which streamline business processes such as loan approval and mortgage, as demonstrated by ICICI Bank. In 2016, ICICI Bank became India's first bank to deploy RPA, AI, Chatbots, and other emerging technologies to ensure sustainable growth. In addition, AI enhances ESG data analysis and reporting by automatically collecting and interpreting ESG information to meet banks' requirements regarding classifying ESG risks, as seen in the Sberbank (Russia). Sber is promoting using AI to achieve sustainable development that would benefit humankind and society (The Economic Times, 2024).

Chatbots and virtual assistants enhanced customer engagement by providing personalized feedback and recommendations on sustainable financial products, exemplified by the First Bank of Nigeria (Nigeria) use of AI-powered chatbots. AI also contributes to innovation in green fintech solutions (Kuang et al., 2023), such as Ecofy (India), which partners with people and businesses who want to monitor their carbon footprint and participate in the green economy. AI supports climate risk modeling and scenario analysis, enabling banks to anticipate and prepare for climate-related financial risks, as Banco do Brasil (Brazil) demonstrated.

Integrating AI with blockchain technology is emerging as a crucial move to ensure transparency and traceability in green finance. Technology integration is needed to manage green bond investments and provide funds for environmental purposes and real environmental projects. These evolving trends prove AI to be a significant tool for achieving the global sustainability goal in the economy through managing ecological risks, enhancing efficiency, increasing production productivity, and enhancing transparency. Trending AI in global green banking unveils how AI is revolutionizing the approach to the sustainable finance sector. Important ones are enriched environmental risk evaluation, green financial products through AI, green banking systems through automation, ESG data, enhanced customer interaction, innovative green fintech solutions, climate risk evaluation, and blockchain in green finance.

4. Opportunities and Applications of AI in Green Banking

4.1. Risk Assessment and Management

AI technologies made risk assessment and management in green banking easy since ML algorithms and data analysis made it easy for banks to forecast risk by predicting specific scenarios. AI algorithms and ML models can detect unusual patterns and correlations in data that human analysts can oversee. These technologies can access and process vast datasets that enable green banks to assess risks related to credit assessment, climate change, compliance, and operations.

4.2. ESG Reporting

AI applications enable monitoring changes in ESG frameworks and their compliance, reducing the possibility of regulatory and legal risks and improving the quality of ESG report filings. In addition, AI-integrated communication platforms also enhance the transparency of communications and information in ESG reporting. These put ESG data, trends, and performance metrics into easily accessible dashboards, enabling investors, regulators, customers, and communities to get real-time updates on the banks regarding sustainability activities and their ESG performance (Bukhari et al., 2020).

4.3. Investment Identification

AI solutions in green banking provide several methods for assessing the sustainability of investment propositions. Using data analysis, ML algorithms, real-time analysis, and natural language processing (NLP), AI improves business decision-making and directors' investments influenced by ESG factors (Murshudli, 2023). Data analytics is essential in green banking since the volume of data linked to green impact assessments, sustainability reports, filing, and market trends involves AI. It allows for filtering out those companies and projects that pay significant attention to their environmental impact, carbon emission levels, energy efficiency, waste management standards, and the corporation's compliance with environmental legislation. AI helps minimize wastage by presenting data analysis that assists portfolio managers in making a favorable investment decision that aligns with sustainability principles (Chen et al., 2022).

4.4. Customer Engagement and Education

AI is used in green banking to engage and raise customers' awareness of environmentally sustainable banking services. Among the ways AI achieves this is through using personalized communication with specific recipients. AI-enabled chatbots and virtual assistants are now considered essential tools in customer care. AI systems give prompt, round-the-clock replies and hence bring much satisfaction to customer expectations. For example, if customers want to know more about green loans, they can converse with a chatbot that provides all relevant information and even helps them apply. Further, AI can determine customer data to develop specific messaging techniques to deliver sales communications emphasizing environmentally friendly banking products compatible with their preferences.

4.5. Operational Efficiency

AI helps banks run their businesses sustainably and at a lesser cost with their four areas of application, which include process automation, resource management, increased use of analytics, and better decision-making. It is, therefore, clear that AI-driven automation is one of the powerful enablers of improving operational productivity for green banking. For instance, routine customer service activities can be performed efficiently with facial recognition, virtual personal assistants, recommendation engines, and chatbots. This not only increases the level of customer satisfaction but also relieves human resources to deal with jobs of higher degree and complexities. Furthermore, AI plays a role in performing back-end operations, which include data input and processing, compliance analysis, and transactions. This cuts down on paperwork and other activities that are prejudicial to the environment, reducing the cost implication.

4.6. Fraud Detection and Prevention (Greenwashing)

The areas of sustainability that need focus include fraud detection and prevention, more so when it comes to greenwashing. Greenwashing is the act of disseminating information while pretending that one's business is environmentally conscious. AI improves the recognition of greenwashing since the corresponding assessments can be based on comparably large datasets to identify discrepancies between the companies' environmental disclosures and activities. For instance, ML algorithms such as NLP can use the companies' annual reports, press releases, and social media posts to check the validity of such claims. These algorithms can compare the stated environmental impacts with the factual information from published sources, including environmental reports, web databases owned by government departments, independent bodies, etc.

5. Techniques of AI Used in Green Banking

5.1. ML and Predictive Analytics

ML involves modeling data from the past to predict future occurrences. By conducting risk analysis, such models can predict climate change risks that could affect investment and regulatory risks influencing environmentally sustainable investments by banks. These technologies help assess environmental risks since they take time to analyze large amounts of data to determine what may constitute an ecological risk concerning lending and investment to avoid funding projects likely to harm the environment (Elshamly et al., 2023; Singh & Zaheer, 2023). For example, prediction algorithms expect climate effects on the value of assets and the rate of loan delinquencies through banks like the SBI (see Box 13.1 for detailed work of SBI).

Box 13.1. SBI: ML and Predictive Analytics for Green Banking.

SBI, India's largest public sector bank, has moved significantly toward sustainable practices. It has established a dedicated unit on ESG and Climate Finance Unit to achieve its commitment toward carbon neutrality. SBI has adopted emerging technologies such as ML, AI-based solutions, and business analytics to provide products and services and enhance customer experience. Several sustainability initiatives SBI took are target of Carbon neutrality, community, and CSR initiatives, green term deposits and green portfolio, green energy initiatives and products, financing re-initiatives, ESG due diligence along with credit risk assessment and green/ESG borrowing through lines of credit.

Sustainability Targets:

Net zero-aligned targets: SBI is working toward aligning key sectors of its financing portfolio with net zero emissions by 2055 as part of its broader sustainability strategy. For this purpose, SBI has prioritized financing renewal energy, clean energy, and sustainable agriculture practices.

Community and CSR initiatives: SBI has also spent Rs. 502.32 Crores on community initiatives, which include 55 lakh CSR beneficiaries. This demonstrated SBI's commitment to social responsibility.

Green term deposits and green portfolio: SBI raised green term deposits to finance green initiatives such as renewable energy, pollution reduction, and green infrastructure. SBI also targeted a green portfolio ratio of 75% in domestic advances by 2030. These initiatives will enable SBI to channel the funds to environmentally responsible projects, significantly contributing to a sustainable future.

Technology as Sustainability Enabler:

Technology has become a key enabler of sustainability in the banking sector. SBI has modernized its infrastructure to improve business and operational efficiency via real-time data analytics and big data, which support operational efficiency and sustainability goals. SBI has significantly changed the branch models by combining physical and digital channels, ensuring customers can access better customer services through multiple touchpoints. Expanding digital footprints will enable banks to achieve sustainability targets by reducing energy consumption and paper usage (SBI, 2024). Generative AI also plays a crucial role in enhancing SBI's service quality and operational efficiency. Generative AI will result in better lead generation, faster response times, personalized customer interactions, and efficient service delivery. With AI technologies, SBI automates repetitive tasks, significantly reducing energy consumption and streamlining workflows.

5.2. Natural Language Processing

NLP is revolutionizing green banking by offering textual data to enhance sustainable banking and organizational processes in the financial sector. In the industry, through NLP algorithms, the SBI is using the algorithms to improve sustainability reporting by automatically determining ESG metrics from textual sources, including financial reports and corporate disclosures. Not only does this shrink the time it takes to complete reports, but it also increases the quality of the information and compliance with legal requirements. Furthermore, NLP is critical in analyzing the customer attitude toward green banking products and services. Through collecting data from customer complaints, social media presence, and surveys, the banks can understand the customers' new needs regarding sustainable finance and thus work toward improving their customer satisfaction and the overall push toward green banking. In the same way, NLP can also assist in managing risks by tracking public opinion and regulation changes regarding environmental policies, allowing banks to avoid reputational risks and conform to environmental laws and rules.

5.3. Robotic Process Automation

RPA entails deploying artificial intelligent software robots to perform conventional and standard methodical tasks, and thereby RPA is a futuristic tool for green banking. Some of the benefits of RPA include lower consumption of papers through customer onboarding, compliance checks, data entry forms, and many others. This automation creates an environment that enables the banks to reduce their impact on the environment while at the same time improving their performance. In addition, RPA allows banks to enhance their approaches to ESG issue reporting and analysis by integrating various sources, such as financial statements and filings. This capability not only helps in integrated sustainability reporting and integrate and green reportage practices, but it also triples up the accurate and proper sustainability reporting and disclosures. Furthermore, RPA helps sustainable finance by automatically assessing loan requests for renewable energy and sustainable infrastructure. Through credit assessment, risk evaluation, and compliance checks, RPA shortens the time for green financing, thereby enhancing the effectiveness of the investment in environmentally friendly projects.

5.4. AI-powered Chatbots and Virtual Assistants

Intelligent chatbots and virtual assistants are now becoming the change agents in green banking because they improve customer engagement. With such robust tools, the banks can talk to the customers, answer questions regarding green financial products, and even direct customers to appropriate green investment avenues. One instance of such chatbots and virtual assistants is "EVA" (Electronic Virtual Assistant) of HDFC Bank, which was built by Senseforth AI Research Pvt Ltd in 2017. This chatbot uses NLP and AI technologies to provide customers with an authentic conversational experience on websites, mobile sites, and portals for bank customers. Similarly, "iPal" from ICICI uses AI and ML to address customers' queries and offer micro financial transactions such as bill payment, fund transfer, account view, and recharge. These chatbots support green banking initiatives by enhancing operational efficiency and reducing resource consumption.

6. Challenges and Dilemmas in AI-driven Green Banking

6.1. Ethical Dilemmas in AI-driven Green Banking

Applying AI in green banking brings numerous benefits to banks, such as efficiency, better decision-making, and enhanced customer experiences. Still, it raises some ethical dilemmas that should be addressed carefully to ensure sustainable banking practices. Some common ethical dilemmas associated with green banking are transparency and accountability, bias and fairness, privacy and data security, unemployment, environmental concerns, equality in access, preventing and detecting fraudulent activities, and systemic risks.

Ensuring transparency and accountability in AI-driven green banking is a significant concern because AI algorithms are based on ML, which operates as black boxes. This system made it difficult for shareholders, customers, and regulators to understand how decisions are made, creating mistrust in green banking institutions' practices. The appropriate strategy for handling this dilemma is to prioritize the explainability of the AI system, which can be developing models that can be interpreted and clearly explained for AI-driven decisions in green banking.

AI algorithms also bring some biases because they are trained on historical data and are based on several assumptions. These algorithms weigh people, events, or things differently based on purpose. Hence, while using AI in green banking, it is necessary to address these inherent biases; otherwise, these will lead to inefficiencies in banking operations in the form of biased credit scoring, loan approvals, or investment decisions. Financial institutions should adopt appropriate strategies such as diverse and representative datasets, bias detection and prevention mechanisms, and regular AI algorithms and systems monitoring.

Unauthorized access, data breaches, and misuse of personal information raise privacy and data security concerns in green banking, severely affecting individuals and institutions. In a time when the importance of data is undeniable, it is paramount for banks to protect customers' personally identifiable information (Shekhar & Hobbs, 2023). Hence, green banks should implement robust cyber security measures and data compliance frameworks when dealing with vast amounts of data with ML algorithms. However, these measures add complexity and cost to implementing AI in green banking practices, especially in emerging markets where AI is nascent (Rahman et al., 2023).

In some cases, AI can affect employment in the banking sector due to job displacement, mainly where there are routine and repetitive tasks. This can raise ethical concerns about AI implementation's social and economic consequences. However, green banks can address this issue by investing in reskilling and upskilling their employees and assigning them roles where human expertise is required.

AI also brings major issues to green banking operations due to high electricity demand while implementing AI. AI algorithms require significant electricity due to massive computational requirements and storage, increasing energy consumption. To address this concern, green banks should focus on energy-efficient hardware, optimization algorithms, and renewing energy sources for data centers (Liu et al., 2025).

6.2. Regulatory Considerations in AI-driven Green Banking

While implementing AI, several regulatory concerns arise due to data privacy violations, governance issues, and lack of trust. Hence, there is a need for regulatory measures to develop confidence and mitigate privacy risks when it comes to the application of AI in banking operations, which deals with large amounts of personal data. The General Data Protection Regulation (GDPR) is the most known data protection regulation. GDPR provides a comprehensive framework for individuals' data privacy across the European Union (EU) and the European Economic Area (EEA). Under GDPR, organizations must appoint a data protection officer to deal with sensitive personal data. This regulation also restricts the transfer of personal data outside the EU/EEA and mandates that data protection impact assessments be conducted for sensitive data. However, there is not much-established data protection regulation in emerging markets. However, several countries, including Brazil, China, and Singapore, have made some efforts to implement AI regulations in general principles, guidelines, and non-binding principles-based approaches. For instance, Brazil and China have general AI legislation to be finalized, Singapore has nonbinding principles, and India has no general AI legislation. Common reasons for bringing regulation in AI applications include those related to banking services: transparency, personal autonomy, human dignity, accountability, technical robustness and safety, diversity, non-discrimination, fairness, data governance, and social well-being.

6.3. Technological and Implementation Challenges

As banking services transform digital, green banks face several technological challenges, including scalability, interoperability, and governance issues. Since the banking system works on an inflexible legacy, challenging its adaptability and effectiveness across a large scale. Hence, legacy system transformation in modernized structure and architecture, effective data management, and continuous testing are required to ensure scalability, enhance customer experience, and protect against cyber threats.

Another technology hurdle in implementing AI in green banking systems in emerging markets is interoperability issues and immature technology, making it difficult for green banks to establish compatibility with existing financial systems. The lack of interoperability leads to a fragmented AI system, which makes it difficult for AI to access complete data sets accurately, thereby hampering customer personalization and risk analytics.

7. Conclusion

The combination of green banking and AI is rapidly proving to be one of the core forces behind creating the new economy. This partnership shows a new trend of combining sustainable economic approaches in the light of current issues backed up by advanced technological solutions. AI integration in green banking distinguishes itself from conventional solutions, creating new opportunities to enhance sustainable banking practices' effectiveness, accuracy, and transparency. Green banking mainly examines how ESG indices may be incorporated into investment decisions, describes their dynamics, analyzes patterns, and accurately forecasts the results. Innovations in AI allow financial institutions to better evaluate the risk and sustainability of environmental investments than in the past. AI-enabled analytics enables the tracking of ESG performance indicators in real-time and offers assurance of compliance with regulations and the stakeholders' trust. Among all these opportunities, several challenges and dilemmas of green banking should be taken into consideration by green banks, which will lead to AI becoming more innovative, resistant, and engaged in the shift to a more sustainable and inclusive world economy.

References

Abdulla, Y., Ebrahim, R., & Kumaraswamy, S. (2020). *Artificial intelligence in banking sector: Evidence from Bahrain.* Retrieved July 10, 2024, from https://www.semanticscholar.org/paper/Artificial-Intelligence-in-Banking-sector%3A-Evidence-Abdulla-Ebrahim/1f15d20456d4f2627aae0668263e6b1244b9bf87

Alam, M., & Akhtar, S. (2024). Introduction to green finance and technology integration. In S. H. Jafar, R. V. Rodriguez, H. Kannan, S. Akhtar, & P. Plugmann (Eds), *Harnessing blockchain-digital twin fusion for sustainable investments* (pp. 1–19). IGI Global.

Alam, M., Akhtar, S., & Bettencourt, A. (2024). Introduction to Fintech in industry 5.0: Companion or antagonist. In S. H. Jafar, K. Hemachandran, S. Akhtar, P. A. Khan, H. Chaarani (Eds.), *The adoption of fintech* (pp. 1–16). Productivity Press.

Bukhari, S., Hashim, F., & Amran, A. (2020). Green banking: A road map for adoption. *International Journal of Ethics and Systems*, *36*(3), 371–385. https://doi.org/10.1108/IJOES-11-2019-0177

Chen, J., Siddik, A. B., Zheng, G. W., Masukujjaman, M., & Bekhzod, S. (2022). The effect of green banking practices on banks' environmental performance and green financing: An empirical study. *Energies*, *15*(4), 1292. https://doi.org/10.3390/en15041292

Elshamly, A., Rehman, S. U., Rahman, M. M., Hameed, R., & Jameel, Z. (2023). AI-based green banking technologies and bank stability: Moderating role of climate change. *Journal of Namibian Studies: History, Politics, Culture*, *35*, 217–228. https://doi.org/10.59670/jns.v35i.3406

Global Business Outlook. (2022). *How digital solutions can power 'Sustainable Banking'?* Retrieved July 9, 2024, from https://globalbusinessoutlook.com/banking-and-finance/how-digital-solutions-can-power-sustainable-banking/

Guang-Wen, Z., & Siddik, A. B. (2022). Do corporate social responsibility practices and green finance dimensions determine environmental performance? An empirical study on Bangladeshi banking institutions. *Frontiers in Environmental Science, 10*. https://doi.org/10.3389/fenvs.2022.890096

Gunawan, J., Permatasari, P., & Sharma, U. (2022). Exploring sustainability and green banking disclosures: A study of the banking sector. *Environment, Development and Sustainability*, *24*(9), 11153–11194. https://doi.org/10.1007/s10668-021-01901-3

Jafar, S. H., Akhtar, S., & Johl, S. K. (2023). AI in insurance. In K. Hemachandran & Rodriguez R. V. (Eds), *Artificial intelligence for business* (pp. 164–173). Productivity Press.

Jafar, S. H., Hemachandran, K., Akhtar, S., Khan, P. A., & El-Chaarani, H. (Eds.). (2024). *The adoption of fintech: Using technology for better security, speed, and customer experience in finance*. CRC Press.

Jafar, S. H., Rodriguez, R. V., Kannan, H., Akhtar, S., & Plugmann, P. (Eds.). (2024). *Harnessing blockchain-digital twin fusion for sustainable investments*. IGI Global.

Khan, P. A., Johl, S. K., & Akhtar, S. (2021). Firm sustainable development goals and firm financial performance through the lens of green innovation practices and reporting: A proactive approach. *Journal of Risk and Financial Management, 14*(12), 605.

Khan, P. A., Johl, S. K., & Akhtar, S. (2022). Vinculum of sustainable development goal practices and firms' financial performance: A moderation role of green innovation. *Journal of Risk and Financial Management, 15*(3), 96.

Kuang, M., Kuang, D., Rasool, Z., Saleem, H. M. N., & Ullah, M. I. (2023). From bytes to sustainability: Asymmetric nexus between industrial artificial intelligence and green finance in advanced industrial AI nations. *Borsa Istanbul Review*. https://doi.org/10.1016/j.bir.2024.03.010

Kumar, S. (2024). *Sustainable banking: Charting the future with AI and data analytics*. Forbes. Retrieved July 15, 2024, from https://www.forbes.com/sites/forbestechcouncil/2024/01/18/sustainable-banking-charting-the-future-with-ai-and-data-analytics/#:~:text=AI%20can%20now%20aid%20sustainable,assessments%20for%20informed%20decision%2Dmaking

Liu, X., Faura, J. C., Zhao, S., Wang, L., & Yao, J. (2025). Impact of artificial intelligence technology applications on corporate energy consumption intensity. *Gondwana Research, 138*. https://doi.org/10.1016/j.gr.2024.09.003

McKinsey Sustainability. (2023). *Green growth: Unlocking sustainability opportunities for retail banks*. McKinsey & Company. Retrieved July 15, 2024, from https://www.mckinsey.com/capabilities/sustainability/our-insights/green-growth-unlocking-sustainability-opportunities-for-retail-banks

Mir, A., & Bhat, A. (2022). Green banking and sustainability – A review. *Arab Gulf Journal of Scientific Research, 40*(3), 247–263. https://doi.org/10.1108/AGJSR-04-2022-0017

Murshudli, F. (2023). Green banking for sustainable development. *Foresight and STI Governance, 17*(2), 82–94. https://doi.org/10.17323/2500-2597.2023.2.82.94

Naseema, N., Akhtar, S., & Al Hinai, A. A. (2024). Disrupting financial services: A case study on Capital One's Fintech Odyssey. In S.H. Jafar, R. V. Rodriguez, H. Kannan, S. Akhtar, & P Plugmann (Eds), *Harnessing blockchain-digital twin fusion for sustainable investments* (pp. 363–383). IGI Global.

Park, H., & Kim, J. D. (2020). Transition towards green banking: Role of financial regulators and financial institutions. *Asian Journal of Sustainability and Social Responsibility, 5*(5). https://doi.org/10.1186/s41180-020-00030-2

Putri, P. I., Rahayu, K. N., Rahmayani, D., & Siregar, M. E. S. (2022). The effect of green banking and financial performance on banking profitability. *Quality – Access to Success, 23*(191), 38–45. https://doi.org/10.47750/QAS/23.191.05

Rahman, M. H., Rahman, J., Tanchangya, T., & Esquivias, M. A. (2023). Green banking initiatives and sustainability: A comparative analysis between Bangladesh and India. *Research in Globalization, 7*, 100184.

SBI. (2024). *Synergizing sustainability within and beyond* [Sustainability report 2023-24]. https://sbi.co.in/documents/43752844/44015013/010824-Final+SBI+Sustainable+AR+12+07+2024.pdf/9ce94c6b-6c0e-c2ac-c0a1-0205b2d84ade?t=1722489643684

Sharma, M., & Choubey, A. (2022). Green banking initiatives: A qualitative study on the Indian banking sector. *Environment, Development and Sustainability, 24*(1), 293–319. https://doi.org/10.1007/s10668-021-01426-9

Shekhar, V., & Hobbs, B. (2023). *What banking directors should ask about AI and machine learning risks*. Ernest and Young. https://www.ey.com/en_us/board-matters/banking-risks-from-ai-and-machine-learning

Siddik, A. B., Yong, L., & Sharif, A. (2024). Do sustainable banking practices enhance the sustainability performance of banking institutions? Direct and indirect effects. *International Journal of Bank Marketing*, *42*(4), 672–691. https://doi.org/10.1108/IJBM-02-2023-0109

Singh, A., & Zaheer, A. (2023). Review on the impact of AI on green banking towards sustainability with special reference to Indian public and private banks. *Journal of Survey in Fisheries Sciences*, *10*(4S), 2475–2492.

The Economic Times. (2024). Artificial intelligence will become a vital resource for achieving sustainable development goals. *The Economic Times*. https://economictimes.indiatimes.com/news/international/world-news/artificial-intelligence-will-become-a-vital-resource-for-achieving-sustainable-development-goals/articleshow/116368737.cms?from=mdr

United Nations Conference on Trade and Development (UNCTAD). (2014). *World investment report: Investing in the SDGs: An action plan*. Retrieved July 10, 2024, from https://unctad.org/system/files/official-document/wir2014_en.pdf

Zhang, X., Wang, Z., Zhong, X., et al. (2022). Do green banking activities improve the banks' environmental performance? The mediating effect of green financing. *Sustainability*, *14*(2), 0989. https://doi.org/10.3390/su14020989

Chapter 14

The Ripple Effects of Climate Policy Uncertainty on Global Financial Markets

Faisal Usmani[a], *Mohsin Khan*[a], *Mohd Afjal*[b] *and Sinem Derindere Köseoğlu*[c]

[a]*Department of Commerce, School of Social Sciences and Language, Vellore Institute of Technology, Vellore, India*
[b]*VIT Business School, Vellore Institute of Technology, Vellore, India*
[c]*Transportation and Logistics Faculty, Istanbul University, Istanbul, Turkiye*

Abstract

Climate policy uncertainty (CPU) has become a crucial factor influencing global financial markets, particularly in emerging stock and bond markets and the rapidly expanding green investment sector. This chapter explores the role of CPU as a key driver of volatility, investment risk, and portfolio diversification challenges. By analyzing market fluctuations, return dynamics, and green asset behavior during periods of financial stress, the study provides comparative evidence on the short- and long-term implications of CPU in emerging and green markets. The findings indicate that heightened uncertainty results in increased short-term volatility and reduced returns in emerging markets. Over time, however, markets adapt to regulatory shifts, potentially yielding higher returns. Notably, green assets exhibit strong return spillovers during distress periods, reflecting their growing integration into sustainable investment strategies. The chapter underscores the importance of strategic investments in green bonds and dynamic portfolio reallocation to mitigate the adverse effects of CPU. A particular focus is placed on emerging markets such as Vietnam, where substantial investments in sustainability underscore the relevance of these strategies. By distinguishing the impact of CPU on traditional and green assets, this study provides valuable insights for investors and policymakers aiming to enhance market resilience and sustainability. The findings contribute to the

Climate Risk and Emerging Markets: Valuation, Volatility, and Portfolio Strategies, 213–224

doi:10.1108/978-1-83708-088-520261041

broader discourse on financial stability in the face of evolving climate policies, offering actionable strategies to navigate uncertainty while fostering sustainable economic growth.

Keywords: Climate policy uncertainty; emerging markets; stock market volatility; green bonds; risk management

1. Introduction

Climate change is something very real now and not a possible future event. Uncertainty is becoming critical in relation to global financial dimensions with the appraisal on climate policies. Uncertainty concerning climate policy (CPU) implies ambiguity in judgment concerning both the regulatory actions put in place and the polices being instituted to mitigate climate change. This type of uncertainty alters investor behavior and affects asset valuations and investment strategies across sectors and regions.

These same policies can be seen to hold sway globally through international policies such as the Paris Agreement or domestic measures like different countries' versions of the Green New Deal. They're really important factors to economies across the world. CPU has many sources, including political instability, ambiguous commitment of countries to the climate change goals, and the rapid pace of green technologies, all of which contribute to fluctuations in financial markets, which determines returns and risks in investments.

Emerging markets are on the receiving end when it comes to the CPU impacts because they are still under development and have a high exposure to climate change risks. Since "long-term investments are often turned off" by fluctuations in climate policy-induced investment flow into these markets, so reactions to such policy changes will attract "short-term speculative investment" based on the general perception of clarity and reliability of such policies.

Moreover, as sustainability with environmental, social, and governance (ESG) creed becomes more manifested on investment decisions, it is imperative to understand how CPU impacts green investments and sustainable finance (Khan et al., 2022). Green investments are classified into different categories like green bonds, renewable energy stocks, and other ESG assets (Alam & Akhtar, 2024). Typically, these types of investments are very sensitive to changes in climate policy and reveal a complex relationship between expectations and reactions in the market.

The origin of this chapter is the way CPU is conceptually related to broad financial markets, notably emerging markets, but also green assets and strategies to be employed by investors to mitigate associated risks. It aims at building intellectual capacity among investors, policymakers, and financial analysts to utilize effectiveness on challenges posed by CPU by studying the interplay between CPU and market dynamics. This will further help develop an understanding of how climate-related policies mold financial markets thereby proposing strategies to make financials grow stronger and encourage investment practices.

2. CPU and Stock Markets

In many emerging markets, the investment decisions that derive from risk management and portfolio diversification strategies tend to be highly influenced by CPU. On the one hand, the unpredictability of climate regulations adds the volatility needed for the markets concerned; on the other, such unpredictability creates deep financial linkages, particularly affecting green and sustainable assets. Thus, necessitating the strategic adoption of measures by investors and financial analysts to capably manage risks and enhance returns amid the flux of regulation. This portion of the study looks into the effects of CPU on stock market behaviors and spills over into the diversification and risk management strategies.

3. Impact of CPU on Stock Markets

Research indicates that changes in legislation and policies have a pronounced impact on market volatility and returns, especially in developing markets. In China, increased CPU coincides with decreased stock market returns but increased volatility in the very short term, while this volatility stabilizes over time as investors adjust to new policy regimes (Xu et al., 2023). In a more general context, increases in CPU depress short-term returns in the United States, but increases might instead always be associated with good returns in the long run. The very character of volatility introduced via CPU will appear over many timescales thereby inflecting additional layers of complexities onto market behavior (Xu et al., 2023). Moreover, CPU has different influences on green assets, increasing return spillovers among them primarily during market extremes. The sensitivity of green assets to CPU underlines their unique roles in the market and their interconnections with mainstream financial instruments (Pham et al., 2024). Thereby the excess return for stocks is given on those that are less sensitive to CPU and the more sensitive ones offer a premium to investors during the policy shifts. Climate policies change while the investors, therefore, have to quickly adapt and strategically manage the exposure to CPU risk. Integration of green financial products, dynamic portfolio adjustment, and refining risk assessment frameworks would help market actors much better deal with sustainable long-term goals.

4. Implication and Consideration

From stock market performance and portfolio management, CPU creates a space for innovative adaptation. Indeed, one can observe a positive correlation between CPU and green activities in the emerging markets like Vietnam, which indicates that CPU may egg companies to develop greener practices (Hong et al., 2024). In addition, as the impact of CPU on carbon trading prices signifies the compelling need for governments to curb expectation management and uncertainty reduction so as to stabilize their financial systems, it also projects some urgency for governments (Su et al., 2024). Therefore, these findings underscore the critical importance of integrating CPU into policy design and investment strategies, ensuring greater financial stability and long-term sustainability.

5. Impact of CPU on Market Volatility

Among several economic sectors, it is in CPU that the greatest impact can be felt on market volatility. Diverse responses characterize these sectors, ranging from real estate to even cryptocurrencies (Jafar, Hemachandran, et al., 2024). Therefore, stakeholders in both the investing and policy worlds need to understand the multidimensional nature of the impact of CPU.

5.1. *Real Estate Market*

CPU is a significant factor impacting the volatility of the real estate markets, particularly in energy-intensive sectors such as industrial and residential properties. As such, coastal properties, which are most vulnerable to climate change-related risks, are sensitive to CPU and must be viewed in terms of long-term investments in such areas.

5.2. *Bond Markets*

Along the same lines, the turbulence of sovereign bonds becomes increasingly petrified with uncertainties emanating from climate policy events such as the most recent one – the Paris Agreement. In fact, emerging markets have proved that green bonds are the best hedge against CPU, thus justifying their role in the promotion of sustainable investment (Guo et al., 2024).

5.3. *Cryptocurrency Market*

CPU affects the cryptocurrency market in a singular way; indeed, it lowers Bitcoin's turbulence. In other words, it means that cryptocurrencies would not be a reliable hedge against CPU. The unique interaction of cryptocurrencies with climate policies is worth nothing (Jafar, Rodriguez, et al., 2024; Mahjoubi & Henchiri, 2024)

5.4. *Commodity Markets*

A strong CPU index shows its strong influence on the volatility of different commodities including aluminum, cocoa, and wheat, which also shows the large extent to which climate policies affect economic activities of this sector (Lasisi et al., 2024).

5.5. *Airline Stocks*

Differential impact of CPU on airline stocks with some airlines experiencing considerable volatility while others show far less influence. Models based on CPU have predicted airline returns more accurately, indicating their effectiveness in evaluating asset pricing in the sector regarding CPU (Marobhe & Kansheba, 2024).

Although the threats posed by CPU tend to increase market volatility, the extent of this threat varies between sectors and asset classes. This fact indicates that while some markets are likely to develop good hedging strategies against CPU, others will remain exposed, necessitating some kind of sector-specific risk management.

6. Sectoral Vulnerabilities to Climate Policy Changes

Changes in climate policy directly affect energy, manufacturing, and agriculture sectors, among others. With more stringent emissions regulations, traditional energy companies are often impeded while renewable energy firms may find new opportunities. Such sectoral performance insights are essential to investors and policymakers for risk and opportunity identification, especially in often emerging market scenarios.

6.1. Energy Sector

The effects of climate policies in the energy sector vary considerably in terms of regional prejudice. Firms in countries facing a higher climate risk would bear the consequence of adverse financial impacts under climate policies, while firms with lower climate risks generally would sustain better prospects. Climate policies are fast-tracking a transition to renewable energy in favor of companies producing green energy. Investment flows into renewables are rising as global regulations increasingly favor cleaner energy sources, and this is changing the financing environment of global energy markets by redirecting capital toward sustainable projects.

6.2. Manufacturing Sector

The stringent climate policy environment has created considerable challenges for the manufacturing industry, where rising operational costs and regulatory compliance requirements are eroding profitability and increasing the need for sector-specific support. Operational cost and regulatory compliance are adversely affecting the manufacturing sector's profitability and directly calling for sector-specific support. This sector cannot afford to be ignorant of the environmental situation. The very existence of the sector critically depends on its adaptation to climate change in order to reduce further operational inefficiencies and competition. Unless targeted policies are in place that will ameliorate the impact, the manufacturing sector will find it hard to remain operational in a changing climate context.

6.3. Agricultural Sector

Agriculture has been, and it continues to be, a highly vulnerable sector with most climatic variability affecting temperature and rainfall to directly affect crop productivity. In this perspective, the developing nations experience conspicuous challenges, with full brunt felt over different time scales. Clearly, however, climate policies also present the opportunities of resilience through sustainable agricultural practices and technological innovations that enhance productivity while minimizing risks in these most vulnerable areas.

7. Role of Portfolio Diversification in Mitigating Climate Risks

According to Reboredo et al. (2017), investors highly valued environmentally friendly investment even though it is usually less financially attractive than other investment types and tends to offer little protective disguise during bad economic conditions. Technological advancements in clean energy innovation and an increase in investments after the 2015 UN climate change conference in Paris have made investments in renewable energy projects much more attractive. These changes are also expected to reduce the negative risk premium associated with these investments, which will put their risk profile in closer proximity to social responsible investment and corporate mutual funds.

8. CPU and Green Bonds

According to Gyamerah et al. (2024), the authors conducted a non-linear ARDL model to determine the effects of green bond return, geopolitical risk, and CPU from January 2016 to August 2022. The findings suggest an increase in short-term geopolitical risk, which adversely affects green bond returns, while a decrease in such risks tends to improve returns in the long run and vice versa. Interestingly, CPU does not tent toward a linear unidirectional effect on green bond returns in those periods.

Green bonds are much more volatile in emerging markets and get agitated with announcements concerning critical events relating to climate policies such as the Paris Agreement (Guo et al., 2024). Green bonds are highly interlinked with other sustainable markets that often transmit shocks to those sectors, which are worsened under situations of CPU that interfere with market dynamics and diversification strategies (Özkan et al., 2024).

In addition, in the sovereign bond markets for emerging economies, green bonds have also been effective hedging instruments. They help to increase the potential hedging against volatility caused by CPU in diversified portfolios. Investment strategies using green assets' interdependencies especially developed in responding to CPU have proven their superiority over traditional buy-and-hold strategies in optimizing risk-adjusted returns (Guo et al., 2024; Pham et al., 2024). This result supports the argument that green bonds play a complex, albeit substantive, role in addressing uncertainties across new climate policies.

9. Green Innovation as a Hedge Against Policy Uncertainty

The coupling between CPU and green markets is an emerging area of studies. In recent investigations, for instance, by Ren et al. (2023), the time-dependent Granger test has been employed to investigate the presence of bidirectional causality between CPU and green markets, where the emergence of strong policy variation or extreme climate events would magnify these interplays.

According to Amzallag (2022), concentration risks posed in some brown-fund contexts are relatively diversifiable, while green funds will suffer less risk against each other due to these concentration risks. This observation implies quite diversified risks and behaviors related to investments in the set of environmentally conscious financial products.

From the European Investment Bank's initiation of the green fund investment in 2007, the world has watched rapid growth toward green investments, signaled by the Climate Bonds Initiative which displayed this rapid growth by green bond issuance rising from $37 billion in 2014 to $509 billion in 2021 (Piñeiro-Chousa et al., 2021). According to Su et al. (2024) provided more information on the issue and explained that during times of economic uncertainty, investor sentiment toward green bonds positions them as safe-haven assets, therefore influencing trends in the market and, in the global recognition of the important role of green bonds in a transition to a low-carbon economy, countries are setting carbon neutrality goals requiring colossal private sector investment.

Green bonds are exceptional in that their proceeds purposefully fund eligible green projects that require due diligence, management of proceeds, and annual reporting on environmental impact. Increasingly attracting attention from mainstream as well as niche investors, green bonds are helping to mitigate climate change while promising stable long-term returns. This evolving dynamic emphasizes the role of financial systems in accelerating environmentally responsible investing practices and supporting further sustainability goals.

10. Geopolitical Factors Influencing CPU

While climate policies are derived from the socio-political, economic, and socio-economic environments in which they are conceived and implemented, it is these very geopolitical conditions and stakeholders' dynamics that decide their successful implementation.

Conversely, tangles between economic complexity and geopolitical risks work adversely to environmental quality, meaning that environmental degradation may become more acute as geopolitical tensions escalate. According to Balsalobre-Lorente et al. (2023) discussed the deleterious effects of economic policy uncertainty on ecological and carbon footprints, leading to the conclusion that these uncertainties may effectively interrupt positive developments wherever environmental quality is concerned.

11. Behavioral Finance Perspectives on Climate Policy Risks

To realize and recognize behavioral biases and sentiments it is the prerequisite for the effective prescription of climate policies and the sustained stability of financial markets (Naseema et al., 2024). The way in which people and entities respond to climate risks depends significantly on perception, and this at best impacts not only how well the policy is able to function but also – much more importantly – pushes with severe impact market movements (Khan et al., 2022).

Behavioral economics focuses on nudging sustainable decisions so they become easier and more attractive for citizens to join in climate actions. It focuses, rather, on behavioral insights in designing nudges that can guide people's choices without heavy-handed and restrictive measures (Alam et al., 2024). Climate sentiments, again, have a significant role in shaping and driving the fortunes of financial markets with respect to investment decisions and movement toward green assets. Such initiatives as carbon taxes and green subsidies would also further advance investments in low-carbon technologies but would also generally have risks to financial stability, especially in the banking sector (Dunz et al., 2018).

Research has established an irrefutable proof that indeed climate risk has a major impact on investments and financial markets. This was further revealed by studies conducted by Cepni et al. (2023), which suggested holding a diversified portfolio involving ESG equities portfolio hedged against physical climate risks besides ESG bonds that manage transition risk exposures arising from policy changes or adaptations of business models with the investor.

The greatest challenge within the field refers to the stranded asset risk associated with a potential "carbon bubble," which would mean that investment in fossil fuel would become worthless due to very stringent measures in climate change regulations. Such misalignment between the two could lead to severe revaluation of assets, with the attendant destabilizing effect on economies overall (Folkers, 2024). Climate-related financial policies would thus be considered as tracking things to deal with a low-carbon transition while the responses of markets against such risks are highly diverse. Among others, it has been shown that climate events can trigger asset revaluations with the need to develop predictive models toward future price movements.

Behavioral finance addresses psychological hurdles to such actions, including skepticism among the public and perceived costs of political action (Chuahan & Chavda, 2024). Cooperation between both public and private groups may channel funds toward sustainable goals. For example, it can be done through increasing the acceptance of climate-friendly policies like carbon taxes with increased social norms and peer influence. Although behavioral insights are good potent weapons, they should be included into traditional policy instruments to prevent possible unintended consequences like financial disruption or inequitable social outcomes. A fair and sustainable transition will need to capture all the socioeconomic realities, in combination with the behavioral dynamics.

12. Integration of Climate Risk Assessment in Portfolio Management

Given that changes in climate will bring in some predictabilities and many uncertainties – not really predictably – the adjustments of these changes with respect to financial impacts and economic impacts are terribly complex and not fully predictable themselves. Thus, such uncertainties become major for investors, for climate risk could allow multiple interpretations of stock prices. For example, there is a varying intensity of climate risks among different sectors and companies in the stock returns. One such risk is a cause of concern for physical risks that result from direct effects, such as natural disasters, disrupting business activities, and causing volatility with cash flow (Cepni et al., 2022). It can include risks related to transition due to changes that are driven to comply with climate regulations or carbon neutrality, so that, no company exhibits similar results as another with respect to impacts or outcomes on stock returns and exposure to physical transition risks. In finality, climate risk assessment has to take place at portfolio management points for measuring and reducing exposure to investment portfolios' vulnerability.

On the studies conducted by Gyamerah et al. (2024), the authors advance the importance of carbon neutrality as a precondition for the formation of specialized financial instruments for green investments. This transition allows diversification avenues for the investors to infuse sustainability into their investment strategies under green finance. However, significant uncertainties form the basis of large risks – climate policy unpredictability and geopolitical risks. These risks have been further exacerbated with unpredictable developments with respect to future legislative and regulatory frameworks, in turn, making investment decisions even more challenging in the green finance sector.

Su et al. (2024) discuss how Green Bond Investments affect both positively and negatively investment strategies. These authors postulate that investors' need to make strategic adjustments to their portfolios would lessen any instability arising in the market. Under the continuing global economic and financial uncertainties, green bonds become critical investment assets that could provide contrasting benefits of stability and sustainability.

13. Policy Recommendation for Enhancing Stability in Emerging Markets

An all-encompassing strategic approach would be recommended for emerging markets in rebuffing against the economic challenges posed by geopolitical uncertainties and so on.

With a strong consideration of the standing of geopolitical risks in influencing carbon emissions and the viability with which businesses work, the ability to strengthen regulatory transparency and investor confidence would be deemed important. Strengthening climate policy with simultaneous reduction of geopolitical risks will facilitate sustainable development.

The creation of green financial products like green bonds will serve robust support by providing stable investment options in good or bad market times. This will enable developing countries to link their finance laws with sustainability objectives and attract responsible investments, thereby mitigating their exposure to external shocks. It is also crucial to diversify the economic base and stop relying on a highly volatile sector like fossil fuels. Sustaining a sound regulatory environment buoyed up by coherent policies fosters resilience, thereby maintaining the appeal of financial markets to both domestic and international investors.

14. Conclusion

It is critical to adopt a holistic strategy for resilience, which nourishes financial well-being, mitigates geopolitical risk, and spurs sustainable growth in emerging markets. Governments could develop a sound and attractive investment climate through regulatory transparency, an expansion of green finance initiatives, and diversification of the economic base. Geopolitical uncertainties must be proactively addressed if these markets are to navigate and adjust effectively to the market uncertainties that surround them.

They are strengthening the institutional frameworks that promote regional cooperation to secure economic safety and further make invitations to emerging markets for overseas investors and businesses. They seem to be built on the fact that, as future challenges, these economies manage emerging reality, that is, the new world order defined as a global economy and yet develop progressively. The last interrelationship is geopolitical dynamics, climate policy, and financial innovation, which will present both challenges and opportunities; therefore, care needs management.

They take the necessary strategy combination of these factors, making their political illusion come alive into the economic world that should be able to sustain over time not only preserving resistance to volatility, but eventually sustainable growth. With the passage of time, an emphasis on stability, sustainability, and building investor confidence would allow emerging markets to enhance their stature in the future and enable ongoing economic progress.

References

Alam, M., & Akhtar, S. (2024). Introduction to green finance and technology integration. In S. H. Jafar, R. V. Rodriguez, H. Kannan, S. Akhtar, & P. Plugmann (Eds.), *Harnessing blockchain-digital twin fusion for sustainable investments* (pp. 1–19). IGI Global.

Alam, M., Akhtar, S., & Bettencourt, A. (2024). Introduction to fintech in industry 5.0: Companion or antagonist. In S. H. Jafar, H. Kaanan, S. Akhtar, P. Alam Khan, & H. El-Chaarani (Eds.), *The adoption of fintech: Using technology for better security, speed, and customer experience in finance* (pp. 1–16). Productivity Press.

Amzallag, A. (2022). Fund portfolio networks: A climate risk perspective. *International Review of Financial Analysis*, *84*, 102259. https://doi.org/10.1016/j.irfa.2022.102259

Balsalobre-Lorente, D., Nur, T., Topaloğlu, E. E., & Evcimen, C. (2023). The dampening effect of geopolitical risk and economic policy uncertainty in the linkage between economic complexity and environmental degradation in the G-20. *Journal of Environmental Management*, *351*, 119679. https://doi.org/10.1016/j.jenvman.2023.119679

Cepni, O., Demirer, R., Pham, L. N., & Rognone, L. (2023). Climate uncertainty and information transmissions across the conventional and ESG assets. *Journal of International Financial Markets, Institutions and Money*, *83*, 101730. https://doi.org/10.1016/j.intfin.2022.101730

Cepni, O., Gupta, R., & Ji, Q. (2023). Sentiment regimes and reaction of stock markets to conventional and unconventional monetary policies: evidence from OECD countries. *Journal of Behavioral Finance*, *24*(3), 365–381.

Chuahan, R., & Chavda, K. (2024). Unveiling the nexus: Exploring the impact of behavioral finance on green finance initiatives. *Journal of Environmental Economics and Sustainability*, *1*(2), 1–12.

Dunz, N., Monasterolo, I., Monasterolo, I., & Raberto, M. (2018). *Don't forget climate sentiments: Real and financial markets' reactions to climate risks*. Social Science Research Network. https://doi.org/10.2139/SSRN.3264181

Folkers, A. (2024). Calculative futures between climate and finance: A tragedy of multiple horizons. *The Sociological Review*, *73*(5), 1104–1121. https://doi.org/10.1177/00380261241258832

Guo, N., Jia, S., & Liu, Y. (2024). Climate policy uncertainty and its impact on the volatility, correlation, and hedging of sovereign and green bonds. *Journal of Environmental Management*, *370*, 122953. https://doi.org/10.1016/j.jenvman.2024.122953

Gyamerah, S. A., Agbi-Kaiser, H. O., & Gil-Alana, L. A. (2024). Do climate policy uncertainty and geopolitical risk transmit opportunity or threat to the green market? Evidence from non-linear ARDL. *The Journal of Economic Asymmetries*, *30*, e00379. https://doi.org/10.1016/j.jeca.2024.e00379

Hong, N. T. H., Kien, P. T., Linh, H. G., Thanh, N. V. H., Tuan, N. L., & Anh, P. D. (2024). Do climate policy uncertainty and economic policy uncertainty promote firms' green activities? Evidence from an emerging market. *Cogent Economics & Finance*, *12*(1), 2307460.

Jafar, S. H., Hemachandran, K., Akhtar, S., Khan, P. A., & El-Chaarani, H. (Eds.). (2024). *The adoption of fintech: Using technology for better security, speed, and customer experience in finance*. CRC Press.

Jafar, S. H., Rodriguez, R. V., Kannan, H., Akhtar, S., & Plugmann, P. (Eds.). (2024). *Harnessing blockchain-digital twin fusion for sustainable investments*. IGI Global.

Khan, P. A., Johl, S. K., & Akhtar, S. (2022). Vinculum of sustainable development goal practices and firms' financial performance: A moderation role of green innovation. *Journal of Risk and Financial Management*, *15*(3), 96.

Lasisi, L. A., Ngwu, F. N., Taliat, M. K., Olaniran, A. O., & Nnamdi, K. C. (2025). Modelling commodity market volatility with climate policy uncertainty: A GARCH-MIDAS approach. *SN Business & Economics*, *5*(3), 29.

Mahjoubi, M., & Henchiri, J. E. (2024). The effect of policy uncertainty on the volatility of bitcoin. *Journal of Financial Economic Policy*, *16*(4), 429–441.

Marobhe, M. I., & Kansheba, J. M. (2024). Airlines and climate policy uncertainty: Are the sector's stocks soaring or stalling? *Journal of Air Transport Management*, *115*, 102536.

Naseema, N., Akhtar, S., & Al Hinai, A. A. (2024). Disrupting financial services: A case study on Capital One's Fintech Odyssey. In S. H. Jafar, R. V. Rodriguez, H. Kannan, S. Akhtar, & P. Plugmann (Eds.), *Harnessing blockchain-digital twin fusion for sustainable investments* (pp. 363–383). IGI Global.

Özkan, O., Adebayo, T. S., & Usman, O. (2024). Dynamic connectedness of clean energy markets, green markets, and sustainable markets: The role of climate policy uncertainty. *Energy*, *303*, 131957. https://doi.org/10.1016/j.energy.2024.131957

Piñeiro-Chousa, J., López-Cabarcos, M. Á., Caby, J., & Šević, A. (2021). The influence of investor sentiment on the green bond market. *Technological Forecasting and Social Change*, *162*, 120351.

Pham, S. D., Nguyen, T. T. T., & Do, H. X. (2024). Impact of climate policy uncertainty on return spillover among green assets and portfolio implications. *Energy Economics*, *134*, Article 107631. https://doi.org/10.1016/j.eneco.2024.107631

Reboredo, J. C., Quintela, M., & Otero, L. A. (2017). Do investors pay a premium for going green? Evidence from alternative energy mutual funds. *Renewable & Sustainable Energy Reviews*, *73*, 512–520. https://doi.org/10.1016/J.RSER.2017.01.158

Ren, X., Yan, H., & Gozgor, G. (2023). Climate policy uncertainty and idiosyncratic volatility: Evidence from the non-financial listed Chinese firms. *Journal of Climate Finance*, *5*, 100026.

Su, C., Song, X., Qin, M., Lobonţ, O., & Umar, M. (2024). Optimistic or pessimistic: How do investors impact the green bond market? *The North American Journal of Economics and Finance, 102248*. https://doi.org/10.1016/j.najef.2024.102248

Xu, X., Huang, S., Lucey, B. M., & An, H. (2023). The impacts of climate policy uncertainty on stock markets: Comparison between China and the US. *International Review of Financial Analysis*, *88*, 102671. https://doi.org/10.1016/j.irfa.2023.102671

Chapter 15

Building Financial Resilience in the Face of Climate Change: Innovations in Climate Finance and Risk Mitigation

Ram Singh[a], *Vinay Pal Singh*[b] *and Fazla Rabby*[c]

[a]*Symbiosis University of Applied Science, Indore, India*
[b]*Quantum University, Uttarakhand, India*
[c]*Stanford Institute of Management and Technology, Sydney, Australia*

Abstract

Traditional financial systems cannot properly manage the climate change risks that challenge the current financial stability. New tools in climate finance such as green bonds, carbon pricing, and climate insurance tools emerged to help build financial resilience because of identified challenges. Various tools and sustainable investment strategies function to strengthen financial systems against climate-related risks, according to this chapter. The chapter combines multiple disciplines to investigate climate finance mechanisms through both empirical research and policy analysis in order to assess their performance. This study investigates the revolutionary advantage of blockchain and artificial intelligence (AI), digital technology to make the climate finance process automatic, enhancing transparency as well as scalability and operational efficiency. The research shows how environmental, social, and governance (ESG) factors play a significant role in robust sustainability goals with financial systems. Emerging climate finance strategies show their capacity to mitigate climate threats while enhancing financial system resilience. The research illustrates how both public and private institutions need to formulate sustainable policies through adaptive methods in order to achieve sustainability. Through its evaluation, the research shows that digital technologies boost conventional financial instruments to create stronger accountable system frameworks. The discussion ends by stressing the need for adaptable financial systems because

Climate Risk and Emerging Markets: Valuation, Volatility, and Portfolio Strategies, 225–241

Published under exclusive licence by Emerald Publishing Limited
doi:10.1108/978-1-83708-088-520261045

they will ensure economic stability on our climate-challenged planet. The chapter delivers practical recommendations about uniting modern financial advancements with digital resources under policy frameworks to develop stronger climate sustainability. The research delivers specific operational instructions about technology-sustainable finance integration by offering its distinctive analysis of these elements.

Keywords: Climate finance; financial resilience; climate risk mitigation; sustainable investment; ESG

1. Introduction

1.1. Financial Resilience

The concept of financial resilience allows financial systems and organizations together with individuals to successfully survive economic shocks and maintain both stability and continuous operations. Within the climate change setting financial resilience requires organizations to develop plans for protecting against the risks triggered by environmental events like large-scale weather patterns and resource shortages and enduring changes in climate patterns. The concept highlights the need to create shock-absorbent systems which promote sustainable recovery together with growth potential (Batten et al., 2020). At the systemic level, policies, rules, and institutions must be changed to make them more financially stable while also lowering risks and allowing long-term economic activities. Global financial entities as well as central banks and regulators started using climate risk evaluations as part of their stress tests to determine financial institution preparedness for climate-driven market disruptions (UNEP, 2021). The implemented measures work to stop potential widespread dangers, support market liquidity, and sustain investor belief during crisis periods. The financial resilience of organizations requires them to spread their revenue across multiple streams while actively deploying risk reduction measures combined with operationally sustainable implementation. Organizations focusing on ESG factors maintain better financial stability since they efficiently manage extended risks and address stakeholder requirements (Morningstar, 2022). Through their implementation of climate insurance, investment organizations shield their financial position from possible losses created by climate-based disruptions (Linnerooth-Bayer et al., 2019). The ability to withstand financial risks caused by climate uncertainties becomes essential for managing the growing climate challenges.

1.2. Factors of Financial Resilience in the Face of Climate Change

Building the creation of financial resilience to climate change requires multiple interconnected elements within a system. These factors enable individuals as well as organizations together with financial systems to resist climate-induced disruptions so they can recover and maintain sustainable practices:

- *Integration of Climate Risk Assessments*: Financial strategies need the full adoption of climate risk assessments for building organizational resilience. Financial institutions and central banks, together with regulators, conduct stress tests on institutions to determine their climate shock exposure. For risk evaluation purposes, financial institutions need to analyze three categories of risk, which include credit risk, market risk, and operational risk related to extreme weather events and temperature change and resource limitations (Batten et al., 2020). Evaluation activities help organizations create advanced planning and reduction strategies.
- *Diversification of Financial Instruments*: Financial instruments with various forms create resilient systems because they distribute risks between different elements. The financial initiative known as green bonds provides money for green projects as carbon pricing implements economic measures to encourage emission reduction efforts. Climate insurance provides financial protection against disaster damage through which businesses, along with individuals, can maintain stability (Linnerooth-Bayer et al., 2019).
- *Adoption of Digital Technologies*: The emerging technologies, along with blockchain and AI develop new tools that actively enhance resilience levels. Blockchain technology offers complete transparency and accountability features for green finance, while AI systems optimize climate risk evaluation, leading to enhanced decision-making capabilities. The technologies solve financial system inefficiencies, which enables better adaptation to climate uncertainties, according to Zhang et al. (2021).
- *ESG*: Investing with ESG criteria leads to enhanced resilience because it supports sustainable practice implementation. Investors choose ESG-aligned companies since their preparedness for long-term risks improves their appeal in the market. According to Morningstar (2022), research findings demonstrate that portfolios based on ESG compliance perform better than conventional investments during market unstable times.
- *Public–Private Partnerships (PPPs):* Collaboration between governments and private entities fosters large-scale resilience initiatives. Public-sector policies establish conditions for innovation development by supporting private-sector investments that execute plans. The Indian collaboration between public and private entities in renewable energy projects shows how these partnerships decrease pollution levels and maintain financial stability, according to the IEA (2023).
- *Access to Inclusive Financial Services*: Inclusive financial services enable individuals, together with small businesses, to acquire microcredit, savings, and insurance, which helps them manage climate-induced shocks. The combination of financial literacy training with social safety welfare programs increases resilience capabilities because it equips disadvantaged communities to handle economic challenges efficiently (OECD, 2021).
- *Sustainable Policy Frameworks*: Financial systems need strong stability combined with market liquidity to survive crises in order to demonstrate resilience.

Financial institutions need central bank support along with adequate liquidity during times when climate volatility becomes severe. Systemic disruptions can be avoided and investor confidence can be protected through this process (World Bank, 2022).

- *Financial System Stability and Liquidity*: Financial systems need strong stability combined with market liquidity to survive crises in order to demonstrate resilience. Financial institutions need central bank support along with adequate liquidity during times when climate volatility becomes severe. Systemic disruptions can be avoided as well as investor confidence can be protected through this process (World Bank, 2022).

Climate change presents an overwhelming challenge to established financial institutions that initially lacked suitable mechanisms for managing disruptions caused by it, leading to an existential crisis in the traditional financial infrastructure. The financial systems suffer destabilization because climate change produces economic effects that increase natural disaster occurrences while disrupting supply chains and causing persistent environmental deterioration (Batten et al., 2020). Financial systems face intensified risks because they did not develop enough resilience to respond to unanticipated climate-related shocks even though they previously centered on predictable market cycles. The financial sector needs an active transformation to overcome its exposed vulnerabilities, since this transformation will create immediate system stability while establishing sustainable systems for the future (Alam & Akhtar, 2024; UNEP, 2021). Green bonds have become extremely popular because they fund projects that deliver environmental benefits across the globe, where issuance surpassed $500 billion in 2023 (Climate Bonds Initiative, 2023). Key climate mitigation programs alongside adaptation initiatives receive funding from carbon pricing policies, which include carbon taxes as well as emissions trading regimes (World Bank, 2022). Lack of climate insurance is now necessary to protect both weak communities and economies in areas with high climate risks. This is because it shifts the financial risks that come from natural disasters (Jafar, Rodriguez, et al., 2024; Linnerooth-Bayer et al., 2019).

These mechanisms need equal support from public authorities together with private sector entities to achieve their desired results. Governments take the primary position in shaping supportive policies and providing economic benefits to develop these mechanisms alongside private companies that provide money and technology along with market-driven solutions (OECD, 2021). The partnership between public and private entities in India proves successful for implementing extensive renewable energy initiatives that both cut carbon pollution and draw major private funding (IEA, 2023). Sustainable financial stability depends on group efforts between public and private entities. Climate finance has experienced a transformation through emerging digital technologies, including blockchain and AI and financial and policy-based tools. Blockchain ensures transparent tracking of green investments through secure, impenetrable records, and AI helps to develop elaborate risk assessment systems and predictive analytics for efficient decisions (Jafar et al., 2023; Zhang et al., 2021). These emerging technologies eliminate persistent challenges in climate finance services because they resolve operational efficiency problems and information distribution issues while facilitating fair resource distribution.

2. Review of Literature

Batten et al. (2020) contend that climate change evolved into an economic problem since traditional financial systems fall short in adapting to climate-caused disruptions. Stern (2006) previously observed the considerable economic damage that emerged from failing to adapt to climate change. Resilience growth starts with the development of new financial instruments. The introduction of green bonds as investment tools has brought substantial changes to the market because they guide resources toward sustainable ecological projects. The Climate Bonds Initiative has documented explosive growth in their bond emission to demonstrate their worldwide value usefulness. Linnerooth-Bayer et al. (2019) studied climate insurance which functions as a key instrument to communicate financial hazards to places under disaster risk. Policy frameworks maintain an essential position in this matter. As per UNEP (2021), the creation of strong policies serves to integrate financial systems with sustainability objectives. World Bank (2022) explains the economic transformation from carbon pricing systems which produce resources to support climate mitigation efforts between taxes and cap-and-trade frameworks. PPPs represent an effective system through which organizations address climate resilience issues. According to analyses published by the International Energy Agency (IEA) (2023) Indian renewable energy projects demonstrate the most effective manner to merge sustainability and economic development through PPPs. OECD (2021) emphasizes that teamwork constitutes a vital element for executing broad climate change policies.

The essential component of digital transformation currently exists in the contemporary business world. Zhang et al. (2021) demonstrate how blockchain technological systems maintain transparency in climate finance operations along with AI-generated predictive models for risk management control systems. The technological breakthroughs help eliminate operational issues, thus enabling financial systems to adapt better to climate uncertainties. The interest now focuses on ESG investment strategies Morningstar (2022), ESG-related portfolio shows superior returns during market fluctuations, which proves that sustainability is essential for financial planning. According to Ghosh (2020), ESG integration makes it possible for firms to combine effective stewardship practices with business profitability. The ability of people to withstand financial stress relies fundamentally on their access to financial services that include all groups. Research by Beck and de la Torre (2007) shows that microfinance serves as a powerful tool to give disenfranchised people economic instruments for avoiding financial disasters. Banerjee et al. (2015) demonstrate that communities can overcome climate-related disasters through educational training about finances and savings programs. A wide range of experts within the literature have started to agree about systemic changes required throughout the system. TCFD (2017) created an evaluation system that dictates financial institutions connect climate risks to organizational governance functions and strategic planning. Clark et al. (2018) confirm that institutions act as key drivers of systemic change according to their research. International collaboration as a solution continues to appear throughout the discussion. Study results by Pottier et al. (2020) demonstrate that the Paris Agreement (2015) established the foundation for worldwide climate cooperation, which changed how global money functions. Financial resilience stands as an absolute requirement for today's modern climate, while all experts agree on this matter.

2.1. Research Gap

Despite many limitations exist within the existing research related to financial resilience in relation to climate change even though substantial advancement has occurred in both areas. The use of green bonds and climate insurance instruments receives research emphasis and distinct studies exist yet evidence shows their extended effectiveness in diverse economic situations limits especially in developing nations (Climate Bonds Initiative, 2023; Linnerooth-Bayer et al., 2019). It hasn't been looked into enough how scalable and easy it is to use ESG integration with blockchain and AI tools (Morningstar, 2022; Zhang et al., 2021). Researchers have not studied the mechanisms which would allow public-private alliances and international agreements like the Paris Agreement to continue when political and economic conditions become unstable (IEA, 2023; Pottier et al., 2020). Research needed to fill these existing gaps enables full recognition of how financial systems can best respond to and minimize multiple climate change impacts.

3. Objectives and Methodology

This chapter examines how new financial tools and sustainable investment practices can strengthen financial systems to withstand climate-related risks. The study analyzed collaborative financial strategies for sustainability goals between public and private sectors in building resilience in long run. This chapter evaluates cutting-edge digital technologies such as blockchain and AI that are used to improve transparency and efficiency levels of climate finance.

4. Financial Tools and Sustainable Investment Practices

Analysts must study innovative financial instruments along with sustainable investment practices to make more resilient against climate-related risks to strengthen the global climate impacts.

4.1. Green Bonds and Sustainable Financing

Green Bonds signify the foremost mechanism to obtain climate-friendly project financing. Green bonds serve as direct finance tools toward environmentally friendly projects which consist of renewable energy platforms as well as green efficiency systems and agricultural sustainability measures. The Climate bonds Initiative (2023) mentions that the increase in market activity in green bonds is fueled by the collection of large amounts of money for low-carbon economy programs. The use of green bonds in financing sustainable projects enables the financial systems to address various climate risks through the implementation of resilient environmentally friendly systems. These instruments serve as dual functions as signals to investors which promote organizations to focus more intensely on protecting the environment.

4.2. Climate Insurance for Risk Mitigation

Insurance products that are proposed to cover climate risk mainly related to weather and natural calamities. Climate insurance mitigates the economic impact on vulnerable sectors by paying them after climate events have occurred (Linnerooth-Bayer et al., 2019). This not only reduces the likelihood of a financial shock, enabling quicker recovery and preventing the loss of capital that would undermine the broader financial systems stability. As climate risks grow, traditional insurance models must integrate climate related risks since climate risks are escalating thereby improving resilience for private and public sectors.

4.3. Carbon Pricing and Emission Reduction Mechanisms

Carbon pricing in the form of carbon taxes and cap and trade is another important tool against climate change. Putting a price on carbon emissions, these mechanisms encourage businesses and industries to reduce their carbon footprints. Carbon pricing has been a strong tool to internalize the environmental externalities of carbon emissions and promote low-carbon technology investment as per World Bank (2022). Carbon pricing provides a clear economic indicator that supports the transition to green technologies and ensures that investments are reallocated away from high-risk, high-carbon sectors and invested in clean, climate -resilient sectors that are less vulnerable to climate change.

4.4. ESG Investment Practices

Sustainable practice investment criteria such as ESG are to be initiated by financial institutions around the world as these institutions generally build financial resilience over the long-term. According to Morningstar (2022) ESG-focused investment portfolios have performed better than traditional investment especially when the market was volatile. The investment community is increasingly aware of the long-term implications of climate risks, understanding that sustainability issues are essential in modern investment approaches. Companies that effectively manage climate risks enable ESG investments to create robust financial frameworks and drive economic transformation toward greater resilience. This indicates that the investors are becoming more conscious of the long term threats that climate change and the significance of incorporating sustainability into investment plans. ESG investments strengthen the financial system stability and aid in the shift toward a more resilient economy by giving preference to business that successfully manages climate risks.

4.5. Innovative Digital Technologies in Financial Resilience

New age digital inventions namely blockchain technology and AI create substantial opportunities for increasing efficiency and transparency in climate finance systems. Through blockchain technology, investors can monitor the funding progress of climate projects by ensuring correct usage and maintaining financial transparency. The introduction of AI enhances risk modeling because it delivers better predictions regarding how climate affects financial operations. AI analytics systems develop new methods of understanding climate risks enabling financial institutions to allocate their assets while better managing their risks according to Zhang et al. (2021). Financial institutions use these technologies to create better alignment between conventional financial methods and developing climate resilience needs thus strengthening overall stability at the system level.

5. Financial Strategies for Sustainability and Long-Term Resilience

Sustainability goals and long-term resilience development rely heavily on both the public and private sectors' purposes within financial strategies.

5.1. The Public Sector's Role in Financial Resilience

The public sector maintains essential responsibility to develop regulatory standards together with basic infrastructure which facilitates financial resilience development. Governments have a duty to develop framework policies and regulatory systems and provide incentives which lead financial resources toward sustainable investments while controlling climate change risks. The IEA (2023) states that suitable government policies remain essential for a low-carbon economy transition because such policies create essential long-term stability and certainty needed to attract major investments. The public sector through its carbon pricing policies and its provision of subsidies to clean energy businesses and tax benefits for green investments, respectively, creates vital mechanisms to unite financial operations with sustainability goals. The main public sector activity involves developing financial mechanisms to reduce climate risk exposures. Public projects which tackle climate change receive funding through green bonds that governments can issue according to Climate Bonds Initiative (2023). Developing nations can benefit from publicly funded insurance programs together with climate resilience bonds which serve as extra risk coverage against climate-related disruptions. The public sector needs to make financial systems resistant to forthcoming climate shocks. Companies should follow TCFD recommendations (2017) by establishing climate risk disclosure requirements that force firms to expose their climate vulnerabilities and display their risk management practices.

5.2. The Private Sector's Role in Financial Resilience

Financial markets rely primarily on the private sector for both innovative development and investment decisions and risk control functions. Most climate projects require funds, especially for renewable energy or sustainable infrastructure. Private investors, financial institutions, and asset managers need to put their money into these projects. They work together to make investments with align to global sustainability goals. These financial groups realize that climate change can make a significant on their investments. So they are using ESG standards which mainly focus on environmental, social, and governance issues. Morningstar (2022) states that ESG investing looks at these factors that keep the businesses strong. Financial institutions are also creating tools to protect against climate risks. They have come up with things like climate insurance, catastrophe bonds, and loans linked to sustainability. These tools help the companies and governments in reducing the financial risks from climate impacts and making the overall financial system stronger (Linnerooth-Bayer et al., 2019).

5.3. Public–Private Collaboration for Long-term Resilience

Sustainable finance needs combined efforts of public and private sectors to meet the sustainability goals and build the strength. PPPs are a great way to achieve this. Renewable energy PPPs have made possible large-scale infrastructure projects that public and private financing separately cannot fund according to Pottier et al. (2020). The two sectors successfully combine their unique capabilities to produce sustainable remedies which yield advantages for universal social progress. The collaboration between public authorities and private organizations leads to the creation of financial instruments which strengthen climate resilience. Public authorities establish product regulations but private enterprises discover new financial tools and develop the essential instruments required by these standards. Public institutions can encourage green bond and sustainable investment fund creation through tax benefits along with governmental backing which private institutions will use to develop and distribute financing products. Public–private collaborative arrangements need to focus on making sure climate finance effectively reaches the most vulnerable demographic which includes developing countries. The government functions as a financial guarantor through subside programs whereas profitability-critical companies handle fund management with their technical know-how. The approach contributes to developing financial systems that serve every segment of society while being independent of climate change damage in vulnerable areas (Banerjee et al., 2015). The public together with private sector entities maintain essential responsibilities to develop financial platforms which stand against climate change impacts. The regulatory mechanisms and institutional structures come from public-sector institutions yet private-sector entities handle resource allocation throughout innovation processes.

- *Long-term Effectiveness of Financial Instruments*: The effectiveness of green bond investments and climate risk insurance varies throughout different geographical areas especially within developing nations. Future research must evaluate diverse economic environments to determine how well these instruments create enduring value and meet local challenges particularly those caused by inadequate infrastructure and limited capital access (Climate Bonds Initiative, 2023; Linnerooth-Bayer et al., 2019).

- *Scalability and Accessibility of Digital Technologies*: Additional research is required to advance blockchain and AI technologies in climate finance so they can enter different financial systems. Research must find solutions to enhance accessibility of technology implementation barriers within developing and lower-income nations because this step would strengthen the global economy (Zhang et al., 2021). Research about infrastructure limitations and regulatory barriers and cost implications should serve as the main driver for extensive deployment of these technological systems.
- *Sustainability of PPPs*: Research remains inadequate to understand how PPPs can continue successfully through political and economic instabilities (IEA, 2023) even though they succeed in renewable energy projects (IEA, 2023). Accommodating functional partnerships in altering policies and changing political environments and market situations requires understanding of necessary elements for continued effectiveness. Analysts should study institutional frameworks together with financial structures and governance models that make PPPs more flexible in challenging environments (Pottier et al., 2020).
- *Intersectionality of Financial Resilience with Socio-economic Factors*: Research has not extensively examined the connection between climate resilience and socio-economic elements which include gender as well as income differences and educational access. Researchers should investigate the specific financial shock experiences of vulnerable populations who are both women and financially disadvantaged. Targeted financial products, microfinance and social protection mechanisms must be investigated to empower marginalized groups as part of developing inclusive financial systems (Banerjee et al., 2015).
- *Policy and Regulatory Frameworks for Resilience*: The current research lacks examination of how particular national and international regulatory policies can be designed to maximize financial resilience. Additional research needs to investigate how public spending measures and governance standards with financial rewards can boost climate adaptation efforts together with risk reduction toward climate change. Research about implementing environmental policies with economic growth preservation efforts in mind remains poorly investigated by both UNEP (2021) and World Bank (2022).

6. Innovations in Climate Finance and Risk Mitigation

Financial institutions need important innovation in climate finance and risk management systems to establish resilience against increasing climate change threats. This section analyzes essential innovations which fall under climate finance and risk mitigation strategies.

6.1. Green Bonds and Climate-aligned Financial Instruments

The climate finance sector has seen green bonds emerge as its most noticeable development because they let governments and companies access special funding for environment-positive operations including renewable energy projects and enhancements in energy efficiency and the development of adaptation methods. Green bonds experienced notable growth in the last decade until they reached a $1 trillion global market accordingly to Climate Bonds Initiative in 2023. The designated environmental sustainability funds of green bonds activate private capital investments while directing those funds to climate change solutions. The evolution of financing instruments has led to sustainability-linked bonds being developed along with green bonds. These sustainability-linked bonds establish interest rate links to issuer environmental performance. These bonds give financial benefits to companies that achieve particular sustainability objectives. The World Bank (2022) explains that these newly created financial instruments mirror global trends which unite markets with sustainability and climate-based objectives. These climate instruments build transparency through their capital-raising mechanism with direct climate measures which also boosts financial accountability.

6.2. Carbon Pricing and Risk Mitigation Mechanisms

The financial impact of climate risks gets reduced through the implementation of Climate insurance as an innovative product. Climate insurance products are increasing due to more intense weather-related disasters such as floods, droughts and hurricanes. Existing insurance mechanisms are insufficient in covering climate risks. Weather indexed insurance is becoming popular for paying out when certain climate events exceed predetermined thresholds. These policies insure agricultural stakeholders, whose harvests are weather dependent. In developing nations, weather-indexed insurance is offered by the international Finance Corporation (2023) to render farmers financially stable due to crop loss in developing nations. The insurance industry employs parametric insurance with predetermined parameters such as wind speeds or rain intensities for rapid disaster-related payouts.

6.3. Climate Insurance

Climate insurance mitigates the economic burden of climate risk. It is increasing due to increase in the frequency and intensity of weather-related disasters such as floods, drought, and hurricanes. The current insurance methods fail to cover climate risks effectively so new advanced insurance solutions are emerging to meet this need. Weather-indexed insurance policies that trigger payouts based on pre-established thresholds for climate events now become more popular among the market. The IFC (2023) clarifies that they help farmers in developing countries to remain financially secure during weather disasters and enhance their resilience against poverty because of crop loss.

7. Digital Technologies and Climate Risk Assessment

Emerging modern digital technology that includes AI, machine learning, and blockchain elements transforms both climate finance systems as well as risk management activities. Digital technologies have powerful abilities to enhance both operational efficiency as well as levels of transparency and efficiency of climate finance management systems. AI predictions combined with machine learning models help financial institutions in gaining better insights about the impact of climate change on their investment portfolios.

8. PPPs for Climate Finance

PPPs are a significant tool to mobilize climate finance in developing countries. They combine public funding and private capital to fund massive climate projects. The partnerships prove crucial in developing nations because these nations have restricted access to capital for climate-related projects. The International Finance Corporation (2023) demonstrates how PPPs serve as crucial tools for creating renewable energy facilities like wind and solar projects in developing economic markets. Through such alliances the financing deficit receives support while public entities access private-sector technology and knowledge which enhances sustainable climate resilience construction. Resilient financial systems need innovations in climate finance together with risk mitigation solutions to face the rising climate change-related hazards. Sustainable projects gain funding through green bonds coupled with carbon pricing methods and climate insurance programs that leverage digital technologies with PPPs. Finances must be integrated with these innovations in order to build long-term sustainability and resilience due to rising insect effects of climate change on global economies.

9. Findings

9.1. Emergence of Green Bonds and Sustainability-Linked Instruments

The market value for green bonds and climate-aligned financial instruments experienced substantial growth in the last few years. The effective capital distribution tools have shown strength in channeling funds toward sustainable projects that include renewable energy and climate adaptations. The green bond market expanded to over $1 trillion during 2022 according to Climate Bonds Initiative 2023 because investors showed advanced interest in climate goal-related projects.

9.2. Carbon Pricing in Risk Mitigation

Economical signals which motivate companies to minimize their carbon footprint effectively emerge from carbon pricing systems which comprise carbon taxes and cap-and-trade policies. Through carbon pricing enterprises and governments can both manage climate-related risks while investing into low-carbon technology solutions because it makes them bear the environmental expenses of their carbon emissions. The adoption of carbon pricing exists in more than 60 nations across the world which collectively controls approximately 20% of global emissions (World Bank, 2022). The growing use of carbon pricing across numerous economies represents a vital response to cut down climate change financial threats.

9.3. Growth of Climate Insurance Solutions

Modern climate insurance products called weather-indexed insurance along with parametric insurance now help businesses control extreme weather financial risks. The products deliver special advantages to agricultural industries which face high exposure to climate change risks. Developing countries have gained security against crop failure through weather-indexed insurance policies according to International Finance Corporation (2023).

9.4. Transparency and Efficiency

The transformation of climate finance occurs through emerging digital technologies such as AI along with blockchain and machine learning which enhance data analyses for risk evaluation alongside transaction transparency. The implementation of AI in climate risk prediction has improved prediction accuracy to enable better financial choices (Zhang et al., 2021). Through blockchain technology climate finance receives transparent transaction records which provide immune protection and effective fund distribution with reduced cases of misallocation and fraud (World Economic Forum, 2022).

9.5. Climate Resilience

PPPs function as an effective tool for gathering financial resources that support large climate resilience initiatives. The partnerships play a crucial role in developing countries since these markets generally face restricted funding options for climate-related projects. PPPs enable public regulatory support to join forces with private investment and expertise for financing renewable energy projects and building infrastructure and adapting to climate risks (International Finance Corporation, 2023).

10. Suggestions

10.1. Green Bonds and Climate-aligned Financial Instruments

State institutions together with banking entities need to enhance their collaboration for increasing the volume of green bond issues alongside sustainability-linked bond allocation and alternative climate-minded financial tools. The addition of tax exemptions together with investment guarantees should serve as inducements to attract more investors to these marketplaces. A more extensive green bond market can supply the required funding needed for climate adaptation activities and mitigation projects which supports the low-carbon economic transition (Alam et al., 2024).

10.2. Expanding Carbon Pricing Mechanisms Globally

The lasting sustainability of climate financial programs requires global expansion of carbon pricing programs. Government policies need to support the creation of carbon taxes and cap-and-trade mechanisms throughout developed economies and developing economies. International investment in low-carbon technologies would increase when carbon pricing receives global coordination which establishes an equal competitive environment. Weather-resistant programs in vulnerable areas should use carbon pricing income as funding streams.

10.3. Climate Insurance for Vulnerable Communities

Developing countries require expanded climate insurance solutions which should serve to protect their most vulnerable populations. Governments need to provide financial motivation for creating affordable climate-based insurance products available to smallholder farmers and low-income communities and businesses operating in vulnerable industries.

10.4. Digital Technologies for Climate Risk Management

Public and financial institutions need to back digital technology adoption including AI and machine learning as well as blockchain to boost climate risk prediction together with climate finance transparency. AI operates to enhance climate modeling as well as risk prediction activities while blockchain functions to guarantee effective allocation of funds toward climate-related projects (Naseema et al., 2024).

10.5. Public–Private Collaboration for Climate Finance

Future development of PPPs should be promoted to overcome financial challenges in climate resilience projects. The government must establish an optimal regulatory structure which promotes private enterprise investments into climate solution development. Public service institutions should provide guarantees simultaneously with co-financing mechanisms that reduce investment risks and enable private sector companies to deliver technical assistance and financial resources (Jafar, Hemachandran, et al., 2024).

10.6. Climate Risks into Financial Regulations

Financial regulatory bodies must adopt climate risk evaluation policies to force financial organizations reveal climate threats as well as potential benefits within their investment strategies. Financial institutions should be motivated to adopt ESG criteria for their investment plan (Khan et al., 2022).

10.7. Climate Finance for Developing Countries

Developed countries require an expansion of their financial support programs to help developing nations manage climate adaptation along with mitigating environmental impact. Climate resilience projects in developing nations can access financial support through mechanisms comprising the Green Climate Fund (Khan et al., 2021).

11. Conclusion

In conclusion, the innovative financial tools examined during research together with green bonds and carbon pricing and climate insurance and digital technologies form essential frameworks to boost financial resilience toward climate change adaptation. These instruments allow both public and private institutions to enhance their capability to address climate-related perils together with establishing financial systems that connect with sustainability targets and establishing enduring climate adaptation and mitigation plans. These innovative solutions when implemented in financial planning strengthen the transition to low-carbon operations and operate as a stable structure to manage unpredictable climate-related financial losses. Implementing these solutions meets resistance when it comes to mass deployment alongside achieving fair distribution of financial aid for climate purposes especially in less-developed nations. The existing gaps require innovative techniques together with policy advancement and collaborative efforts between institutions for their resolution.

12. Directions for Further Research

Studies should examine how to increase the large-scale potential of unique climate finance methods across various economic scenarios especially among emerging and developing nations. The study needs to investigate how digital technology advances enable more efficient and transparent operations of climate finance systems in depth. The research needs to investigate whether PPPs succeed in funding major climate resilience projects through studies also showing how financial institutions can improve their climate risk assessments. The study of financial innovation's economic and demographic effects on susceptible people would create essential knowledge for developing climate finance approaches that promote equality.

References

Alam, M., & Akhtar, S. (2024). Introduction to green finance and technology integration. In S. H. Jafar, R. V. Rodriguez, H. Kannan, S. Akhtar, & P. Plugmann (Eds.), *Harnessing blockchain-digital twin fusion for sustainable investments* (pp. 1–19). IGI Global. https://doi.org/10.4018/979-8-3693-1878-2.ch001

Alam, M., Akhtar, S., & Bettencourt, A. (2024). Introduction to Fintech in Industry 5.0: Companion or antagonist. In S. H. Jafar, K. Hemachandran, S. Akhtar, P. A. Khan,

& H. El-Chaarani (Eds.), *The adoption of Fintech: using technology for better security, speed, and customer experience in finance* (pp. 1–16). Productivity Press.

Banerjee, A., Karlan, D., & Zinman, J. (2015). Six randomized evaluations of microcredit: Introduction and further steps. *American Economic Journal: Applied Economics, 7*(1), 1–21. https://doi.org/10.1257/app.20140287

Batten, S., Sowerbutts, R., & Tanaka, M. (2020). Climate change: Risk to financial stability. *Bank of England Quarterly Bulletin, 2020*(Q2), 1–10. https://www.bankofengland.co.uk/

Beck, T., & de la Torre, A. (2007). *The basic analytics of access to financial services* [World Bank Policy Research Working Paper No. 4026]. World Bank.

Clark, G., Reed, J., & Sunderland, T. (2018). Bridging funding gaps for climate and sustainable development. *Sustainability, 10*(12), 4334. https://doi.org/10.3390/su10124334

Climate Bonds Initiative. (2023). *Annual green bond market report*. Climate Bonds Initiative. https://www.climatebonds.net/

Ghosh, S. (2020). ESG investing: Performance and prospects. *Journal of Sustainable Finance & Investment, 10*(4), 427–442.

International Energy Agency (IEA). (2023). *India's path to net zero: Role of public-private partnerships*. International Energy Agency. https://www.iea.org/

International Finance Corporation (IFC). (2023). *Weather-indexed insurance in emerging markets*. https://www.ifc.org/

Jafar, S. H., Akhtar, S., & Johl, S. K. (2023). AI in insurance. In *Artificial intelligence for business* (pp. 164–173). Productivity Press.

Jafar, S. H., Hemachandran, K., Akhtar, S., Khan, P. A., & El-Chaarani, H. (Eds.). (2024). *The adoption of fintech: Using technology for better security, speed, and customer experience in finance*. CRC Press.

Jafar, S. H., Rodriguez, R. V., Kannan, H., Akhtar, S., & Plugmann, P. (Eds.). (2024). *Harnessing blockchain-digital twin fusion for sustainable investments*. IGI Global.

Khan, P. A., Johl, S. K., & Akhtar, S. (2021). Firm sustainable development goals and firm financial performance through the lens of green innovation practices and reporting: A proactive approach. *Journal of Risk and Financial Management, 14*(12), 605.

Khan, P. A., Johl, S. K., & Akhtar, S. (2022). Vinculum of sustainable development goal practices and firms' financial performance: A moderation role of green innovation. *Journal of Risk and Financial Management, 15*(3), 96.

Linnerooth-Bayer, J., Mechler, R., & Hochrainer-Stigler, S. (2019). Insurance against climate risks. *Nature Climate Change, 9*(9), 637–639. https://doi.org/10.1038/s41558-019-0560-3

Morningstar. (2022). ESG investing performance trends. *Morningstar Research Report, 12*(4), 15–27. https://www.morningstar.com/

Naseema, N., Akhtar, S., & Al Hinai, A. A. (2024). Disrupting financial services: A case study on Capital One's Fintech Odyssey. In S. H. Jafar, R. V. Rodriguez, H. Kannan, S. Akhtar, & P. Plugmann (Eds.), *Harnessing blockchain-digital twin fusion for sustainable investments* (pp. 363–383). IGI Global.

Organisation for Economic Co-operation and Development (OECD). (2021). *Mobilizing finance for climate action*. OECD Publishing. https://www.oecd.org/

Paris Agreement. (2015). *UNFCCC*. https://unfccc.int/

Pottier, A., Landa, G., Vernier, C., & Hourcade, J. C. (2020). The implications of the Paris Agreement for global financial systems. *Energy Policy, 137*, 111173. https://doi.org/10.1016/j.enpol.2019.111173

Stern, N. (2006). *The Stern review: The economics of climate change.* [Database]

Task Force on Climate-related Financial Disclosures (TCFD). (2017). *Recommendations of the task force on climate-related financial disclosures*. https://www.fsb-tcfd.org/

United Nations Environment Programme (UNEP). (2021). *Climate change and financial systems: Building resilience*. United Nations Environment Programme. https://www.unep.org/

World Bank. (2022). *State and trends of carbon pricing 2022*. World Bank. https://www.worldbank.org/

World Economic Forum. (2022). *Blockchain for sustainable finance: Unlocking potential*. https://www.weforum.org/

Zhang, Z., Wang, C., & Li, F. (2021). The role of blockchain and AI in climate finance. *Journal of Sustainable Finance & Investment*, *11*(2), 157–172. https://doi.org/10.1080/20430795.2020.1861086

Chapter 16

Climate Resilience in Emerging Markets: A Comparative Study of Selected States' Climate Initiatives

Aliza[a], Furquan Uddin[b] and Muhammad Usman[c]

[a]*Faculty of Commerce, Banaras Hindu University, Uttar Pradesh, India*
[b]*Department of Management & Business Administration, Aliah University, Kolkata, India*
[c]*International Business Strategy, University of Lancashire, Preston, UK*

Abstract

The growth of emerging economies, when accompanied by the development of their population and industries, stands to make significant contributions to international efforts that are geared toward tackling climate change. However, such efforts have to cope with difficulties in several emerging markets like inadequate infrastructure, limited funding, and governance issues. This chapter used case studies to focus on the risk-mitigation strategies of three southern Indian states (Maharashtra, Tamil Nadu, and Karnataka) for achieving development goals amid the pressing need for climate action plans. Further, a comparative analysis was also conducted for these three state-level climate initiatives – Maharashtra State Action Plan on Climate Change (MSAPCC), Tamil Nadu State Action Plan on Climate Change (TNSAPCC), and Karnataka State Action Plan on Climate Change (KSAPCC). While much progress has been made, challenges such as funding limits, data shortages, and intersectoral collaboration remain to be overcome for climate action plans to be a success. However, these state-level action plans serve as an important example of how methods for climate change mitigation and adaptation can be incorporated into regional development processes. The practical implications are wide-reaching and are useful for governments and communities in addressing climate change. The chapter informs the creation of effective climate policies by identifying

Climate Risk and Emerging Markets: Valuation, Volatility, and Portfolio Strategies, 243–256

Published under exclusive licence by Emerald Publishing Limited
doi:10.1108/978-1-83708-088-520261048

the most efficient strategies that are used by the government for climate resilience. The chapter emphasizes that decentralized approaches and local solutions must be promoted to tackle short-term vulnerabilities with an eye for longer-term sustainability.

Keywords: Climate resilience; climate action plan; climate change; emerging markets; state action plan on climate change

Introduction

Climate resilience is defined as the ability of systems such as people, ecosystems, and economies to predict, prepare for, respond to, and recover from climate change effects. It involves reducing vulnerability to climate hazards like extreme weather occurrences, adapting to long-term climate shifts, and implementing measures such as improved infrastructure, disaster preparedness, sustainable practices, and strengthening social institutions. Sharma et al. (2020) highlight how climate change drives migration, disrupting regional growth and disproportionally affecting economically vulnerable areas. However, defining environmental migration remains a challenge, limiting coordinated efforts. Hence, a well-defined framework could help unify isolated initiatives and foster collaboration across international, national, and local levels. Warner and Weisberg (2023) describe "loss and damage" in climate policy as unavoidable climate impacts like rising sea levels, increasing temperatures, and biodiversity loss.

Developing nations face climate change challenges alongside financial constraints, which hinder their ability to adapt. Climate risk assessment often points to inadequate adaptation capacity, largely due to governance shortcomings (Olsson et al., 2006). Wildowicz-Szumarska and Owsiak (2024) confirm the link between climate change and economic inequality, noting that poor nations struggle more with mitigation and adaptation to climate change.

This study analyzes state-level climate action plans, which function as subsets of India's National Action Plan on Climate Change (NAPCC). Launched in 2008, NAPCC integrates climate concerns into national development, promoting sustainability through eight missions covering solar power, energy efficiency, sustainable agriculture, water conservation, and emissions reduction through urban planning and industrial processes (Pandve, 2009). Recognizing India's diverse geography, social inequalities, and development needs, states were directed in 2009 to create State Action Plans on Climate Change (TERI, 2014). This comparative study examines Maharashtra, Tamil Nadu, and Karnataka – three large other states with similar geography and biodiversity – analyzing how their climate policies align with national strategies while addressing local vulnerabilities.

Literature Review

This section provides a review of prior literature in the field of climate resilience.

Concept of Climate Resilience

Climate resilience refers to the ability of individuals, communities, ecosystems, and economies to adjust to and recover from climate change. It involves anticipating climate hazards, mitigating vulnerabilities, and adapting to extreme weather, rising sea levels, and shifting weather patterns. Climate change exacerbates poverty in developing countries, pushing vulnerable populations into hardship (Jafar, Hemachandran, et al., 2024; Tompkins et al., 2013). Until recently, economic research on climate resilience in underdeveloped countries was limited (Stage, 2010). Eyckmans et al. (2016) argue that developed countries must provide grants to developing countries to address climate change challenges. Resources for international development are under pressure as climate challenges grow, making cost-effective assistance increasingly urgent (Nakhooda, 2013). Okere and Uche (2024) highlight the disproportionate impact of climate change on poorer countries. Warner and Weisberg (2023) note that inadequate mitigation by industrialized countries imposes an unjust burden on developing countries, necessitating financial responsibility from wealthier nations.

Climate Resilience Issues in Emerging Markets

Emerging countries face significant climate resilience challenges due to inadequate financial grants, poor infrastructure, and vulnerability to extreme weather. Many already struggle with poverty, growing urbanization, and weaker governance, complicating climate adaptation efforts. Dependence on climate-sensitive industries like agriculture and tourism further increases risks. Various studies explore climate resilience in different economies and sectors. Ayers et al. (2011) analyzed Nepal's Pilot Program for Climate Resilience to understand how stakeholders interpret its global objectives. Rai et al. (2014) used the "building blocks" concept to compare Bangladesh's Climate Change Resilience and Trust Fund, assessing their progression from planning to funding and execution. Meerow (2017) examined "double exposure" in a Philippines city, emphasizing how climate change affects infrastructure and mitigation efforts. Hirons et al. (2018) conducted a multi-scalar analysis of Ethiopia's coffee sector and climate resilience strategies. Friend and Thinphanga (2018) found Thailand's institutions lacking significant climate action. Later, Garschagen and Marks (2019) stress the need for vulnerability assessments regarding climate change resilience to achieve long-term risk reduction in Asian cities. Ngarambe et al. (2022) investigate the link between mortality and local climate changes in Seoul, finding that higher male mortality rate at extreme temperatures (over 60°C). Muchiri and Opiyo (2022) studied climate adaptation in Kenya's Korogocho settlement, emphasizing community-driven literacy and local experiential knowledge. Ferranti et al. (2022) propose an analytical methodology for assessing urban transport resilience to current and future weather in Rio de Janeiro. Jamali et al. (2023) revealed that the socio-cultural component is very important in creating capacity for urban climate resilience, in addition to eco-environmental and economic components. Recently, Li et al. (2024) investigated the status and impediments to climate resilience governance in China's coastal megacities, with a particular emphasis on Shanghai's policies and plans.

Climate Resilience Issues and Practices Across Sectors

Climate resilience issues vary by sector, with each facing unique challenges in adapting to climate change. In agriculture, shifting weather patterns, such as erratic rainfall and high temperatures, endanger food production and farmers' lives, especially in underdeveloped countries. Lim-Camacho et al. (2017) used a value chain-based technique to evaluate supply chain elasticity in the event of disturbance caused by climate-related challenges and advocated for proactive adaptation to balance supply chain efficiency and cost reduction against resilience and long-term sustainability. Khumalo et al. (2024) examine the impact of climate-smart agriculture (CSA) practices and climate adaption techniques on food and income possibilities. Similarly, Zougmoré et al. (2018) demonstrate the effectiveness of CSA in improving climate resilience among smallholder farmers in sub-Saharan Africa, while Lipper et al. (2014) highlight the role of CSA in reducing greenhouse gas emissions and improving productivity.

In the energy sector, risks include the availability of renewable resources, such as water for hydropower, and infrastructure damage from extreme weather events. Also, rising sea levels, flooding, and heatwaves challenge urban resilience, affecting infrastructure, public health, and housing. The water sector is also dealing with changes in precipitation patterns, which affect water supply and quality. Furthermore, businesses that rely on natural ecosystems, such as tourism and fisheries, are vulnerable to climate-related disturbances like coral bleaching and dwindling fish populations. Kristl et al. (2020) address the building sector's core climate resilience concerns, such as climate adaptation plans, energy efficiency, and mitigation strategies. To address such issues, Lim-Camacho et al. (2017) used a value chain-based technique to assess supply chain resilience to climate disruption, emphasizing proactive adaptation to balance efficiency, cost reduction, and long-term sustainability. Ssekyanzi et al. (2024) investigate the potential of innovative rainwater storage systems to manage rainwater challenges sustainably by analyzing important success criteria. Khumalo et al. (2024) examine the impact of CSA practices and climate adaption techniques on food and income possibilities. Besides, the relevance of the garbage sector has the potential to greatly contribute to climate change and has a damaging influence on the local ecosystem.

Efforts for Boosting Climate Resilience in Emerging Markets

Previous initiatives to strengthen climate resilience in emerging markets have concentrated on upgrading infrastructure, disaster preparedness, and incorporating climate adaptation into national strategies. International organizations have contributed financial and technical assistance in implementing CSA and early warning systems. However, challenges like limited resources and political instability have hindered progress. Current efforts emphasize long-term, sustainable approaches to building resilience at local and national levels. Dasgupta and Shaw

(2015) developed a five-point climate resilience evaluation model and an amalgamated resilience indexation technique to monitor climate-related disasters, focusing on communities living in the rural coastal plains of the world. Argyroudis et al. (2022) and Alam et al. (2024) highlighted the role of digital technologies in enhancing infrastructure resilience through efficient decision-making before, during, and after hazard occurrences. Pereira et al. (2024) found that green infrastructures and design measures improve quality of life by mitigating heatwave impacts. The adoption of sustainability concepts by communities will help to address climate challenges effectively (Raza et al., 2023). Vinata et al. (2024) underscored the role of coastal ecosystems in climate adaptation and mitigation.

Role of Technology for Climate Resilience in Emerging Markets

Technology and innovation contribute to the climate resilience capacity in emerging economies by providing risk mitigation and management solutions. Technologies like climate modeling and satellite modeling, with the help of data analytics, enhance early warning systems for weather disasters. In agriculture, drought-resistant crops and precision farming techniques amid climate change (Alam & Akhtar, 2024). Renewable energy resources, like solar and wind power, provide alternatives to fossil fuels, reducing the dependence and vulnerability to conventional resources. Technology may aid emerging markets to enhance resource management, better infrastructure, and create more climate-resilient communities. Mosleh et al. (2023) developed a "Stormwater Green Infrastructure" resilience assessment tool to identify issues and help stakeholders to address climate challenges. Pandeya et al. (2024) highlight that CSA as a path to sustainability and resilience. Also, Mondal et al. (2024) explore AI's role in carbon neutrality through digital inclusion for developing markets. While nature-based solutions could address climate change, they receive little attention in low-income nations. Jafar, Rodriguez, et al. (2024), Naseema et al. (2024), and Wu (2024) highlight that FinTech increases energy efficiency via digital transformation and significantly reduces regional carbon emissions.

Suggestions for Boosting Climate Resilience in Emerging Markets

The future could see initiatives that educate, train, and raise awareness programs regarding sustainability, empowering communities to manage climate change vulnerabilities in emerging economies. Investment in climate-smart infrastructure like flood defenses, renewables, and water management technologies is essential to protecting vulnerable people. Collaboration with international private organizations can assist in mobilizing financial resources and technical skills to strengthen resilience toward weather change on a small-scale level. Additionally, urban design, agricultural, and disaster response systems will benefit from climate resilience included as a part of the strategy that is sustainable and more integrated. Finally, helping increase resilience by encouraging innovation and development of locally adapted technology can provide new economic opportunities. Liu et al. (2016) provided a methodology for assessing the economic benefits of "climate resilient development" that included three models: a "home benefit cost model", a "diffusion model," and a "regional benefit cost model." Saxena et al. (2018) highlight that resilience and transformation are a top-down and donor-driven process that needs to be a shared vision of all stakeholders. At the same time, they note that actors do not agree on what the terms "resilience" and "transformation" entail, where they tend to define "resilience" as "bounce back" capacity from extreme events and "transformation" as disruption of the socioeconomic and political structures. The present indicators for efficient and effective measures can build on the agriculture sector's resistance to climatic hazards to make the agricultural sector climate hazards resilient.

Findings

Case Study 1: MSAPCC

Overview: Maharashtra is one of India's most populous states covering an area of 307,713 km^2 with a rich geographical diversity, comprising coastal districts bordering the Arabian Sea, Sahyadri mountain range, and extensive agricultural plains. Climate change in the form of irregular rainfall patterns, rising temperatures, numerous droughts, and more frequent cyclonic storms is extremely sensitive to the state. However, risks are avoiding these and dealing with the impacts of climate change therefore, to plan the way for sustainable development, the MSAPCC was developed. The state's adaptation and mitigation techniques should be incorporated into state policy and development plans. It also aims to strengthen resilience for climate change-sensitive sectors in agriculture, water resources, health, and ecosystems. It helps build climate-resilient urban planning and sustainable infrastructure development aimed at achieving low-carbon development through promoting renewable energy technology and energy efficiency measures to reduce greenhouse gases. The Maharashtra State Climate Change Mission (MSCCM) manages MSAPCC with the support of government departments, local bodies, and other stakeholders for action coordination. Implementation is accomplished using the contributions of technical groups, experts, and local authorities. The progress against pollution reduction, water conservation, and increasing renewable energy capacity can be tracked with clear markers.

Case Study 2: TNSAPCC

Overview: Tamil Nadu is among the most industrialized states of India and ranks first in agricultural production. But it is the geographical location of India adjacent to the Indian Ocean and dependence on seasonal rainfall that enhances the climatic risks it faces. The TNSAPCC was created as a response measure to tackle climate change impacts while building its capacity for adaptation and mitigation in the most affected sectors. It made an endeay at boosting the adaptive capacities of the state in relation to climate change effects on agriculture, water, coastal areas, and public health at large. Besides, it promotes a changeover from fossil fuels to green energy, encourages energy efficiency throughout all sectors, and making sure that climate action is in tune with the development goals set by the state for climate change and development. TNSAPCC was established to pursue an intensive approach for climate change impacts, including adaptation, mitigation, and capacity building in sensitive sectors. The objectives of the TNSAPCC include strengthening the adaptation capacity of the state with respect to adverse impacts of climate change on agriculture, water, coastal regions, and public health. It also pushes for the transition to renewable energy sources and increases energy efficiency in all sectors as well as broadens its scope to include climate change efforts toward the state development agenda by addressing sustainability and economic growth. Furthermore, it strives to raise the level of climate literacy among people so that they are engaged in planning and implementing climate action at the local level. The TNSAPCC would also promote consultations with a broader range of stakeholders in the fight against climate change through government civil society organization and local community engagement.

Case Study 3: KSAPCC

Overview: This south Indian state has great potential for reserves, and agriculture as well as a burgeoning acropolis. On the matter of climate issues, the state has several critical problems, such as changes in rainfall regime, dry years, and increasing temperatures. To address these risks Karnataka State Climate Change Action Plan Committee aims to increase the resilience and low-carbon development in various sectors in the state. Overall, the KSAPCC aims at building climate change resilience for sectors including agriculture, water, urban, and ecosystems, supporting the deployment of low-carbon technologies and renewable energy across industrial, residential, and commercial sectors, improving the capacity for climate change adaptation through urban and agricultural planning, water management, and through research, data, and skill development. Government agencies, local authorities, non-government organizations, and the corporate sector also help the Karnataka State Climate Change Action Plan Committee implement the Climate change responses which have been coordinated by the KSAPCC. Through the reviews, progress in the implementation of the action plan is assessed while other tools such as performance indicators are used in the assessment of climate resilience measures.

Comparative Analysis of Maharashtra, Tamil Nadu, and Karnataka State Action Plans on Climate Change (MSAPCC, TNSAPCC, KSAPCC)

The MSAPCC, TNSAPCC, and KSAPCC address each state's unique climatic vulnerabilities and development demands. These state-level action plans have numerous common goals, including lowering greenhouse gas emissions, increasing resilience to climate effects, and supporting sustainable development, but they range greatly in their methodologies, strategic focus, and problems. A comparison of these three programs reveals their respective strengths, shortcomings, and possibilities for success in combating climate change.

Key Focus Areas

The climate action plans have its focuses on the following sectors:

MSAPCC: Focuses strongly on agricultural resilience, coastal protection, and enhancing forest cover to combat climate change. Its diverse geography demands region-specific interventions. The key focus areas include agriculture, water resources, coastal management, and renewable energy.

TNSAPCC: Tamil Nadu stands out with its focus on public health resilience, given the state's vulnerability to heatwaves and vector-borne diseases, along with its leadership in renewable energy. The key focus areas include agriculture, water resources, coastal management, renewable energy, and health.

KSAPCC: Karnataka emphasizes urban resilience and sustainable city planning, leveraging its progress in renewable energy while addressing drought-prone areas through water management practices. The key focus areas include agriculture, water resources, urban development, and energy.

Strategic Objectives

The transition to renewable energy is a fundamental component of all three programs, with each state focusing on increasing solar and wind power generation. All three states place a premium on strengthening resilience to climate-related risks in areas such as agriculture, water, and health. All the plans ensure that climate initiatives are integrated with larger development goals, encouraging sustainable growth while lowering carbon emissions. However, the plans have unique objectives as mentioned below:

Maharashtra: The MSAPCC emphasizes the need to strengthen coastal ecosystems and promote afforestation and reforestation for carbon sequestration.

Tamil Nadu: The TNSAPCC prioritizes public health, trying to develop infrastructure to deal with heatwaves, vector-borne diseases, and other health concerns caused by climate change.

Karnataka: The KSAPCC stresses the importance of climate-resilient urban design, with a focus on lowering the urban "heat island effect" and ensuring that cities can withstand extreme weather events.

Key Challenges

Each state faces unique challenges in tackling climate adversities and in the implementation of the scheme which are as follows:

Maharashtra: The state faces financial constraints in securing adequate funds for large-scale climate action, particularly for agriculture and water management. Maharashtra's long coastline makes it highly vulnerable to cyclones and rising sea levels, which require extensive protective measures. The lack of granular, localized climate data for effective decision-making hampers targeted action.

Tamil Nadu: Tamil Nadu's coastal areas are highly vulnerable to climate impacts, and managing the displacement of communities affected by coastal erosion is a key challenge. Rapid urbanization and the pressure on infrastructure create significant challenges for adapting urban areas to the impacts of climate change. Strengthening public health systems to deal with climate-induced health risks, particularly in rural areas, requires substantial investment.

Karnataka: The state has to deal with conflicting priorities while balancing the growth of industries with the need for climate action, particularly in areas like agriculture, which remains a key challenge. Also, securing consistent funding for long-term climate adaptation projects, especially for rural areas, is a challenge. Karnataka faces issues related to the availability of localized climate data, which is critical for tailoring climate adaptation measures.

Strengths

A climate action plan's strength stems from its capacity to establish clear, verifiable emissions reduction objectives, create collaboration among governments, corporations, and communities, and prioritize sustainable practices. The strength of the plans is mentioned below:

Maharashtra: The MSAPCC covers a wide range of sectors from agriculture to energy, with specific programs to address the state's geographic diversity. In addition, given Maharashtra's vulnerability to coastal impacts, the action plan's emphasis on protecting coastal ecosystems is a critical strength.

Tamil Nadu: The TNSAPCC's inclusion of health as a key pillar is particularly important, given the rising risks of climate-induced health issues in the state. Also, the state is a leader in renewable energy, particularly wind energy, and the action plan builds on this with an aggressive expansion strategy.

Karnataka: Karnataka's focus on making urban areas more resilient to climate change through sustainable urban planning is highly innovative. The state's substantial progress in solar and wind energy is reinforced in the KSAPCC, making it a model for other states.

Discussion

Climate resilience serves to mitigate possible damages and assures that systems can bounce back and prosper in the face of persistent environmental difficulties by reinforcing infrastructure, implementing sustainable practices, and encouraging adaptive methods. The protection of current and future generations from climate change threats calls for resilience building. Addressing climate resilience in developing markets necessitates combining sustainable development, investing in adaptable infrastructure, and strengthening local capacity to respond to climate effects, all while gaining financial support for long-term solutions. Strengthening the role of communities and multi-stakeholder coalitions is critical to reducing the injustices and inequalities inherent in anthropogenic climate change (Seleguim, 2021). Resilient communities are better prepared to deal with the difficulties of climate change, safeguarding their long-term well-being and sustainability (Garschagen & Marks, 2019). However, financial constraints are the prime hurdle in achieving the targets of climate resilience. Trundle (2020) shows how to build on the resources, networks, and latent capacities of urban informality to improve the climate resilience of urban systems. Cekan and Legro (2022) investigated how public funders and lenders assess the viability of environmental and other sectoral development projects.

There are plenty of global and regional initiatives to mitigate the ill consequences of climate change. However, their success depends on various factors. Biagini and Miller (2013) advocated for stronger public–private partnerships that will help to improve climate resilience while also creating business opportunities. Further, keeping in mind the vast number of corporations, the engagement of corporate institutions to tackle climate change risk, responses and adaptation to adverse weather situations must be put to top focus. Sharma et al. (2020) suggested that a participative model could make national programs more effective, international efforts more targeted, and local techniques transferable. The programs aimed at poverty reduction and resilience development should be synergized to effectively utilize funds and other resources.

Climate resilience in emerging countries requires a comprehensive approach to adopt sustainability and mitigate the risk of climate change. To protect communities from extreme weather disasters, start by developing climate-resilient infrastructure such as flood defences, sustainable water systems, and disaster-resistant structures. Strengthening governance and institutions is also critical, as it ensures that climate risk management is integrated into national and local policies, allowing for both proactive planning and responsive action to climate consequences. Moreover, it also supports sustainable agriculture and good resource management including climate-smart inclusive development of agriculture, and water management, among others, and improves food security and safeguards ecosystems. Climate resilience can be achieved through climate neutrality. However, the sustainability of climate neutrality cannot be achieved by existing sociotechnical structures, for example, energy and urban systems (EEA, 2019). Using such synergy among these aspects, countries of developing economies can improve their ability for resilience to climate change, and at the same time, they can strengthen their development through sustainability and alleviate vulnerabilities.

Conclusion

Developed for Maharashtra, Tamil Nadu, and Karnataka, the MSAPCC, TNSAPCC, and KSAPCC are essential frameworks to combat the effects of climate change and promote sustainable development. The different plans of each state are a result of its vulnerabilities and aspirations, but all state plans stress the need for renewable energy, sustainable agriculture, and climate-resilient infrastructure. While much progress has been made, challenges such as funding limits, data shortages, and intersectoral collaboration remain to be overcome for this to be a success. However, these state-level action plans serve as an important example of how methods for climate change mitigation and adaptation can be incorporated into regional development processes. Improving execution depends on how well one can work around budget limits, inter-department cooperation, and the rising need for localized data for better execution. Meeting these commitments requires access to climate funds to invest in green efforts via public–private partnerships and global climate funds. Community engagement and education are finally critical, as giving local populations knowledge and resources helps them to better understand the "what" and "why" of climate hazards, and to be more active participants in adaptation activities. While these states advance with their climate action measures, their experiences offer valuable lessons on how state-level action is likely to impact India's wider national climate objectives. Innovation, resilience, and social equity in such policies have the potential to lead to revolutionary change in climate mitigation while also benefiting long-term environmental and economic sustainability.

References

Alam, M., & Akhtar, S. (2024). Introduction to green finance and technology integration. In S. Jafar, R. Rodriguez, H. Kannan, S. Akhtar, & P. Plugmann (Eds.), *Harnessing blockchain-digital twin fusion for sustainable investments* (pp. 1–19). IGI Global Scientific Publishing. https://doi.org/10.4018/979-8-3693-1878-2.ch001

Alam, M., Akhtar, S., & Bettencourt, A. (2024). Introduction to fintech in industry 5.0: Companion or antagonist. In S. H. Jafar, K. Hemachandran, S. Akhtar, P. A. Khan, & H. EL-Chaarani (Eds.), *The adoption of fintech* (pp. 1–16). Productivity Press.

Argyroudis, S. A., Mitoulis, S. A., Chatzi, E., Baker, J. W., Brilakis, I., Gkoumas, K., Vousdoukas, M., Hynes, W., Carluccio, S., Keou, O., Frangopol, D. M., & Linkov, I. (2022). Digital technologies can enhance the climate resilience of critical infrastructure. *Climate Risk Management, 35*. https://doi.org/10.1016/j.crm.2021.100387

Ayers, J., Kaur, N., & Anderson, S. (2011). Negotiating climate resilience in Nepal. *IDS Bulletin, 42*(3), 70–79.

Biagini, B., & Miller, A. (2013). Engaging the private sector in adaptation to climate change in developing countries: Importance, status, and challenges. *Climate and Development, 5*(3), 242–252. https://doi.org/10.1080/17565529.2013.821053

Cekan, J., & Legro, S. (2022). Can we assume sustained impact? Verifying the sustainability of climate change mitigation results. In *Transformational change for people and the planet: Evaluating environment and development* (pp. 105–122). Springer International Publishing.

DasGupta, R., & Shaw, R. (2015). An indicator based approach to assess coastal communities' resilience against climate related disasters in Indian Sundarbans. *Journal of Child and Family Studies, 24*(3), 85–101. https://doi.org/10.1007/s11852-014-0369-1

EEA. (2019). *Trends and projections in Europe 2019: Tracking progress towards Europe's climate and energy targets*. Retrieved February 21, 2020, from https://www. eea.europa.eu/publications/trends-and-projections-in-europe-1

Eyckmans, J., Fankhauser, S., & Kverndokk, S. (2016). Development aid and climate finance. *Environmental and Resource Economics, 63*(2), 429–450. https://doi.org/10.1007/s10640-015-9883-3

Ferranti, E. J. S., Oberling, D. F., & Quinn, A. D. (2022). Transport resilience to weather and climate: an interdisciplinary view from Rio de Janeiro. *Proceedings of the Institution of Civil Engineers: Urban Design and Planning*, *175*(3), 103–121. https://doi.org/10.1680/jurdp.21.00006a

Friend, R., & Thinphanga, P. (2018). Urban water crises under future uncertainties: The case of institutional and infrastructure complexity in Khon Kaen, Thailand. *Sustainability (Switzerland)*, *10*(11). https://doi.org/10.3390/su10113921

Garschagen, M., & Marks, D. (2019). Towards an agenda for profound urban climate resilience in Southeast Asia. In A. Daniere, & M. Garschagen (Eds.), *Urban climate resilience in Southeast Asia. The Urban Book Series*. (pp. 223–228). Springer. https://doi.org/10.1007/978-3-319-98968-6_11

Hirons, M., Mehrabi, Z., Gonfa, T. A., Morel, A., Gole, T. W., McDermott, C., Boyd, E., Robinson, E., Sheleme, D., Malhi, Y., Mason, J., & Norris, K. (2018). Pursuing climate resilient coffee in Ethiopia – A critical review. *Geoforum*, *91*, 108–116. https://doi.org/10.1016/j.geoforum.2018.02.032; https://www.moef.gov.in/state-action-plan-on-climate-change

Jafar, S. H., Hemachandran, K., Akhtar, S., Khan, P. A., & El-Chaarani, H. (Eds.). (2024). *The adoption of fintech: Using technology for better security, speed, and customer experience in finance*. CRC Press.

Jafar, S. H., Rodriguez, R. V., Kannan, H., Akhtar, S., & Plugmann, P. (Eds.). (2024). *Harnessing blockchain-digital twin fusion for sustainable investments*. IGI Global.

Jamali, A., Robati, M., Nikoomaram, H., Farsad, F., & Aghamohammadi, H. (2023). Urban resilience and climate change: Developing a multidimensional index to adapt against climate change in the Iranian capital city of Tehran. *Urban Science*, *7*(1). https://doi.org/10.3390/urbansci7010007

Khumalo, N. Z., Sibanda, M., & Mdoda, L. (2024). Implications of a climate-smart approach to food and income security for urban Sub-Saharan Africa: A systematic review. *Sustainability (Switzerland)*, *16*(5). Multidisciplinary Digital Publishing Institute (MDPI). https://doi.org/10.3390/su16051882

Kristl, Ž., Senior, C., & Temeljotov Salaj, A. (2020). Key challenges of climate change adaptation in the building sector. *Urbani Izziv*, *31*(1), 101–111. https://doi.org/10.5379/urbani-izziv-en-2020-31-01-004

Li, C., Yang, H., Yao, Q., An, N., & Meng, H. (2024). Governing urban climate resilience (UCR): Systems, agents, and institutions in Shanghai, China. *Sustainability (Switzerland)*, *16*(7). https://doi.org/10.3390/su16072648

Lim-Camacho, L., Plagányi, É. E., Crimp, S., Hodgkinson, J. H., Hobday, A. J., Howden, S. M., & Loechel, B. (2017). Complex resource supply chains display higher resilience to simulated climate shocks. *Global Environmental Change*, *46*, 126–138. https://doi.org/10.1016/j.gloenvcha.2017.08.011

Lipper, L., Thornton, P., Campbell, B.M., Baedeker, T., Braimoh, A., Bwalya, M., Caron, P., Cattaneo, A., Garrity, D., Henry, K., & Hottle, R., 2014. Climate-smart agriculture for food security. *Nature Climate Change*, *4*(12), 1068–1072.

Liu, S., Connor, J., Butler, J. R. A., Jaya, I. K. D., & Nikmatullah, A. (2016). Evaluating economic costs and benefits of climate resilient livelihood strategies. *Climate Risk Management*, *12*, 115–129. https://doi.org/10.1016/j.crm.2015.11.005

Meerow, S. (2017). Double exposure, infrastructure planning, and urban climate resilience in coastal megacities: A case study of Manila. *Environment and Planning A*, *49*(11), 2649–2672. https://doi.org/10.1177/0308518X17723630

Mondal, S., Das, S., & Vrana, V. G. (2024). Exploring the role of artificial intelligence in achieving a net zero carbon economy in emerging economies: A combination of PLS-SEM and fsQCA approaches to digital inclusion and climate resilience. *Sustainability (Switzerland)*, *16*(23). https://doi.org/10.3390/su162310299

Mosleh, L., Negahban-Azar, M., & Pavao-Zuckerman, M. (2023). Stormwater green infrastructure resilience assessment: A social-ecological framework for urban stormwater management. *Water (Switzerland)*, *15*(9). https://doi.org/10.3390/w15091786

Muchiri, C. N., & Opiyo, R. O. (2022). Community adaptation strategies in Nairobi informal settlements: Lessons from Korogocho, Nairobi-Kenya. *Frontiers in Sustainable Cities*, *4*, 932046.

Nakhooda, S. (2013). *The effectiveness of international climate finance* [ODI Working Paper, iii + 22 pp].

Naseema, N., Akhtar, S., & Al Hinai, A. A. (2024). Disrupting financial services: A case study on capital one's fintech odyssey. In S. Jafar, R. Rodriguez, H. Kannan, S. Akhtar, & P. Plugmann (Eds.), *Harnessing blockchain-digital twin fusion for sustainable investments* (pp. 363–383). IGI Global Scientific Publishing. https://doi.org/10.4018/979-8-3693-1878-2.ch015

Ngarambe, J., Santamouris, M., & Yun, G. Y. (2022). The impact of urban warming on the mortality of vulnerable populations in Seoul. *Sustainability (Switzerland)*, *14*(20). https://doi.org/10.3390/su142013452

Okere, K. I., & Uche, E. (2024). Climate change resilient strategies for greener Africa: The perspectives of energy efficiency and eco-complexities. *Sustainable Futures*, *8*. https://doi.org/10.1016/j.sftr.2024.100397

Olsson, P., Gunderson, L. H., Carpenter, S. R., Ryan, P., Lebel, L., Folke, C., & Holling, C. S. (2006). Shooting the rapids: navigating transitions to adaptive governance of social-ecological systems. *Ecology and Society*, *11*(1), 18.

Pandeya, S., Gajurel, A., Mishra, B. P., Devkota, K., Gyawali, B. R., & Upadhaya, S. (2024). Determinants of climate-smart agriculture adoption among rice farmers: Enhancing sustainability. *Sustainability (Switzerland)*, *16*(23). https://doi.org/10.3390/su162310247

Pandve, H. T. (2009). India's national action plan on climate change. *Indian Journal of Occupational and Environmental Medicine*, *13*(1), 17–19.

Pereira, C., Flores-Colen, I., & Mendes, M. P. (2024). Guidelines to reduce the effects of urban heat in a changing climate: Green infrastructures and design measures. *Sustainable Development*, *32*(1), 57–83. John Wiley and Sons Ltd. https://doi.org/10.1002/sd.2646

Rai, N., Huq, S., & Huq, M. J. (2014). Climate resilient planning in Bangladesh: A review of progress and early experiences of moving from planning to implementation. *Development in Practice*, *24*(4), 527–543. https://doi.org/10.1080/09614524.2014.908822

Raza, M. W., Rasheed, A., & Uddin, F. (2023). What affects the consumers' green purchasing behaviour? A study from an emerging market. *International Journal of Productivity and Quality Management*. https://doi.org/10.1504/IJPQM.2023.10059145

Saxena, A., Qui, K., & Robinson, S. ann. (2018). Knowledge, attitudes and practices of climate adaptation actors towards resilience and transformation in a 1.5°C world. *Environmental Science and Policy*, *80*, 152–159. https://doi.org/10.1016/j.envsci.2017.11.001

Seleguim, F. B. (2021). How do community responses from global south contribute to climate justice and resilience debate? *Ambiente e Sociedade*, *24*. https://doi.org/10.1590/1809-4422asoc20210148vu2021L5RS

Sharma, A., Bracken, G., & Balz, V. (2020). Environmental migration and regional livelihood planning: A livelihood planning approach to circular migration. *Environmental Justice*, *13*(5), 173–180. https://doi.org/10.1089/env.2020.0010

Ssekyanzi, G., Ahmad, M. J., & Choi, K. S. (2024). Sustainable solutions for mitigating water scarcity in developing countries: A comprehensive review of innovative rainwater storage systems. *Water (Switzerland)*, *16*(17). Multidisciplinary Digital Publishing Institute (MDPI). https://doi.org/10.3390/w16172394

Stage, J. (2010). Economic valuation of climate change adaptation in developing countries. *Annals of the New York Academy of Sciences, 1185*, 150–163. https://doi.org/10.1111/j.1749-6632.2009.05168.x

TERI. (2014). *Assessing climate change vulnerability and adaptation strategies for Maharashtra: Maharashtra State Adaptation Action Plan on Climate Change (MSAAPC)*. https://www.moef.gov.in/uploads/2017/09/Maharashtra-Climate-Change-Final-Report.pdf

Tompkins, E. L., Mensah, A., King, L., Long, T. K., Lawson, E. T., Hutton, C., Hoang, V. A., Gordon, C., Fish, M., Dyer, J., Bood, N. (2013). *An investigation of the evidence of benefits from climate compatible development* [Centre for Climate Change Economics and Policy Working Paper No. 124]. Sustainability Research Institute, University of Leeds.

Trundle, A. (2020). Resilient cities in a Sea of Islands: Informality and climate change in the South Pacific. *Cities, 97*. https://doi.org/10.1016/j.cities.2019.102496

Vinata, R. T., Kumala, M. T., & Setyowati, P. J. (2024). Blue carbon ecosystems for climate resilience in Indonesia: A study of adaptation strategy. *Environmental Policy and Law, 54*(1), 43–51. https://doi.org/10.3233/EPL-230049

Warner, K., & Weisberg, M. (2023). A funding mosaic for loss and damage. *Science, 379*(6629), 219.

Wildowicz-Szumarska, A., & Owsiak, K. (2024). Impact of climate change on income inequality. implications for rich and poor countries. *Economics and Environment, 89*(2). https://doi.org/10.34659/eis.2024.89.2.684

Wu, Q. (2024). From bits to emissions: how FinTech benefits climate resilience? *Empirical Economics, 67*(5), 2009–2037. https://doi.org/10.1007/s00181-024-02609-9

Zougmoré, R. B., Partey, S. T., Ouédraogo, M., Torquebiau, E., & Campbell, B. M. (2018). Facing climate variability in sub-Saharan Africa: Analysis of climate-smart agriculture opportunities to manage climate-related risks. *Cahiers Agricultures (TSI), 27*(3), 1–9.

Chapter 17

Financial Terrains: Analyzing the Changing Territory of Climate Risks and Opportunities

Muneer Shaik[a], *Vidya Suresh*[b], *Mahmood Shaik*[c] *and Medhansh Bairaria*[a]

[a]*School of Management, Mahindra University, Hyderabad, India*
[b]*Department of Finance and Accounting, College of Banking and Financial Studies, Muscat, Oman*
[c]*EEE Department, Chaitanya Bharathi Institute of Technology, Hyderabad, India*

Abstract

Climate change poses significant financial risks, particularly for emerging markets that are highly exposed to environmental degradation, resource scarcity, and extreme weather conditions. This chapter examines the impact of climate risks on financial assets, market stability, and investment strategies. Estimates indicate that by 2100, approximately 2% of global financial assets could be at risk due to climate change, with worst-case scenarios projecting potential losses of up to 10%. The study employs a combination of empirical research and financial modeling to assess climate-related risks across emerging economies. Analyzing historical economic losses, sovereign credit ratings, and asset pricing, provides insights into the financial vulnerabilities these economies face. Drawing from data sourced from global financial institutions and market analyses, the chapter presents a structured approach for investors, asset managers, and policymakers to integrate climate risk considerations into their financial decision-making processes. Findings reveal that climate change led to an estimated $2.8 trillion in global economic losses between 2000 and 2019, equivalent to roughly $16 million per hour based on the report of World Economic Forum. Countries such as Bangladesh, Brazil, India, and Indonesia are particularly at risk, with adverse climate events affecting investment

Climate Risk and Emerging Markets: Valuation, Volatility, and Portfolio Strategies, 257–271

Published under exclusive licence by Emerald Publishing Limited
doi:10.1108/978-1-83708-088-520261051

inflows, economic growth, and creditworthiness. This chapter bridges the gap between theoretical research and practical financial applications by providing actionable recommendations for mitigating climate-related financial vulnerabilities. It underscores the need for sustainable investment strategies to enhance resilience in emerging markets.

Keywords: Climate risks; opportunities; financial terrains; emerging markets; global impact

1. Introduction

In 2023, the world witnessed unprecedented heatwaves that ravaged Europe, torrential floods that inundated parts of Asia, and infernal wildfires that scorched North America, and brought about tremendous suffering to human beings and severe economic chaos. These events were not random isolated incidents but represented dark signs of a planet badly strained. As human civilization tries to address the climate crisis, those implications have begun to cross environmental concerns and permeate the governance of corporations, disturb the financial markets, and modify the global economic order.

The financial landscape has been changing, and more so now than ever with climate change influencing the economic future trajectories, especially within at-risk emerging markets. As recent research warns, by 2100, as much as 10% of the global financial assets will be lost because of disruptions caused by climate changes. More conservative estimates place in jeopardy 2% of the world's financial assets, too significant to ignore in today's interconnected world where risks cascade quickly across borders and industries. Extreme weather events are not only damaging physical capital but also reverberate in financial markets, causing currency instability, credit risk augmentation, and triggering large insurance payouts. A recent survey conducted by the Task Force on Climate-related Financial Disclosures (TCFD) showed that almost 60% of the world's 100 largest publicly traded companies expect climate-related risks to have a significant impact on their operations within the next five years (Chua et al., 2022). This shift in perspective brings out an urgent need to include climate into decision-making in finance.

Climate-change-related disasters resulted in economic losses of $2.8 trillion between 2000 and 2019, in turn averaging $16 million per hour, as indicated by the World Economic Forum. However, a fair playing field does not exist. Emerging markets that frequently face infrastructure deficits and limited climate funding resources account for a significant portion of these losses. This creates a paradox in which the nations that contributed the least to past greenhouse gas emissions are currently experiencing the most serious consequences.

We discuss the disproportionate exposure to the ill effects of climate change among emerging countries like Bangladesh, Brazil, India, and Indonesia which together form nearly a quarter of the world's GDP. Bangladesh alone loses an estimated 2% of its GDP annually due to cyclones and floods (Islam et al., 2022).

In Brazil, the deforestation and shifting rainfall patterns undermine the agricultural sector (de Souza Batista et al., 2023). On the other hand, in India, agriculture is the source of livelihood for 45.5% of the workforce, where crop yields are deteriorating and water scarcity undermines food security and economic stability (Konda, 2018).

Despite the risks, there are many wonderful opportunities. The phenomenon of climate change is accelerating innovation in renewable energy, sustainable finance, and green infrastructure, thus opening new ways for economic growth and investment. For instance, global investment in renewable energy surpassed $673 billion in 2023. In the meantime, the green bond market has grown exponentially as well. By the end of 2024, total issuances are anticipated to reach $3.1 trillion, according to the World Solar Investment Report.

These changes are clear in the growing acknowledgment by investors and leaders that minimizing climate risks has become both essential and strategically vital. The choices made today will either confine emerging markets in a pattern of risk and stagnation or propel them as leaders in the global shift toward sustainability. This chapter intends to offer a strong foundation for understanding and maneuvering through the intricate overlap of financial systems and climate risks.

2. Literature Review

This review of literature highlights the development of climate risk concepts, their economic implications, and adaptive financial approaches – especially in emerging markets – by highlighting major contributions to the debate.

2.1. Climate Risks and Economic Vulnerabilities

Developing countries, especially in South Asia, Sub-Saharan Africa, and Latin America, are extremely susceptible to climate threats as they are agriculture, forestry, and fisheries dependent (IPCC, 2022a). Weak adaptive capacity aggravates their exposure, exacerbating global disparities as increased temperatures affect economic stability (Alam & Akhtar, 2024; Dell et al., 2012; Jafar et al., 2024).

Climate disasters also contribute to long-term macroeconomic effects, especially in nations with weaker institutions (Cavallo & Noy, 2011). Small island states are extremely vulnerable, with events like Hurricane Maria (2017) resulting in economic devastation (Naseema et al., 2024; Sircar et al., 2024). Building resilience through adaptive policy and global collaboration is crucial to minimize these risks.

2.2. Asset Valuation and Market Stability

Research by the London School of Economics (Dietz et al., 2016) indicates that the projected "climate value at risk" (climate VaR) of global financial assets today is 1.8% on a business-as-usual emissions trajectory. Applying a standard estimate of global financial assets, this equates to approximately $2.5 trillion. However, most of the risk is in the tail. This is in line with the study by Campiglio et al.

(2018), who noted that stranded assets-investments that lose value because of the transition to a low-carbon economy pose significant risks to portfolios dependent on fossil fuels or carbon-intensive industries.

2.3. Emerging Opportunities in Green Finance

While much of the literature tends to focus on risks, there are also opportunities for mitigating climate change through innovative financial instruments. Fig. 17.1 shows the rapid emergence of corporate green bonds which exemplifies the growing opportunities for green finance, with the issuance surging from only $5 billion in 2013 to a spectacular $95.7 billion by 2018 as corporations increasingly commit to sustainable investments (Alam et al., 2024; Flammer, 2021).

In the context of emerging markets, Wang and Zhi (2016) explored the role of blended finance in mobilizing private capital for climate-resilient infrastructure projects. Their observations showcase that public–private partnerships can cater to credit gaps, particularly in areas with limited fiscal capacity.

2.4. Integrating Climate Risks into Financial Models

Climate-aware financial modeling has become a key focus in modern research. Bolton et al. (2020) emphasized the need to integrate climate scenarios into stress-testing frameworks to assess systemic risks. While central banks in nations such as the UK and the Netherlands have embraced this solution, emerging markets are severely challenged by data gaps and a scarcity of technical skills. But efforts such as the climate policy initiative are attempting to ameliorate these challenges through capacity-building initiatives and standardized risk assessment tools.

Climate risks, such as natural disasters and resource shortages, have long-term economic consequences. They affect consumer expenditure, saving behavior, and migration choices, especially in vulnerable areas, where families tend to move toward precautionary savings, lowering aggregate economic activity (IMF, 2019).

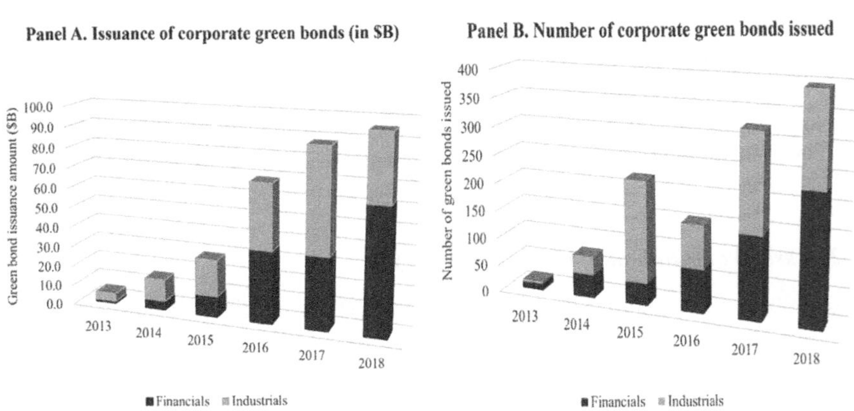

Fig. 17.1. Corporate Green Bonds. *Source*: Flammer (2021).

2.5. *Knowledge Gaps and Future Directions*

Though there is much useful information contained within the literature that has already been developed, much still remains to be researched – specifically the cascading effect of climate risk on integrated financial systems in the Global South, which has had relatively little focus. The body of scholarly work further reinforces that climate change is not just an environmental challenge but also an economic and financial one. Its effects are strongly linked with global finance, causing market volatility while, at the same time, promoting innovation opportunities. The studies have concentrated on green bonds' linkedness with other financial assets in times of extreme events (Billah et al., 2024; Khan et al., 2022; Rabbani et al., 2023, 2025). This chapter attempts to delineate these fundamental concepts while proposing a unifying framework for understanding and responding to climate-related financial risks in emerging markets. By combining academic research and real-world practice, stakeholders are able to navigate an evolving financial landscape characterized by the uncertainties of climate change.

3. Climate Risk Integration in Financial Decision-making

Climate change is not anymore an environmental issue; it's one of the most pressing fiscal issues of our time. While the Earth bears the impacts of climate change – more intense hurricanes, destructive floods, and rising seas higher – financial institutions have come to appreciate that such risks cannot be ignored anymore. In fact, climate risks are increasingly being integrated into financial decision-making across the board, from boardrooms of companies to investment portfolios (Khan et al., 2021). This shift is changing the way we understand value, risk, and opportunity in the financial markets.

3.1. *Physical and Transition Risks*

Understanding what climate risks are and explaining this would be important. A definition of climate risks: TCFD was first initiated by the Financial Stability Board in 2017, which divided the types of climate risks relevant to be measured by the financial sector into two broad categories; these include physical risks and transition risks (Board, 2017).

Physical risks are immediate tangible impacts of climate change, including extreme weather: floods, wildfires, hurricanes, which can damage infrastructures, disrupt supply chain, and increase insurance-just like Hurricane Katrina in 2005, that damages worth an estimated $160 billion and dramatically impacted the economy. Transition risks are the economic shocks that occur as the world transitions in to a low-carbon economy.

3.2. *Regulatory Shifts and Institutional Changes*

The integration of climate-related risks into their decision-making frameworks has increasingly become a necessity for financial institutions and governmental bodies. One of the key catalysts for this change is the regulatory reforms of entities such as the European Union and central banks worldwide. For instance, in 2021, the Bank of England was the first central bank to conduct climate stress tests on leading financial institutions (Reuters, 2021). The Bank of England has integrated climate risk analyses into its comprehensive financial review to ensure that banks and insurance companies better account for climate-related financial risks better. Governments and financial institutions also adjust policies to address climate-driven shifts in societal behavior. For instance, climate risks have accelerated the adoption of green insurance models and resilience-focused urban planning (OECD, 2024).

3.3. The Shift in Investment Strategies: Adapting to Climate Risk

Global financial markets are increasingly prioritizing sustainability, with institutional investors integrating climate risk into their decision-making. BlackRock CEO Larry Fink's 2020 warning about the financial consequences of neglecting climate risks has accelerated this shift (Sorkin, 2020). Sustainable investment funds, such as BlackRock's climate transition exchange traded funds, have outperformed traditional markets, reinforcing the financial viability of climate-conscious investing. While green finance presents vast opportunities, implementation barriers such as high capital costs, weak regulatory frameworks, and limited institutional capacity in developing markets hinder adoption. Many emerging economies struggle to access climate funds efficiently due to bureaucratic delays and inadequate financial infrastructure (IFC, 2023).

3.4. The Road Ahead: A New Era in Financial Decision-making

In the future, incorporating climate-related risks into financial decision-making would shift from being an exception to becoming the norm. The former Governor of the Bank of England, Mark Carney, famously warned us that we face a "tragedy of the horizon," meaning that the financial sector has failed to take into account the long-term risks associated with climate change. However, the situation is changing (Carney & Benjamin, 2015). Financial institutions are increasingly realizing that climate-related risks are financial risks and are changing their models to address this change. Be it through stress testing, scenario analysis, or issuance of green bonds, the financial sector is getting better equipped to deal with the consequences of climate change. Climate change presents financial opportunities as well as challenges.

4. Analyzing the Changing Terrain of Climate Risks

Global financial institutions, sectors, and economies are becoming more complex as a result of climate challenges. This section examines how asset value, sovereign credit ratings, and global financial stability are evolving, with a focus on emerging markets.

4.1. The Escalating Frequency and Severity of Climate Events

Natural disasters have become more numerous and intense in the past few years, and the risks from climate change have also escalated. According to the World Meteorological Organization (WMO), in the period 1970–2019, there were $3.64 trillion direct economic losses brought about by the steep increase in climate-related catastrophic events within the last 50 years (WMO, 2021). These catastrophes, once a rare threat, have evolved into frequent issues are more prone to hit weak markets. Climatic threats have evolved from unusual occurrences to increasingly frequent and severe events. They manifest as natural disasters that devastate economies, primarily hitting weak regions.

4.2. Implications for Sovereign Credit Ratings

Impacts of climate hazards on sovereign credit quality are very significant. The impact of climate change has precipitated credit downgrades for other emerging market economies because it exposes them to natural disasters and dampens their resiliency (Moody's, 2022). To illustrate, a hurricane named Hurricane Maria struck the island nation Dominica in the year 2017, amounting to an equivalent of 226% damage of the country's GDP with a drastic downgrading of the country's credit rating (Sircar et al., 2024).

Risks from climate change are changing how sovereign creditworthiness is currently being evaluated, with a lowering for more vulnerable countries because they have less capacity to adapt and weather climate shocks. Their financial problems are heightened by downgrades, which raise their challenge of getting financing affordably priced and foreign investment.

4.3. Stranded Assets and Market Volatility

One of the financial risks that comes with global warming is a new concept known as stranded assets: investments whose value becomes zero instantly when the world transitions to a low-carbon economy. Zhou et al. (2023) in their study find that climate catastrophes lead to sharp declines in stock and bond markets, particularly in financially constrained regions. This uncertainty threatens long-term investment portfolios, and therefore, it is essential to incorporate climate risks into investment decisions. Shifting to a low-carbon economy can pose significant risks of stranded assets, which adversely affect the value of investment in high-carbon businesses. Nations such as India and Nigeria have challenges in shutting down coal plants because of employment issues and infrastructural needs (IFC, 2023).

4.4. Cross-border Impacts and Global Financial Stability

Climate risks transcend borders, disrupting global supply chains and financial markets. The 2011 Thailand floods caused $45 billion in losses, crippling the automotive and electronics sectors (World Bank, 2011). Similarly, the 2021 Texas winter storm led to a semiconductor shortage, affecting industries worldwide (BCS, 2023).

Emerging economies are particularly vulnerable, as they rely heavily on agriculture and natural resources. The Food and the Agricultural Organization (FAO) warns that a 30% decline in agricultural output in Sub-Saharan Africa by 2050 could intensify food insecurity and economic instability (IPCC, 2022b). Recognizing these risks, the IMF promotes financial innovations to de-risk climate investments, while global climate funds like the Green Climate Fund (GCF), Collective Investment Fund, and Global Environment Facility enhance financial access for developing nations (Green Climate Fund, 2023; IMF Blog, 2022).

A highly interconnected global economy amplifies these disruptions, necessitating coordinated international efforts to strengthen resilience and ensure financial stability.

4.5. The Growing Importance of Adaptation and Resilience

Developing countries are therefore particularly vulnerable to such "tipping cascades," in large part because their food systems are highly vulnerable through reliance on agriculture and mineral extraction. The FAO warns that food insecurity could get worse and economic instability could get worse if agricultural production declines by as much as 30% by 2050 in Sub-Saharan Africa (IPCC, 2022b).

The interconnected nature of the world economy further aggravates the effects of climate-related threats. Weather occurrences that are extreme and catastrophic interrupt supply and trade systems, affecting many industries and regions. Emerging markets are more sensitive to shifts in the global economy due to limited diversification and heavy dependence on agriculture and natural resources. The worldwide impact of these consequences highlights the necessity for cooperative frameworks to enhance global resilience.

5. Addressing Climate Risks: Financial Impacts and Real-Life Case Studies

5.1. Real-life Case Study: Hurricane Sandy and New York City's Resilience

In 2012, Hurricane Sandy caused damages worth $19 billion in New York City, severely impacting infrastructure and the economy (NYC Comptroller, 2022). In response, the city launched a $20 billion OneNYC Resilience Plan, which focused on protecting coastal areas and critical infrastructure (The City of New York, 2016).

5.1.1. Financial Measures Taken

- The city installed flood barriers and strengthened transportation systems, reducing the risk of future disruptions.
- Allocated $500 million for resilient energy systems to ensure continued power supply during extreme events (NYC Comptroller, 2022).

5.1.2. Impact

- Insurance premiums in vulnerable areas are reduced by approximately 15% due to enhanced risk mitigation (NYC Comptroller, 2022).
- Estimated savings of $3 billion annually in potential avoided losses from future extreme weather events (NYC Comptroller, 2022).
- Increased investor confidence as infrastructure projects attracted private funding from entities like BlackRock, supporting further urban development (NYC Comptroller, 2022).

5.2. Real-life Case Study: Australian Wildfires and Corporate Resilience

The 2019–2020 Australian bushfires caused economic losses of $2.8 billion, impacting industries such as tourism while also impacting other industries such as agriculture due to supply chain disruptions (University of Sydney, 2024). Companies like Qantas and BHP implemented climate-resilience strategies post-disaster to mitigate financial risks.

5.2.1. Financial Measures Taken

- Qantas allocated $50 million toward carbon offset programs, reducing its exposure to environmental regulations and carbon pricing (Qantas, 2019).
- BHP-integrated climate-risk assessments into its investment decisions, redirecting $400 million toward renewable energy projects (BHP, 2019).

5.2.2. Impact

- Qantas achieved a 20% reduction in operational disruptions from extreme weather by 2023, saving approximately $1.2 billion (Qantas, 2023).
- BHP saw an 18% increase in institutional investments as its environmental, social, and governance (ESG) rating improved post-intervention (BHP, 2024).

6. The Role of Financial Innovation in Mitigating Climate Risks

Advanced financial tools and systems are critical in solving the economic effects of climate-related risks. These instruments not only manage financial disturbances but also market investment in sustainable options.

6.1. Green Bonds: Catalyzing Climate Action

Sophisticated financial instruments and systems are vital in addressing the economic impact of climate-related risk. These tools not only stabilize financial shock but also invest in sustainable choices.

Case example: The European Investment Bank (EIB) issued the first green bond, the Climate Awareness Bond (CAB), in 2007, laying the foundation for a €2.2 trillion market. EIB remains a leader, with over €50 billion in CABs and €9 billion in Sustainability Awareness Bonds (SABs). In India, NTPC Limited issued ₹2,000 crore ($250M+) in green bonds in 2021 to fund solar and wind projects, targeting a 3% annual carbon reduction (NTPC, 2021).

Impact: Advancing Sustainable Investments:

- Green bonds attract capital for climate initiatives while offering issuers lower borrowing costs through a 10–20 basis point "greenium." They accelerate the transition to a low-carbon economy, proving that sustainability-focused investments can drive both financial and environmental benefits.

6.2. Catastrophe Bonds (CatBonds): Risk Transfer Mechanisms

Catastrophe bonds enable insurers and governments to transfer climate risks to capital markets. By linking payouts to specific climate events, these bonds provide timely liquidity in disaster-stricken regions.

Case Example: The World Bank (IBRD) has issued a new catastrophe (cat) bond, providing $175 million in additional insurance coverage for Mexico against Pacific-side named storms. This new bond significantly increases Mexico's Pacific hurricane risk coverage, which had previously been $125 million under an expired cat bond. Alongside three other cat bonds issued by the World Bank for Mexico earlier this year, the country's total cat bond-backed insurance protection for 2024 now stands at $595 million, marking a substantial boost in financial resilience against natural disasters. The African Risk Capacity (ARC) utilized cat bonds to provide drought insurance, with payouts helping countries like Malawi avert food crises during severe droughts in 2019 (African Risk Capacity, 2020).

Impact:

- Cat bonds ensure quick recovery, limiting economic shocks from natural disasters.
- They reduce government fiscal pressure by sharing the financial burden with private investors.

6.3. ESG Investing and Climate Risk Integration

The rise of ESG investing has incentivized companies to adopt robust climate strategies. Several studies focused on the role of ESG and its integration with other financial assets (Saha & Shaik, 2024; Shaik & Rehman, 2023). Asset managers like BlackRock have integrated climate risks into their investment frameworks, influencing global capital allocation.

Impact:

- Over $35 trillion in assets are now managed under ESG principles, accounting for 36% of global professionally managed investments (Bradford, 2021).
- Companies with strong ESG ratings attract higher institutional investment, lowering their cost of capital and boosting long-term shareholder value.

7. Bridging Climate Data Gaps: Strengthening Risk Assessment and Resilience in Emerging Markets

Assessing climate risks in emerging markets is hindered by a widespread lack of high-quality, standardized data. Financial institutions, policymakers, and investors struggle to integrate climate risks into decision-making due to inconsistent reporting frameworks and insufficient technological capabilities (IMF, 2022). In regions like Africa and South Asia, weak weather observation networks severely hamper disaster forecasting and economic planning (Ramadane et al., 2024). Without reliable data, these economies face heightened financial instability and limited capacity to implement effective adaptation strategies.

The Climate Risk Index 2025, published by Germanwatch, identifies nations most affected by extreme weather events, including Bangladesh, Pakistan, and Mozambique. Evaluating economic losses, fatalities, and population impact, the index underscores the urgency for vulnerable economies to strengthen climate resilience (Climate Risk Index, 2025). Still, when a nation drops below 60% data coverage, determining climate risks is much more difficult (Bonnisseau, 2022). Almost 100 nations, with 106.6 million inhabitants, have not got good enough data for climate modeling and disaster analysis (Bonnisseau, 2022). Although proxy indicators and region aggregation are useful alternatives, they are still not good enough to replace direct data gathering.

To remedy these gaps, emerging markets need to invest in strong data infrastructure, such as satellite-based climate observation, predictive analytics powered by AI, and upgraded ground sensors (Financial Stability Board, 2021). These technologies allow for more accurate risk estimation, enhancing financial planning and disaster management. No less important is the implementation of standardized climate risk disclosure guidelines, such as those proposed by the TCFD, to promote consistency and comparability across markets (IMF, 2024).

8. Conclusion

Climate risks have evolved from an environmental concern to a powerful driver of financial markets, investment choices, and economic resilience. As highlighted in this chapter, climate-related catastrophes, stranded assets, and shifting investor preferences are already impacting sovereign credit ratings, supply chain disruptions, and increasing financial volatility. These risks are no longer theoretical threats but immediate challenges that require policymakers, investors, and financial institutions to act with haste.

At the same time, climate risks provide an opportunity to innovate and adapt. The rapid growth in green finance, sustainability-linked bonds, and ESG-driven investments demonstrates that financial markets are capable of adjusting to support a low-carbon world. Institutions such as the World Bank, GCF, and IMF are committing capital to build climate resilience, but challenges such as gaps in funding, inefficiencies in regulation, and inequalities in financial access remain, especially in emerging economies.

In order to enable the transition to a more climate-resilient economy, policymakers must establish clear rules that promote green investments, ensure efficient deployment of climate funds, and integrate climate risk analysis into national financial plans. Investors must update asset pricing models to integrate climate risks, reallocate capital to resilient sectors, and utilize blended finance models to support big-ticket green projects. The banking industry must enhance climate stress tests, develop creative financial instruments such as catastrophe bonds, and align lending policies with long-term sustainability goals.

However, implementation is the biggest challenge. Bureaucratic inefficiency, fragmented policies, and feeble risk evaluation frameworks make it difficult for climate finance to find its way to the most vulnerable. Increasing global cooperation, strengthening climate data transparency, and engaging financial institutions in integrating climate aspects into decision-making will be necessary in order to overcome these barriers.

The finance industry stands at a crossroads. Decisions today will determine whether economies remain vulnerable to climate instability or become global leaders in green finance. By encouraging innovation, adopting international collaborations, and incorporating climate risk into financial systems, we can create a financial system that not only survives climate shocks but also supports long-term economic prosperity and stability.

References

African Risk Capacity. (2020). *African Risk Capacity annual report 2020*. https://www.arc.int/sites/default/files/2021-10/ARC-Ltd_Annual-Report_2020-final.pdf

Alam, M., & Akhtar, S. (2024). Introduction to green finance and technology integration. In S. Jafar, R. Rodriguez, H. Kannan, S. Akhtar, & P. Plugmann (Eds.), *Harnessing blockchain-digital twin fusion for sustainable investments* (pp. 1–19). IGI Global Scientific Publishing. https://doi.org/10.4018/979-8-3693-1878-2.ch001

Alam, M., Akhtar, S., & Bettencourt, A. (2024). Introduction to fintech in Industry 5.0: Companion or antagonist. In *The adoption of fintech* (pp. 1–16). Productivity Press. https://doi.org/10.4324/9781032644165-1

BCS. (2023, March 3). *Understanding the global chip shortage |BCS*. BCS, The Chartered Institute for IT. Retrieved December 8, 2024, from https://www.bcs.org/articles-opinion-and-research/understanding-the-global-chip-shortage/

BHP. (2019, July 23). *BHP to invest US$400m to address climate change*. https://www.bhp.com/news/media-centre/releases/2019/07/bhp-to-invest-us400m-to-addr ess-climate-change

BHP. (2024, August 27). *BHP annual report 2023–24*. https://www.bhp.com/-/media/documents/investors/annual-reports/2024/240827_bhpannu alreport2024.pdf

Billah, M., Shaik, M., Hadhri, S., & Balli, F. (2024). Unveiling the impact of oil price shocks on global sukuk markets: A focus on quantile coherence and time-frequency connectedness. *Applied Economics*, 1–27. https://doi.org/10.1080/00036846.2024.2424500

Bolton, P., Després, M., Pereira da Silva, L., Samama, F., & Svartzman, R. (2020). Green Swans': Central banks in the age of climate-related risks. *Banque de France Bulletin, 229*(8), 1–15.

Bonnisseau, N. (2022, October 24). *The implications of data gaps in climate science – Berlin*. Plan A. Earth. Retrieved March 2, 2025, from https://plana.earth/academy/data-gaps-climate-science

Bradford, H. (2021, July 19). *Sustainable investment assets hit $35 trillion, 36% of all managed assets*. https://www.pionline.com/esg/sustainable-investment-assets-hit-35-trillion-36-all-managed-assets

Campiglio, E., Dafermos, Y., Monnin, P., Ryan-Collins, J., Schotten, G., & Tanaka, M. (2018). Climate change challenges for central banks and financial regulators. *Nature Climate Change, 8*(6), 462–468.

Carney, M., & Benjamin, N. (2015). *Breaking the tragedy of the horizon – climate change and financial stability – speech by Mark Carney*. Bank of England. Retrieved March 2, 2025, from https://www.bankofengland.co.uk/speech/2015/breaking-the-tragedy-of-the-horizon-clim ate-change-and-financial-stability

Cavallo, E., & Noy, I. (2011). Natural disasters and the economy—A survey. *International Review of Environmental and Resource Economics, 5*(1), 63–102.

Chua, W. F., James, R., King, A., Lee, E., & Soderstrom, N. (2022). Task force on climate-related financial disclosures (TCFD) implementation: An overview and insights from the Australian Accounting Standards Board Dialogue Series. *Australian Accounting Review, 32*(3), 396–405.

City of New York. (2016, April 20). *OneNYC: Mayor de Blasio Announces Progress on New Coastal Resiliency Efforts in Most Vulnerable Communities*. https://www.nyc.gov/office-of-the-mayor/news/370-16/onenyc-mayor-de-blasio-progress- new-coastal-resiliency-efforts-most-vulnerable

Climate Risk Index. (2025, February 12). *Climate risk index 2025*. Germanwatch e.V. Retrieved March 2, 2025, from https://www.germanwatch.org/sites/default/files/2025-02/Climate%20Risk%20Index%202025.pdf

de Souza Batista, F., Duku, C., & Hein, L. (2023). Deforestation-induced changes in rainfall decrease soybean-maize yields in Brazil. *Ecological Modelling, 486*, 110533.

Dell, M., Jones, B. F., & Olken, B. A. (2012). Temperature shocks and economic growth: Evidence from the last half century. *American Economic Journal: Macroeconomics, 4*(3), 66–95.

Dietz, S., Bowen, A., Dixon, C., & Gradwell, P. (2016). 'Climate value at risk' of global financial assets. *Nature Climate Change, 6*(7), 676–679.

Financial Stability Board. (2021). *The availability of data with which to monitor and assess climate-related risks to financial stability*. https://www.fsb.org/2021/07/the-availability-of-data-with-which-to-monitor-and-assess-climate-related-risks-to-financial-stability/

Financial Stability Board. (2017). *Recommendations of the task force on climate-related financial disclosures*. https://assets.bbhub.io/company/sites/60/2021/10/FINAL-2017-TCFD-Report.pdf

Flammer, C. (2021). Corporate green bonds. *Journal of financial economics, 142*(2), 499–516.

Green Climate Fund. (2022). *GCF in brief: Adaptation planning*. https://www.greenclimate.fund/document/gcf-brief-adaptation-planning

Green Climate Fund. (2023). *Climate Funds unite to enhance access to climate finance and increase impact*. https://www.greenclimate.fund/news/climate-funds-unite-enhance-access-climate-finance-and-increase-impact

IFC. (2023). *Challenges of green finance*. https://documents1.worldbank.org/curated/en/099717411212328052/pdf/IDU0d3c2f00d0 351404d7c08cc40cd0b621a7d59.pdf

IMF. (2019). *Economics of climate*. International Monetary Fund (IMF). Retrieved March 2, 2025, from https://www.imf.org/external/pubs/ft/fandd/2019/12/pdf/fd1219.pdf

IMF. (2022, November 28). *Bridging data gaps can help tackle the climate crisis*. International Monetary Fund (IMF). Retrieved March 2, 2025, from https://www.imf.org/en/Blogs/Articles/2022/11/28/bridging-data-gaps-can-help-tackle-the-climate-crisis

IMF. (2024). *G20 data gaps initiative*. International Monetary Fund (IMF). Retrieved March 2, 2025, from https://www.imf.org/en/News/Seminars/Conferences/g20-data-gaps-initiative

IMF Blog. (2022). *How blended finance can support climate transition in emerging and developing economies*. https://www.imf.org/en/Blogs/Articles/2022/11/15/how-blended-finance-can-support-climate-transition-in-emerging-and-developing-economies

IPCC. (2022a). *Chapter 5: Food security — Special report on climate change and land*. IPCC. Retrieved December 8, 2024, from https://www.ipcc.ch/srccl/chapter/chapter-5/

IPCC. (2022b). *Climate change 2022: Impacts, adaptation and vulnerability*. IPCC. Retrieved December 4, 2024, from https://www.ipcc.ch/report/ar6/wg2/

Islam, M. S., Samreth, S., Islam, A. H. M. S., & Sato, M. (2022). Climate change, climatic extremes, and households' food consumption in Bangladesh: A longitudinal data analysis. *Environmental Challenges*, *7*, 100495.

Jafar, S. H., Hemachandran, K., Akhtar, S., Khan, P. A., & El-Chaarani, H. (Eds.). (2024). *The adoption of fintech: Using technology for better security, speed, and customer experience in finance*. CRC Press.

Khan, P. A., Johl, S. K., & Akhtar, S. (2021). Firm sustainable development goals and firm financial performance through the lens of green innovation practices and reporting: A proactive approach. *Journal of Risk and Financial Management*, *14*(12), 605.

Khan, P. A., Johl, S. K., & Akhtar, S. (2022). Vinculum of sustainable development goal practices and firms' financial performance: A moderation role of green innovation. *Journal of Risk and Financial Management*, *15*(3), 96.

Konda, C. (2018). Climate change and food security in India: Some issues and challenges. *International Journal of Creative Research Thoughts*, *2018*, 477–488.

Moody's. (2022). 2022 TCFD report. https://www.moodys.com/sites/products/ProductAttachments/Sustainability/2022-tcfd-report.pdf

Naseema, N., Akhtar, S., & Al Hinai, A. A. (2024). Disrupting financial services: A case study on Capital One's Fintech Odyssey. In S. Jafar, R. Rodriguez, H. Kannan, S. Akhtar, & P. Plugmann (Eds.), *Harnessing blockchain-digital twin fusion for sustainable investments* (pp. 363–383). IGI Global. https://doi.org/10.4018/979-8-3693-1878-2.ch015

NTPC. (2021).*GREEN BOND INFORMATION REPORT*. NTPC Limited. Retrieved December 8, 2024, from https://ntpc.co.in/sites/default/files/inline-files/Post-Issuance-Report.pdf

NYC Comptroller. (2022, October 13). *Ten years after Sandy: Office of the New York City comptroller Brad Lander*. NYC Comptroller's. Retrieved December 8, 2024, from https://comptroller.nyc.gov/reports/ten-years-after-sandy/

OECD. (2024). *Climate adaptation and resilience*. OECD. Retrieved March 2, 2025, from https://www.oecd.org/en/topics/policy-issues/climate-adaptation-and-resilience.html?utm_source=chatgpt.com

Qantas. (2019, November 11). *Qantas Group to slash carbon emissions*. https://www.qantasnewsroom.com.au/media-releases/qantas-group-to-slash-carbon-emissions/#:~:text=Qantas%20will%20invest%20%2450%20million,currently%20almost%20d ouble%20the%20price

Qantas. (2023, September 20). *Annual report 2023–24*. https://investor.qantas.com/FormBuilder/_Resource/_module/doLLG5ufYkCyEPjF1tpgyw/file/annual-reports/2023-Annual-Report.pdf

Rabbani, M. R., Billah, S. M., Shaik, M., Rahman, M., & Boujlil, R. (2023). Dynamic connectedness, spillover, and optimal hedging strategy among FinTech, Sukuk, and Islamic equity markets. *Global Finance Journal, 58, 90*, 100901.

Rabbani, M. R., Hassan, M. K., Billah, S. M., Shaik, M., & Halim, Ż. A. (2025). Religion vs. ethics: Tail dependence between Sukuk, green bond, Islamic Fintech, and fourth industrial revolution assets. *Pacific-Basin Finance Journal*, 102683.

Ramadane, M., Prentice, A., & Lewis, B. (2024, November 14). *Africa grapples with forecasting challenge as weather disasters loom.* Reuters. Retrieved March 2, 2025, from https://www.reuters.com/sustainability/africa-grapples-with-forecasting-challenge-weather-disasters-loom-2024-11-14/

Reuters. (2021, June 8). *Bank of England launches climate stress test for banks and insurers.* https://www.reuters.com/business/sustainable-business/bank-england-launches-climate-stress-test-banks-insurers-2021-06-08/

Saha, K., & Shaik, M. (2024). Dynamic nexus between Sharia and ESG indices and ETFs in India. *Cogent Economics & Finance, 12*(1), 2409423.

Shaik, M., & Rehman, M. Z. (2023). The dynamic volatility connectedness of major environmental, social, and governance (ESG) stock indices: Evidence based on DCC-GARCH model. *Asia-Pacific Financial Markets, 30*(1), 231–246.

Sircar, A., Thomas, A., Serdeczny, O., Jattansingh, S. (2024). A review of loss and damage in the Caribbean (1994 to 2024). *Climate Analytics.* chrome-extension://efaidnbmnnnibpcajpcglclefindmkaj/https://ca1-clm.edcdn.com/publications/Review-of-loss-and-damage-in-the-Caribbean-1994-2024.pdf?v=1717576292.

Sorkin, A. R. (2020). *BlackRock C.E.O. Larry Fink: Climate crisis will reshape finance.* https://www.nytimes.com/2020/01/14/business/dealbook/larry-fink-blackrock-climate-cha nge.html

University of Sydney. (2024, January 31). *Black summer bushfires wiped $2.8 billion from tourism supply chains.* https://www.sydney.edu.au/news-opinion/news/2024/01/31/black-summer-bushfires-austr alia-wiped-billions-from-tourism-supply-chains.html

Wang, Y., & Zhi, Q. (2016). The role of green finance in environmental protection: Two aspects of market mechanism and policies. *Energy Procedia, 104*, 311–316.

World Bank. (2011, December). *The World Bank supports Thailand's post-floods recovery effort.* http://www.worldbank.org/en/news/2011/12/13/world-bank-supports-thailands-post-flood s-recovery-effort

World Meteorological Organization (WMO). (2021, August). *Weather-related disasters increase over past 50 years, causing more damage but fewer deaths.* https://wmo.int/media/news/weather-related-disasters-increase-over-past-50-years-causing-more-damage-fewer-deaths

Zhou, F., Endendijk, T., & Botzen, W. W. (2023). A review of the financial sector impacts of risks associated with climate change. *Annual Review of Resource Economics, 15*(1), 233–256.

Part IV

Case Studies

Chapter 18

Pioneering Firms in India and Their Climatic Challenges: A Case Study of ITC Limited

Sujit Singh[a], *Ezutah Udoncy Olugu*[b] *and Sumit Gupta*[c]

[a]*School of Management, Woxsen University, Hyderabad, India*
[b]*School of Mechanical, Industrial and Aeronautical Engineering, University of the Witwatersrand, Johannesburg, South Africa*
[c]*Amity School of Engineering and Technology, Amity University, Uttar Pradesh, India*

Abstract

This chapter presents a case of one of the pioneering corporations, Indian Tobacco Company (ITC) Limited's sustainable business strategy to address the effects of climate change. ITC's sustainability initiatives in water stewardship, renewable energy, climate-smart agriculture, and paperboard recycling are comprehensively explored. The results of the study are based on the data collected from ITC's financial and socio-cultural projects which aimed at enhancing agricultural production, empowering women and creating rural employment. Some of the key milestones that ITC has achieved include water positivity, over 50% renewable energy, and climate-smart agriculture, all because of their sustainable approach. The company also reduced its environmental effects while increasing its socio-economic value, particularly in rural areas of India. This case points out the necessity of the stakeholder's approach and the long-term perspective for a sustainable business. This chapter provides a rich and practical understanding of how organizations can incorporate sustainability strategies to tackle climate change and thrive. The practices of ITC are exemplary, and this case provides a clear understanding of how sustainability can be incorporated into business strategies. The study adds to the growing discussion on corporate sustainability. This study offers insights for other companies on managing the conflict between profit, people, and the environment.

Climate Risk and Emerging Markets: Valuation, Volatility, and Portfolio Strategies, 275–289

Published under exclusive licence by Emerald Publishing Limited
doi:10.1108/978-1-83708-088-520261054

Keywords: Sustainability; climatic challenges; ITC Limited; water stewardship; climate resilience

1. Introduction

Pioneering Indian businesses have been vital to the country's financial growth as they have risen to the challenge of environmental stewardship (Roy, 2023). They influence job creation, wealth generation, and positive social and environmental change. Pioneering companies have been essential to the economy's development of robust industries, promotion of innovation, and rise to global competitiveness (Karim & Said, 2024). For example, Indian corporate giants such as Tata Group, Reliance Industries, and ITC Limited have made significant contributions to the gross domestic product (GDP) growth of India and have gained global recognition. This commercial success has helped the government in accomplishing its development goals of lowering poverty and enhancing living conditions by directly and indirectly creating jobs (Fallah Shayan et al., 2022). From an environmental viewpoint, these businesses are leading India's transition to sustainability. Among India's most pressing environmental concerns include pollution, deforestation, and significant greenhouse gas emissions. Businesses who were early adopters have acted rapidly to reduce these consequences. ITC Limited is one business that has advanced sustainability; it is now both carbon positive and water positive (Banerjee & Chakraborty, 2020). The extensive use of renewable energy sources by Indian businesses has also put the country well on its way to attaining its ambitious net-zero goals by 2070 (Chaturvedi et al., 2024).

Government laws such as the Companies Act of 2013 have made it even more important for businesses to participate in attending to social and environmental issues (Schedule, 2013). Through these investments in corporate social responsibility, which are required by this regulation, businesses are advised to connect profits with societal benefits. Programs for community development, garbage reduction, and renewable energy are becoming increasingly more essential parts of the business goals of numerous leading corporations. However, the obstacles are enormous. India's increasingly industrializing population directly adds to the increasing needs on the country's natural resources. Finding a balance between profitability and environmental practices is particularly challenging for smaller enterprises (Prabhakar & Brar, 2024). Nevertheless, the ingenious businesses' commitment to socially responsible and sustainable development highlights their critical function in bridging India's environmental goals with its developmental needs. These businesses have an influence on India's economy both now and in the future. They are setting an example for other countries to follow in their fight against climate change and development, and their activities align with global sustainability objectives.

Since its establishment over a century earlier, ITC has been active in a vast array of industries, including IT, paperboards, hotels, fast-moving consumer goods (FMCG), and agriculture (Patel & Thakrar, 2024). ITC is in a strong position to fix the complicated environmental concerns associated with its diverse industries and promote sustainable business practices since to its substantial portfolio (Bottriell, 2023). India's vulnerability to climate change, which includes unpredictable monsoons, rising temperatures, and a shortage of resources, presents significant hurdles for businesses operating there. ITC's reliance on natural resources, like as water and agricultural inputs, has made it harder to maintain operating stability. These challenges are worsened by regulatory requirements, shifting consumer expectations, and the need to fix up environmental responsibility with financial progress (Sarangi & Jabbal, 2024).

ITC has adopted a business strategy that integrates sustainable development principles (Limited, 2024). For over two decades, ITC has been a leader in sustainability, exceeding water and carbon neutrality targets. By using innovative ideas in waste management, sustainable agriculture, and renewable energy, ITC achieves both environmental protection and responsible economic growth in rural areas (ITC, 2025). This case study explores ITC's climate risk mitigation strategies and its role as a sustainability model.

2. Overview of ITC Limited

One of the biggest companies in India is ITC Limited, previously the Indian Tobacco Company. It was established in 1910. Initially focused on the tobacco sector, the corporation's growth is characterized by a purposeful growth in to several industries. ITC invested a substantial quantity of time making cigarettes and other tobacco products (Jairath, 2014). The 1970s were the time when ITC started its diversity journey by venturing in to the FMCG sector with brand names like Sunfeast (biscuits), according to Ramachandran and Manikandan (2012). This shift enabled ITC to shift away from tobacco and toward a more ethical and ecologically responsible business model. ITC started offering hotels and paperboards in the 1980s, declares Kaul (2019). While the paperboards and packaging sector turned into one of India's leading paperboard producers, the ITC Hotels brand helped the company establish a strong name in the hotel sector (Maheshwari, 2019). ITC's innovative attitude and dedication to sustainability enabled it to accomplish the groundbreaking carbon-positive, water-positive, and zero-waste-to-landfill status (Sarkar, 2024).

ITC's FMCG business is vital to its profitability and future growth. ITC is a major player in the agricultural industry, renowned for its sourcing and processing of agricultural products. Mukerji's 2020 work showcases E-Choupal, a company program fostering sustainable farming and rural progress. Among ITC's many products are popular brands such as Bingo and Aashirvaad atta (wheat flour). Indian farmers supply the ingredients for potatoes and Sunfeast cookies. The company's paperboard division is recognized for its environmentally friendly practices, such as recycling and sustainable forestry, having received several awards (Anbarasan & Sushil, 2018). FMCG and other sectors leverage ITC's packaging solutions to maintain a competitive advantage. India's top hotel chains include ITC Hotels, which boasts prestigious properties such as the ITC Maurya and ITC Grand Chola. Shanti (2016) notes the company's hotels are known for their sustainable practices, including water conservation and renewable energy

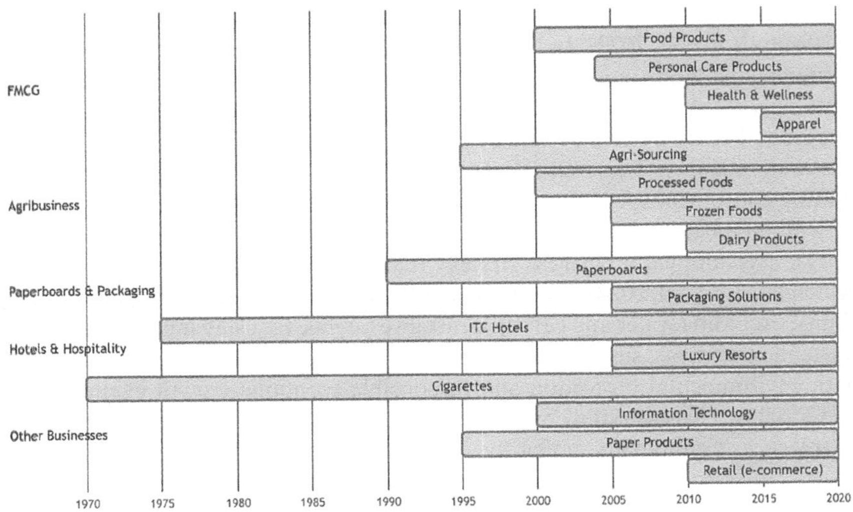

Fig. 18.1. Timeline of ITC Portfolio Expansion. *Source*: Authors' creation based on ITC (2025).

use (Maitra, 2024). ITC Infotech, the company's IT subsidiary, has driven significant growth in the information technology sector by providing software and IT services globally. ITC Infotech offers a wide array of services encompassing analytics, digital transformation, and business consulting (Javaid et al., 2022).

With its varied businesses and global leadership, ITC Limited makes a substantial contribution to India's economy. This portfolio highlights ITC's commitment to sustainable practices and its capacity for adaptation. ITC is crucial to India's progress, contributing significantly to job creation, rural improvement, and fostering innovation as one of India's most prominent and sustainable companies. ITC directly or indirectly employs countless people in the hotel, FMCG, and agriculture sectors (Mahadevan, 2013).

ITC's e-Choupal initiative has raised the earnings and productivity of countless farmers, providing a competitive edge in the agricultural industry (Mukerji, 2020). Farmers' lives have been considerably improved by the company's dedication to rural development, which helps them much better discover prices and decreases their need for middlemen. Products that ITC offers to the public have substantially affected India's GDP and urged development in related industries like manufacturing and logistics. ITC's focus on sustainability aligns with India's wider goals of reasonable development and ecological preservation. The time line of ITC portfolio expansion is provided in Fig. 18.1.

3. Climatic Challenges Facing Indian Businesses

Businesses are under regulatory pressure to adhere to stricter environmental rules created to address climate change (Dwivedi et al., 2023). Three of the most crucial problems are pollution, water scarcity, and changing weather condition patterns.

In India, extreme weather condition events consisting of heat waves, floods, and unplanned monsoons are becoming increasingly regular. A vital part of the agricultural calendar for a long time, the southwest monsoon produces over 70% of the country's annual rains (Natarajan et al., 2022). With serious downpours alternating with dry periods, the monsoons are now less predictable (Srinivasarao et al., 2020). This has led to stopping working harvests, concerns about food security, and damage to facilities. The impact of erratic rains on agricultural output in India's Uttar Pradesh and Maharashtra locations serves as one illustration. Rural hardship and food inflation are the outcomes of this (Sharma & Sen, 2021). Heatwaves are happening more regularly and with greater strength in northern and main India. As individuals try to cool themselves, the record-high temperature levels in places like Delhi and Chennai are burdening public health and raising energy demands (Agarwal & Goyal, 2021). These heat waves are contributing to the pressure currently put on infrastructure by raising the demand for water and power.

One of India's most pushing concerns is the extreme water tension triggered by shortages, which affect about 600 million people (Mahato et al., 2022). The issue is made worse by components including extreme groundwater extraction, poor water management, and dry spells. Climate change, which has altered rainfall patterns and decreased water materials in essential locations, has made these concerns even worse. Significant rivers like the Ganga and Yamuna are getting increasingly contaminated, and groundwater levels in areas like Tamil Nadu, Rajasthan, and Punjab have dropped to alarming levels (Kumar et al., 2024). Since the agricultural sector utilizes over 70% of India's freshwater resources, it is ending up being more susceptible to altering rainfall patterns (Sikka et al., 2022). Cities like Bengaluru, Mumbai, and Chennai are facing severe water shortages as a result of urbanization, population growth, and increasing water demands in the domestic and commercial sectors (Ghosh, 2021). Climate change is intensifying the situation by modifying the quantity of water readily available throughout the year, making it more difficult for businesses and federal governments to forecast and plan for water lacks.

Air pollution is a significant problem in populous areas like Delhi, which is often ranked as one of the most polluted cities on the planet. Unhealthy air quality is caused by a variety of sources, including building dust, industrial effluent, vehicle emissions, and burning agricultural leftovers in neighboring states. Because of this, respiratory diseases are prevalent, particularly in more youthful and elderly people. According to a World Health Organization (WHO) assessment, outside air pollution triggers practically 1.2 million deaths yearly in India (WHO, 2021). The poisoning of water sources including rivers, lakes, and groundwater by untreated sewage and industrial effluents is another growing problem. For instance, the Ganga River is one of the most contaminated rivers in the world since it receives a lot of raw sewage and neglected hazardous waste. Human and aquatic health are affected by this. Food security and agricultural productivity are both impacted by soil contamination brought on by extreme use of pesticides and fertilizers.

These environmental issues are having an influence on the Indian economy. Agriculture is perhaps the sector in India most susceptible to the effects of climate change. Weather events that were previously predictable, such as seasonal rainfall, temperature patterns, and water accessibility, are ending up being increasingly unpredictable because of climate change. Unforeseeable rains patterns and protracted dry spells have resulted in crop failures and reduced yields, particularly in areas like Maharashtra, Uttar Pradesh, and Madhya Pradesh that greatly rely on monsoon rains. The Indian Council of Agricultural Research estimates that by 2050, agricultural yields of staple crops including rice, wheat, and maize may drop by 30%, leading to food insecurity and financial losses (Pathak, 2023).

Climate risks also pose significant obstacles to India's manufacturing sector. Çevik (2024) asserts that extreme weather condition occasions like heatwaves, floods, and cyclones have a harmful effect on supply networks, industrial schedules, and employee efficiency. Steel, chemical, and textile sectors are disproportionately impacted by these disturbances. Textile workers in Ahmedabad and Surat are vulnerable to heat and floods, affecting productivity. The scarcity of essential materials jeopardizes the industry's supply chain. Because of water shortages, industrial operations in Tamil Nadu and Karnataka are curtailing production or significantly increasing capital expenditure on water conservation measures, elevating operational expenses. The automotive sector also faces challenges because of climatic conditions. Escalating energy costs and climate-change related disruptions are diminishing the profitability of industrial facilities.

4. ITC's Response to Climatic Challenges

The sustainability initiatives of ITC Limited are based on a "Responsible Luxury" model, which incorporates environmental sustainability, social responsibility, and economic growth using a comprehensive "triple bottom line" (TBL) framework (Bharwani & Mathews, 2023). For ITC, "Responsible Luxury" signifies the creation of premium products through ethical and ecologically responsible practices throughout their lifecycle. ITC exemplifies this approach through its initiatives in waste management, water conservation, eco-responsible manufacturing, and sustainable procurement (Kaith & Sachdeva, 2024). The sustainable practices of ITC's luxury hotels, for example, the ITC Grand Chola and ITC Maurya, are showcased through their environmentally conscious design, renewable energy sources, and water conservation programs. These leading establishments embody responsible luxury, demonstrating a commitment to both high-quality service and environmental stewardship.

ITC's commitment to social responsibility is underscored by its community development programs. As a sophisticated digital platform, E-Choupal serves as a prime example of a system connecting farmers and consumers worldwide, offering resources related to agriculture, climate change mitigation, and sustainable farming methods (Bakshi, 2023). The initiative demonstrably improved income and productivity levels for over four million Indian farmers (Mukerji, 2020).

This company surpasses sustainability benchmarks, achieving water positivity through replenishment exceeding consumption and carbon positivity via carbon footprint reduction. To maintain biodiversity and advance sustainable forestry practices, ITC has undertaken additional initiatives such as afforestation and the development of green supply chains. The company's packaging and paperboard divisions utilize circular economy principles, as noted by Sahoo (2024). The company's commitment to waste minimization is demonstrated through extensive recycling programs and the employment of sustainably harvested materials. In collaboration with local populations, the ITC Social Forestry Program engages in the reforestation of damaged lands, thereby contributing to a considerable initiative. Fostering sustainable living and generating employment contribute positively to the economic and environmental well-being of rural areas.

ITC's water stewardship program aims to improve water consumption efficiency and reduce the company's overall water impact (Basfore, 2022). This includes company-wide water-saving initiatives, wastewater treatment plants, and recycling programs. Water conservation is a key goal, not just for production but also for the company's supply chains and the local community. To reduce usage, ITC, for instance, has built water-efficient technology in its factories and hotels, such as zero-liquid discharge systems, water recycling facilities, and reverse osmosis systems. These are only a handful of the several actions the business has taken to increase the efficiency of its water consumption. Water waste may be decreased and reused more easily thanks to these technical developments. Techniques for sustainable agriculture: ITC's e-Choupal initiative encourages water-efficient farming practices, like as drip irrigation and drought-tolerant crop varieties, to enable farmers in the regions it serves use less water. Rainwater harvesting is a key component of ITC's water management strategy (Gupta et al., 2021). Rainwater collecting systems are installed in several of the corporation's facilities.

ITC Limited has made significant strides in using renewable energy as part of its initiatives to advance sustainability and reduce its carbon impact. The company has made large investments in renewable energy sources like solar and wind in an effort to decrease its dependence on non-renewable fuel sources. Solar thermal systems and rooftop solar panels offer the majority of the electrical energy needs in much of its buildings that include hotels, offices, and enterprises. The enormous solar energy facility developed by ITC's Bhadrachalam Paperboards & Packaging Department works as one such. By producing renewable energy for both domestic usage and export to the national grid, the company helps improve India's energy balance. ITC has likewise expanded into wind energy as part of its devotion to sustainable energy. The company has invested heavily in wind farms across Tamil Nadu, Gujarat, and Maharashtra to meet its renewable energy goals. These efforts support India's ambitious renewable energy goals. The company's long-term goals include improving energy efficiency, increasing renewable energy capacity, and achieving net-zero emissions. ITC aligns its renewable energy initiatives with the UN's Sustainable Development Goals, especially SDG 7 (Affordable and Clean Energy), to contribute to global climate action (Sonpatki & Kathuria, 2023). Table 18.1 provides a comprehensive overview of ITC's performance metrics across various categories, including financial outcomes, agricultural practices, waste management, and environmental impact. It compares baseline or target values with current achievements, highlighting significant improvements in areas such as farmer income, climate-smart agriculture, water conservation, and women empowerment.

Table 18.1. ITC Sustainability Performance Metrics.

Category	Metric	Target (for Year 2030)	Achieved (As on 2024)
Net income/year/farmer	From agriculture	₹ 99,700	₹3,47,426
	From fruit trees	₹ 0	₹47,000
	From livestock	₹ 0	₹ 1,30,000
	PM KISAN scheme	₹ 0	₹ 6,000
Total net income/year/farmer		₹ 99,700	₹5,30,426
Adoption and access	Adoption of climate smart agriculture practices	0%	87%
	Access to irrigation	40%	91%
	Adoption of on-farm diversification	10%	54%
	Adoption of off-farm diversification	50%	85%
	Association with farmer institutions	30%	75%
	Linkage to targeted schemes	50%	90%
Community well-being	Having bank account	74%	99.60%
	Having health insurance	26%	53%
	Having ration card	70%	93%
	Medical check-up	18%	81%
	Financial literacy training	29%	72%
Climate smart agriculture	Area covered	40 lakh acres	27.94 lakh acres
Climate smart village	Area covered	30 lakh acres	19 lakh acres

Table 18.1. (*Continued*)

Category	Metric	Target (for Year 2030)	Achieved (As on 2024)
Watershed development	Area covered	22 lakh acres	16.38 lakh acres
Water harvesting structures	Number of structures	50,000	32,400
Storage potential of water	Volume	60 million kl	54.26 million kl
Crop water use efficiency	Water saved	2,000 million kl	1,090 million kl
Biodiversity conservation	Area covered	10 lakh acres	4.70 lakh acres
Social forestry	Area covered	6.30 lakh acres	4.90 lakh acres
Linkages with government programs	Number of linkages	50 lakh	24.75 lakh
Agri-business centers	Number of centers	2,000	1,158
Farmer producer organizations	Number of organizations	4,000	1,660
Support to education	Children covered	20 lakh	15.31 lakh
Infrastructure support to schools and anganwadis	Number of institutions	4,000	3,914
Vocational training	Youth trained	2.25 lakh	1.12 lakh
Household toilets constructed	Number of toilets	40,000	43,804
Waste management	Households covered	75 lakh	50.59 lakh
Maternal child health and nutrition	Beneficiaries covered	15 lakh	14.61 lakh
Women empowerment	Women covered	2.50 lakh	1.92 lakh

Source: ITC Sustainability Report (2024).

Through its operations, logistics, and procurement, ITC Limited has been a leader in building an environmentally responsible and sustainable supply chain. A sustainable supply chain is a major goal for ITC, and this is being achieved through sustainable sourcing practices. ITC's operations in FMCG, paperboard, and agribusiness depend on sustainably licensed suppliers to provide their raw materials. Working with farmers via programs like e-Choupal, the company is committed to sustainable and ethical sourcing of rice, grains, and pulses. To guarantee ethical and eco-conscious sourcing, ITC collaborates with suppliers certified by organizations such as Fairtrade and the Rainforest Alliance, particularly for food and personal care items. In addition, ITC is attempting to lower its environmental effect by promoting environmentally friendly packaging options. Nowadays, a great deal of the company's line of product are packaged in environmentally friendly, recyclable, or biodegradable materials.

ITC's sustainability programs exemplify responsible corporate behavior through efficient water management and renewable energy integration. The operational model employed by ITC could be emulated by other firms through the implementation of carbon offset programs, improvements in energy efficiency, the adoption of green supply chain management, and the pursuit of sustainable sourcing initiatives. These steps, when implemented, contribute to decreased environmental impact, the advancement of sustainable development, and the attainment of global climate goals within the business sector. Numerous awards recognize ITC Limited's commitment to sustainable and eco-friendly practices, establishing its leadership within the Indian business sector.

5. Key Lessons Learned

ITC Limited offers considerable leadership to Indian businesses in steering climate change challenges and integrating sustainability into their operational strategies. The company has set the normal for sustainability in India's business setting in terms of corporate responsibility, resource efficiency, and mitigating climate challenges. Other considerable takeaways from this for other Indian businesses comprise:

5.1. Integrate Sustainability into Core Business Strategy

ITC's adopts TBL approach, which focuses on revenue, people, and the environment first. It is a great example. Indian businesses include sustainability as a necessary element of their operations.

5.2. Promote Climate-resilient Supply Chains

The ITC has controlled the carbon emissions by employing innovative approach to procure raw materials. Further, these approaches have been extended to handle shipments in an environmentally friendly way. The industrial and agricultural sectors should integrate the practices associated with waste decrease, energy-efficient transportation, and sustainable farming practices.

5.3. Water Stewardship and Efficiency

Their commitment to rainwater collection, wastewater treatment, and water replenishment may act as a design for other companies.

5.4. Adopt Renewable Energy Solutions

The requirement of resolving energy-related climate threats is a key lesson to be gained from ITC's investments in renewable energy sources. Setting up solar panels, wind turbines, and other energy-efficient equipment might assist businesses end up being carbon neutral, improve sustainability, and lower energy costs. As ITC's activities reveal, even small and medium enterprises (SMEs) can consist of renewables into their operations through collaborations and green funding. They are able to save considerable in advance expenses as a result.

5.5. Innovate in Sustainable Products and Services

Eco-friendly packaging and responsibly sourced raw materials are among ITC's key sustainability achievements. Recyclable or eco-friendly packaging, sustainable production methods, and environmentally friendly consumer products are all considered environmentally responsible.

5.6. Collaborate with Stakeholders and Build Capacity

ITC's commitment to sustainability underscores the necessity of collaboration among suppliers, stakeholders, and local communities (Flammer et al., 2021).

6. Implications for Policy Makers

Integration of sustainability and climate resilience initiatives into business operations decreases risks while promoting long-term competitiveness. Indian businesses can steer climate challenges, build resilience, and promote sustainability by implementing ITC's strategy. ITC focuses on renewable energy, water management, innovative products, and supply chain sustainability.

6.1. Incentivize Green Technologies and Renewable Energy

Governments should promote the businesses to adopt renewable energy and green technologies through grants, tax rebates, aids, and policies. This might include renewable energy sources like solar, wind, biogas, and batteries. India's National Solar Objective is one sector that has actually had success with the adoption of renewable energy pressed by policy.

6.2. Strengthen Regulatory Frameworks for Sustainability Reporting

Governments have the authority to force sustainability disclosures from businesses, following the example set by global organizations like the Task Force on

Climate-related Financial Disclosures and the Global Reporting Initiative. By requiring businesses to monitor and report environmental damage, governments may encourage more transparency and responsibility. Moreover, this would support climate-resilient investments and assist line up corporate enterprises' operations with national climate objectives.

6.3. Support Sustainable Supply Chain Development

Sustainable supply chains cause cooperation between governments and the private sector. Sustainable sourcing may be promoted among businesses through collaborative initiatives such as eco-labeling and fair-trade certification. A framework assisting SMEs in developing sustainable supply chain competencies would be beneficial. Sustainable farming, with a focus on water conservation and less pesticide use by small farmers, may be a key area for public–private partnerships.

6.4 Foster Research and Development (R&D) for Climate Solutions

Public funding of R&D initiatives fosters innovation in the private sector, leading to advancements in climate-friendly technologies, energy efficiency, and resilient agriculture. Public–private partnerships may prioritize R&D in emerging areas such as carbon sequestration technologies, enhanced recycling methods, and environmentally conscious agricultural practices. Strategic investment in climate innovation may enable India to assume a leading role in global sustainable development.

6.5. Create Climate Risk Financing Mechanisms

Collaborative efforts between governmental bodies and financial institutions facilitate the development of financial instruments to mitigate climate-related risks, encompassing climate insurance, sustainability-linked lending, and green bonds. By including climate threat into their financial decision-making procedures, businesses may be inspired to adopt more climate-resilient policies.

7. Conclusion

To combat the effects of climate change, such as unpredictable weather patterns and droughts, effectively, Indian businesses need to learn from game-changer firms such as ITC. ITC is a model of how Indian firms can embrace climate resilience, circular economy, and sustainable development as their strategic strategies in fulfilling national and global climate goals. To make India climate-resilient in the future, climate resilience needs to be embedded in climate-risk industries such as manufacturing and agriculture. ITC's climate-resilient technologies and new business models can help drive economic growth and reduce the impacts of climate change.

Climate action and sustainable development are the key drivers of ITC Limited's strategy as a business leader. ITC's green initiatives over the past few years have cut across industries such as paperboard, hospitality, agriculture, and FMCG. The company uses less water and carbon than it recovers and offsets, and therefore is water-positive and carbon-positive. ITC's search for sustainability is also evident in its frugal use of resources, use of renewable energy, and water conservation. Various Indian companies look up to ITC as a model for ethical luxury, projecting a TBL strategy where profit, people, and planet are accorded equal importance. ITC's search for sustainability is a model of how business success can go hand in hand with environmental stewardship.

References

Agarwal, R., & Goyal, O. (2021). *The crisis of climate change: Weather report.* Taylor & Francis.

Anbarasan, P., & Sushil. (2018). Stakeholder engagement in sustainable enterprise: Evolving a conceptual framework, and a case study of ITC. *Business Strategy and the Environment*, *27*(3), 282–299.

Bakshi, A. (2023). ITC's e-Choupal as a benchmark for rural transformation: A case study. *Academy of Marketing Studies Journal*, *27*(5), 1–9.

Banerjee, S., & Chakraborty, D. (2020). Role of eco-efficiency in evaluating environmental performance and in accomplishing sustainable development goals case study of ITC Ltd. *The Management Accountant Journal*, *55*(12), 95–101.

Basfore, R. (2022). Green practices of top Indian FMCG companies. *Indian Business@ 75: Research on Trends and Prospects*, 319–331.

Bharwani, S., & Mathews, D. (2023). Sustainable luxury: From an oxymoron to a tautology – The case of the Indian luxury hospitality industry. *Worldwide Hospitality and Tourism Themes*, *15*(3), 231–248.

Bottriell, K. (2023). Multistakeholder roundtables and voluntary standards. *Smallholders*, 405–438.

Çevik, V. A. (2024). Impacts of climate change on logistics and supply chains. *Afet ve Risk Dergisi*, *7*(2), 368–391.

Chaturvedi, V., Ghosh, A., Garg, A., Avashia, V., Vishwanathan, S. S., Gupta, D., Sinha, N. K., Bhushan, C., Banerjee, S., Datt, D., Bansal, J., Pathak, M., Dhar, S., Singh, A. K., Khan, N., Rashmi, R. R., Agrawal, S., Agarwal, D., Singh, A., ... Prasad, S. (2024). India's pathway to net zero by 2070: Status, challenges, and way forward. *Environmental Research Letters*, *19*(11), 112501.

Maheshwari, S. (2019). *Engage!: Co-creating Organizational Vitality and Individual Fulfilment*. SAGE Publications Pvt. Ltd.

Dwivedi, A., Sassanelli, C., Agrawal, D., Moktadir, M. A., & D'Adamo, I. (2023). Drivers to mitigate climate change in context of manufacturing industry: An emerging economy study. *Business Strategy and the Environment*, *32*(7), 4467–4484.

Fallah Shayan, N., Mohabbati-Kalejahi, N., Alavi, S., & Zahed, M. A. (2022). Sustainable development goals (SDGs) as a framework for corporate social responsibility (CSR). *Sustainability*, *14*(3), 1222.

Flammer, C., Toffel, M. W., & Viswanathan, K. (2021). Shareholder activism and firms' voluntary disclosure of climate change risks. *Strategic Management Journal*, *42*(10), 1850–1879.

Ghosh, P. (2021). Water stress and water crisis in large cities of India. In R. K. Mishra, R. B. Singh, & A. Dubey (Eds.) *Sustainable climate action and water management* (pp. 131–138). Springer.

Gupta, H., Jain, A., & Mahavidalaya, A. (2021). A CSR initiative of ensuring water sustainability: FMCG sector in India. *International Journal of Creative Research Thoughts (IJCRT)*, *9*(7), 113–120.

ITC Limited. (2024). *ITC sustainability integrated report 2024*. https://www.itcportal.com/sustainability/itc-sustainability-vision-and-strategy.aspx

ITC Limited. (2025). *History and evolution*. Retrieved April 3, 2025, from https://www.itcportal.com/about-itc/profile/history-and-evolution.aspx

Jairath, J. (2014). ITC limited: Diversifying for growth – A case study. *International Journal of Management, IT and Engineering*, *4*(3), 218–228.

Javaid, M., Haleem, A., Singh, R. P., Suman, R., & Gonzalez, E. S. (2022). Understanding the adoption of Industry 4.0 technologies in improving environmental sustainability. *Sustainable Operations and Computers*, *3*, 203–217.

Kaith, A., & Sachdeva, G. (2024). Green HRM for sustainable business: Insights from ITC and ONGC initiatives in India. In M. Valeri, & B. Sousa (Eds.) *Human relations management in tourism* (pp. 141–162). IGI Global.

Karim, A., & Said, F. (2024). Discussion on Malaysia's globalization journey from resource-based economy to global player. *Journal of Business and Economic Options*, *7*(1), 29–38.

Kaul, V. K. (2019). Introducing business and economy. In A. Yadav, & B. K. Sarkar (Eds.) *Understanding the environment of business*. Pearson Publication.

Kumar, R., Goyal, M. K., Surampalli, R. Y., & Zhang, T. C. (2024). River pollution in India: Exploring regulatory and remedial paths. *Clean Technologies and Environmental Policy*, *26*, 2777–2799.

Mahadevan, B. (2013). *The immutable self within us*. https://www.iimb.ac.in/sites/default/files/pdf/19%20The%20immutable%20self%20within%20us_0.pdf

Mahato, A., Upadhyay, S., & Sharma, D. (2022). Global water scarcity because of climate change and its conservation strategies with special reference to India: A review. *Plant Archives (09725210)*, *22*(1).

Maitra, R. (2024). Reducing carbon footprints through green technology in the tourism industry: A review of selected hotels in Delhi. In D. Sharma, H. Abdullah, & P. Singh (Eds.), *Sustainable tourism, Part B* (pp. 105–121).

Mukerji, M. (2020). Re-examining strategic and developmental implications of e-Choupal, India. *The Electronic Journal of Information Systems in Developing Countries*, *86*(4), e12132.

Natarajan, V. A., Tamizhazhagan, V., Tangudu, N., & Kumar, M. S. (2022). Analysis of groundwater level fluctuations and its association with rainfall using statistical methods. *Journal of Algebraic Statistics*, *13*(3), 1895–1904.

Patel, R. R., & Thakrar, N. (2024). *A comprehensive analysis of corporate social responsibility practices of selected companies of India*. https://shodhgangotri.inflibnet.ac.in/bitstream/20.500.14146/7918/1/synopsis.pdf

Pathak, H. (2023). Impact, adaptation, and mitigation of climate change in Indian agriculture. *Environmental Monitoring and Assessment*, *195*(1), 52.

Prabhakar, A. C., & Brar, G. P. (2024). Green revolution, agricultural performance with sustainability and bio-diversity: Special reference to India. *International Journal of Economic Performance*, *7*(1), 281–318.

Ramachandran, J., & Manikandan, K. (2012). *ITC limited: India first*. https://www.itcportal.com/about-itc/profile/history-and-evolution.aspx

Roy, K. (2023). *Political governance, economic pursuit, global hegemony, and environment; China, India, and the World*. Balboa Press.

Sahoo, B. (2024). Social forestry: A national and international issue. *Jamshedpur Research Review*, 69–74.

Sarangi, N. C., & Jabbal, D. (2024). The role of business leaders in promoting sustainable practices and the SDGS-experience from India. *Journal of Lifestyle and SDGs Review*, *4*(2), 1–37.

Sarkar, S. D. (2024). *Environmental management and corporate social responsibility in India: The missing block in sustainability*. Paper presented at the Proceedings of the NDIEAS-2024 International Symposium on New Dimensions and Ideas in Environmental Anthropology-2024 (NDIEAS 2024). https://www.atlantis-press.com/proceedings/ndieas-24/126000695

Schedule, V. (2013). *Under Section 135 of the Companies Act, 2013*. Ministry of Corporate Affairs.

Shanti, J. (2016). A study on environmental sustainability practices of star hotels in Bangalore. *Asian Journal of Business Ethics*, *5*, 185–194.

Sharma, A., & Sen, S. (2021). Impact of drought on economy: A district level analysis of Madhya Pradesh, India. *Journal of Environmental Planning and Management*, *64*(6), 1021–1043.

Sikka, A. K., Alam, M. F., & Mandave, V. (2022). Agricultural water management practices to improve the climate resilience of irrigated agriculture in India. *Irrigation and Drainage*, *71*, 7–26.

Sonpatki, R., & Kathuria, A. (2023). *Navigating the storm: Business resilience in the age of climate change* [Paper presentation]. Workshop on e-Business.

Srinivasarao, C., Rao, K., Gopinath, K., Prasad, Y., Arunachalam, A., Ramana, D., Ramana, D. B. V., Ravindra Chary, G., Gangaiah, B., Venkateswarlu, B., & Mohapatra, T. (2020). Agriculture contingency plans for managing weather aberrations and extreme climatic events: Development, implementation and impacts in India. *Advances in Agronomy*, *159*, 35–91.

World Health Organization. (2021). *Mapping opportunities for training in air pollution and health for the health workforce*. World Health Organization.

Printed and bound by CPI Group (UK) Ltd, Croydon, CR0 4YY

13/09/2026

14961064-0008